Emerald Thread

TIMOTHY BOHEN

Published October 2024 by Bohane Books, LLC

Edited by: Kimberly Blessing, Jenn Fecio McDougall, Phil Nyhuis, and Karen Brady Borland
Book designed by: Kris Miller
Author photo: KC Kratt
Front cover photo: Collection of the Buffalo History Museum

ISBN: 978-0-9886912-1-6

Printed in Buffalo, New York by Keller Bros. & Miller, Inc.

For more information, please visit: www.timothybohen.com

To my wife, Kimberly; my mother, Betsy; and my late father, Timothy

For generations, Ireland has been the emerald thread in the fabric of American history and national life.

—Nancy Pelosi, Speaker of the United States House of Representatives, in an address to the Irish Parliament on April 17, 2019

Contents

Introduction

The Irish were among the poorest, most wretched immigrants to wash up on American shores. They faced fierce bigotry from the Protestant establishment, yet they continued emigrating from Ireland to make Buffalo their home. Within a few generations, these hardworking, determined immigrants transformed the city and staked their claim to the American Dream.

Frightened by the waves of Irish Catholic immigrants streaming into Buffalo during and after the Great Famine (1845-1850), the Protestant establishment tried to oppress the Irish. At the same time, politicians enacted laws intended to limit their rights. Newspaper editorials mocked the Irish, characterizing them as drunks and simpletons, reflecting a general nativist sentiment that ran throughout the city of Buffalo.

The American Party, known as the Know-Nothings, ran on the most anti-immigrant platform in United States history. Their decision to elect Buffalonian Millard Fillmore as their presidential candidate in 1856 reflected the strong nativist sentiment in Buffalo. The Know-Nothings targeted Catholics, mainly the Irish. They campaigned to enact laws restricting citizenship, voting rights, and the ability to hold public office. Although Fillmore lost the election, bigotry toward the Irish persisted for decades.

Despite nativist efforts to block the Irish from participating in the political process, the rebellious Irish leaned in. They realized early on that seizing political power was, among other things, a sure way to secure civil service jobs that would improve the lives of their constituents. Starting as ward bosses, the Irish moved on to the halls of Congress and eventually into the governor's mansion.

Many believe that the building of the Erie Canal brought the Irish to Buffalo in 1825, but that's only the beginning of the story. While hundreds of Irish laborers were forced to work on the most dangerous sections of the canal, resulting in countless injuries and deaths, most of those earliest immigrants moved on to other canal projects in different parts of the country. It was the Irish who arrived in Buffalo in large numbers during and after the Famine who went on to shape the city.

When Famine immigrants arrived, many worked on the waterfront as manual laborers, helping Buffalo become one of the country's largest centers for milling flour and one of its busiest grain transshipment hubs. Other Irish immigrants built Buffalo's railroads, turning the city into one of the nation's largest railroad hubs. As a result, Buffalo produced some of the wealthiest industrialists in the nation. At the same time, Irish immigrants living in waterfront neighborhoods suffered extremely harsh conditions, including brutally high infant mortality rates and unsanitary drinking water. While wealthy Anglo-Americans built lavish homes and summer retreats in and near Buffalo, Irish women toiled as domestic servants.

When Irish-American Bishop John Timon came to Buffalo in 1847 and the Sisters of Charity the following year, they built a safety net for thousands of impoverished immigrants and city residents. Many of these institutions, including a network of churches, schools, and charitable organizations, still exist today. The Irish Sisters of Charity opened Buffalo's first hospital. During several cholera outbreaks, it saved the lives of scores of Catholics and non-Catholics. Additionally, impoverished immigrants were cared for in a mental asylum, pregnant women were tended to in maternity hospitals, and homeless boys and girls were taken into orphanages, all supported by the Catholic Church.

With this safety net in place, Famine immigrants and their descendants, unlike their earlier compatriots, levied political power to secure better jobs critical to the future success of the Irish. Instead of working as servants and manual laborers, the Irish found better-paying jobs as teachers, firefighters, and police officers. Taking advantage of Buffalo's booming economy, ambitious Irish immigrants learned skilled trades and started businesses—some became multi-millionaires. Over time, Buffalo became a more Irish city.

Today, we can find the imprint of the Irish throughout Buffalo. Given their natural gifts for the written and spoken word, the Irish landed jobs as reporters, editors, and newspaper publishers who advocated on behalf of the less fortunate. Ripe with a sense of injustice suffered in their motherland, they became lawyers and judges, working to create a more just and equitable society in their new land. Performers and entertainers drew on their well-established traditions in music and dance to enrich Buffalo's arts and cultural institutions. The Irish were also fierce competitors, producing national stars in rowing, baseball, and boxing, and they played a crucial role in shaping professional football in Buffalo. Architects and landscapers shaped the physical landscape of our city, designing and building many familiar structures and sites throughout downtown Buffalo. Finally, brave Irish-American soldiers enjoyed careers in the military, with several individuals becoming national heroes.

This is the story of Buffalo's Irish—the emerald thread woven into the fabric of our fair city. Céad míle fáilte.

The Book's Purpose and Methodology

This book came about as the result of research for my first book, *Against the Grain: The History of Buffalo's First Ward* (2012). In that work, I focused on ordinary and extraordinary men and women, many Irish, living in the First Ward. However, many Emerald Isle immigrants and their descendants who lived outside this Irish neighborhood also shaped our city.

Here, I use mainly biographies to tell the story of Buffalo's Irish community— one of the largest Hibernian centers in the United States. I hope to reveal the extent to which the Buffalo Irish made outsized contributions to the Queen City and the nation.

Regarding methodology, determining who counts as being "Irish" was complicated. Surnames do not necessarily indicate Irish ancestry, making it especially difficult to identify Irish women. I did extensive research on each individual I chose to include in this book, and most have significant Irish ancestry on their paternal or maternal side or both. Readers will also find that some of the named "Buffalo Irish" in this book were born in Western New York and went on to achieve fame elsewhere, while others born outside of this area helped shape our city's history. *Emerald Thread* is organized by subject matter, so I encourage readers to meander and pick the people or material that interests them most. Hopefully, when you are done reading this book, it will be impossible to imagine Buffalo without the Irish.

CHAPTER ONE

Pioneers and Canal Builders

Samuel Wilkeson—A King Among Men

While walking through the northwestern section of Buffalo's Forest Lawn Cemetery, visitors cannot miss a prominent pink obelisk on a hill next to a tall flagpole, surrounded by a black, wrought iron fence. Tourists often gather at the site, some taking photographs, for this is former U.S. President Millard Fillmore's final resting spot. He was the 13th president of the United States, and historians rate Fillmore's performance as mediocre at best. As a founder of numerous institutions in Buffalo, however, he was remarkable.

There are no crowds on the hill north of Fillmore's, in section K, just an occasional squirrel darting around. On that hill stands a nondescript granite obelisk, one side bearing the Latin inscription: *Urbem Condidit*—"He Built the City." This monument is the final resting place of Samuel Wilkeson, the "Father of Buffalo." Were it not for Wilkeson's efforts in building Buffalo's harbor, the city's history may have been drastically different. We begin our story about the Irish in Buffalo with him.

Samuel Wilkeson, born in Carlisle, Pennsylvania in 1781, was the son of two immigrants from the north of Ireland who had settled in the United States in 1760. They were Scots Irish, part of the first wave of immigrants from Ireland who arrived in America before the start of the American Revolutionary War in 1775. John Wilkeson, Samuel's father, was forced to emigrate from Ireland because of a scarcity of farmland to divide among himself and his brothers. Over the next century and a half, thousands more Irish immigrants from the south and west of the Emerald Isle fled for the same reason. In addition to a shortage of land, the Scots Irish, usually Presbyterians, also fled Ireland because of religious discrimination from policies implemented by the British who ruled over Ireland at the time.

In the spring of 1784, when young Samuel was a small child, his parents, along with twenty other pioneering Scots-Irish families, traveled over the Allegheny Mountains on pack horses with all of their worldly possessions. After settling in the wilderness of western Pennsylvania, south of Pittsburgh, the Wilkesons erected a log cabin, plowed the virgin land, and began farming corn, potatoes, and flax.[1] While establishing their homesteads, these new settlers also contended with natural hardships, lack of supplies, and Native American raiding parties. [2]

As a child, young Wilkeson attended school for a mere two weeks before starting work on the family farm. At age twenty-one, equipped with the lessons of resilience and hard work, Wilkeson set out on his own. He married Jane Oram, daughter of a Scots-Irish immigrant, and they eventually had six children—many of whom would later leave an imprint on Buffalo and beyond. Wilkeson built a farm and grist mill in southwestern Ohio, but the restless and ambitious son of immigrants was yearning for more. Around 1807, he moved his family to Chautauqua County, New York, and built a fleet of keel boats. With his vessels, he transported nails, glass, and bar iron on rivers from Pittsburgh to Lake Erie and then up the lake to the fledgling village of Buffalo. From there, he returned to Pittsburgh with boats loaded with salt.

One year after the start of the War of 1812 with Great Britain, U.S. General William Henry Harrison, a future president of the United States, commissioned Wilkeson to build a fleet of ships in northern Ohio to assist him with his impending invasion of Canada. The previous contractor had failed to deliver the needed boats, so Harrison implored Wilkeson to finish the job quickly. After hiring a team of carpenters to assist him, he built the fleet to specifications on time and did not disappoint the future president. Looking for another adventure, he immediately joined the Chautauqua militia and hurried to Buffalo to battle the British. Ultimately, it was a losing cause for the Americans: the British burned Buffalo to the ground. When Wilkeson and a companion returned to the charred village a few days later, they found nothing living except a cat prowling among the ruins. He returned home, however, satisfied that he had personally "slain a few of the enemy."

In April 1814, while the war against Britain was still raging, Wilkeson moved his family to Buffalo because his instincts told him this was the place to make his fortune. After loading a lake boat with the framing and roof for a store, as well as materials for a house, the Wilkesons relocated to the small village on the eastern end of Lake Erie. He constructed his shop at the corner of Main and Niagara Streets in Buffalo and his residence nearby. After the war ended in 1815, unemployed American soldiers from the campaign encamped unlawfully in Buffalo, becoming a menace to the local citizens. Desperate to deter the lawbreakers, the villagers unanimously elected the tall, stern Wilkeson as justice of the peace. He quickly restored order, forging his reputation as a natural leader and a man of action. In one biographical sketch, the author used Old Testament language to describe Wilkeson's actions: he was a "terror to evil-doers," and "utterly fearless...he smote the rascals and ruffians brought before him."

Wilkeson Builds a Harbor

Within a few years, Wilkeson participated in another Buffalo battle. This one, however, did not involve fighting the British. When the construction of the Erie Canal commenced in 1817, the New York State Canal Commission had not yet decided on the Canal's western terminus. The villages of Buffalo and Black Rock soon emerged as the two contenders. Based on the outcome of this contest, massive fortunes would be won or lost. The Holland Land Company, which owned land in both villages, did not own the area at the water's edge, so they had no incentive to develop a harbor in either place. The Dutch investors were also indifferent about which village won and understood that they would prosper handsomely—by selling high-priced lots—in either municipality.

In the early years of this battle, it looked like Black Rock had the upper hand. They had a more well-known advocate and champion in General Peter B. Porter and a rudimentary harbor protected from the lake winds because of Bird Island and Squaw Island (now called Unity Island). Black Rock also had a one-hundred-foot black rock outcropping, which could serve as a wharf and a place for boats to dock.[5] Buffalo had a silt-filled Buffalo Creek where it joined Lake Erie, and strong lake currents made navigation challenging. The creek was only waist-high in some parts and was not deep enough to accommodate tall sailing ships. In addition, a dense forest of elms, sycamores, black walnuts, basswoods, and oaks lined the banks of the waterway. Much of this forest had to be razed. Adjacent to the forest was a mosquito-infested swamp that terminated at the tall cliffs, or bluffs (since demolished), separating the village from the lake. Creating a harbor in Buffalo would be an arduous undertaking in the best of conditions, and near impossible when the village leaders discovered that no Buffalo residents had any harbor-building experience. Tools and heavy equipment were also scarce. Despite these shortcomings, however, Buffalo had Wilkeson as their champion.

Since there was also no federal money to build a harbor, a small group of Buffalonians went to Albany to secure a loan. Government finances were paltry at this time because of the costly War of 1812. Still, New York State offered a $12,000 loan to be paid back in twelve years, secured by a bond and a mortgage. In December 1819, seven of the nine original supporters backed out of the deal, fearing the plan would fail. Not part of the original group of financiers, Samuel Wilkeson came forward and pledged his support to the two remaining bondholders, Charles Townsend and Oliver Forward. The three men agreed to cover the state loan with their personal property as collateral. If the canal leaders chose Buffalo as the Lake Erie terminus, the state would forgive the loan; if they selected Black Rock, the three men had ten years to pay it off. This agreement was a risky proposition for the 39-year-old Wilkeson. But it was also the chance of a lifetime.

In May 1820, the three financiers were ready to begin the harbor construction. It would soon become clear, however, that securing the financing was the easy part of this project. While Wilkeson's partners offered financial resources, they had nothing to contribute to the construction phase. Townsend apparently had a disability, and Forward had no experience supervising such a project. Neither did Wilkeson, but it did not stop this dynamo from volunteering to be the superintendent. William Peacock, a Holland Land Company engineer, had already surveyed the harbor two years before and had recommended building a 1,000-foot pier into the lake. So, at least Wilkeson had a starting point. To construct the dock, Wilkeson needed to hire some workers. Struggling to find enough men willing to do the job, he offered $2 a month more than the prevailing wage. Employment at the higher rate included the stipulation that they would work six days a week from morning to night, regardless of the weather.

After erecting a boarding house for the laborers, the building of the harbor required two primary operations. First, they had to construct the pier that Peacock proposed, which served a dual purpose. It would allow larger lake vessels to dock and unload their goods in deeper water, avoiding the shallow water closer to shore. Also, the pier would limit sand accumulating at the mouth of the Buffalo Creek. In the first year of construction, they erected a 900-foot-long timber pier that extended from the mouth of the creek into Lake Erie. This project was no small feat because Buffalo had no pile driver available. So the industrious Wilkeson assembled one using a cast-iron mortar shell that had been leftover from the recent war. A blind horse, trained to walk in a circle, was used to power the pile driver, which required one hundred strokes of the mortar shell to drive each pile into the creek bed. The men then constructed stone-filled timber cribs to keep the pier supports from washing away during the frequent lake storms. After finishing this arduous task, they anxiously waited to observe whether the pier would survive a Western New York winter. Fortunately, it did.

The second challenge involved deepening the creek so boats would not become lodged on the sand bar. To do this, Wilkeson and his men constructed a dam, which had two purposes, in the spring of 1821. First, the dam would raise the water level by three feet and, when released, would create enough force, in theory, to straighten the angle of the mouth of the creek. This enhancement was necessary so boats did not have to make sharp turns entering the lake. The second purpose of the dam was to trap the melted winter ice and spring rains which, when released, would dredge a deeper channel.

Once the workers assembled the dam, they released water several times, which slowly reoriented the water's path and cleared the channel. Before they could complete the process, however, Buffalo's weather wreaked havoc. On one relatively calm day, a rare and violent lake tidal wave emerged without warning, and Wilkeson's workers barely escaped with their lives. While no one was hurt, the wave destroyed a significant portion of the dam, threatening to collapse the entire structure. The Scots-Irish leader quickly galvanized his workers and recruited a sizeable contingent of villagers to aid in the dam repair project. If the dam had collapsed, it could have jeopardized the entire harbor project. Wilkeson inspired and led his men, many of whom worked waist-deep in the powerful creek current while battling torrential rains. After twelve straight hours, including some in the dark, the exhausted men finally made the necessary repairs, preserving the dam's integrity. Even though the rains continued overnight, fortune was on Wilkeson's side. A strong northeast wind lowered the lake level and replenished the dam's water level. When the water was released, it washed out 20,000 cubic feet of gravel.[6] This event created the desired channel: five feet deep, ninety feet wide, and large enough to accommodate several lake boats daily. Wilkeson and his men had persevered and created the first man-made harbor on the Great Lakes. The Buffalo Creek, later enlarged and renamed the Buffalo River, would never be the same. Neither would Buffalo.

The Western Terminus

The harbor was now complete, but there was still no guarantee that the canal commissioners would choose Buffalo as the Canal's Lake Erie terminus. Between 1819 and 1821, various state canal board members and engineers arrived in Western New York, reviewed the two villages, and made preliminary recommendations. Some recommended Black Rock, some Buffalo. Citizens in each village were on edge, eagerly awaiting the final decision. Wilkeson traveled to Albany to plead Buffalo's case with fellow Irish descendant Governor DeWitt Clinton, with whom he met a dozen times. One can only wonder what assurances, if any, Clinton gave to Buffalo's canal champion. Wilkeson knew that the decision wasn't solely Clinton's. But he also knew his politicking could only help his case.

In June of 1822, the canal commissioners arrived at Benjamin Rathbun's Eagle Tavern on Main Street in Buffalo to meet with the leaders of each village to make their decision. In a small room in the tavern, Wilkeson argued in favor of Buffalo. Utilizing maps of the waterways and an extensive knowledge of winds, waves, and currents, he made a compelling case that they should choose Buffalo. He also regaled them with the harrowing tales of building the harbor despite harsh weather conditions and setbacks.

Although a skilled debater, Wilkeson faced a tough competitor. The esteemed General Porter presented Black Rock's advantages to the commissioners. After careful deliberation, the canal board and five engineers made their final choice for the western terminus: Buffalo won. This decision had monumental consequences. As a result, instead of becoming a grand city, Black Rock became just another stop on the canal—and the villagers' aspirations of wealth and prestige evaporated. The embittered General Porter eventually moved to Niagara Falls. In 1853, Black Rock was quietly annexed by the city of Buffalo and relegated to a mere neighborhood. Buffalo, by contrast, became one of America's wealthiest nineteenth-century cities, the sixth-largest port in the world and, by 1900, the eighth-largest city in the United States. Wilkeson, of course, became a legend.

Politician, Businessman, and Colonization Agent

Wilkeson excelled at almost every challenge he encountered. In addition to successfully building the harbor and winning the terminus battle, he served Buffalo in various political and government roles. As previously mentioned, he served as justice of the peace, Erie County's first judge, a New York State assemblyman, and a New York State senator. In 1836, his fellow citizens elected him the fifth mayor of Buffalo. All the while, he simultaneously managed several commercial enterprises. He owned a fleet of vessels, a freight-forwarding business, a small cotton textile mill, warehouses, Buffalo's first iron foundry, and a company that manufactured steam engines and stoves.

If there is one cloud over Wilkeson's legacy, it is his involvement with the American Colonization Society (ACS), which his close friend Millard Fillmore also supported. Founded in 1816, the purpose of the ACS was to facilitate the passage of free American Blacks to Liberia to create a permanent settlement in West Africa. In 1838, Wilkeson relocated to Washington, D.C., to become the general agent for the ACS and editor of its newspaper, the *African Repository*. The following year, Wilkeson edited a 90-page booklet, *A Concise History of the American Colonies in Liberia*, which he used to paint a positive assessment of the conditions of Blacks in the colony and raise funds for his organization.[7] Wilkeson also established commercial links between Liberia and the American cities of Baltimore and Philadelphia, overseeing the recruitment of southern Blacks to be transported to Liberia.[8]

Wilkeson claimed to be deeply moved by the condition of enslaved people and reportedly haunted by fears that white southerners would "exterminate" the freed Blacks.[9] In his mind and the minds of many others of his time, it would be better to send the Blacks back to Africa where, in his words, they would have hope to see "their race rise."[10] However, he was also opposed to abolition because he feared it would fracture the union between the states. Instead of a wholesale freeing of the slaves, Wilkeson advocated for gradual emancipation, coupled with the ACS scheme to send the freed slaves back to Africa.[11] However, most free Blacks did not want to return to Africa, and several prominent Black leaders, like Frederick Douglass, condemned the ACS as "diabolical." Douglass's biographer asserted that nothing raised the orator's ire like enthusiasm for returning Blacks to Africa.[12] In Douglass's view, the organization's real motive was just to remove Blacks from society, which would lead to the "extermination" of his people.[13]

Historians should undoubtedly judge Wilkeson's efforts with the ACS based on the context of the era in which he lived. A more thorough examination of his writings for the *African Repository* and local newspapers of the time is needed to understand his true motivations.[14]

Wilkeson's Legacy

In the 1820s, Wilkeson and his wife built a beautiful mansion on Niagara Square, and it stood for almost a century as a monument to one of Buffalo's most remarkable citizens. (When it was torn down in 1915, the stately house was replaced by a "new necessity of the times"—a gas station.) In July of 1848, Wilkeson traveled to Tennessee to visit his daughter—but fell ill on the way. He did not survive his journey. Nor did he live to see the Civil War that he feared would erupt—but eight of his grandsons fought for the Union Army when it commenced. Two of them died in battle. After his death, his friends and contemporaries ascribed to him superhuman qualities, elevating him to a mythical status. Other male peers in Buffalo were praised, but not with the reverence reserved for Wilkeson.

So, did Samuel Wilkeson build the city? Some historians would argue that Joseph Ellicott, the surveyor and land agent for the Holland Land Company, built the city. By 1804, Ellicott surveyed and laid out the village of Buffalo. His radial street design, modeled after Pierre L'Enfant's design of Washington, DC, is still intact today. Others could make the case that Millard Fillmore is the "Father of Buffalo." His influence is significant: a founding member of the University of Buffalo, the Buffalo Historical Society, Buffalo General Hospital, the Buffalo Club, and a contributor to the Buffalo Fine Arts Academy. However, it was Samuel Wilkeson who established the foundation and the structure of Buffalo by building its harbor and winning the battle for the terminus of the Erie Canal. Wilkeson's efforts, not Ellicott's or Fillmore's, made Buffalo the Queen City of the Great Lakes. His epitaph, "He Built the City," engraved on his memorial stone in Forest Lawn Cemetery, rings true.

Wilkeson was a "king among men." He grew up in the wilderness with no training in manners or formal education. He became a successful farmer, soldier, merchant, forwarding agent, harbor builder, judge, state senator, mayor, ship owner, foundry owner and head of a national organization. He was a natural leader with iron resolve who could inspire others to accomplish seemingly impossible tasks. To steal a line from the late Irish poet Seamus Heaney, Wilkeson was "a natural force masquerading as a human being."[15]

In 2013, the city of Buffalo built a popular new waterfront park named Wilkeson Pointe in his honor. Other reminders of Buffalo's builder include a large bas-relief sculpture of him on the South Elmwood Avenue side of Buffalo's City Hall, and a student housing complex at the University at Buffalo named Wilkeson Quadrangle. Samuel Wilkeson was just one of many Irish Americans to shape Buffalo. Other Irish Protestants—such as William H. Glenny and John B. Manning—made fortunes in Buffalo and contributed to its civic life. By Wilkeson's death, Irish Catholics were settling *en masse* in Buffalo. They would make an even more significant contribution to the city.

Mary Lynch O'Rourke-Pioneering Irish Settler

The first Irish Catholic settler in the Buffalo area was likely Con O'Neill, a ferryman who worked in Black Rock in about 1800.[16] There is no other information about him besides his name and occupation, and he has disappeared into history. Thomas Moore, the famous bard, lyricist and author of *The Irish Melodies*, may have been the first Irish Catholic visitor to the village of Buffalo. In July of 1804, Moore visited John Crow's log tavern near the corner of what are now Exchange and Washington streets on his tour of North America. Apparently, this former resident of Dublin and London was underwhelmed by what he saw of this fledgling village on the shores of "Erie's stormy lake."

The O'Rourkes, Patrick and Mary, were almost certainly the first Irish Catholic couple to settle in Buffalo.[17] They arrived in 1815, just a few years after the British razed the village. At their arrival, historical records state that only forty-three families were residing there. The only other Catholics were the family of the French nobleman Louis Le Couteulx.

Mary (Lynch) O'Rourke, born in Albany on St. Patrick's Day in 1785, was the eldest child of two Irish immigrants from County Roscommon. Details about her early years are scarce, except for the fact that she received a formal education and spoke both English and Irish. In 1802, at age seventeen, she married Patrick O'Rourke, a merchant from Albany. The O'Rourkes moved to Schenectady, then Palmyra, and finally settled in Buffalo. It is unclear why they moved to the western edge of New York State, but the financial opportunities connected to rebuilding the village may have attracted Patrick O'Rourke, like Samuel Wilkeson a year earlier.

According to family lore, Patrick O'Rourke's stock of retail goods was burned and destroyed by the British sometime during the War of 1812, but it is unclear where or when this happened.[18] O'Rourke's grandson, John McManus, claimed his grandfather never recovered from the event and was disconsolate until he died in 1825.[19] His depression or mental illness had forced Mary O'Rourke to find the means to support her family—which she did by operating the Erin Harp House, a boardinghouse at 123 Main Street (near the present-day Marriott Courtyard at Canalside). The Widow O'Rourke, as she was known from 1825 forward, set an example for countless Buffalo Irish women who followed her—she provided for the family after an Irish husband had died, abandoned the family, or suffered an injury.

Mary O'Rourke was a Buffalo pioneer in terms of her Irish heritage and Catholic faith. In her early years, she and her family endured extended periods without access to church services. She had to travel to Michigan or Albany to have her children baptized. Her home was apparently a destination for priests and bishops traveling from Albany to Buffalo.[20] It was also reportedly the site of Buffalo's first official Catholic Mass, but no year was given.[21] In 1821, Philadelphia Bishop Henry Conwell passed through town and baptized one of the O'Rourke children.[22] In the same year he visited, Irish priest Father Patrick Kelly celebrated Mass at St. Paul's Episcopal Church in Buffalo. Kelly's Mass, which presumably the O'Rourkes attended, was the first *public* Catholic Mass in Western New York since Father Louis Hennepin arrived in Niagara Falls in 1678. Kelly continued to minister to the Catholics of Western New York for about two years, but it was not until 1829 that Buffalo had its first permanent priest.[23]

Mary O'Rourke was noted for her financial charity—which was remarkable considering that she cared for her large family on her presumed meager earnings from operating a boardinghouse. She generously donated to the construction of St. Joseph's Cathedral but died just before it was dedicated. One of the Sisters of Charity described her as a woman full of sweetness and charm.[24] The same religious sister wrote that "Strangers in a strange land found a refuge with her [O'Rourke]" and noted that the widow often looked after the spiritual and temporal needs of young immigrant girls.[25] She added that O'Rourke never refused to help anyone who solicited her.

O'Rourke was described as a handsome woman with a charming personality and a sweet smile.[26] She loved Ireland and enjoyed singing Irish melodies. On March 17, 1839, Buffalo's first public observance of St. Patrick's Day occurred at the O'Rourke home.[27] In later years, O'Rourke looked forward to Sunday Mass, where she socialized with her friends, sometimes communicating in Irish.[28] Her grandson recalled her bountiful network of friends. Not all were Irish, but certainly most were Catholic. Some of the Irish surnames of her friends included Rowan, Cannon, McDonough, McHenry, McGowan, Brennan, Cronin, and Flanagan.[29] Early Irish settlers stayed close to those who shared their heritage and faith.

Widow O'Rourke suffered the typical tragedies of other nineteenth-century women. As mentioned earlier, her husband passed away at a young age, and from then on, newspapers and city directories simply referred to her as "Widow O'Rourke." Within a few years of her husband's death, she had to provide shelter for two of her daughters who became widows themselves; one of the daughters had four children who had to be cared for, as well. O'Rourke also lost her favorite grandson, Francis Milton, whom she had raised after her daughter passed away. The bright young man was in his sixth year in a Catholic seminary in Montreal when he succumbed to an illness.[30] Another of her grandsons claimed this was a crushing blow and may have precipitated a decline in her health.

In December 1853, the sixty-eight-year-old woman passed away. In her obituary, the writer commended her charitable works and noted that she was one of the city's most senior residents.[31] Her funeral at St. Patrick's Church in downtown Buffalo was overflowing with friends and admirers. The Sisters of Charity, whose institutions were beneficiaries of her generosity, attended with a group of handsomely dressed orphans who surrounded O'Rourke's coffin.

Mary Lynch O'Rourke certainly witnessed some remarkable events in Buffalo's history including the rebuilding of Buffalo after its destruction by the British; the building of the harbor and construction of the Erie Canal; deadly cholera epidemics—including the 1832 wave that killed one of her sons-in-law; the financially devastating Panic of 1837; the 1844 deadly lake seiche; the creation of a new Catholic diocese, and the installation of its first bishop, as well as an influx of famished Irish refugees. Perhaps she was also acquainted with some of Buffalo's famous citizens of her day, such as Millard Fillmore, Samuel Wilkeson, or Louis Le Couteulx.

Mary O'Rourke and her family set a good example—to the skeptical Buffalo Protestants—that the Irish could contribute positively to their adopted city. Several of her grandchildren (McManus and Milton families) became prosperous and civic-minded citizens of the Queen City. However, not all of the Irish arrivals to Buffalo who followed them would set such a virtuous example.

The Erie Canal Workers

At its opening in 1825, the Erie Canal was the most impressive engineering feat in America's young history. In terms of size, it was the second-longest canal in the world. More importantly, it revolutionized transportation by reducing the cost of shipping a ton of goods from Buffalo to New York City from roughly $100 by road to just $10 by canal. It also cut the travel time from Buffalo to Albany in half. The cities along the canal—Buffalo, Rochester, Syracuse and Albany—attracted legions of immigrants, including thousands of Irish. The success of the canal eventually made New York the most important commercial and political state in the Union, with New York City becoming the nation's financial capital. The Canal also became the nation's first "highway," which facilitated the settlement of the Midwest by thousands of immigrants, most of whom traveled through Buffalo.

The section of the canal around Lockport, twenty-eight miles north of Buffalo, was one of the most difficult of the entire canal project. There were two significant obstacles. First, a dual-set of five locks—now called the Flight of Five—needed to be built to lift and lower canal boats fifty feet over the Niagara Escarpment. When completed, it was an engineering triumph. The second operation, the Deep Cut, involved cutting a channel through the ridge of bedrock in Pendleton just south and west of Lockport. This wall of limestone, sometimes thirty feet higher than Lake Erie, prevented the water from running downhill from Buffalo to Lockport. Without a steady flow of water, the Lockport locks would be inoperable. This monumental task of removing the wall of rock, which delayed the opening of the canal until the fall of 1825, was its last and costliest operation. The entire Deep Cut was seven miles long, but the most arduous stretch was a section of solid rock that extended for two miles. Irish workers had to dig and blast a channel twenty-seven feet wide and anywhere from thirteen to thirty feet deep.[32] To complicate matters, this was the pre-dynamite era, so much of the work, at first, was done by Hibernian hands. Later, blasting powder, reformulated by E.I. DuPont, was utilized, but its performance was sometimes unpredictable and dangerous.

Some historians have wrongly downplayed the role of the Irish in building the Erie Canal (1817-1825). Their view stems from an 1819 report that claimed three-fourths of canal workers were native-born. But this report was from the 1818 season, and the canal still had seven more years of construction. Many of the canal contractors were American-born, but their workforce, especially after 1820, was overflowing with Irishmen. The phrase "Yankee ingenuity and Hibernian brawn" was used to describe the construction of American canals like the Erie.[33] As certain canal sections became more challenging and hazardous to construct—such as Lockport, the Irondequoit Valley, and the Montezuma marshes—contractors increasingly recruited the Irish. Historians estimate that as many as 1,200 Irishmen labored at Lockport alone. According to one canal report, as many as 1,000 workers, many from the Emerald Isle, were sickened by a mosquito-borne illness as they labored in the Montezuma marshes, west of Syracuse, in muddy water up to their knees.

Unfortunately, extensive biographies of these Lockport Irish canal workers are scarce or non-existent. However, we can make some generalizations from newspaper articles and diaries of Lockport residents and visitors. Newspaper publishers relished reporting on Irish misbehavior—and there was plenty of that in this segment of the canal. Two significant riots erupted during the building of the Erie Canal, and both transpired in Lockport due to the Irish.

On Christmas Eve in 1822, a dispute arose between the Lockport residents and the Irish workers—many of whom had consumed too much whiskey. The Hibernians were allegedly looking for more liquor, so they shattered the window of J.P. Lawes' tavern in the village. They also reputedly tried to raze several buildings in town. Local townspeople came out to defend their shops from the Irish lawbreakers, who were armed with clubs and stones. Several people were seriously wounded as flying rocks filled the streets. A large stone was embedded in one resident's skull, and with no local doctor available, another resident had to remove it with a jackknife. By Christmas morning, two local citizens were killed, and fourteen laborers, most with Irish surnames, were arrested; another twenty hired hands fled to Canada before dawn.

A jury indicted a total of eight of the workers for the murder of Lockport resident John Jennings. The main defendant in the clash was an Irishman named James Kelly, sometimes spelled Kelley. At his trial, he was initially acquitted on the charge of murder, but he was then retried, found guilty of manslaughter, and sentenced to several years in the state penitentiary. Historian Patrick McGreevy points out that both the courts and the newspapers were overly sympathetic to the townspeople. They portrayed the Hibernians as violent, drunk, and irrational. The newspaper accounts neglected to disclose the dreadful conditions the laborers endured on that section of the canal that could have provoked such drunken, violent rage.[35]

Canal Living and Working Conditions

Many Irish immigrants who landed in New York City were hired to work on Clinton's Ditch.[36] Agents for the canal contractors arranged for the workers to journey up the Hudson River to whatever section of the canal needed men. From 1816 to 1819, more than 10,000 Irish emigrants landed in New York City, and many found work on the canal.[37] In January 1821, ads appeared in New York City newspapers soliciting 1,200 laborers for the Lockport project.[38] That same year, due to a shortage of willing workers, Irish laborers were also recruited from the state prison. On at least two occasions, Governor DeWitt Clinton released prisoners on the condition that they agreed to serve out their term by digging the Erie Canal.

In his book *Stairway to Empire: Lockport, the Erie Canal and the Shaping of America* (2009), Patrick McGreevey masterfully details the deplorable living and working conditions of the Irish laborers. The first element they faced was distrust and disdain from the Lockport residents. Many native-born Protestant residents feared these foreign men—some who spoke only Irish and many who followed the Roman Pope. These men from Erin were isolated in small settlements along the edge of the canal, living in hovels and rustic lean-tos. One Lockport resident described how the Irish would cut down a tree, lean it onto a building, and then live underneath the tree branches. Other dwellings included wooden cabins with dirt floors and a cutout in the roof for a chimney. No matter what structure they resided in, the workers suffered in the harsh Western New York winters and humid summers. Irish settlements such as the one in Lockport helped shape the derogatory phrase "Irish shanties" and perpetuated the term "Wild Irish."[39]

In terms of wages, many contractors recruited hired hands at $12 a month, which included room, board, and whiskey rations. Later, they changed their pay to a simple daily wage of 75 cents.[40] While the higher daily rate seemed more advantageous for workers than the flat monthly rate, the employees were now responsible for their own room and board. This new arrangement also transferred the financial risk from the contractors to the workers if there were work stoppages or if the workers were injured or sick. Of course, there was no death benefit in the event of a workplace fatality. Still, they had no option but to agree to the arrangement because employment opportunities were limited.

The six-day work schedule was grueling: 12 to 14 hours a day in the summer and 10 hours a day in the winter.[41] It was also dangerous. The limestone blasting went on all day, and men and boys were sometimes maimed or killed from falling stones or accidents at the blasting site.[42] The men drilled holes into the dense layers of rock, packed it with blasting powder, lit the fuse and then ran. On occasions when the powder failed to explode, the workers returned to relight the fuse, which sometimes led to horrific outcomes.

In her memoir, Edna Smith, the wife of a Lockport doctor, remembered that "on some days the list of killed and wounded would be almost like that of a battlefield."[43] Another visitor recounted how "the Irish laborers grew so reckless that at the signal for blasting, instead of running to the shelter provided for them, they would just hold their shovels over their heads to keep off the shower of smaller stones and be crushed every now and then by a big one."[44]

The physical environment along the Lockport section was chaotic. One resident recalled a sky filled with the "smoke of burning powder." With trees uprooted and rocks piled high along the Deep Cut area, it looked like a hurricane had cut a path through the region. Of course, the area was replete with Irish shanties and shacks, most lacking proper sanitation.[45] Others described the work environs as a war zone with rocks flying everywhere and continuous explosions all day.[46]

Drunkenness and fights added to the unsettling Lockport atmosphere. Alcohol consumption was an integral part of the Irish laborers' daily routine. The men drank throughout the workday, where they were served by "jigger bosses"—young boys who were responsible for doling out whiskey rations at set times throughout the day. Drinking in the evenings as well as on Sundays was the custom. Labor historians estimate that each laborer consumed between twelve and twenty ounces of whiskey during the workday.[47] The men, especially Catholics, also lacked any access to church services. No priests were nearby to minister to the workers, celebrate Sunday Mass, or comfort the sick and dying. In fact, only one priest ministered to all of Western New York at that time.

As the 1822 riot demonstrated, it did not take much for violence to erupt. On the morning of July 12, 1824, Protestant Irishmen assembled in the village to commemorate the Battle of the Boyne—the 1690 clash in Ireland where Protestant King William of Orange defeated Catholic King James II. In Lockport, an armed gang of about three hundred Catholic working men confronted the celebratory Protestants and, at the sight of the mob, the non-Catholics quickly returned to their canal work.

But that was not the end of the conflict. The Catholics had been antagonized and were now reminded of hundreds of years of Protestant domination in their homeland. So they marched down the Canal line to a beating drum, assaulting the William of Orange supporters wherever they found them. The attacks lasted into the evening, and several men received serious injuries. Unable to maintain order, the town officials called in the militia to restore the peace. Labor historian Peter Way claims it was the first time in North American history that authorities summoned the militia to calm a canal disturbance.[48]

After enduring five years of deplorable working and living conditions, the laborers finally finished the Lockport section. On the morning of June 24, 1825, Lockport hosted a ceremony to commemorate the completion of this astonishing feat. Reverend Francis Cumming, the first Episcopalian pastor of Rochester, was the event's primary speaker. Cumming praised everyone involved in constructing the locks and supervising the Deep Cut. He thanked the commissioners, the engineers, and even the apprentices. But he did not mention the twelve hundred Irish laborers who did the dreadful work of blasting and removing miles of stone.[49] To Cumming, and others like him, the Hibernian hired hands were just an extension of the tools used to complete this monumental task, no different than the horses, cranes or wheelbarrows on the job site.

Being overlooked or forgotten was not uncommon for the early nineteenth-century Irish. They rarely garnered a mention in the newspapers except when they broke the law or caused trouble. In recent years, with the help of New York

State Assemblyman Matthew Murphy, Jr. and the Ancient Order of Hibernians, a prominent monument and plaque now commemorates the Irish diggers. The plaque reads: *In Memory of the Many Irish Immigrant Laborers Whose Endurance In The Construction Of The Grand Erie Canal Brought Untold Wealth To The Area In Which They Settled.* In 2020, life-size bronze statues of nineteenth-century Irish lock tenders created by artist Susan Geissler were installed to honor Michael Hennessey, Martin Noonan and Tom O'Hara. The following year, Geissler and her team installed five more statues at the site.

Finishing the Rest of the Erie Canal

While the Lockport section was still under construction, work started on the Tonawanda-Black Rock-Buffalo segment in 1823. For this part of the canal, contractors recruited Irishmen from eastern New York at a rate of eighty cents a day (nearly double the national prevailing wage) and regular whiskey rations.[50] The Tonawanda-to-Black Rock segment included a dam-building project on the Tonawanda Creek near the Niagara River. Later that year, the Buffalo canal section commenced. On August 9, 1823, Major John G. Camp, who won the contract for two of Buffalo's canal segments, presided over a groundbreaking ceremony there. People from all over Western New York were encouraged to participate in the festivities, which included public prayers, music, cannon fire, and plenty of flag-waving.[51] Farmers were encouraged to bring their plows and animals to assist in cutting through the soil. Camp also provided a barrel of whiskey as a refreshment to energize and encourage his workers. However, Camp and his crew did not complete most of the Buffalo canal segment until 1825.

At the end of May 1825, workers completed the nine-mile Tonawanda to Black Rock canal section and, on June 4, they released water from the Niagara River to fill the canal all the way to Tonawanda. General Peter Porter, who *still* had not given up on his village being declared the western terminus, hosted a large celebration in Black Rock that he optimistically called the "Termination of the Grand Canal."[52] But this was a desperate, last-ditch effort. Within two months, the contractors finished Buffalo's canal segment, and now Lake Erie water from this village filled the canal to points east.[53] The Black Rock residents' aspirations to be chosen as the terminus officially ended.

One legend about the Buffalo section has persisted over the years. As an incentive for the Irish workers to finish this final segment quickly, the contractors put whiskey barrels at regular intervals. Once the men reached the barrel, they were free to consume it and then encouraged to dig until they arrived at the next barrel.[54] While this may seem far-fetched, other contractors did put barrels of whiskey along the route so that parched-throated men could refresh themselves, but not necessarily as an enticement to work more swiftly. But using whiskey as an inducement to finish the last leg was a real possibility.

The same day that the villagers from Black Rock were celebrating the canal opening, Buffalo was preparing for its own festivities. On June 4, the Marquis de Lafayette, a Frenchman and beloved Revolutionary War hero, arrived in Buffalo to greet the residents and offer a public speech. In front of hundreds of people gathered from all over the countryside, he spoke about the remarkable progress and growth he witnessed in this former frontier village.[55] He delivered his speech on a platform in front of Benjamin Rathbun's Eagle Tavern, located along Buffalo's most prominent public square—it was later named Lafayette Square in his honor.[56] Early in the morning on the following day, the famous military hero left Buffalo and arrived in Black Rock, where he was feted by General Porter. Later that day, on the *Seneca Chief* boat, the same vessel DeWitt Clinton would take several months later, Lafayette cruised to Tonawanda, eventually arriving in Niagara Falls by carriage.[57]

By the fall of 1825, Samuel Wilkeson, Buffalo's most prominent canal champion, was named chairman of Buffalo's Erie Canal delegation, which welcomed Governor DeWitt Clinton on his trip to inaugurate the canal. On October 26, Wilkeson accompanied the governor on the *Seneca Chief* packet boat as it traveled on a ten-day journey from Buffalo to New York City. The delegation placed a barrel of Lake Erie water onboard the *Seneca* so that Clinton could dump it into New York's harbor—forever uniting the Great Lakes with the Atlantic Ocean. In November of the same year, they reversed the process as Judge Wilkeson returned from New York City on the *Seneca* with a keg of salt water from the Atlantic. At 10 a.m. on November 23, with throngs of Buffalo citizens cheering, Wilkeson stepped up to the edge of the boat and poured the salt water into Lake Erie and then proclaimed, "The waters of the Lake were mingled with those of the Ocean; and we, in return, now reunite those of the Ocean with the Lake." New York State would never be the same. Canal historian Peter Bernstein wrote that Wilkeson earned this ceremonial honor because he was "the most aggressive of Buffalo's aggressive citizens in the struggle [for Buffalo] to be named the terminus of the Canal."[58]

Irish Migration to Buffalo

After constructing the canal, some claim that many of those working in Lockport and Buffalo settled there, shaping its civic life for years to come.[59] It is unclear, however, how they would have sustained themselves since there was not yet a surge in new jobs from the completed canal. As day laborers, the men had to keep working in order to survive. Many of them likely migrated to new canal projects in Ohio or Pennsylvania, or crossed the border to Ontario, Canada. An analysis of the 1828 Buffalo village directory supports the fact that few canal workers stayed in Buffalo. In that year, just three years after the opening of the canal, only about 50 out of 960 males, or 5% of the total male population, had typical Irish surnames.[60] Four years later in 1832, seven years after the canal's opening, there were only about 130 Irish surnames out of 3,223 males listed in the city directory.[61] Interestingly, 78% of them were employed in skilled or semi-skilled occupations (e.g., tailors, teachers, clerks, merchants, grocers, cabinet makers, etc.), so it does not appear that there were legions of unskilled Irish laborers in Buffalo at this time. Buffalo's strategic location on the Great Lakes meant that Buffalo became a transshipment colossus. Thousands of men were needed to load and unload goods such as grain, flour, and lumber. So Buffalo's thriving port, not the building of the canal, brought waves of Irish to the Queen City.

The Erie Canal had to be enlarged starting in 1836. The enlargement project, which went on for years, was completed with a predominantly Irish labor force, some of whom remained in Buffalo. However, the author of *The History of the Catholic Church in Western New York* (1904) claimed that the first significant Irish migration to Buffalo was in 1841 with the Boston and Buffalo Railroad construction project.[62] Buffalo would eventually become an important national rail center, employing thousands of Irish men and women. Incidentally, the same year the railroad project commenced, the growing Buffalo Irish community formed a parish for themselves: St. Patrick's Church, located on a lot at the corner of Ellicott Street and Batavia Street (now Broadway).

Grain Elevator

Many Irish immigrants came to Buffalo due to Joseph Dart and Robert Dunbar's invention of the world's first steam-powered grain elevator in 1843. This innovative elevator reduced the time needed to unload the Midwestern grain ships. What previously took seven days on the backs of Irish longshoremen to unload now took *just* two hours with this invention. A grain transshipment revolution was underway, eventually leading to Buffalo becoming the grain capital of the world. Within a little more than a decade, there were ten of these massive elevators along the banks of the Buffalo River, requiring more unskilled workers to operate them. Laborers were also needed in the hulls of lake ships and onshore, where they loaded grain into canal boats and railcars for transport to points east. Grain scooping required about 1,000 workers yearly; roughly ninety percent were Irish. In later years, as Buffalo expanded into milling and grain processing—especially cereal, flour, and animal feed—thousands more jobs were created. Even after the Famine years,

Irish farmers from the south and west of Ireland continued to migrate to Buffalo to secure these positions.

Buffalo Irish Settlements

As the Irish flocked to Buffalo, they settled in an area called The Flats, situated just south of present-day Lower Terrace Street, down to the Inner Harbor. Histories of Buffalo claim the pioneering families included the O'Rourkes (as previously mentioned), the Bowens, the Doughertys, and the Mooneys. The settlement grew over time and, by 1840, the Irish were so overcrowded in this neighborhood that it forced some to migrate south and southeast of the downtown district. Some single laborers started to settle on Ohio Street and further into the First Ward where, in 1859, they formed St. Bridget's Parish. Others established homes along the shore of Lake Erie in an area called the Beach, and still others shifted east on Seneca and Swan Streets into the Second Ward, where they started a new St. Patrick's Church in 1853.

A more affluent group moved north up Niagara Street into what was initially called the Third Ward (it eventually became the Eighth Ward in the 1850s). In 1859, this group of merchants, professionals, and skilled laborers founded Holy Angels Parish on Porter Avenue. In contrast, some of the poorest and most desperate Irish made their home in the Canal District, or the "Infected District" as it was often called. This area—wedged in between the Commercial Slip, the Erie Canal, and the Buffalo River—was a lively, rough-and-tumble area. Sailors and canallers would come to blow off steam at one of the 108 saloons in the neighborhood or partake of the temptations luring them into one of the District's seventy-five storied brothels. The next chapter will discuss colorful stories about the Irish in this Canal Street area.

The 1855 New York State census revealed the number of Irish people living in Buffalo had exploded compared to the previous census. According to the census that year, 56% of the Irish in Buffalo arrived between 1850 and 1851.[64] By that accounting, there were 2,400 Irish heads of household and a total of 10,000 Irish in Buffalo, including women and children—more than half of whom lived near the water in the First Ward or in the Eighth Ward off Niagara Street.[65] These Famine immigrants, however, were different from the pioneer Irish settlers. Of the Great Hunger refugees (arrivals from roughly 1845-1855), only 17% were employed in skilled or semi-skilled positions compared to 78% just twenty years earlier.[66] Most of the Buffalo Famine immigrants were farmers, farmhands, or fishermen from the west of Ireland, and were, therefore, only qualified for laboring positions. We turn to one of them now.

Daniel Guiney and the Famine Immigrants

There is more biographical information on the Famine-era Buffalo Irish than those in the Canal era. Professor Kerby A. Miller has collected hundreds of letters Irish immigrants in America wrote to their families back home. These letters contain valuable information about the experiences of the new arrivals. Twenty-three-year-old Buffalo settler Daniel Guiney wrote one of these letters to his family in County Cork. After landing in New York City from Liverpool on July 24, 1850, he arrived in Buffalo two weeks later with fourteen other travelers from Ireland.

Besides the letters, there is much background information about Guiney, his family, and his companions because they were part of a British state-aided emigration scheme. The property where Guiney and his family lived and farmed was a Crown-owned estate called Kingwilliamstown in North Cork. By the time the potato blight arrived in the 1840s, a few hundred Irish Catholics had toiled as tenant farmers on this British monarchy-owned land. During the Great Hunger, many tenants and their families suffered financial hardships, could no longer pay their rent, and were at risk of eviction. At the same time, the Crown Estate commissioners determined there were too many farmers (a "surplus population" was the term they used) for too little land, so they came up with a solution. They would pay the tenants' one-way passage to New York City if they volunteered to leave the estate permanently.

One hundred ninety-one people signed up for the offer and emigrated in four separate groups. Each group took about six weeks to travel from Cork to Liverpool and then to New York City.[67] Several of the Kingwilliamstown families settled in Buffalo. According to the detailed British recordkeeping, we know about the meager rations allotted to every adult passenger for their Atlantic crossing. It consisted of the following weekly rations: two and a half pounds of bread, one pound of wheat flour, three pounds of oatmeal, one half pound of sugar, one half pound of molasses, and two ounces of tea, as well as three quarts of water daily. Due to confusion while loading the ship in Cork, some passengers on the first journey received no provisions on the way to Liverpool; three tenants died on that short journey to England. Others complained about smaller rations than promised after setting sail on the Liverpool to New York expedition.

Daniel Guiney arrived in the United States in the second group in 1850. After landing in New York City, part of his group sailed to Albany and journeyed to Buffalo for eight days by canal boat. He wrote a letter home shortly after his trip describing his impressions and thoughts. Regarding his canal journey, he commented on how expensive milk and bread were compared to home, but wrote that he was able to walk along the canal and eat freely from the bountiful apple trees. Guiney was also impressed by the large number of sheep, horses, and cows he observed throughout central New York and wrote, "The Yankees are the wisest men in the world in respect of doing business."[68]

When Guiney arrived in Buffalo, he was warmly welcomed by Matthew Leary and Dennis Danihy, former neighbors from the Cork estate who had come to Buffalo the year before. When he reached the Danihy house, the new arrival was shocked to see a feast of potatoes, meat, butter, bread, and tea for dinner. After dinner, they purchased two dozen bottles of small beer, a gallon of gin and whiskey and drank well into the morning. Guiney remarked in his letter that based on the fine clothes worn by his former Irish neighbor Dennis Reen, one would think he was a boss or supervisor instead of a former farmer. He noted that the Irish-speaking girls (probably the Danihy girls) who used to "be trotting on the bogs at home" now spoke excellent English, after only a year in the United States. In his letter home, Guiney notes being astonished at how plump and healthy Denis Danihy appears compared to his weakened condition a year before in Famine Ireland.

Guiney stated that jobs were plentiful in his new home and implied the daily wage was twice that of Ireland. He noted that opportunities existed to make even more money if they left Buffalo, but many preferred to remain there together. After landing in the Queen City, Guiney expressed an optimistic and joyful tone in his letter home—especially for someone who had presumably just witnessed so much misery from the potato blight. Despite his upbeat tone, many immigrants in Buffalo had difficult lives due to workplace injuries and fatalities, disease, alcoholism, or violence. But we know the end of Guiney's story, and it is a happy one.

Like thousands of other immigrants from European countries, Buffalo was just a stepping stone to a new adventure in the Midwest. Guiney, his mother, and his brothers left Buffalo in the early 1850s for Detroit, which was becoming its own boomtown. His 1891 obituary declared that he was one of the best-known residents in Detroit and had a large circle of friends. He had built a successful grocery business—which left his family financially well off—and had served as a Detroit councilman and the overseer of highways.[69]

From the heroic accomplishments of Samuel Wilkeson building Buffalo's harbor to the legions of Irish Catholics and Protestants who risked their lives constructing the Erie Canal in Lockport and its environs, the Irish played a critical role in the public works projects in Western New York and beyond. They built the infrastructure—canals, railroads, and roads—contributing to New York's immense wealth. They toiled as poorly paid laborers who generated incredible fortunes for their employers. These Hibernian laborers earned a reputation for being rough and rowdy.

The multitudes of immigrants who came to Buffalo due to the Great Hunger were some of the poorest, most wretched people to ever seek refuge in America. They were perceived as primitive people deserving their poor lot in life. It would take decades for the Irish to overcome these negative stereotypes.

CHAPTER TWO

Saints and Sinners

The Irish were among the most desperate immigrants who ever landed in the United States. Those who arrived in Buffalo during the 1840s and 1850s were predominantly penniless, and they spread diseases, packed the poorhouse, committed crimes, lacked education, drank excessively, and lived off of government assistance more than any other previous ethnic group. One historian wrote, "The [Irish] famine immigrants were the most impoverished, destitute, unskilled group ever to arrive in the United States. Eighty to 90 percent of them were classified as unskilled laborers. Ninety percent were Catholics, as many as a third spoke only Gaelic, and few came with any savings."[1] One Irish-American journalist noted that the Famine immigrants seemed like a different race than the Irish who preceded them by even just ten years. "Dire wretchedness, appalling want and festering famine have tended to change their character."[2] One historian asserted, "For a long time they were fated to remain a massive lump in the community, undigested, undigestible."[3]

The Irish Potato Famine was a watershed event in Ireland's history that devastated its people, causing traumas that left lingering effects for generations. An American historian who has specialized in collecting and examining letters from Irish immigrants in America found that among those from the south and west of Ireland, as well as the lower classes, there was "an enormous sense of loss, of loneliness and of exile..." from their emigration experience.[4] Unlike other immigrants, they were not leaving their homeland with optimism for better opportunities, but out of sheer necessity because they were starving to death. For individuals who survived the Irish Famine, anger over their circumstances manifested itself in domestic violence, alcoholism, and family abandonment. The Great Hunger also led to a profound hatred for the English, which for some persisted into the twentieth century.

The Desperate and Destitute Buffalo Irish

Statistics of the Buffalo Irish in the poorhouse, jail, hospitals, and insane asylum tell the story of why the Irish were viewed as inferior and defective. Below are just some of the highlights that convey their dire situation.

Employment

In the 1855 New York State census, 46 percent of the Irish in Buffalo did not list any regular occupation, and another 20 percent were "outdoor or general laborers" with no fixed place of employment.[5] Put another way, two-thirds of the men lacked a steady, year-round job. Most worked seasonally in demanding manual labor roles, such as laying railroad tracks, digging canals, or loading and unloading goods along the waterfront. Only 16.5 percent of the Irish were skilled workers compared to 37 percent of the Germans.[6] Many Irish women worked as domestics and laundresses and ran boarding houses to supplement their family's income.

The Erie County Poorhouse

In 1849, during the height of the Famine wave, the Irish made up 63 percent of poorhouse inmates.[7] After that, during the 1850s, they constituted 51.2 percent of the Erie County poorhouse residents, yet they never reached more than 20 percent of the population.[8] More than 50 percent of the Irish-born residents of the Erie County poorhouse were women.[9] In some periods during the 1850s-1870s, there were two to three times as many Irish-born as German-born in the poorhouse, even though the German population was significantly larger.[10] In 1855, only 23 percent of Irish owned their own homes, compared to 54 percent of German immigrants.[11]

Relief provided by Buffalo Poor Department

In 1866, nearly 1,900 individuals of Irish descent needed relief from the Overseer of the Poor compared to 1,641 Germans and only 427 native-born Americans.[12] Even in 1880, three decades after the end of the enormous Famine wave, the Irish led those receiving relief: 506 Irish families, 505 German, 302 American, 106 English, and 26 Black families.[13] But not all Buffalonians were happy about spending money on these poor immigrants. In 1880, the annual *Buffalo Commerce and Manufacturing* magazine published various statistics about Buffalo. When they wrote about Buffalo's Poor Department, the editors complained that it was "…the most burdensome of all the branches of the City's work, since in a pecuniary point of view, it is all expense without any corresponding return."[14] This view—that aid to the poor led to no return on investment—probably represented the views of many in the Protestant merchant and professional class to whom the magazine appealed.

Crime

During the 1850s, roughly 40 percent of the prisoners in the county jail were Irish. Most were convicted of intoxication, vagrancy, or disorderly conduct.[15] The Germans, by contrast, averaged only 12 percent annually, with a much larger share of the city's population. In 1866, 33 percent of all arrests in Buffalo were Irish-born citizens, and most were public order offenses.[16] At this time, Irish-born individuals made up only 10 percent of Buffalo's residents, so they had three times the expected number in jail based on their share of the population.[17] Even in 1881, out of 9,012 arrests in Buffalo/Erie County, 1,580 were Irish-born and, as usual, they led all other immigrant groups. Germans, whose population was twice the size of the Irish, were arrested 800 times, half of the number of Irish arrests.[18] In 1880, 76 percent of the inmates at the Providence Lunatic Asylum were Irish born or Irish descendants.[19] Even three decades after the end of the Famine, many Irish were still desperately struggling and in need of assistance.

The Sisters of Charity—The Famine-Era Heroes

At noon on June 3, 1848, six Catholic religious sisters arrived at Buffalo's Exchange Street train station, wearing all-black dresses, short capes, caps with crimped borders, and ties.[20] Many of the onlookers had probably never seen a religious sister before. Bishop John Timon, who had begged and pleaded with the women to come to Buffalo to found a hospital, was not at the train station to greet them. He reportedly asked his messenger, "Are they Irish?" The boy responded that "they were [Irish] or might well as be"–in other words, they were from Ireland or were second-generation Irish.[21] Almost all of the six who arrived in June and two additional sisters who came shortly after were of Irish descent. They included Sister Ursula Mattingly, the hospital administrator; Sister Hieronymo (Veronica) O'Brien, the Chief of Staff for Sister Nurses, as well as Ann de Sales Farren, Anacaria Hoey, Clare McDurby, Mary Aloysia Lilly, Mary Eliza Dougherty, and Agatha O'Keefe. In short order, these women and dozens of others would provide much-needed comfort to thousands of destitute immigrants.

A Sisters of Charity historian described the dire circumstances of the immigrants. "Many people needed medical assistance due to epidemics…, construction and railroad accidents, illnesses common to poor housing environments, and indigent people already weakened from malnutrition and in poor health."[22] The journey across the Atlantic Ocean taxed their health, and when they arrived, many were exposed to tuberculosis, typhus, cholera, and respiratory problems.[23] In 1848, when the Sisters opened their hospital, 87 percent of the inmates at the county almshouse—the only institution to care for them—were foreign-born citizens, primarily Irish and German Catholics.[24]

As Buffalo rapidly grew in the 1850s, the Protestant elite were less concerned with charity and primarily focused on lucrative commercial opportunities. They were not interested in creating a network of charitable institutions to help immigrants. The prevailing Protestant-American ideology advocated for personal responsibility, which obviated their obligation to care for these destitute new arrivals, most of whom were Catholic.[25] Before the Sisters founded their hospital, Protestant businessmen had discussed building a hospital in Buffalo for seven years, but they never built it.

Within two months of their arrival, the Sisters of Charity, who had arrived in Buffalo penniless, built their hospital at the corner of Virginia and Pearl Streets. In August 1848, after the city leaders tried unsuccessfully to block the opening of the Catholic hospital, the Sisters received their first patients—six ill mariners from the Sailor's Home.[26] The Sisters' mission was to care for the "sick and destitute of the City of Buffalo" regardless of the patient's religion.[27]

The Sisters Hospital in Buffalo was ground-breaking in at least three aspects. First, it could accommodate up to one hundred patients, much larger than a typical hospital in this era. Second, the Sisters accepted public funds to help manage it.[28] Protestants did not want their money supporting a Catholic institution even though people of all religions were treated there. Third, they treated children, which was not a widespread practice at the time. The Irish-American Catholic sisters, with the creation of Sisters Hospital, established the first institutionalized healthcare network in Western New York. Historian Jean Richardson claimed, "The successful establishment of the Sisters of Charity Hospital led to a network for social welfare institutions in antebellum Buffalo."[29]

The timing of their hospital was exceptionally fortuitous. The following year, in 1849, Buffalo was struck particularly hard by a cholera outbreak caused by infected water sources. The most severely impacted people, many Irish and German immigrants, were those who lived near the Erie Canal and the Hydraulics neighborhood. Of the known ethnicity of the cholera dead, 42 percent were Irish.[30] After this epidemic passed, the *Buffalo Medical Journal* praised the Sisters' efforts. Out of 134 patients, 82 recovered, a success rate much higher than that of the county's public facility. The efforts of the Sisters were described as "a matter of astonishment not less than admiration. Night after night…they were at their post, never manifesting weariness or diminished zeal."[31] In addition to saving lives, their success garnered respect from skeptical city leaders.

Not everyone was delighted with the Sisters and their hospital. The prominent Reverend John C. Lord, close friends with Samuel Wilkeson, objected to state funds helping support a Catholic institution. Even the Superintendent for the Poor, Lester Brace, vehemently challenged their endeavor, including writing a public editorial in the *Commercial Advertiser*. Brace, who was responsible for caring for the poor inmates—more than half of whom were Irish—was a cruel Buffalo bigot who defamed Catholics. In October 1849, Father Bernard O'Reilly responded to Brace's attack, but the *Commercial Advertiser* wouldn't publish the rebuttal, so the *Courier* did. In his editorial, Brace explained why he refused to transfer poorhouse inmates to the Sisters of Charity Hospital. O'Reilly replied that this was detrimental to the inmates because the Sisters offered better care at no additional cost to the county. O'Reilly described Brace as unconcerned with the welfare of those under his care, dismissive of the high mortality rate at the poorhouse, and exhibiting a hatred for many under his supervision. The county poorhouse was, in O'Reilly's words, "more comfortless…than a farmer's corn house, its poor suffering inmates badly attended, and badly provided for, whilst the flies feasted on the countenances of the dying…"[32] O'Reilly added that one unnamed superintendent at the poorhouse, when asked about extending relief to the deserving poor, callously declared, "We can bury them cheaper at the poorhouse."[33] Throughout the nineteenth century, the idea that poverty resulted from immoral behavior was widespread. It was not until the end of the nineteenth century that reformers such as Irish writer George Bernard Shaw argued that the poor were immoral *because* they were poor.

Within three years of the hospital's opening, the Sisters treated more than seven hundred patients there. In the 1848-1850 period, true to the Sisters' mission, 57 percent of the 1,428 people they treated were charity cases.[34] Hundreds of ailing patients, many of whom had no other place to go, were treated with dignity by the Sisters. In 1856, of the 487 patients at Sisters Hospital, 216 were from Ireland, 144 were from Germany, and 63 were born in the United States.[35] This was further evidence that the Irish were indeed in need of assistance.

Sister Hieronymo (Veronica) O'Brien

Sister Hieronymo (Veronica) O'Brien, born in 1819 in Washington, D.C. and one of the founders of Sisters Hospital, was one of Buffalo's Famine-era heroes.[36] She left such an impact on charitable and social service institutions in Western New

York that Gerald M. Kelly wrote an entire book on her life. Both of O'Brien's parents, Michael O'Brien and Catherine (Mackin) O'Brien, were born in Ireland. In 1841, Veronica O'Brien joined the Sisters of Charity, taking the religious name Hieronymo. After working in Pittsburgh and New York City, she was selected for a leadership role, as the "Chief of Staff Sister Nurses," at the Buffalo hospital. Her managerial skills were quickly tested by the surge of cholera patients needing care. She and her fellow Sisters tirelessly treated over a hundred critically ill patients.

O'Brien developed a reputation as an excellent nurse during her career, and her talents did not go unnoticed. In September 1857 during the onset of the Panic of 1857, Timon dispatched her to found Rochester's first Catholic hospital: St. Mary's Hospital (Rochester was then part of the Buffalo Diocese). She opened the critically needed institution in December of that year with two other Sisters and almost no money. As they prepared the hospital from September to December, the Sisters subsisted on water thickened with flour and slept on straw bedding in a rat-infested room.[37] Once again, O'Brien's timing was fortuitous: the 1857 financial depression devastated countless unemployed immigrants in Rochester and beyond. She also petitioned the federal government to allow her to open a ward in her hospital to care for sick seamen and canal workers. Not long after, she secured an Army contract to care for ill and injured Union soldiers during the Civil War; it is estimated that she and her sisters treated between three and five thousand soldiers before the war ended.[38] O'Brien was just one of the hundreds of Irish and Irish-American religious sisters who made a lasting impact on Buffalo.

Sister Rosaline Brown

Sister Rosaline Brown, born in 1814 near Philadelphia to two Irish immigrants, was another hero to Buffalo's Famine immigrants.[39] She was not raised Catholic but converted and later joined the Sisters. She founded Detroit's first hospital in 1845, and then transferred to Buffalo in about 1850. She became the Superior of St. Vincent's Orphan Asylum in Buffalo, and established St. Mary's Infant Asylum and Maternity Hospital in 1854.[40] However, in 1859, after a visit to the Erie County poorhouse, she was so moved by the terrible treatment of the inmates that she was inspired to open an institution to treat those with a mental illness. At the county institution, she witnessed mentally ill people chained or tied to posts and others strapped to benches. The patients' clothing was scant; some were half-naked, and their food was inedible. In her opinion, these vulnerable people were treated more like animals than humans.[41] The following year, in 1860, Sister Brown pleaded with Bishop Timon to open a center to treat Buffalo's mentally ill and those suffering from substance abuse. Timon quickly approved her plan.

Brown then had to beg and borrow from local citizens to start her retreat, even writing newspaper editorials soliciting money.

Prominent citizens, including railroad magnate Dean Richmond and future President Grover Cleveland, donated money to her cause. She secured thirty acres of land at Main Street and Humboldt Parkway, and founded the Providence Insane Asylum—later called the Providence Retreat. At that time, it was the only asylum west of Utica, New York for those declared insane. The asylum was so far from downtown that potable water had to be brought in barrels daily, and candlelight provided the only illumination.

In 1880, five of the nine Sisters running the Providence Asylum were of Irish descent, and the other four were Germans. According to the census of that year, of the 91 inmates listed as insane, 76 percent were Irish or of Irish descent, a much higher rate than their proportion of the city's population. Forty-three percent of the 91 inmates were born in Ireland and had lived through the Famine years— further proof of the trauma caused by the Great Hunger. The Sisters operated the facility for over eighty years, caring for thousands of patients suffering from depression, dementia, and psychotic illnesses.[42]

In 1885, at age 71, Sister Rosaline Brown died from stomach cancer. Her obituary on the front page of the *Buffalo Evening News* stated, "Few more devoted and untiring laborers in the cause of Christ ever lived than the lamented Sister Superior, and her memory will long be kept green in the hearts of the poor whom she aided and indeed by the entire community."[43] Brown was remembered for her incredible business sense, intelligence, charm, and a magnetic personality that attracted people to her and her causes. It took a nineteenth-century Irish *woman*—not a bishop or a wealthy Protestant businessman—to have the vision and determination to establish an institute for those suffering from mental health issues.

St. Vincent's Orphanage

While three of the Sisters were forming Sisters of Charity Hospital in 1848, another three busied themselves establishing St. Vincent's Orphan Asylum. The devastating cholera epidemic in 1849 quickly filled up their orphanage—at least forty children entered the facility that year. One wonders what would have happened to the children without the orphanage. In the early 1850s, the Sisters divided the boys and girls into two facilities. St. Vincent's Female Asylum, located next to St. Patrick's Church at Ellicott and Broadway, housed the girls. The boys' orphanage, eventually called St. Joseph's Male Orphan Asylum, was no longer run by the Sisters of Charity. It moved to different locations before it was ultimately located at Limestone Hill, in what is now Lackawanna.[44] For thirty years, the Sisters remained at the Ellicott Street site, but in 1885, in need of more space, they relocated the orphanage to the Robinson-Squier House at Main and Riley Streets. Demand continued to grow and, in 1899, they built a new asylum that could accommodate 250 young girls at that site.

At that time, the institution was progressive because the Sisters taught the girls skills that allowed them to be independent. An 1859 article in the *Buffalo Republic* newspaper praised the education and skills the young women received, in addition to instruction in virtue and morality. Some girls learned to be proficient as seamstresses, cooks, and dressmakers—it was noted that affluent women from all over the city came to the asylum to get their gowns and dresses made.[45] Before she could leave, each girl had to be matched with a family, or a place of employment to ensure she had the means to support herself. The Sisters were proud that few women "went astray" and attributed this to the fact that the discharged orphans were self-supporting.[46] Since 1848, when the Sisters founded the asylum, they enriched the lives of thousands of young, vulnerable women in Western New York.

St. Mary's Infant Asylum and Maternity Hospital

In 1854, the Sisters also founded St. Mary's Infant Asylum and Maternity Hospital on Edward Street, which was Buffalo's first hospital for pregnant women as well as a place for unwed mothers and young orphans. In 1856, the *Buffalo Courier* claimed that the Queen City had been in need of an asylum to care for poor widows, orphaned children, and expectant mothers. The *Courier* editor suggested that the number of abandoned children had been growing and was hopeful that a house like this could keep children away from crime and vice.[47] St. Mary's took care of the youngest abandoned infants—foundlings, as they were then called—most of whom were under the age of two, and not old enough for a traditional orphanage.[48] Each child was eventually matched with a willing family or transferred to St. Vincent's or St. Joseph's orphanages.

In 1865, the Sisters reported patient statistics at St. Mary's for 1854-1864. They claimed that before they opened St. Mary's, it was common to find abandoned children "living, dying or dead on the stoops along the streets, in alleys and bye-ways."[49] By 1864, they had aided 1,932 women and children who were cared for by private donations, not government funds. Almost 25 percent of their patients were not from Western New York, but instead were desperate immigrants traveling through Buffalo. Immigrants who were either sick or without money found themselves stranded in Buffalo because it was a gateway city between the east and west, and some needed care for their newborns or essential maternity services.[50]

The rest of the patients were from all over Western New York, from Buffalo to Canandaigua, New York. Of the 1,932 patients, 927 were discharged, 265 were sent to other asylums, 106 were adopted, 535 were deceased, and 105 remained at St. Mary's. Their twenty-five percent mortality rate is quite astonishing from our modern point of view, proving that the lives of mothers and young children in that era were fragile. By 1915, the Sisters had cared for thousands of children, many of whom were given up by penniless mothers who themselves had been abandoned by their husbands.[51] By 1948, more than 10,000 girls had been cared for by the Sisters.

Legacy

By 1860, the Sisters, not the bishop or lay trustees, controlled the hospital board of trustees and administration. Catholic hospitals allowed women to be leaders outside the home, and Irish women welcomed the opportunity. First and second-generation Irish Sisters led the hospital for its first fifty years, and more than half the Sisters who staffed the institution were Irish.[52]

In addition to managing Sisters of Charity Hospital and St. Mary's Infant Asylum and Maternity Hospital, the Sisters also established Emergency Hospital, Buffalo's first emergency hospital. By 1880, the Sisters had treated 35,000 patients, half of whom were charity cases, at their hospitals. Sisters Hospital also played an essential role in training local physicians with its connection to the Buffalo Medical College and later the Niagara Medical School. In 1889, the Sisters also founded a nursing school in Buffalo, which, when it closed in 1999, had graduated 3,500 students.

The Sisters of Charity, who were not paid for their labor, cared for people of all creeds, including men, women, and children. Paying particular attention to women, they took care of orphans, abandoned girls and infants, widows, aged women, and unwed mothers. Life would have been far worse for so many desperate immigrants and their descendants if it weren't for the Sisters of Charity.

A Nativist Press

Throughout the nineteenth century, the Protestant-owned newspapers in Buffalo had an overt bias against the Irish. Their anti-Irish sentiment ranged from routine jokes portraying Hibernians as simpletons to editorial content antagonistic to their race. As early as 1817, the *Buffalo Gazette* published a joke with the headline: "Irish Humor." A Buffalo merchant had turned his business sign upside down to garner attention. One day, he witnessed a local Irishman standing on his head in a violent rainstorm. When the merchant asked the Hibernian what he was doing, the Irishman replied, "I am trying to read the sign."[54] Sometimes the papers published multiple Irish jokes per day. On November 11, 1826, the *Buffalo Emporium* published four anti-Irish jokes scattered throughout the paper's third page.[55] If you search the word "Irish" in the *Buffalo Patriot and Commercial Advertiser* in the 1830s, you will commonly find Irish jokes. Most of the humor seemed harmless but reinforced the stereotype that Irish men and women were simple.

Bigotry against the Irish Catholics accelerated as Famine immigrants descended on the Queen City. The newspaper jokes persisted even throughout the Famine—as a million people perished. In October 1850, the *Courier* published this one: An Irish student was once asked what was meant by "posthumous works?" "They are such works," says Paddy "as a man writes after he is dead."[56] The *Express*, one of Buffalo's leading newspapers in the mid-nineteenth century, enjoyed baiting the Irish and the Catholic Church.[57] During the early 1850s, Almon M. Clapp, the editor of the *Express*, "increasingly denounced the Catholic church and immigrant—especially the Irish—bloc voting…" By the 1850s, the *Express* and the *Commercial Advertiser* were both patently anti-Irish. In 1857, in a court case, Clapp was accused of once declaring that Irishmen are "traitors and thugs that owed an allegiance to a foreign Government." He added, the Irish "are dogs and ruffians, that had no idea of liberty than what a glass of rotten whiskey inspired." This was during a trial where Clapp and some of his nativist friends were accused of preventing an Irish-born Buffalonian, James O'Grady, from voting in a June 1857 election. O'Grady took a swing at Clapp and blackened his eye. Under oath, Clapp did not deny that he had once uttered his bigoted statement. Nevertheless, O'Grady was found guilty of assault and nothing happened to Clapp.[58]

The other two papers, the *Courier* and the *Republic*, were slightly more sympathetic to the Irish, but still primarily critical of them. An analysis of *Courier* articles about the Irish in 1850 puts them mainly in the anti-Irish camp with the frequent publication of anti-Irish humor. It was hard to find a piece that put the Irish in a positive light, especially in light of the horrors of the Famine.

Nothing distressed the editors of the local newspapers more than how the Irish voted as a bloc for their candidates. On November 13, 1855, the editor of Buffalo's *Morning Express* questioned the intelligence of the Irish and used words like "herd" and "droves" to portray them as animals. He compared the Irish to the Germans, whom he asserted were ruled by reason.

> The elections just determined show that the great mass of Irish people in this country vote for the name democracy without a single thought as to whether they are voting for or against their own personal interests and the

interests of the country. The Germans think, deliberate, consider, but the mass of Irish move in droves under whatever impulse controls them... It is needless to appeal to their reason, they are clannish and herd together...They pour out on election day in herds and droves, no one thinking for himself but following their leaders...These droves of men completely under the control of the demagogues might some day or other be used for purposes inconsistent with equal rights and free principles of citizenship.

Likewise, in an 1857 *Commercial Advertiser* editorial, the editor was incensed that the First Ward Irish voted overwhelmingly for the Democratic candidate, who won the election. The newspaperman asserted that the residents in the First Ward are "made up *en masse* of the veriest tag-rag and bob-tail who ever got drunk at a wake, men who infallibly choose a location in a swamp, and live in a shanty with pigs under the bed and chickens roosting on the headboard...these fellows are hewers of wood and drawers of water, not from motives of patriotism, but simply because they are coarse, drunken wretches, without the ambition or the brains to better their conditions."[61]

Millard Fillmore and the Nativists

It was not only the press pitted against the Irish. The American Protestants had a deeply embedded contempt for Catholics, and many espoused a belief in the intellectual superiority of Anglo-Saxons over the Celts. Similar to Boston and Philadelphia, Buffalo became a hotbed of nativism. After all, its most famous citizen, Millard Fillmore, ran for the U.S. presidency on the American Party ticket, the most anti-immigrant platform in the country's history.

As early as 1844, Fillmore objected to the influence of the foreign-born vote in American politics. When he lost the 1844 New York gubernatorial election, he blamed it on immigrants, stating "Contrary to our expectations the foreign vote of Erie County went almost unanimously against us." He declared, "The abolitionists and the foreign Catholics have defeated us in this state...A cloud of gloom hangs over the future...May God save the country from the effects of foreign influence."[62] Eleven years later, in 1855, Fillmore wrote to a friend after the defeat of his Know-Nothing gubernatorial candidate in New York. "I have looked with dread at the corrupting influence which the contest for the foreign vote is exerting upon our elections...it is demoralizing the whole country and converting the ballot-box into an unmeaning mockery, where the rights of native-born citizens are voted away by those who blindly follow mercenary leaders."[63] Fillmore also lamented the high proportion of foreigners holding political office, especially Irish and German Catholics.

The American Party, known informally as the Know-Nothings, was a political movement that sprang out of a fraternal organization called the Order of the Star Spangled Banner. It was America's first anti-immigration party. In order to become a member of the Know-Nothings, one had to be a native-born citizen, a Protestant, born of Protestant parents, reared under Protestant influence, and not united in marriage with a Roman Catholic. There were no exceptions. The group started a Buffalo chapter in the spring of 1854. The *Commercial Advertiser*, sympathetic to the views of the nativists, published an article announcing this new organization. The aim of the Know-Nothings "was the exclusion from office, and perpetual war on the Catholic religion," and they reminded their readers you had to be "opposed to the Catholic religion" to be a member.[64] The publisher of the paper wasn't critical of their explicitly anti-Catholic platform. The editor wrote, "We attach no great importance to the Know-Nothing organization, but it will probably serve a useful purpose by calling attention to the influence of so vast a foreign population as we have."

In 1854, Buffalo lawyer Gustavus Scroogs was elected New York State chairman of the American Party, and ran for Lieutenant Governor that year, losing by just a few votes. While he lost, Buffalo voters elected three other Know-Nothing candidates to the New York State Assembly. That year, the nativist candidate for New York State governor secured 42 percent of the Buffalo vote, proof that this was not a fringe party, and that bigotry was widespread in the Queen City. In April 1855, local chapter president Charles G. Irish, Jr. wrote an editorial in the *Morning Express*.[65] He asserted that it was a "fact that our best and learned Judges of the United States have declared a Roman Catholic in belief and principle cannot become a citizen, though he may have taken... the oath of allegiance."[66]

Charles Irish also declared that every Protestant must free the country "from that monster [the Catholic Church] which has long since made its appearance in our midst and is only waiting for the hour to approach to plant its flag of tyranny, persecution and oppression among us."[67] This same man was previously the city's Overseer of the Poor, and responsible for the neediest residents, the majority of whom were Catholics (German and Irish). In July 1855, the local nativists were gaining strength and hosted a mass meeting attended by many prominent Buffalonians. At the gathering, they promoted the slogan, "Americans ruling America" and admonished the city's Poor Master for caring for the Irish paupers.

Some of the Buffalo Irish defied the antagonistic rhetoric from the nativists and resolved to fight back. On July 14, 1854, a nativist preacher came to Buffalo to embolden the Know-Nothings. The Irish fought several of his followers on Main Street across from the American House. According to a report in the *New York Times*, "seven or eight Irishmen's heads were broken, but no one was killed. Five Irishmen were arrested and fined $25 each."[68]

In 1855, former President Millard Fillmore, a Buffalo resident and a Whig party member while in the White House (1850-1853), joined the secretive Know-Nothing organization.[69] Fillmore's apologists claim he was not a bigot, but believed he could use the American Party to save the Union from an impending civil war over slavery. At best, he was an opportunist who risked the social peace by associating with known bigots during a volatile time.[70] At worst, Fillmore was as intolerant as many of the party's leaders, but intelligent enough to let them spread their loathsome messages so that he could appear beyond reproach. This was, after all, the man who signed the detestable Compromise of 1850, which included the Fugitive Slave Act. In later years, he always insisted he was personally against slavery. But as president, he intervened to ensure that more than forty men were indicted for treason, simply because they refused to act as slave catchers.[71]

At their 1856 convention in Philadelphia, the Know-Nothing leaders adopted a platform that championed substantial restrictions on immigrants' ability to obtain citizenship and the right to vote. They also decreed no paupers would be allowed into the country, and advocated that only native-born American citizens could hold federal, state, or municipal office, as well as government jobs.[72] Most importantly, they unanimously selected Millard Fillmore as their presidential candidate, and he enthusiastically accepted. Fillmore traveled across New York State to campaign for the upcoming election. In a speech in Newburgh, New York, he exclaimed, "Americans should govern America. I regret to say that men who come fresh from the monarchies of the old world, are prepared neither by education, habits of thought, or knowledge of our institutions, to govern America." He later added, reinforcing his point, "Americans will and shall rule America."[73]

Democratic candidate James Buchanan crushed Millard Fillmore and the Know-Nothing Party in the 1856 presidential election. Fillmore won only a single state: Maryland. After the humiliating election loss, even the local newspapers distanced themselves from Fillmore. The *Morning Express* changed its tune about the Know-Nothing Party and declared that if Fillmore hadn't run with the American Party, he would have done better with the voters. The paper added that had he "entered the canvass on the side of freedom and kept his spirit free of the...intolerance that is attached to his party, he would have found himself under a more auspicious sun...." They claimed, "We opposed the American [Party] organization because of its bigotry, intolerance, oath-binding, as well as on account of infringement of constitutional rights of men in religious tests."[74] In the two years leading up to his election loss, their editorials and others in the *Commercial* were very sympathetic to the nativists.

One year after the devastating loss, the nativists regrouped and selected Buffalo's Jesse Dana as their New York state president. Once again, like Scroogs two years earlier, a Buffalo Protestant led the entire state organization. Locally in

Buffalo, two Know-Nothing candidates won their races in 1858. But the issue of slavery started to bubble up, and the American Party began to lose members to the nascent Republican Party. While the Irish Catholics were spared from a formally bigoted party, they now had to contend with a more veiled narrow-mindedness in members of the Republican Party. The thawing of antagonisms between the nativists and the Irish did not dissipate until the early twentieth century. In fact, it wasn't until the 1960 presidential election of John F. Kennedy, more than one hundred years after Fillmore's defeat, that the Irish could finally win the office of the President.

Riots, Violence and Gangs

While the Buffalo Irish certainly encountered bigotry, their own behavior contributed to the negative perceptions other Buffalonians held about them. Regular newspaper reports of drunken public brawls, assaults, and domestic violence, especially in the Canal District, solidified the "Wild Irish" stereotypes. Even occasional workplace strikes—while often justified—were viewed as threatening to the civic peace. The newspaper editors at the time reported on these disturbances with relish. All of the local newspapers covered one particular incident with colorful language. It was a Sunday afternoon riot, on August 9, 1835, near the Commercial Street Bridge in the Canal District. After church services, a crowd gathered to watch a fight between two Irish men. Another group of onlookers raced across the bridge to glimpse the fisticuffs. But the original crowd of Hibernians did not want their company, so a brawl ensued. At least two hundred Irishmen and boys—some reports suggested more—savagely fought with stones and clubs for over an hour. Too few police were at the scene to disperse the crowd, so the Irishmen fought on until a dozen men were seriously injured, a few were "maimed for life," and twenty were arrested.[75]

Irregular hours, unsteady employment prospects, and low wages added to the stress many people living and working in the waterfront district felt. In January 1849, six hundred Irish canal workers, working on a canal improvement project between Buffalo and Black Rock, went on strike for higher wages (they wanted an increase from 62.5 cents a day to 75 cents a day), but the contractors refused. The bosses escalated the situation by hiring strikebreakers—many of them German laborers. The Irish responded by rioting and guarding the towpath with rifles and pitchforks. The authorities summoned multiple militia companies to quell the riot, which the newspapers called the "Tow-Path Rebellion."

Another demonstration occurred the following year, in March 1850, when Buffalo Irish canal workers working on an enlargement project went on strike for several days. They demanded a reduction to a ten-hour work day. The *Buffalo*

Courier in an article entitled "Almost A Riot" snidely referred to the striking laborers as "malcontents."[76] The Irish canal workers tried to entice the other ship canal laborers to join their strike, but the contractors disbanded the strikers before it could expand. A little more than a week later, however, on March 16, in an article entitled "Riot," the reporter claimed a large group of Irish strikers went back on a walkout, and it prevented one hundred and fifty other laborers from returning to work. This time, fistfights erupted, and the mayor and police were called to the site to restore order.

However, the darkest chapter of the Irish labor disturbances occurred in July 1863. Once again, Irish dockworkers went on strike for better wages, and the business owners responded by hiring Black replacement workers. On July 6, the Irish waterfront laborers exploded with rage at losing their jobs to non-Irish workers and sought out and terrorized any Black man they could find. Several Blacks were severely beaten with bricks, and two of them were drowned in the Buffalo River by Irish attackers.[77]

Gangs

Not all of the violence on the waterfront was labor-related, and the local press also loved to cover these stories. In the Canal District, small Irish gangs often operated with impunity. One well-known squad was the Kirby Gang. Members included Irishmen Frank Carey, David Carey, "Blind" Higgins, Henry Frawley, William Ryan, and Patrick Kelly. The *Buffalo Republic* claimed "robbers, burglars, pickpockets, sneak-thieves, dock rats, pimps, crimps and cutthroats gravitate to that neighborhood as water runs downhill."[78] One evening in 1885, the drunken gang stumbled out of a saloon. Patrolman Mahoney was waiting to arrest them, and he shot and killed nineteen-year-old member David Carey. The young thief had been arrested eight times before the incident and served time in prison.[79] The newspaper article describing the incident claimed that the Canal Street area was the worst in the city in terms of crime, and possibly one of the worst in the country. Petty thieves such as the Kirby Gang did not improve the reputation of the Buffalo Irish.

There were other reports of Irish gangs that did not have the tragic ending of David Carey. In the 1860s, a band of primarily Irish pirates was active along Buffalo's waterfront. The Beach Guerillas, as they were then known, were led by a man known only as "Dublin." He and his comrades Jimmy "The Cotton Hook Man," "Leary" Ready, and "Billy the Mugger" worked Buffalo's harbor. They would board a ship, disperse its crew, and steal as much cargo as possible. The understaffed police force could not capture the men; even if the gang was in trouble, a gang member would blow a whistle, and more recruits would arrive to neutralize the authorities.[80] One day in 1862, Dublin, who was bored of the usual *modus operandi*, devised a new and daring scheme. They boarded the *Mercedes*—moored along the Buffalo River—and steered it a mile down the lake. They renamed it the *Annie* by painting over its previous nameplate and sailed the pirated ship to safe harbor in Canada. No one ever heard from Dublin and his crew again, and the disappearance of the *Mercedes* remained one of the great unsolved Buffalo harbor mysteries.[81]

Around the same time that Dublin and his gang were terrorizing ship crews, Charles Darcy, the son of an Irishman, was named chief of police in 1862. He was later named Sheriff of Erie County. During and immediately following the Civil War, Buffalo attracted some nefarious characters—many of them Irishmen—who settled along the waterfront on the island (now called Kelly Island) near Michigan Street and on the Beach neighborhood nearby. These vagabonds survived by stealing from unsuspecting citizens along the waterfront. Prominent Buffalo citizens such as William Fargo, Grover Cleveland, and Dean Richmond wanted these violent thieves apprehended. Mayor Fargo, who referred to the men as the "buccaneers on the Island," was even willing to enlarge the jail to keep them off Buffalo's streets. Chief Darcy, with a limited team, was tasked with clearing these men out of town, forcing them to take respectable jobs, or sending them to prison. After a handful of mass arrests of up to fifty men at a time, he put an end to the Buffalo Beach guerillas. Rogues and scoundrels, such as "Dublin" and "Billy the Mugger," did nothing to endear the Irish to the citizens of Buffalo.

Murderers—Patrick Morrissey and John Gaffney

In 1835, an Irish laborer, Michael Kelly, after a long night of drinking, returned to his Buffalo home, began arguing with his wife, and plunged a butcher knife into her chest. Kelly was found guilty of murder and sentenced to hang. He is reputedly the first man hanged in Buffalo since it had become a city in 1832. But he was not the last.[83] Almost twenty years later, in 1853, Buffalo's Lawrence Fogarty, a native of County Limerick, was hanged for the drunken murder and robbery of John Brown. But two murders by Irishmen in the 1870s eventually made national news.

Patrick Morrissey, an Irish immigrant, was convicted of Buffalo's first matricide. On June 23, 1872, Morrissey's aged mother, Ann Haley, was cooking him dinner when he arrived home demanding money. She refused. Morrissey, who was drunk and agitated, grabbed a seven-inch carving knife and plunged it into his mother's breast. It penetrated her lungs, piercing the left common carotid artery and killing her almost instantly. Morrissey ran out of the house screaming, "I've killed my mother."[84] When he eventually sobered up, he didn't even remember the incident. The 28-year-old Morrisey was convicted of murder and sentenced to hang at the hands of the Erie County sheriff—none other than the future president of the United States, Grover Cleveland.

There is extensive biographical information about Morrissey, unlike many other Irish laborers of the time, because of the nature of his heinous crime. He was born in Neenah, County Tipperary, in 1844, the year before the start of the Great Hunger. The Famine severely impacted Tipperary, so he and his parents emigrated to the United States. As a young child, Morrissey worked as a ferry boy on the Buffalo River. When Morrissey committed a criminal offense at eleven years old, a judge declared him a delinquent and sent him to the Western House of Refuge in Rochester. With almost no formal education, Morrissey worked as a sailor on the Great Lakes at age fourteen. He later sailed across the globe to faraway places such as Amsterdam, Brazil, Russia, Sicily, and San Francisco.[85] By twenty-one, he was convicted of burglary and robbery, and sentenced to three and a half years in the state prison.

Morrisey's father passed away when he was young, and his mother remarried. She supported the family by running a boarding house and a saloon near the Commercial Street bridge in the Canal District. During the trial, it was noted that young Morrissey was exposed to some "low character" people in her boardinghouse. Several people testified that his mother, who was often inebriated, had a violent nature; one witness said Mrs. Haley had the worst temper he had ever seen. Even on the afternoon of the event, an eyewitness recalled that Mrs. Haley called her son a "bastard" and "a son of a bitch." Another witness shared that Haley abused her son in the past, presumably physically and emotionally. Three of his sisters remarked that they left home at a young age because their mother was such a violent drunk, and one sister reminded the jury that her mother once threw an axe at her.[86] All of the children had physical scars from wounds inflicted by their mother. The defense attorney also informed the jury that the defendant had suffered a head injury at sea seven years prior and, as a result, liquor had a powerful effect on him. They pled for temporary insanity due to alcohol.

But Morrissey's legal strategy was ineffective. The jury delivered a quick verdict: guilty of murder in the first degree. The judge, in turn, swiftly gave his sentence: death by hanging. Nominally Catholic, Morrissey spent the next few weeks turning to God. While Morrissey was in prison, Bishop Stephen Ryan confirmed him. On the morning of the execution, the former sailor consumed his last meal of poached eggs and mackerel and then received communion from Bishop Ryan. Three Irish priests, Fathers Quigley, Lanigan, and Malloy, arrived to give him solace while his three sobbing sisters said their final goodbyes. Seventy witnesses gathered in the yard of the Old Courthouse to watch Morrissey hang. He was led out of jail, where he was allowed to embrace another Irishman on death row, John Gaffney. The two of them hugged and kissed each other goodbye.

Morrissey was led to the gallows where they placed a black robe on him and secured the noose. He read a prepared statement, possibly written by his spiritual director, that urged his fellow man to avoid liquor, stay away from evil associations, and attend to their religious duties.[87] At 12:10 pm, the hood was draped over his head, and Sheriff Grover Cleveland released the lever. Morrissey dropped six feet, and the force killed him almost instantly. He was pronounced dead two minutes later, and they placed his body into a black walnut casket. It would be forty-four years before Buffalo experienced another case of matricide.

John Gaffney, the man Morrissey said goodbye to on his way to the gallows, was another tragic character. On the evening of May 7, 1872, shots rang out at the corner of Canal and Evans Streets outside of Sweeney's tavern. As police arrived, they witnessed the body of Irishman Patrick Fahey in a pool of blood. After an extensive investigation, they determined that John Gaffney had shot Fahey, who died of his wounds at home. On the night of the murder, James Quinn and Gaffney went to Sweeney's saloon to play cards. Fahey arrived at about four o'clock in the morning, and Gaffney accused him of starting trouble in his own saloon the previous evening. After a heated discussion, "Red Jack" Farrell, who was standing at the bar, showed Gaffney his pistol in his pocket. Gaffney grabbed it and shot Fahey in the back, piercing the victim's left lung.[88]

John Gaffney was born in Buffalo in 1844 to two Irish immigrants. His father, James Gaffney, died in the Mexican War when Gaffney was two, and his mother, Eileen Murphy, who reportedly worked as a prostitute, died of cholera in the early 1850s. After that, he had no one to look after him, so he fended for himself by peddling on the streets. At age fourteen, with little education, Gaffney became a sailor on the lakes like Morrissey. Eventually, he opened a tavern near the Erie Canal. Gaffney had a history of violence but no convictions until the Fahey murder. At his trial, the prosecutor revealed the saloon owner's violent past. He had shot at his first wife intending to kill; he had shot and struck Rose Kilbride through her Canal Street home window, and he had savagely beaten a Black man in Fort Erie.[89] He had also bashed a man's head in with a brick, and just months before the Fahey shooting, he had shot at a man on Carroll Street. According to the *Courier* reporter, alcohol was involved in all of these incidents.[90] Even more remarkable, despite his violent past, the residents in that part of town were furious that the well-liked saloon owner was sentenced to death.

After a plea of insanity that failed, Gaffney was sentenced to death by hanging. Sheriff Grover Cleveland was once again the hangman. Incidentally, both of these hangings were used against Cleveland in his presidential campaign when he acquired the moniker, "The Buffalo Hangman," and he was the only U.S. president to execute someone. But Cleveland had a progressive political mindset, and in other instances he worked to save two other Buffalo Irish murderers. Grain scooper Martin Flanagan was sentenced to death for killing his foreman, and Cleveland appealed the case to the authorities in Albany—the sentence was eventually reduced.[91] One of Grover Cleveland's last acts as New York's governor was to commute the sentence of longshoreman Jim Kelly, who had been convicted of murdering a stranger at a saloon at Ohio and Michigan Streets.[92] Cleveland believed it was an unintentional act.

Buffalo's "Bad Bridgets"—Prostitution[93]

The authors of the highly entertaining and informative *America's Crossroads: The Making of A City*, detailed the colorful characters who inhabited the Canal District, or the Infected District, as it was often called, because of the prevalence of vice, crime, and disease in the neighborhood. The district included the area between lower Main Street to Terrace Street to Erie Street down to the harbor. But most of the newsworthy events happened near Canal Street, which ran parallel to the terminus of the Erie Canal.

Most of the stories up to this point have been about men, but just as many women were trying to survive in that area of Buffalo. Due to hopeless circumstances, hundreds of women turned to prostitution to survive. The typical sex worker in the mid-nineteenth century was a young, foreign-born immigrant. Many of these desperate women ended up in the Canal District. Two of the most notorious brothel owners, Mother Cary, who ran a bordello on Canal Street, and Pug-Nose Cora, employed nearly four hundred women.[94] Other women worked independently from their homes or rented flats. Roughly 60 percent of the houses on Canal Street between Erie and Commercial were known places of prostitution.[95] Even as late as 1893, the number of known brothels in the Canal District, according to a report by the Christian Homestead Association, was seventy-five.[96]

The life of prostitutes in the Infected District was nasty, brutal, and, all too often, short. In the 1850s, the average New York City prostitute survived for about four years in her profession before succumbing to an early death.[97] It is doubtful that many Buffalo street workers survived much longer. The prostitutes often didn't have a home, so they had to sleep wherever they could find space: canal boats or alleyways.[98] Venereal diseases, as well as diphtheria and scarlet fever, were rampant. Violence against women by their clients and boyfriends was widespread.

While Irish surnames are prominent in arrest records and Buffalo newspaper articles about the Infected District prostitutes, detailed ethnic statistics of the street workers is unknown. An 1858 study of New York City prostitutes reports that Irish-born immigrants made up 28 percent of the New York City population, but 35 percent of all prostitutes. Using the New York City data, we can deduce that if the Irish made up 20 percent of Buffalo's population, they probably made up at least 20-25 percent of the prostitutes. The fact that in 1855 Bishop Timon established the Home of Good Shepherd, a reformatory school for those who had already engaged in crimes such as prostitution, was evidence that it was prevalent among Irish and German Catholic girls.[99]

Not all of the Canal District prostitutes, however, had the same work experience. There was a hierarchy based on the clients they serviced. The lowest were the "common whores" who took care of the towpath canal workers—the men who were often unskilled laborers, violent and drunk. The next tier of sex workers engaged with the lakeshore men, and they were considered "sophisticated."[100] Their clients had higher-paying jobs so they could solicit higher-end prostitutes. At the top of the pyramid were the courtesans who sold their services to the wealthy Buffalonians and well-heeled visitors to the Queen City. One of these courtesans became notorious.

"Irish Lize"—Eliza Quirk

On January 1, 1869, the *Buffalo Courier* listed the most notable events for the prior year, 1868. On this list of important happenings for December 22 was the "Death of Eliza Quirk *alias* Irish Lize." Other events of the time included William Fargo's election to president of the Buffalo Club and Edwin Booth's performance of *Hamlet* at the Academy of Music. The list included the deaths of politicians, judges, and other prominent Buffalonians. But Quirk was different from the rest—she was a well-known courtesan. Making this exclusive list of significant events was proof that she was a fixture in Buffalo society.[101]

Most Irish prostitutes did not stray much from the Canal District. But Irish Lize, who had once had an address near the Canal, quickly separated herself from the common prostitutes and became a courtesan. The early years of her life are lost to history except that she was born in Ireland in 1812, and eventually emigrated to the United States. She likely landed in New York City and made her way to Buffalo. During her years in Buffalo, she regularly appeared in the newspapers for arrests and fines for sex work. Often the penalty would be a $25 charge for a "disorderly house" or a "house of ill-favor."[102] Despite these legal infractions, she was relatively successful. In 1848, she saved enough money to build a house away from the seedy waterfront. Her brick boarding house, built at 72 Sycamore Street, is one of the oldest structures still standing in Buffalo. She likely rented some of the rooms to other prostitutes, making her home a high-end brothel.

In a bizarre story in 1864, toward the end of the Civil War, Irish Lize was associated with former Confederate Captain Charles H. Cole. He was sent by the Confederate high command to the Great Lakes region to spy and act as a saboteur. His orders were to capture the *USS Michigan* and set free four thousand Confederate prisoners stationed on Johnson's Island near Sandusky, Ohio. Next, Cole and his sympathizers in Canada planned to destroy several cities on the Great Lakes, including Cleveland and Buffalo. Cole, who falsely claimed to be an affluent businessman from Philadelphia, smoked cigars, dressed impeccably, and was accompanied by a beautiful woman.[103] At some point in 1864, he traveled to Buffalo and met Irish Lize, who became his "wife in disguise." We will never know whether Lize knew of Cole's military orders, but she accompanied him on his travels throughout New York and Canada.

John Wilson Murray, who spent time in Buffalo as a crew member of the *USS Michigan*, was commanded by his Union Army superiors to uncover a rumored conspiracy involving the freeing of Confederate prisoners. Murray, who worked as a Union detective, followed the couple as they traveled from city to city. While in Montreal, he described Cole's companion, whom he later learned was Irish Lize, in this manner:

> She was an elegant looking lady, big and stately, a magnificent blonde with clothes that are marvel to me. I did not know then, but later she turned out to be the celebrated Irish Lize. The contrast between her and Cole was striking. She was big, stout and fine looking; he was a little, sandy, red-haired fellow, but smart as lightning.[104]

As time passed, Cole befriended and duped one of the Union officers on the *Michigan*, who regularly permitted the spy to tour the coveted military vessel. One evening in September 1864, Cole was supposed to attend an elegant supper on the ship where he planned to drug the officers, allowing him to capture the ship. But Detective Murray had intercepted the Confederate plot, and the authorities arrested Cole and his accomplices before they could enact their bold plan.

Before the plan unraveled, Irish Lize had revealed to Murray, disguised as a fellow hotel guest, that she never wore the same pair of gloves twice, and she proudly showed him a trunk filled with a dozen pairs of gloves—a testament to her success as a courtesan. The Confederate saboteur Cole was held prisoner until the end of the Civil War, while Murray was promoted to the Secret Service in Washington, DC. There was no record of what happened to Irish Lize, but it is assumed she was released and returned to her life in Buffalo.

Within a few years after the Cole episode, on December 22, 1868, the 56-year-old Eliza Quirk died at her home at 72 Sycamore. In her *Courier* obituary, the writer declared that Irish Lize was "one of the most notorious courtesans in the country."[105] The writer added that she had given up her "evil ways" ten years before her death and had found comfort at St. Mary's Church. She was remembered for being generous, but also for the "bold bad life she led for many years."[106] She was buried in the United German and French Cemetery near Buffalo.

Irish Lize's home remains intact. Built in 1848, it is one of the oldest residences in Buffalo, and one of the last examples of Federal-style architecture from the pre-Civil War era. In 2020, preservationists successfully saved her house from demolition, and it is now on the National Historic Register. Rocco Termini, a prominent builder in Buffalo, bought the house and donated it to Preservation Buffalo Niagara (PBN).[107] PBN will raise about $2.1 million to turn her home into three affordable housing units, the headquarters for Heart of the City Neighborhoods, Inc., and a meeting space for PBN.[108] The new owners hope to tell Eliza's story to shine a light on the hundreds of desperate women who had to work in the sex trade to make ends meet.

In the spring of 1899, reformers lost patience with the houses of prostitution throughout the canal area of Buffalo. On March 31, Buffalo police officers raided and cleared out one hundred women who worked as prostitutes, some of whom had lived there for twenty years or more. The surnames of the evicted were a mix of Irish and English. A *Buffalo Express* reporter was on the scene during the evictions and captured a conversation between a haggard older prostitute named Hattie Connors and the police. The police claimed she did not cause them much trouble over the years, but she replied that they had arrested her a thousand times.[109] At the eviction, Connors told another woman that she was either going to "the Poorhouse or hell," and she did not care either way.[110]

Irish immigrants faced unrelenting hardships: bigotry, discrimination, poverty, and disease. To some, life here must have seemed even worse than in their native land. Eventually, their situation began to improve.

CHAPTER THREE

The Catholic Church, Labor Unions, and Public Service

The Irish in Buffalo had three supporting institutions, like three legs on a stool: the Catholic Church, labor unions, and government. The Church provided education and a social safety net. The labor movement and unions agitated for better pay and fewer weekly working hours. And the local and state governments provided hundreds of public service jobs, offering steady, year-round employment. Without these three, it would have taken the Irish much longer to establish themselves in Buffalo, much less shape the Queen City to the extent they did.

The Catholic Church

On April 23, 1847, the Vatican created the Catholic Diocese of Buffalo to minister to the growing number of its members in Western New York. On October 17 of that year, in a pouring rainstorm, 12,000 Buffalonians welcomed Bishop John Timon, a Vincentian priest and son of Irish immigrants from Cavan County, to head the new diocese.[1] A fine carriage was waiting to pick him up, but Bishop Timon decided to walk, carpetbag and umbrella in hand.[2] This act of solidarity with his flock would set the tone for his tenure as bishop.

At the time, the center of the Buffalo Roman Catholic Church, and the presumed home for the new bishop, was the stately St. Louis Church, a French and German parish on Main Street. However, Timon, born of humble beginnings, desired to live near his fellow Irish men and women. He set up residence near the more modest St. Patrick's Church on Ellicott Street.

While roughly 6,300 Irish people lived in Buffalo, only three hundred families were registered at St. Patrick's Church when Timon arrived.[3] The first Bishop of Buffalo confirmed a staggering 4,167 people in Buffalo in his first year—proof that Buffalo was a rich mission territory. When not performing his pastoral duties,

Timon was crafting a plan to create an institutional church to help lift its members out of poverty.

As discussed in the previous chapter, Timon had invited the Sisters of Charity to build a hospital, an orphanage, and a home for wayward and homeless young women.[4] The Sisters also opened a maternity hospital, an infant asylum, and Providence Insane Asylum. Together, the Sisters and Bishop Timon created a social safety network that cared for thousands of Catholics and non-Catholics alike.

Timon was also passionate about improving educational opportunities for his Irish flock. He was concerned, however, that members of the congregation would lose their faith in the public schools, which only hired non-Catholics as teachers and had an anti-Catholic bias. Timon took matters into his own hands. He recruited several religious orders to establish secondary schools, such as the Mercy Sisters (Mercy Academy), the Daughters of the Heart of Mary (Nardin Academy), and the Christian Brothers (St. Joseph's Collegiate Institute). He also recruited the Vincentian Fathers (Niagara University), the Franciscans (St. Bonaventure), and the Jesuits (Canisius College). This network of schools, which became some of the city's most esteemed and sought-after educational institutions, raised the academic level and career prospects for thousands of immigrants, Irish and otherwise, for generations to come.

Churches

Timon created a network of churches to address his followers' spiritual, social, and communal needs. Before his arrival, opportunities to participate in church rituals and sacraments were limited. Thus, the former Vincentian missionary opened dozens of parishes across Western New York. Timon was confident that Buffalo would be prosperous and understood that great cities need impressive cathedrals. In 1849, the Irish bishop traveled to Europe to meet with the pope and tour the Old World's great cathedrals. He used this trip to raise funds for his new cathedral from kings, princes, and archdukes.[5] Raising money and gathering ideas for his house of worship, however, was only part of his challenge.

In 1851, Timon purchased the Webster Garden Estate in Buffalo's "loveliest district with a beautiful park and rolling terraces stretching down to the shores of Lake Erie."[6] Once the Protestants discovered his plans for the site, they quickly tried to repurchase the land. But it was too late.[7] Bishop Timon chose Irish-American architect Patrick Keeley from New York City to design his Gothic-style church, similar to the prominent ones he had visited throughout Europe.

Just blocks away from Protestant cathedrals, Catholics would now have a permanent house of worship.

In February 1851, Timon laid the cornerstone of St. Joseph's Cathedral. Irish laborers did much of the work constructing the bishop's church.[8] After working grueling hours during the day, laborers would come after work to haul stones or provide the masonry work for the project.[9] Obtaining finances for the cathedral was challenging, so Timon continually begged parishioners, foreign dignitaries, and his fellow priests for assistance. Finally, on July 1, 1855, St. Joseph's Cathedral was dedicated to an overflowing crowd of 3,000 people—including many prominent ecclesiastical figures from around the United States. Timon was able to pay off the project within eight years of completion.

While it was not exclusively an Irish parish, for many decades, the rectors of the cathedral were Irish, and many of the parishioners hailed from the Emerald Isle.[10] But the burgeoning Irish community in the First Ward also needed its own church. When it was time to create a parish there, Timon chose the name St. Bridget's to honor the Irish saint. In 1853, a small frame church was built on Fulton Street at Louisiana Street, and five years later a more prominent, brick Romanesque-style church replaced it. Around the same time, Timon also supervised the construction of Holy Angels Church on Porter Avenue to minister to the thousands of Irish residents on Buffalo's West Side.

Over two decades, the indefatigable Bishop Timon built one of America's most important nineteenth-century Catholic dioceses from almost nothing. Buffalo historians have praised Timon for his contributions to the city. Mark Goldman describes Bishop Timon's impact on the Irish immigrants as follows:

> While the Irish had been in Buffalo for over twenty years prior to the arrival of Bishop Timon in 1847, it was not until he came that the rest of the people of Buffalo became daily and seriously aware of them. The Irish churches and religious societies were highly ethnocentric and invisible, and the periodic Irish newspapers had no circulation beyond the confines of the First Ward. Timon's arrival changed all of this. Now, for the first time, Buffalo's Irish working-class population had a brash and bold spokesman who rallied and inspired the Irish and in the process frightened the older German and WASP community.[11]

Another local historian emphasized the importance of Bishop Timon's charitable activities to all Buffalonians:

> Furthermore, because the American Protestant response to poverty and other local welfare needs was, besides the poorhouse, largely non-existent before

1847 and inadequate after it, Timon simultaneously, almost single-handedly, created the institutional foundations of much of local charity.[12]

Timon was remembered for more than his charity. He has been compared to St. Paul; relentless in his travels through the cold and fatigue to preach and administer the sacraments to his flock.[13] And Archbishop Hughes, a contemporary of Timon, considered him the humblest man he had ever met.

Critics of Timon claimed he was uncompromising when faced with opposing viewpoints, unrelenting toward priests he felt were not contributing enough, and unwilling to delegate work and responsibilities more often.[14] Despite those alleged faults, had it not been for Timon's efforts, thousands of immigrants would have suffered greatly from hunger, sickness, and homelessness.

Bishop Timon died on April 16, 1867, two days after preaching the Palm Sunday Mass at St. Joseph's Cathedral. There were enormous gatherings throughout Western New York to commemorate this man, and an estimated 100,000 people in Buffalo turned up to view his body. After the funeral mass, Bishop Timon was buried beneath his beloved St. Joseph's Cathedral.

Timon used to say that even though he was born in America, he was conceived in Ireland.[15] The Irish, particularly those from the poorer neighborhoods, were lifted up by their Irish benefactor. Subsequent bishops would face challenging conditions and situations during their tenure. However, no one would face more obstacles and opposition with such limited resources and still accomplish as much as Bishop Timon.

Overcoming tremendous obstacles and facing fierce opposition, this diminutive figure, who stood just over 5 feet tall, achieved more for the Catholic Church in Buffalo during his tenure than any subsequent ecclesiastical figure. Much of the social care network that he created still exists today.

Other Noteworthy Church Leaders

After Bishop Timon died, the Vatican replaced him with another Irishman. In fact, for the Diocese of Buffalo's first 150 years of existence, popes chose only Irish priests to lead the Buffalo flock, despite large numbers of German, Polish, and Italian Catholics. The Irish and Irish-American bishops included Timon, Ryan, Quigley, Colton, Dougherty, Turner, Duffy, O'Hara, Burke, McNulty, and Head (see Appendix B).

Bishop Stephen V. Ryan, Timon's replacement, was born in 1825 in Ontario, Canada. Ryan, also a Vincentian priest, differed in temperament from his predecessor—he was amiable, cerebral, and calm. Father Patrick Cronin, who knew both prelates, compared them by saying, "Timon's nature was like a torrent rushing down the mountain, crushing every obstacle that impeded its course. Stephen Vincent Ryan resembled the majestic river flowing calmly...."[16]

Like Timon, Ryan quickly founded institutions to assist his congregation. He founded the *Catholic Union and Times* newspaper, a widely-read weekly journal that became the bishop's mouthpiece and helped establish orthodoxy in church teachings. Irish-born Father Patrick Cronin edited the paper for years and wrote extensively on issues relevant to Ireland and Irish Americans.

In 1884, Bishop Ryan, with the help of Catholic laypeople, created the Irish American Savings and Loan Association. Ryan understood that increasing homeownership rates would improve the financial prospects of his Irish flock. This financial institution, referred to as the "poor man's bank," was integral in helping the working-class Irish purchase their own homes. Many of the Association's members were police officers, firefighters, school teachers, and railroad workers. By the 1920s, the organization advertised that it had helped 10,000 members purchase a house, accelerating wealth creation for first and second-generation immigrants.

Ryan, an intellectual fluent in several languages, expanded Timon's educational network. Ryan's supporters credited him with creating a parochial school system with 76 schools and 20,000 students, "equal to any in the country."[17] Bishop Ryan also founded the Young Men's Catholic Association, which hosted debates and lectures to instruct and train future Catholic leaders.

Several Irish-American priests associated with Buffalo became bishops. One of them was James Quigley, Buffalo's third bishop. Quigley was born in Oshawa, Canada, in 1855 to poor Irish immigrants who moved to Rochester, New York, a few years after his birth. In 1865, his parents sent ten-year-old Jimmy to Buffalo to live with his uncle, Father Edward Quigley. James Quigley attended St. Joseph's Collegiate Institute, where he was the favorite student in his class and a star pitcher on the school's baseball team.[18]

After graduating at the top of his high school class, he planned to attend West Point Military Academy. Instead, the charismatic Quigley decided to become a Catholic priest. Bishop Ryan sent the gifted young man to Europe for seminary studies, where Quigley was ordained at Innsbruck, Austria. A rising star in the Buffalo diocese, Quigley was a noted pulpit speaker, and his charisma endeared him to people.[19] After serving at St. Joseph's Cathedral, Quigley asked Bishop Ryan's permission to become rector of St. Bridget's in the First Ward.[20] The bishop honored his request.

During Quigley's tenure at St. Bridget's, he connected with the workers and their families, and his thoughts on the church's involvement in labor issues evolved. Quigley also inspired a young man, William Donovan, a future First World War hero. Donovan later claimed that Father Quigley, who became a champion of the working-class Irish, was his boyhood idol.[21] In December 1896, forty-one-year-old James Quigley became Bishop of Buffalo. It was a proud moment for his fellow Irish men and women. Even non-Catholic newspaper editors wrote favorably about him, describing him as popular, intelligent, progressive, and inclined toward the liberal wing of the Catholic Church.[22] We will learn more about Quigley and the labor movement later in this chapter.

About fifty years after Quigley was installed as bishop, Joseph Aloysius Burke became the first Buffalo-born priest to head the local diocese. Burke was born in 1886 and raised just outside the First Ward. His Irish immigrant father, Joseph S. Burke, worked as a boilermaker and owned a saloon; his mother, Amelia (Howard) Burke, was a homemaker. Burke, described as short in stature, with gray eyes and black hair, was educated by the Mercy Sisters at St. Stephen's School and later by the Jesuits at Canisius High School and Canisius College.[23] He entered the priesthood, studied at the University of Innsbruck in Austria, and then served as an army chaplain with the 91st division on the French and Belgian Front during the First World War.[24]

The Vatican promoted Monsignor Burke to auxiliary Bishop of Buffalo in 1943, and nine years later, he became the ninth bishop of Buffalo. During his decade as head of the diocese (1952 to 1962), he presided over a "Golden Age" of the Church, building or expanding dozens of churches, schools, and rectories. The diocese at the time had 800,000 members who were served by one thousand priests and three thousand religious sisters. Nuns and priests educated 80,000 students in Catholic elementary schools, and thousands of pupils attended thirty-nine Catholic high schools.[25]

During this time, Burke dedicated himself to foreign missions, the Puerto Rican immigrants in Buffalo, and the building of St. John Vianney Seminary in East Aurora. As the son of a laborer, he was also a dedicated advocate for the labor movement. In October 1962, Bishop Joseph A. Burke died from a sudden heart attack at age 76 while attending the first week of the Vatican II Council in Rome.

Sisters of Mercy

Irish Catholic sisters have improved the health and well-being of tens of thousands of Buffalonians for nearly two hundred years. In addition to the Sisters of Charity, Bishop Timon also recruited the Sisters of Mercy, a community of Irish nuns dedicated to educating children and serving the needs of the poor.

One cold February day in 1858, three Irish Sisters and a postulant arrived in Buffalo from Rochester: Mother Mary Teresa Carroll, Sister Mary O'Reilly, Sister Mary Madden, and Mary Ann McGarr, a postulant. When the enthusiastic women arrived at their First Ward dwelling on Fulton Street, which was previously ravaged by fire, Bishop Timon personally assisted the Sisters in gathering necessary materials such as beds, bed linens, and other essential supplies. He watched over them "like a vigilant father."[26] Irish residents in the area were familiar with the "walking Sisters" from the old country and were grateful for their arrival.[27] No one knew then of the impact the Sisters would have on Buffalo over the next century.

The day after their arrival, Timon gave the three Sisters money to set up a soup and bread kitchen for the poor and a pharmacy in the First Ward to assist the immigrants, who were suffering from the effects of a financial crisis, later called the Panic of 1857.[28] In those days, the Sisters went two by two with brown baskets that contained food and medicine to the homes of the sick and poor.[29] Financial support was scarce, forcing them to beg for resources to assist the impoverished. Within a few years, the Sisters established several schools to educate the large Irish populations south of downtown. In 1871, one of their new schools was bursting with over twelve hundred children.[30]

The Sisters, whose first settlement in Buffalo was in the First Ward near St. Bridget's Church, quickly responded to the Irish migration to South Buffalo at the turn of the twentieth century. In 1902, they purchased the Rufus P. Choate estate at Red Jacket Parkway and Abbott Road, across from Cazenovia Park, to build a new motherhouse for their sisters.[31] During this time, Mother Mary Scholastica, the Order's superior, led much of the expansion in South Buffalo. Scholastica, whose birth name was Mary Corbett, was a daughter of Irish immigrants who grew up in the First Ward. Corbett joined the Mercy Sisters at age sixteen, taught at St. Bridget's School for twenty-five years, and served as principal.[32] She also supervised the transition of the motherhouse from Batavia to the new site on Abbott Road.

In 1904, the Mercy Sisters opened Mercy Hospital on Tifft Street, near the newly created Holy Family Church. The hospital served the workers at the steel plant and people in neighborhoods south of downtown. Under Corbett's supervision, the Mercy Sisters also opened Mount Mercy Academy, a girls' high school on Abbott Road. (The school is still operating one hundred and twenty years later.) Three years later, the Sisters also staffed a six-room school at St. Teresa's Parish on Seneca Street. Some Buffalonians thought the school was unnecessary because it was "in the wilderness of South Buffalo." But critics were proven wrong. By the fall of that year, one hundred thirty-five students were enrolled at the Sisters' school.[33] In 1908, the Irish Sisters opened an elementary school at Holy Family Parish, educating several generations of Irish families.

In February 1928, the Sisters of Mercy opened a new $1 million hospital on Abbott Road near their motherhouse and high school. The Sister who oversaw the construction was Mother Superior Mary Agatha, who had previously served as head of Mercy Academy. Sister Agatha was born Julia Manning in 1862 to Irish immigrants and served as the mother superior of the order in the 1920s.[34] Thanks to the Sisters, the foundations and infrastructure were now in place for future generations of the South Buffalo Irish.

Sister Mary Mechtilde O'Connor

Sister Mary Mechtilde O'Connor, a hospital founder and administrator, was another prominent Mercy nun.[35] Anne Margaret O'Connor was born in 1886 to Irish immigrant parents from County Clare. Her parents ran a grocery store on Buffalo's Smith Street and were leaders at St. Stephen's Church. After attending St. Stephen's Elementary School and Central High School, where O'Connor was the basketball team captain, she joined the Mercy Sisters.

After professing vows and taking the name Mary Mechtilde, O'Connor worked as an elementary school teacher and later as a principal at several Mercy schools. In 1930, at age forty-four, she accepted a position as the head administrator of St. Jerome's Hospital in Batavia, New York. As an effective hospital leader there, O'Connor was later chosen to lead the Sisters' flagship hospital, Mercy Hospital. During her tenure at Mercy, she oversaw the construction of three more wings at this critical South Buffalo institution. These experiences prepared her for her most significant career challenge: constructing a new hospital in the Buffalo suburb of Kenmore.

In 1948, O'Connor spearheaded the fundraising and planning efforts for this new 100-bed facility called Kenmore Mercy Hospital. She served as the hospital administrator until 1977, leading several expansion projects and establishing the first helicopter ambulance service in Western New York history. Even into her late 80s, she still worked to guide the hospital through several building projects.

Her life-long charitable work did not go unnoticed. Bishop James McNulty presented her with the *Pro Ecclesiae et Pontifice* medal from Pope Paul VI for "her magnificent contribution to our society as an educator and administrator."[36] For her work, the grocer's daughter was also the first woman to receive the Canisius College President's Medal, and she was awarded the "Most Distinguished Citizen in the Town of Tonawanda." Kenmore Mercy's lobby has a plaque with her picture commemorating her service at the hospital.

Two other Mercy Sisters shaped healthcare in Western New York. Sister M. Helena McLaughlin played a role in establishing Mercy Hospital and paved the way for Mercy Health Services.[37] She was born Mary Rose McLaughlin in Elmira, New York, and joined the Mercy Sisters in 1893. She also served as the head of the Order in the Buffalo Diocese for eighteen years. Another notable woman was Sister Sheila Marie Walsh, one of Mercy Flight's founders. Walsh was one of the prime movers in establishing the emergency medical helicopter service that has saved many lives. Walsh, a South Buffalo native, also served as the administrator of Mercy Hospital in the 1970s.

St. Mary's School for the Deaf

Mary Anne Burke was born in Dublin in 1842, and at the start of the Famine, her parents emigrated to the United States. At age nineteen, Burke entered the Sisters of St. Joseph in Buffalo. In 1861, Bishop Timon sent Burke to Philadelphia to learn the newest teaching methods for children with speech and hearing impairments, so he could open a school for these children. Burke returned the following year, and by that time Timon had constructed a four-story brick structure. At the time, it was the only school for deaf children run by a Catholic diocese in the country.[38] By 1872, the school's reputation had spread, and New York State started to send public school children to her school. With Burke's progressive teaching curriculum, her school grew into one of the elite schools in the country, with many children from out of state boarding at her facility. Burke later led a campaign to raise money to build an even larger facility on Main Street to accommodate all students at one site. From 1862 to 1915, the school had educated over one thousand students.[39]

In addition to articulation and lip-reading, the teachers prepared the children for careers in printing, dressmaking, needlework, and shoemaking.[40] For sixty-five years as principal of St. Mary's School for the Deaf, Sister Anne Burke was a pioneer in her field. She also served as the Mother Superior of Sisters of St. Joseph, where she helped found many schools across the diocese. Sister Anne Burke's school for deaf children on Main Street is still operational one hundred and sixty years later.

Catholic Charities

In 1923, Irish-born Bishop William Turner founded one of Buffalo's largest charitable organizations: Catholic Charities. Turner, the sixth Bishop of Buffalo, was born in County Limerick in 1871. After working as a philosophy professor at Catholic University in Washington, D.C., he was named Bishop of Buffalo in 1919. Turner believed a unified Catholic welfare organization would have better results than the existing system with over twenty independent agencies. Turner served as the chairman of the board of trustees, while Father John C. Carr, the son of an Irish immigrant, was named director of the local organization. In the early years, the organization raised money for four local orphanages, five homes for the elderly, several protective homes for girls, nurseries, and several field agencies.[41]

They expanded the reach of the charitable organization to Niagara, Chautauqua, and Cattaraugus counties. In 1933, the King of Italy awarded Turner one of Italy's highest honors for his tireless work with the Italian immigrants in Buffalo.[42] *The Buffalo News* wrote that Bishop Turner "loomed as another St. Vincent de Paul in caring for the Catholic poor of Western New York."[43]

At the end of the twentieth century, Monsignor John J. Conniff, a grandson of Irish immigrants, led Buffalo's Catholic Charities for thirty years, longer than any previous director. The Irish-American priest also served as the chairman of the national Catholic Charities organization from 1969 to 1973. In the mid-1990s, while Conniff was the leader, the organization annually assisted over 200,000 Western New Yorkers of all faiths. During his tenure, Catholic Charities consisted of over forty organizations and field offices with a staff of over four hundred workers.[44] By this time, the organization had adapted to the needs of the community with programs in counseling, domestic violence, and mental health services. They also focused attention on immigration, helping to resettle hundreds of immigrants and refugees arriving in Buffalo from Africa and Asia. Catholic Charities of Buffalo still assists over 125,000 Western New Yorkers annually.

Father Nelson Baker

If you were to have asked most twentieth-century Western New Yorkers who they would most associate with charitable works, it would undoubtedly have been Father Nelson Baker. While neither his first nor last name sounds Irish, Baker was half-Irish. He was born in 1842 to Lewis Becker (later Baker), a German Lutheran immigrant, and Caroline Donnellan, an Irish Catholic immigrant. All four Baker children, including Nelson, were baptized Lutheran, but he liked attending Catholic church services with his devout mother. One day, when Nelson was nine years old, his mother marched him (and only him) to St. Patrick's Church and baptized him as a Catholic. His Irish Catholic mother's faith shaped Nelson's life's work.

After his schooling, Nelson Baker worked in his father's grocery store until the outbreak of the Civil War. Shortly after, Nelson enlisted with the Union forces, where he fought in the Battle of Gettysburg and was later sent to New York City to help suppress the draft riots. He returned to Buffalo and started a successful grain business, but he experienced a strong calling to become a priest. After seminary studies, Baker was assigned to a parish just outside of Buffalo in Lackawanna (then Limestone Hill). The bishop promoted him to the superintendent of an orphanage at that parish. While there, Father Baker expanded the site's charitable offerings. He built Our Lady of Victory Infant Home for unwed mothers and their children and opened a maternity hospital, which he later transformed into a general hospital. Father Baker also built a farm to feed the hungry and a home for nurses. But his work with thousands of orphaned children brought him the most joy.

Besides his charitable institutions, Baker built a massive church dedicated to Our Lady of Victory. It was completed in May 1926, and five months later, Pope Pius XI elevated it to a basilica, one of only two minor basilicas in the United States at the time.[45] During Baker's lifetime, Buffalo residents referred to him as the "Padre of the Poor." One Father Baker expert wrote that his "commitment to serve the poor, abandoned, lonely, orphaned, hungry, unborn, racial minorities and the sick was tireless and far-reaching."[46] The Buffalo Diocese has pursued Father Baker's cause for canonization. In 2011, Pope Benedict XVI declared the humble Buffalo priest "Venerable" for his heroic virtue. Almost ninety years after Baker's death, his aid organizations, OLV Charities and OLV Human Services, still assist thousands of vulnerable people in Western New York, and his basilica is one of the region's most visited sites.

Niagara University and St. Bonaventure University

In 1855, Bishop Timon requested that Father John Joseph Lynch, a fellow Irish-born Vincentian priest, found a diocesan seminary. Lynch secured two hundred acres of farmland north of Buffalo, in Niagara Falls, to erect a facility to train future priests and educate lay people. The College and Seminary of Our Lady of Angels was renamed Niagara University in 1883. Under the supervision of Irish-born physician Dr. John Cronyn, the college opened one of the first medical schools in Western New York. In its first twenty-five years, the college graduated hundreds of priests and dozens of doctors, lawyers, professors, and merchants.[47] Many Irish immigrants secured professional employment thanks to the educational programs at Niagara University. The college founder, Father Lynch, went on to become the Archbishop of Toronto.[48]

A few years after the Vincentian Brothers formed Niagara University, an Irish immigrant conceived of a Catholic college south of Buffalo. Nicholas Devereux, born in 1791 in County Wexford, and settled near Utica, New York, dreamed of building a utopian city for Irish settlers. He purchased land from the Holland Land Company near Olean, New York to create a commercial, educational, and spiritual center called Allegany City.[49] While his utopian vision never materialized, the Irish immigrant convinced Bishop Timon to allow him to travel to Rome to recruit priests for a Catholic college. The Franciscans agreed to send four friars to Olean, with Devereux donating the land and money to fund the operation. After the school opened in 1858, the friars called it St. Bonaventure College, which is still thriving one hundred and sixty years later, as St. Bonaventure University.

Sister Denise Roche

Sister Denise Roche was the longtime head of one of Buffalo's most successful colleges. Born in Buffalo, Denise Roche was the daughter of Vincent Roche and Mary (Crehan) Roche, both Irish Americans. While Denise's father worked as a salesman, her mother was a trailblazer who worked as an administrator in the Buffalo schools for twenty-two years, juggling a career and raising a family before it was fashionable.[50] Denise graduated from D'Youville College, earned a Ph.D. in sociology from the University of Massachusetts, and joined the Grey Nuns of the Sacred Heart. Sister Roche returned to D'Youville College to teach and work as an administrator. As the head of the sociology department, she added programs in gerontology and criminology.

In 1978, Roche became the college's youngest president at age thirty-six. She took control of a college in crisis with plummeting enrollments and a budget deficit, informing some staff that the college might not open in the fall.[51] This Irish-American sister had a vision for transforming the sleepy college on Buffalo's West Side by growing a program to support the healthcare industry while retaining its focus on liberal arts. The college added professional degrees in occupational and physical therapy, physician assistant, and other healthcare occupations.

Roche erected new buildings around the campus core, including a library, arts and science building, student housing, and a sports complex. Under Roche's tenure, the school added four doctoral programs and twenty-three master's programs. Twenty-five years after she took the helm, the student body more than doubled, and the college was financially stable.[52] In 2004, *The Buffalo News* stated Roche turned D'Youville College into "a significant institution on the West Side," investing $49 million into construction projects in the neighborhood.[53] By 2015, the school had invested $100 million in new facilities, helping to stabilize its West Side community.

In 2016, Sister Denise Roche retired from D'Youville after thirty-seven years at the helm. At the end of her tenure, the student body had tripled, the college budget ($60 million) was ten times larger, and the endowment rose from $1.2 million to $38 million.[54] Roche also served on many local civic and corporate boards. In 2016, Governor Andrew Cuomo nominated the Buffalo Irishwoman as the Niagara Frontier Transportation Authority (NFTA) chairwoman. In this high-profile position, she led the largest Upstate New York transportation system with two international airports, a bus system, and a train service. While she excelled in this endeavor, Sister Denise Roche will always be remembered for transforming a small Catholic college into a major regional institution and gentrifying a historic Buffalo neighborhood.

In the early years of the twenty-first century, Irish-American leaders of local colleges (later named universities) were everywhere. While Sister Denise Roche led D'Youville College for almost four decades, Kevin Sullivan was at the helm of Medaille College for fourteen years, ending in 2001. John Hurley, who received a law degree from Notre Dame Law School and worked as a partner for Phillips Lytle LLP, was president of Canisius College for twelve years. His brother, Paul Hurley, a graduate of Canisius College, was the first lay president of Trocaire College in South Buffalo, where he served for fourteen years. Father James J. Maher, C.M., was president at Niagara University for a decade. At Erie Community College, former congressman Jack Quinn served as president for almost a decade. Finally, Sister Margaret Carney, OSF, was president of St. Bonaventure for twelve years, while Dr. Michael S. Brophy became the leader of Hilbert College in 2019. Bishop John Timon would have been proud of his fellow Irish men and women who presided over many of the institutions he and his successors had built. Despite all the accomplishments of the named men and women in the Catholic Church, we now turn to a darker period of Church history.

The Church's Sexual Abuse Scandal

In the 1960s, nearly one million people in the eight counties of Western New York were affiliated with the Roman Catholic Church; by 2023, it was down to 557,000.[55] Part of this decline was due to the regional population loss. Others left the Church for other faith traditions or no longer affiliated with organized religion. The Church's power and influence waned at the dawn of the twenty-first century. But it would lose more of its membership as a horrific scandal came to light.

On February 27, 2018, Michael Whalen, a brave fifty-two-year-old South Buffalo resident, announced in front of the Catholic Diocese's headquarters on Main Street that Father Norbert Orsolits had sexually abused him when he was fourteen. Whalen claimed that the cleric's abuse "ruined his life" and led him to a life of drug and alcohol abuse.[56] Shortly after Whalen's announcement, *Buffalo News* reporter Jay Tokasz contacted Father Orsolits to verify the claim. Shockingly, the retired priest admitted that he abused "probably dozens" of boys. The number of abused turned out to be at least twenty underaged boys.[57] As details emerged about the Diocese's coverup of the sexual scandal, it turns out that Orsolits was not even the worst offending priest in terms of the number of accusers.

For years before Whalen's announcement, there had been dozens of other local sex abuse allegations. The difference this time was that Father Orsolits admitted to the reporter what he had done in a disturbing, matter-of-fact manner. It was the shot heard around Western New York. Within a short time, other victims stepped forward, alleging abuse from priests. Irish-American Bishop Richard J. Malone was at the helm then, and he was criticized for not being forthcoming in terms of what the diocese knew about the numerous allegations.

Another brave Catholic, Malone's Irish-American executive assistant, Siobhan M. O'Connor, secretly smuggled documents from the diocese headquarters and shared them with the news media. The documents included additional names of abusive priests that had not been previously revealed, including some accused who were still employed by the diocese. In 2018, O'Connor appeared on CBS's *60 Minutes*, exposing the coverup scandal to a national audience. In her interview, she declared, "Just as my name is all Irish, I [Siobhan] have an all-Irish temperament…injustice has always been something that I could not abide by from a young age…" Diocesan leaders realized they had a massive crisis on their hands—first the abuse, then the coverup. Within a year, lay advocates from the Movement to Restore Trust, including Irish Americans such as Thomas Beecher, John Hurley, and Maureen Hurley, led the effort that forced Bishop Richard Malone to resign due to his alleged role in covering up abuse allegations.

As of 2023, over 900 victims have accused priests or employees of the diocese of sexual abuse.[59] Nearly every Catholic parish had at least one Child Victims Act abuse lawsuit.[60] A 2021 *Buffalo News* analysis shows that since 1950, 230 priests who have worked in the Buffalo diocese have been accused of abuse in and outside of Buffalo. During the same time, approximately 2,300 priests have served this area.[61]

Financially, this scandal has devastated the Buffalo diocese. By 2019, it had already paid out $17.5 million to 106 victims on the condition that the survivors promised not to sue the diocese. The local Catholic Church also spent $11 million in legal fees on its Chapter 11 bankruptcy.[62] As of 2023, Buffalo is one of the twenty-six out of 194 U.S. Catholic dioceses (13%) that have filed for bankruptcy. While the ethnic background of the abusive priests is diverse, many of the Buffalo bishops who transferred the abusive priests to other parishes or covered up the abuse were Irish Americans.

Sadly, this scandal has overshadowed the nearly two centuries of goodwill the Catholic Church had built up. It does a great disservice to the thousands of religious sisters and brothers who provided for the spiritual and material needs of the region's residents.

The Irish and the Labor Movement

While the Church provided the Irish with a social safety net, the labor movement improved their wages and working conditions. As discussed earlier, as early as 1822, the Lockport Irish canal workers rioted due to their horrifying working and living conditions. Irish workers expanding the Erie Canal went on strike for higher wages in 1849. The following year, they laid down their shovels to demand a shorter work day of ten-hour shifts. While canal workers had made the most noise up to this point, in 1863, the Irish dockworkers stopped working in an effort to secure better wages. Buffalo Irish laborers also played significant roles in the national railroad strikes of 1877 and 1892. But none of these strikes compared to the one initiated by dockworkers along the Buffalo River during the last year of the nineteenth century.

The Great Strike of 1899

In the winter of 1898-1899, the Lake Carriers' Association, a trade association representing vessels on the Great Lakes, awarded William "Fingy" Conners, an Irish-American saloon owner from Buffalo, control over all the loading and unloading of the grain boats, including the lucrative task of hiring the grain scoopers.[63] Many of the first and second-generation Irish arrivals to Buffalo found jobs scooping grain out of the hulls of ships. Conners, who managed the freight-handling business along the Lake Erie shore, devised a scheme to profit from this new contract. He set up a network of cronies at saloons in the First Ward who added fake names to the roster of workers on each job and then collected the pay themselves. For instance, if thirty scoopers worked a job, the saloon bosses would say there were forty and keep the wages of the ten fictitious workers. The grain scoopers realized this resulted in reduced income for them and threatened to strike. Not wanting any disruptions in his business, Fingy Conners immediately ended the practice. But this was not the end of his scheming.

The year before Conners won his new contract, a grain scooper's pay was based on how many bushels he unloaded. Workers averaged $4.90 daily. Fingy devised a new compensation plan with a fixed rate of 28 cents an hour of work versus the previous wage system based on bushels unloaded.[64] Almost overnight, this resulted in a 50% decline in pay for his fellow Irish Catholics and former neighbors.

To make matters worse, the bosses favored workers who spent money in their saloons. Saturday was payday, and the workers received their wages over the counter at the bar in the evening. The workers' wages were the net of their earnings, less alcohol and boarding fees. If the boss deemed your check too large, he would refrain from hiring you for the next job. This system favored young, single workers who boarded at the saloons and enjoyed liberal libations over married men with families.

The leadership of Local 51, stacked with Conners' loyalists, decided to accept his pay plan, which infuriated most grain scoopers. In late April 1899, the roughly 900 grain scoopers organized a new union, Local 109, at Patrick "P.J." McMahon's saloon on Elk Street.[65] Conners immediately dispatched his thugs to destroy McMahon's family saloon and rough up the union organizers. As the shipping season began in May, the scoopers strike made national headlines for disrupting freight shipments across the Great Lakes. The Great Dock Strike of 1899 had commenced.

Fingy struggled to find replacement workers to assist in unloading the boats. Local Italian and Polish immigrants sided with the strikers, forcing Conners to recruit over 1,000 scabs outside Buffalo and as far away as New York City and Cincinnati. But when they arrived in Buffalo and learned they were hired to be strikebreakers, they, too, defected to the strikers' side.

Despite winning over the scab workers, many grain scoopers still faced an agonizing decision: earn reduced wages by siding with the powerful Fingy Conners or strike and struggle to feed their families with little in the way of government or union safety nets. Despite the uncertainty, most scoopers ultimately sided with the strikers.

Fortunately, the powerless grain scoopers had allies in the Catholic Church and the political arena. Father Patrick Cronin, an Irish Catholic priest and advocate for the workers, wrote several articles in the *Catholic Union and Times*, where he chastised Fingy Conners for his corrupt system. Knowing editorials wouldn't change Fingy's course of action, Cronin convened a meeting of the scoopers at St. Bridget's Hall in the First Ward, where he delivered a passionate speech rallying the workers to stand up to Conners. As Cronin's speech was nearing an end, cheers erupted from the back of the hall as another church official gently pushed through the crowd to the platform. The entire assembly rose to meet the unexpected guest, Bishop James Quigley.

Bishop Quigley delivered a detailed, somewhat dispassionate address to the workers, leaving them with an unequivocal mandate: refrain from working for Conners until he quit the grain business.[66] The Bishop's authority was in part derived from Pope Leo XIII's groundbreaking 1891 papal encyclical *Rerum Novarum*, which, for the first time, officially urged Church leaders to advocate on behalf of workers' rights. The pope declared the Church could no longer be silent regarding matters of labor and the conditions of workers. Eight years after this proclamation, Bishop Quigley was mandated to spearhead the efforts on behalf of the roughly 900 grain scoopers. The strikers finally had a leader who would guide them through this storm.

Despite sharing an Irish Catholic background, Bishop Quigley and Fingy Conners couldn't have been more different. Quigley was well educated and refined, while the crude Conners was schooled on the docks. Quigley, the former rector from the working-class First Ward, relied on persuasion and eloquence to become the chief negotiator and dealmaker for the strikers. At the same time, Conners used fear and intimidation while recruiting a gang of toughs and thugs to execute his orders.

On the political side, Catholic strikers had what appeared to be a traditionally unlikely ally: a former Republican congressman and Episcopalian named Rowland B. Mahany. But Mahany, a son of an Irish immigrant from County Kerry, had previously worked as a Buffalo dockworker. Although he attended elite schools like Hobart and Harvard, he admired the working class.[67] In 1895, the *Catholic Union and Times* endorsed this Republican in his bid for the open congressional seat in Buffalo. More importantly, the Irish Catholics in the southern part of Buffalo— most of them Democrats—elected him to two terms in Congress. During the strike, Mahany, sometimes called "the silver-tongued orator," pleaded the case for the laborers and rallied the workers.[68] He broadened awareness of the plight of the scoopers to the Protestant clergy, who joined the Catholic scoopers' cause.

Meanwhile, Conners' efforts to intimidate the strikers led to more violence, including the death of one of Conners' close associates, William H. Kennedy. Conners was quickly losing control of the strike. The freight handlers had already joined the strike, and the International Seamen's Union, representing the ships' crew members, threatened to join. Union workers from the New York Central Railroad and men from the coal and iron industry also joined them.[69]

The strike was now attracting national attention. Daniel Keefe, the president of the International Longshoremen's Association, came to Buffalo several times during the dispute to assist in the negotiations on behalf of the workers. At the same time, Bishop Quigley urged the workers to maintain peace and order, which contributed to the sympathy exhibited by the wider community.

Commerce on the Great Lakes shut down, and tens of millions of bushels of wheat were stuck on the freight ships; two weeks into the strike, 3.6 million bushels of grain were waiting to be unloaded on forty-three massive vessels.[70] In Duluth alone, grain companies were waiting to ship over 20 million bushels to Buffalo. The strikers in the First Ward had halted the entire grain trade route from the Midwest to the East Coast. If people on the East Coast had not previously heard of the grain scoopers from the First Ward, they had now. Finally, almost a month later, on May 23, the shipping companies could no longer hold out, and they agreed to negotiate directly with Bishop Quigley and the new union, Local 109. William J. Conners had lost his control over the grain scoopers.

Almost immediately, the scoopers voted for P.J. McMahon as president of the new union and drew up a new constitution. The next day, police officers patrolled the docks, checking the workers' union cards to ensure they were members of McMahon's new union. The Irish grain scoopers were satisfied with the terms: their original wage structure was reinstated, they now made about 49 cents per hour, and they were paid at their place of employment, no longer in the saloons.

Within a few years after the Great Dock Strike in 1899, labor unions in the city grew more powerful after being practically nonexistent just a decade earlier. However, some city labor leaders incorporated a socialistic strain in their labor proclamations and tried to organize the unions under a single umbrella called the Erie Labor Council.

Bishop Quigley felt these socialist teachings were hostile to the Church, so in February 1902, he crafted a pastoral letter, which priests on the East Side of Buffalo read to their congregations. Specifically, it condemned socialistic teachings while at the same time protecting a worker's right to join a union. Quigley declared, "A workingman may be a union man and a good Catholic, but he cannot be both a Social Democrat and a Catholic." This pastoral letter was the first time a U.S. bishop publicly denounced the teachings of socialism as it was related to unions.[71]

Quigley quickly emerged as the leading Catholic cleric in the U.S. on the relationship between socialism and labor unions. In January 1903, the Vatican promoted him to Archbishop of Chicago, which at the time was a city at the forefront of the socialist movement.[72] Perhaps Quigley's elevation to archbishop wouldn't have happened if a courageous group of grain scoopers hadn't organized at P.J. McMahon's saloon in the First Ward and stood up to the corrupt Fingy Conners.

After the strike, Rowland Mahany's prominence also rose, and he was named Buffalo's Harbor Commissioner with a mandate to reform the abuses during the pre-strike days. The Irish politician also switched to the Democratic Party, and President Woodrow Wilson named him senior attorney in the Department of Labor from 1918 until 1919. A year later, he was named acting Secretary of Labor in President Warren G. Harding's administration. Despite losing the Great Strike of 1899, William J. "Fingy" Conners capitalized on his diverse business interests and became a multi-millionaire. We will learn more about him in the next chapter.

National Labor Leaders (O'Connor and Molony)

By 1900, Irish Americans dominated many of the labor organizations in the United States. Between 1900 and 1910, Irish Americans were presidents of almost half (50 of the 110) of the affiliate unions of the American Federation of Labor.[73] Buffalo molded a few of these national labor leaders. One of them was Thomas Ventry

(T.V.) O'Connor, who was born in 1871 to an Irish immigrant father. The family settled in Toronto, Ontario, then moved to Buffalo when young Thomas was four. Throughout his childhood, O'Connor's father, who worked as a plasterer, moved the family in and around various Buffalo Irish neighborhoods. As a young man, T.V. O'Connor worked in waterfront occupations such as tug fireman, ferryman, and lake sailor. With a formal education that ended at grammar school, he always carried a book with him to further his schooling. O'Connor was described as a cheerful, friendly person who also could be rough-and-tumble when needed.

O'Connor had a knack for union organizing, starting with his involvement with the Tugmen's Protective Association. In 1906, he became president of this union that spanned the Great Lakes. Two years later, O'Connor was elected to one of the most powerful union roles in the country: president of the International Longshoremen's Association (I.L.A.). The former Buffalo Irish tugboat man now steered the 90,000-member organization through twelve tumultuous years, including being shot at by New York City union gangsters on two different occasions. He added Gulf Coast and Pacific Coast I.L.A. districts to his oversight and managed complex Panama Canal shipping issues after its opening in 1914. During a widespread multi-union strike against the Lake Carriers' Association (L.C.A) in 1909, O'Connor prudently urged his union members not to strike against the powerful L.C.A. In fact, because of O'Connor's foresight, the I.L.A. union was one of the last unions still in existence after the strike. That same year, he moved the I.L.A. headquarters from Detroit to Buffalo.

In 1920, O'Connor supported Republican candidate Senator Warren G. Harding's campaign to become U.S. President. After Harding's election, the president rewarded the former Buffalo waterfront worker by naming him Assistant Secretary of Labor in his administration. O'Connor, a lifelong Democrat, supported the Republican ticket because he believed the Southern-led Democratic Party would be unfriendly to labor.[74] Later, O'Connor caught the attention of President Calvin Coolidge, who appointed him to the prestigious position of chairman of the United States Shipping Board, where O'Connor served until 1933. In this role, he was also instrumental in building up the United States merchant marine.

O'Connor claimed two tenets were keys to his success. First, "Consider the common working man as much as the man who is ten leagues ahead of him." Second, "Never forget to smile your orders as well as your thanks."[75] O'Connor also served under President Herbert Hoover and was said to be friends with three Republican presidents (Harding, Coolidge, and Hoover). Buffalo's T.V. O'Connor died on October 17, 1935, but not before leaving an indelible mark on the International Longshoremen's Association and the national labor movement.

Another top Buffalo labor leader was a native of Ireland. Joseph P. Molony, born in Ennis, County Clare, in 1906, emigrated to the United States at the age of twenty. After working in New York City for a few years, he moved to Buffalo and labored on the Republic Steel ore docks. Molony only had ten years of formal education but was a voracious reader and largely self-taught. As an eighteen-year-old in Ireland, Molony had read Upton Sinclair's *The Jungle*. The description of the working conditions in the Chicago stockyards appalled him so much that he resolved to join the union movement.[76] At Buffalo's Republic plant, he became a key organizer for the Steel Workers Organizing Committee (S.W.O.C.). In 1942, when the SWOC merged with other unions to become the United Steelworkers (U.S.W.), Molony became the director for District 4 (all of New York State). In this capacity, he was responsible for 71,000 members in the second-largest district in the nation.

Molony held the New York State U.S.W. leadership position from Buffalo for two decades. The Irish immigrant was affectionately called "the steelworkers' orator" and the "Irishman with the silver tongue."[77] *The Buffalo News* described him as "a brilliant negotiator, with a quick wit and sunny disposition." While in Buffalo, he also held leadership positions in the Democratic Party, the Buffalo Urban League, and the United Negro College Fund. Molony was elected to three terms as the Niagara Frontier Port Authority chairman. Before the opening of the St. Lawrence Seaway in 1959, Moloney advocated for a deeper port and modern facilities so that large cargo ships would not bypass Buffalo. Although Molony desperately tried to protect waterfront jobs, it was a lost cause. After 1959, most ships did not need to dock in Buffalo on their way from the Great Lakes to the Atlantic Ocean, which resulted in the loss of thousands of local jobs.

In 1965, Molony left for Pittsburgh to become the international vice president of the 1.4 million-member USW union. One of his notable achievements was bringing in more than a half-million new members into the USW from non-steel industries. The former Buffalo labor leader also served as the national coordinator for the twenty-six-union bargaining team for the non-ferrous metals industry and was chairman of the USW's Civil Rights Committee. After four decades in the labor movement, he retired in 1973. Joseph Molony, a significant force in the labor movement, is another example of the Buffalo Irish's impact on improving working conditions across the country.

Another longtime Irish union leader was Michael A. "Mike" Fitzpatrick. Born in South Buffalo, Fitzpatrick was the son of a police officer. At Bishop Timon High School, he was a star running back who once had a 1,000-yard season. For fourteen years, he worked as an ironworker, eventually becoming the leader of the local association. As a union leader, Fitzpatrick backed dozens of downtown building projects, such as the Hyatt Regency Buffalo and the Erie Basin Marina; some of these projects wouldn't have happened without financing from his union.

In 1977, Fitzpatrick was elected to the Erie County Legislature as a Democrat, and he served in that role until 2001. In 1983, he joined the International Association of Ironworkers Union in Washington, D.C. Eventually, the Buffalo ironworker was elected General Secretary of that organization, representing 120,000 members. At Fitzpatrick's death, Congressman Brian Higgins credited Fitzpatrick for assisting Buffalo's development for more than a generation, asserting that Fitzpatrick "left fingerprints on dozens of downtown projects that served as building blocks for what we see today."[79] Mike Fitzpatrick was the latest Buffalo Irish union leader, but he won't be the last.

Public Service, Government, and Lawyers

For first- and second-generation Irish immigrants, jobs outside low-skilled positions were limited. However, by the late nineteenth century, a new field of opportunity propelled many Irish men and women into the middle class: public service. These jobs included positions as firemen, police officers, teachers, and other civil service roles. While not offering high wages, these positions provided job stability and financial security. The Irish in Buffalo, who mainly had aligned with the Democratic Party, claimed a disproportionate share of these government jobs in exchange for their loyalty.

The Irish gravitated toward two of the largest city departments: police and fire. By the late 1890s, the Buffalo Fire Department's leadership changed from German hands to Irish. In 1892, Bernard J. McConnell was appointed Fire Department Chief, Edward P. Murphy was named the Assistant Fire Chief, and John F. Malone was named one of the fire commissioners. As the leadership of this organization changed, so too did the hiring of the rank and file. In 1890, at the First Ward Fire Engine Companies 8 and 10, nineteen of the twenty-four firefighters were Irish or Irish Americans.[80] While these large numbers of Irish were expected in the First Ward, the fact that Irish and Irish Americans comprised 38.2% of the Buffalo Fire Department in 1900 is more surprising since Irish Americans comprised less than 20% of Buffalo's population.[81] By the 1920s, the Irish dominated leadership positions in the city's firehouses, where twenty-five of the fifty-two chiefs had Irish surnames.[82]

The Irish also dominated the police department. By one account, the 1859 police force in Buffalo comprised twenty-five Irishmen out of sixty officers, with a few prominent Irish politicians filling many of these positions with their sons and cousins.[83] By 1890, 50% of the police captains, 45% of the detectives, and 40%

of the patrolmen were Irish or Irish Americans. Over the 140-year history of the Buffalo Police leadership, many commissioners and superintendents were of Irish origin. The first superintendent of the Buffalo Police Department (1872-1879) was Colonel John Byrne, a native of County Wicklow, Ireland.

In 1906, Mike Regan became the superintendent of the Buffalo Police Department.[84] Regan was born March 4, 1859, in County Cork, Ireland, and arrived in Buffalo with his family nine years later. In 1880, the massive young man—reportedly 6'6" tall—became a police patrolman and quickly moved up the ranks to lieutenant and then captain. In 1901, Regan gained national recognition for his role in quelling the lynch mob that gathered at police headquarters to kill Leon Czolgosz, President William McKinley's assassin. "Big Mike" Regan also crusaded against disorderliness in Buffalo's ubiquitous saloons, especially along the waterfront.

Regan retired as superintendent in 1915 and is still the second-longest serving police superintendent in the city's history. He was the first of several Irish First Warders to lead Buffalo's police department. Austin Roche, born on Chicago Street, became Buffalo Police Commissioner in the 1930s, John B. Myers in the 1980s, and Richard T. Donovan in the 1990s.[85] Other police department chiefs with Irish surnames included Doyle, Byrne, Curtin, Higgins, McClellan, Cronin, Cannan, McMahon, Morin, Finney, Cunningham, and Myers.

Sheriff Thomas F. Higgins

In the next neighborhood over from the First Ward, in what is called the Valley, Thomas F. Higgins was born in 1930. Higgins was the second son of Thomas F. Higgins, Sr. and Margaret (nee Power) Higgins. Both of his parents were natives of County Cork. His father, born in 1901, served in the Cork Brigade during the Irish War of Independence and later in the National Army during the Irish Civil War. Years later, in 1925, Higgins Sr. immigrated to Buffalo, looking for better job prospects. Higgins' mother, Margaret Power, was raised in Cobh, just thirteen miles from where his father was born. She arrived in Buffalo in 1926, and a year later, she married Thomas Sr. They raised their family on St. Stephen's Place, and Higgins' father worked various jobs, including a stint at Republic Steel, while his mother raised nine children.

Thomas Higgins Jr. dropped out of South Park High School at age seventeen because he was "tired of being hungry." Higgins toiled in a "dirty job" at the Donner Hanna Coke Company but knew he didn't want to work there for long. The South Buffalo Irishman enlisted in the Marine Corps when the Korean War broke out. After training at Parris Island and Camp Pendleton, the 6'3", 165-pound Higgins shipped out to the front lines in Korea. He served in the artillery unit in a dangerous role as a forward observer. On a bitterly cold Christmas Day in 1951, Higgins was separated from his platoon and was soaked to the bone after falling through an ice-covered stream. With temperatures near zero, he made his way toward a flickering light, where he found a friendly, sixteen-year-old Korean interpreter who provided him with warm clothes and shelter. Higgins was always grateful that the young man saved his life.[86]

After his time in Korea, Higgins returned home and became a Buffalo policeman, moving up the ranks as a detective and helping found the Underwater Recovery Team. A natural-born leader, he was named the head of the police academy. After twenty-one years with the police, Higgins moved to the Erie County Sheriff's Department, where he worked as the undersheriff for nine years. In 1985, Higgins was elected Erie County Sheriff and led the 625-member department. As the top sheriff, one of his first actions was creating a unit called the Family Offense Unit to investigate crimes against children. Higgins' twelve-year tenure as Erie County's top law enforcer coincided with the drug war violence in the 1980s and '90s. He also oversaw the building of the Erie County Holding Center.

Despite dropping out of high school, Higgins earned three college degrees, including a master's degree in history from Buffalo State College, which he earned at age sixty-six. Active at his alma mater, Buffalo State College, he funded an endowed scholarship for criminal justice students and served as president of its alumni association. Higgins was also engaged in several civic organizations, including serving as the Korean War Memorial Committee chairman and the Buffalo and Erie County Naval & Military Park board president.

Throughout his life, Higgins claimed that his Irish heritage shaped him.[87] He remembered marching in his first St. Patrick's Day Parade in Buffalo in 1935. As an active Blackthorn Club member since 1972, he marched with the storied group yearly until he died in 2018. Various Irish organizations, including the Amherst Gaelic League, Friendly Sons of St. Patrick, and the Ancient Order of Hibernians, have recognized his accomplishments with their highest honors. Later in life, the sheriff made twelve trips to visit his parents' native Ireland.

In 2018, United States Congressman Brian Higgins (no relation) announced that the $22 million Bailey Avenue bridge and park, which connects South Buffalo to the rest of the city, would be named in honor of Sheriff Thomas F. Higgins. The congressman cited the former sheriff's forty-two years in local law enforcement and his accomplishments in numerous civic organizations as the reasons for this honor. At Higgins' death, the *Buffalo News* said, "Mr. Higgins ranked as one of Buffalo's best-known figures in not only police and political circles, but throughout the community."[88]

Lawyers and Judges

Since their arrival in Buffalo, the Irish have gravitated to the field of law. As native English speakers, they had an advantage in that field over many other immigrant groups. They also came from an Irish tradition that prized oral and written skills, which served them well in politics and law. One of the most prominent Buffalo lawyers, Irish or not, was John Lord O'Brian. He was born in 1874 to John and Elizabeth (Lord) O'Brian, Irish Episcopalians. John's father served as a justice of the peace and then entered the insurance business. The senior O'Brian's prosperous commercial prospects enabled the family to move from the First Ward to the wealthier Delaware Avenue neighborhood.

Young John graduated from Central High School in 1892 and entered Harvard University at seventeen. During this time, his family lost all their fortune and property during the Panic of 1893. After Harvard, John returned to Buffalo, taught elementary school, studied law, and became a lawyer in 1898. Interested in politics, the Republican O'Brian was elected to the New York State Assembly in 1907. Two years later, President Theodore Roosevelt nominated him to become the U.S. District Attorney for the Western District of New York.

In this capacity, O'Brian enforced the civil service laws in Buffalo, which were being abused.[89] He also dedicated himself to enforcing violations of the Sherman Antitrust Act, such as in a prominent Eastman Kodak case. O'Brian successfully argued that Kodak had created a monopoly in the amateur photography industry by buying competitors, dissolving them, and transferring their assets back to Kodak. He earned a reputation for his antitrust expertise, and President Herbert Hoover appointed him the Assistant Attorney General of the Antitrust Division. The Buffalo Irishman served as chief counsel on many important cases, including the RCA Corporation breakup. During the First World War, as the head of the War Emergency Division, O'Brian enforced the Espionage and Sedition Acts. He was credited for balancing the rights of the millions of German and Austrian Americans in the United States while protecting U.S. citizens and strategic military sites. At the war's end, O'Brian noted that no enemy "alien" set a fire or explosion at a U.S. installation.[90] During the war, O'Brian's sister, Alice Lord O'Brian, served with distinction in an American Red Cross leadership position in France.

Over the years, O'Brian was appointed to various high-level government posts from the Theodore Roosevelt administration to the Harry Truman administration. One of his most noteworthy accomplishments was his successful defense of the Tennessee Valley Authority Act in front of the U.S. Supreme Court in 1938. A *New York Times* columnist, Arthur Krock, once described John Lord O'Brian as the "most distinguished lawyer and classical liberal of our times."[91] The home of the University at Buffalo's Law School is named O'Brian Hall in his honor.

There were several other noteworthy Buffalo Irish attorneys. Daniel J. Kenefick was born to Irish parents in the First Ward during the Civil War. In 1894, Kenefick became the District Attorney for Buffalo at the age of thirty-one. Later, he was elevated to the Superior Court of New York and then to the New York State Supreme Court, where he served nine years. His most noteworthy accomplishment was his monumental effort in 1926 to rewrite the charter of the City of Buffalo. At the time, it was called the Kenefick Commission in his honor, and it sought to modernize city government, including separating the Common Council's legislative duties from the mayor's executive ones to ensure the separation of powers. It was groundbreaking, and it served as a model for other municipalities. Kenefick has a street named after him in South Buffalo, and he received the University of Buffalo Chancellor Medal for being a "Great Citizen of Buffalo."

Charles Stewart Desmond, the son of a saloon keeper and grandson of Irish immigrants from County Cork, was born in Buffalo, in a room above his father's saloon, in 1896. He became one of the most powerful judges to ever emerge from Buffalo. After graduating from Canisius College, Desmond earned his law degree from the University of Buffalo in 1920. After Desmond worked in private practice, New York State Governor Herbert Lehman appointed him to fill a vacancy on the State Supreme Court. Within a year, Buffalo political boss Paul E. Fitzpatrick spearheaded Desmond's nomination to New York's highest court, the Court of Appeals, where he worked for a quarter of a century. He was the youngest person to serve on that court and served as New York State's first-ever chief judge from 1960 to 1966.[94]

A lifelong Democrat, Desmond led the liberal wing of the court. In his career, he wrote over four hundred and fifty opinions, including a decision in 1965 that the police must inform criminal defendants that a lawyer will be assigned to them if they cannot afford one. Senator Daniel Patrick Moynihan, commenting on Desmond's long life and career, said, "Few in all that history have done half so much to sustain and enhance a glorious constitutional tradition."[95]

Judge John Curtin

We end this chapter the same way we started it: with an unassuming, slight Irish Catholic who impacted the lives of thousands of Buffalonians. John Thomas Curtin was born in South Buffalo on August 24, 1921 to Irish-American parents who raised their family on Pawnee Parkway. His father, John J. Curtin, was a superintendent at the Bethlehem Steel plant, and his mother, Ella Quigley, was a bank secretary. The Jesuits educated the young John Curtin at Canisius High School and later at Canisius College. During the Second World War, he was a fighter pilot in the South Pacific theater and survived thirty-five combat missions. After his service, Curtin graduated from the University of Buffalo Law School.

Curtin was described as "a short, slightly built man with twinkling blue eyes, a gentle wit and a humble demeanor."[96] He was also a fearless prosecutor and judge who took on violent gang members, organized crime, and large corporations. He issued rulings that angered thousands, including many of his fellow Irish Americans.

After several years in private practice, in 1961, Curtin was appointed by President John F. Kennedy to be the United States Attorney for the Western District of New York. In this role, he served as the chief federal prosecutor, where he won a case which mandated an increase in minority hiring against Bethlehem Steel, his father's former employer. In 1967, Senator Robert F. Kennedy recommended President Lyndon B. Johnson nominate Curtin to the United States District Court. He served as chief of that court from 1974 to 1989, after which he assumed senior status.

In 1972, Buffalo Common Council member George K. Arthur filed a federal suit against the Buffalo Board of Education, the City of Buffalo, and the New York State Board of Regents. In his case, Arthur alleged that the city and state institutions violated the 14th Amendment for equal protection of the law by maintaining a segregated school system. Four years later, in *Arthur v. Nyquist*, Chief Judge John Curtin ruled in favor of George Arthur. Curtin argued that the Buffalo Board of Education was guilty of "creating, maintaining, permitting, condoning and perpetuating racially segregated schools...."[97] This monumental decision instigated the long and challenging process of desegregating the public schools, where Curtin worked hands-on, monitoring the students' integration. Besides improving the racial balance in schools, the court case led to the creation of magnet schools that focus on a specialized area like performing arts or science. His rulings also led to the increased hiring of minority teachers.

There was some opposition to Curtin's ruling, especially from the white communities where children were bused across the city to achieve the desired racial balance. Curtin received regular death threats and hate mail, but he was undeterred.[98] Despite some threatening letters, Buffalo experienced little violence or "white flight" compared to other cities forced to desegregate, such as Boston. Within a few years, Buffalo was receiving visitors from across the country to witness the success of the process. However, some prominent Black Americans, like Frank Mesiah, the president of the NAACP, felt Curtin and the Board of Education didn't go far enough in their reforms. While Mesiah acknowledged the

magnet schools helped some Black children, he felt Buffalo still segregated most
children of color in underfunded and underperforming schools.[99] Curtin lifted
his orders on school segregation in 1995 because he determined they had made
significant progress.

Judge Curtin's ruling on desegregation of the schools shaped later cases on
integrating the Buffalo police and fire departments. In 1978, the South Buffalo
native ruled that these public safety organizations had to increase opportunities
for minority residents and women. Curtin's orders specified that 50% of new hires
from both departments had to be minorities, and 25% of the police department
had to be women. Irish Americans had been overrepresented in both of these
organizations for at least a century, and some of them felt this ruling was a threat
to the future hiring of members of their group. Within a decade of his decision,
Curtin was content with the progress the police and fire departments had made in
improving minority and female representation.[100]

Many of Judge Curtin's decisions revealed his concern for the underrepresented
and oppressed. *The Buffalo News* claimed that people who knew the judge described
him "as a liberal who tried to make the law work for the downtrodden."[101]
According to Richard Griffin, his friend from Canisius College and a fellow lawyer,
Curtin had "a deep sensitivity to the underprivileged."[102] This guiding principle
was most evident in his desegregation cases and minority hiring quotas but also in
his refusal to hear drug cases in the 1990s because he believed incarceration was
the wrong approach to the problem. However, Curtin showed no mercy regarding
violent gang drug dealers. He sentenced gang leader Donald "Sly" Green to four
terms of life in prison and an additional 121 years.[103]

In the 1980s, Judge Curtin presided over one of the most significant environmental
cases in U.S. history: Love Canal. The Hooker Chemical and Plastics Company,
which Occidental Chemical Corporation later purchased, illegally dumped 22,000
tons of toxic chemicals in a neighborhood in Niagara Falls, New York between
1942 and 1953. Hooker sold the polluted land to a developer who later built tract
housing on the site. By the late 1950s, residents started smelling strong odors and
noticing substances rising from the soil. In 1978, a Niagara Falls news reporter
wrote a story on the health issues Love Canal families were experiencing, such as
cancer and congenital disabilities. After the report, local neighborhood activists
demanded action from the authorities. In 1978, New York State evacuated over
two hundred families from the toxic neighborhood.

After the plaintiffs filed a federal lawsuit, Judge Curtin ruled that Occidental
Chemical was negligent and liable for damages. The company settled with New
York State for $98 million in 1994.[104] Curtin wrote that Occidental's "disposal
practices were at least partially responsible for the release, or threatened release,

of the chemicals from the Love Canal landfill."[105] The company also paid more than $20 million to 1,400 individuals who claimed they experienced health complications from exposure to the waste. Love Canal remains one of the worst environmental disasters in U.S. history, and Curtin's ruling was a model for other such cases.

In 2016, at ninety-four, Curtin retired from the court after serving for forty-nine years. Buffalo historian Mark Goldman wrote, "Judge Curtin is perhaps the most significant person in 20th century Buffalo."[106] Goldman also asserted that Judge Curtin was a "transcendent figure in the history of our city" and that "his legacy is incalculable."[107] The former dean of the University at Buffalo Law School, Nils Olsen Jr., stated that he couldn't imagine "any judge ever having as big an impact on this community [Western New York] as Judge Curtin."[108]

The Catholic Church, labor organizations, and the local government all supported the vulnerable Buffalo Irish. Once in power, the Irish used these institutions to benefit not only themselves but also Polish and Italian immigrants. People of all races and creeds, including immigrants from Asia and Africa today, still benefit from the toils of the Irish in shaping these institutions. The Irish, influenced by the trauma of the Great Famine and bigotry in America, were biased toward justice. This hunger for justice was evident in the works of many religious sisters and priests, labor leaders, lawyers, and judges.

CHAPTER FOUR

Captains of Industry

In 1911, Maurice Courtney, a prominent Buffalo lawyer, wrote a series of articles in Buffalo's *Catholic Union and Times* summarizing the condition of the local Irish. He declared, "Catholics, particularly Irish Catholics, have made wonderful progress in America in the munificence of their religious advancement, in their beautiful churches, and religious institutions; but commercially and in business realms theirs has been but an indifferent success. We may honestly say they are spiritually and religiously strong, while financially and commercially weak."[1] He added that the Irish had made progress in professions such as doctors, lawyers, and dentists.

Earlier in the article, Courtney fondly recounted the numerous Irish shopkeepers who had been in downtown Buffalo when he was young, including McCool's (stylish gentlemen's hats), Robert Forsyth (boots and shoes), Timothy Cochrane (tailor for clothing), William Boland & Son (clothing), William Carland at the Gothic Hall (clothing), McDonnell & Son at 232 Main Street (photo portrait), and Michael Hagen's (books).[2] However, he lamented the lack of manufacturing and banking leaders.

While some of Courtney's memories of earlier years were accurate, by 1911 the Irish were making progress in the business world, gathering steam as the century progressed. Several Irish immigrants in Buffalo had amassed wealth and created commercial enterprises that would have been inconceivable in Ireland and possible only in the United States.

Merchants and Manufacturers—Glenny, Carland, and Keogh

As previously noted, Buffalo's first successful Irish businessman was Samuel Wilkeson. But a fellow Scots-Irishman, William H. Glenny, would be the first to establish a national firm. Glenny was born in 1818 in Northern Ireland, and at the age of eighteen, with no money or patronage, he emigrated to Buffalo. In 1840, Glenny opened a crockery store on Main Street, becoming the first of many Hibernians who amassed great wealth in the dry goods business. Glenny's store, located at 204 Main Street, was stocked with china, glassware, lamps, and chandeliers. In later years, he added sterling silver products, gas fixtures, English pottery, and French clocks to his stock. In a *Courier* ad, Glenny announced that he had just received a European shipment with bronze figures, vases, clocks, Parisian marbles, plated ware, and cut glass.[3] His enterprise initially catered to Buffalo consumers, but he soon marketed his goods across the country—selling exceptionally well to settlers in the western states—and his store eventually became one of the largest crockery businesses in the country.

After enjoying three prosperous decades in the same location on Main Street, Glenny hired Richard A. Waite, one of Buffalo's renowned architects, to design a new building for his wares. At 251 Main Street, Waite designed a five-story cast-iron façade building in the Italian Renaissance Revival style that was completed in 1877. It was such a prominent landmark that the block was eventually simply referred to as the "Glenny Block." When it was completed, it was the tallest cast-iron building in New York State outside of New York City.[4] Today, the Glenny Building is Buffalo's only cast-iron façade building, and it was recently renovated and converted into thirty-six apartments.

Glenny's Midas touch extended beyond the dry goods business. In 1856, he was one of the original founders and directors of Manufacturers & Traders Trust Company (now known as M&T Bank) and a trustee of Erie County Savings Bank (later, the Erie Savings Bank). The Irishman was one of the principal organizers of the Buffalo, New York & Philadelphia Railway and director and manager of the McKean and Buffalo Railroad.[5] Like Wilkeson, he was an active member and generous contributor to his local Presbyterian church.

In Glenny's obituary, he was described as "exacting in business principles, persistent in effort, strong-willed, of strict integrity...."[6] The writer added, "Few men have been so closely identified with the development of Buffalo's commercial interests as has Mr. Glenny."[7] Another obituary claimed he was known by merchants across the nation and in Europe, and he had "few equals and no superior" in Buffalo.[8] In addition to his extant Main Street building, one can still buy W.H. Glenny-engraved silver items and porcelain ware from online merchants. However, Glenny's most important legacy was his involvement with founding M&T Bank, one of the country's largest regional banks.

William Carland

In the mid-nineteenth century, while some new arrivals made a decent living as merchants and small store owners, successful Irish-born Catholic factory owners in Buffalo were rare. According to the 1855 New York State census, there were only two Irish manufacturers with large-scale operations—and William Carland was one of them.[9] William Carland, born in Cork, Ireland, in 1822, settled in Boston twelve years later and moved to Buffalo in 1843. He descended from "cultured ancestors" in Ireland, possessed "charming manners," and was a "great favorite socially."[10] In Boston, he apprenticed in the retail trade, but like other East Coast settlers, he envisioned acquiring his fortune in up-and-coming Buffalo. In 1846, Carland founded Gothic Hall, a clothing company located at 151 Main Street in an ornate building with a Gothic façade. His operation became Buffalo's leading maker of ready-made men's clothing, and he initially employed three hundred tailors, most of whom were German immigrants, not Irish.[11] The Irish businessman claimed to carry fifty thousand garments in stock with the latest fashions from Paris and London.[12] Carland's business motto was "Large sales and small profits."

Carland sold suits, gloves, hats, shirts, cravats, tweed coats, linen collars, socks, and green jackets. In 1849, he enlarged the store from Main Street to Washington Street, and the *Buffalo Courier* claimed it was the most significant business of its kind in the country and one of the "largest, best finished and arranged stores we ever saw."[13] At this point, he employed between four and five hundred workers annually. In addition to a wholesale and retail operation in his store, he also built a museum and a 1,000-seat concert hall on the second floor. But Carland had incurred substantial debts and informed his tailors that he would pay their wages in store credit, not cash. The furious German tailors went on strike and paraded out of the building led by a marching band. The strikers picketed outside his building and even hung an effigy of their Irish employer.[14] Carland, however, sued the strike organizers in court for intimidation and won the suit. Business resumed.

Carland's newspaper advertisements from the time offer a history lesson. In 1849, he urged those going to California during the Gold Rush to shop at his store rather than visiting a store out west because his prices were much lower.[15] Three years later, he was selling a revolutionary new product—the Singer sewing machine, which had been invented only the year before. In 1857, he declared the must-have fashions were fancy cashmere, silk, and Marseilles vests.[16] But, the booming economy quickly reversed and gave rise to a financial depression—the Panic of 1857. In fact, by January 1858, he was selling all goods at cost.[17] In a December 1859 advertisement, he boldly claimed his business was famous from

Maine to Georgia. He added that if the Union dissolved—threats of the South's
secession from the Union were gathering steam—he had no idea how the South
could survive without access to his company's products.[18]

But the financial panic of 1857 and the impending Civil War were not Carland's
only problems. Peter LeCouteulx, a prominent Buffalonian, sued him for unpaid
debts. Carland's personal life was also in turmoil. His wife was committed to an
insane asylum in Baltimore, and his only brother died.[19] In August of 1860, there
was an announcement in the newspapers that the Gothic Hall store inventory,
fixtures, and furniture were being auctioned off, and his business foreclosed soon
after. Three months later, on November 10, Carland and three others died in a
tragic fire at the Clarendon Hotel that started in the hotel's kitchen. The next
day, his charred body was found under a pile of rubble—his head and limbs were
missing.[20] In addition, the fire killed two Irish servant girls, Anne McAuley and
Bridget Mulcahy.

Before his company's foreclosure, he had become the well-to-do businessman
he envisioned. The value of his house was almost fifteen times the average home
price of other prominent Irish immigrants.[21] He was one of Buffalo's most
affluent Irish Catholics, a trustee for Sisters Hospital, president of the Emigrant
Savings Bank, and one of the most generous donors to the building of St. Joseph's
Cathedral. His close friend, Bishop John Timon, for whom Carland and his wife
had named one of their sons, presided at his funeral Mass at St. Joseph's Cathedral.
Gothic Hall, his distinctive building, stood for one hundred and twenty-four years
before it was torn down around 1969 for the construction of the Marine Midland
Center, now called Seneca One Tower.[22]

Augustine Keogh

Augustine Keogh was the other Irish-born manufacturer with a large operation
who had settled in Buffalo, but, unlike Carland, he led a relatively charmed life,
dying a wealthy man at age 95. Keogh and William Carland knew each other and
were both original trustees of the local Emigrant Savings Bank. This bank offered
a safe place for Irish immigrants to keep their money and send remittances home
to Ireland. Keogh was born in Dublin in 1812 and moved to New York City in
the 1830s. He settled in Buffalo in 1849 with his Irish wife, Eliza Donnelly, and
brother, John. The Keogh brothers, Augustine and John, moved their pianoforte
manufacturing business from New York City, where they had achieved considerable
success, to the fast-growing city of Buffalo. They manufactured pianos with a
stylish rosewood finish and had a showroom to display their musical instruments.
Their manufacturing plant was at Pearl and Seneca Street, and, eventually, it
was moved to Washington Street. At some point in the early 1860s, the Keogh

brothers sold their business in Buffalo, purchased land in Pennsylvania, and made a considerable sum during the Pennsylvania oil boom.[23] Keogh engaged in the real estate business in New York City, and, by 1880, he was retired and living on fashionable Lexington Avenue in New York City. At his death in 1905, the *Buffalo Enquirer* claimed he was one of the most prominent figures in Buffalo and that his original pianos were still present in the city at his death, although they were now antiquated.[24]

The Retailers

After William H. Glenny and William Carland succeeded in the retail trade, other Irishmen followed. Retail businesses appealed to the Irish, given the low barrier to entry and the fact that one did not need technical skills to succeed. One man who followed this path was Jeremiah F. Sheehan. Born in County Cork in 1846, at the start of the Famine, he emigrated to the United States at age twenty-one. After starting his career in the dry goods business in New York City, Sheehan, like Carland, hoped to secure his fortune by moving to fast-growing Buffalo. Around 1872, he had established his store, J.F. Sheehan & Co., at 485 and 487 Main Street, where he sold fine dresses, French cashmere, hosiery, corsets, cloaks, silks, laces, and gloves.[25] In addition to establishing his store, he served as one of the organizers of Union Bank and a local railroad.[26] Sheehan's pioneering dry goods store eventually became one of Buffalo's premier retailers: Hens & Kelly.

Patrick Joseph Kelly—Hens & Kelly

Patrick Joseph Kelly was born in 1858 to moderately well-to-do parents in County Roscommon. After completing private schooling at seventeen, he moved to Dublin to apprentice at the city's leading home furnishings firm, where he developed a reputation for exceptional trading abilities. Kelly left Dublin at age twenty-four to seek opportunity and adventure in New York City. Shortly after landing, he met Mathias J. Hens, a German immigrant and buyer for J.F. Sheehan's Buffalo company. They quickly became close friends and remained in contact for several years. In 1887, Hens encouraged Kelly to move to Buffalo to work as a bookkeeper for J.F. Sheehan's company. Sheehan was preparing to retire, so Hens offered to buy his business and form a partnership with his Irish friend, Patrick Kelly. In 1892, they launched their new company, Hens & Kelly, in a small 18-foot by 50-foot store on Main Street.[27] The firm adopted the motto "Good merchandise at the lowest prices."[28] Their company experienced rapid growth; in its first thirty years, sales doubled every four years on average. The two founders had started with just one clerk, and by the 1920s, they employed seven hundred workers. In 1922, they moved into a six-story, 10,000-square-foot building at 478 Main Street. Hens & Kelly, then referred to as Buffalo's oldest dry goods merchants, now occupied the massive space from Main to Pearl Street along Mohawk Street.

In 1925, two years before he died of a heart attack at his summer home in Bay Beach, Ontario, Kelly, who refused to retire, declared, "I would rather wear out than rust out."[29] At the end of his life, he had accumulated considerable wealth and was a member of various local clubs, as well as the exclusive American Irish Historical Society in New York City. His obituary noted that Kelly "rose from a position of obscurity across the sea to one of great prominence in America."[30] After his death, the management of Hens & Kelly expanded beyond their Main Street store and opened stores all over Western New York. The chain closed in 1982 when Federated Department Stores purchased it. Hens & Kelly is remembered as one of Buffalo's largest and most important twentieth-century retailers.

John F. Sweeney

John F. Sweeney was born in Ireland in 1854 and, like Patrick Kelly, worked for some of the premier retail stores in Dublin. He emigrated to the United States in 1874 and worked his way to Lockport, New York where he founded one of the leading dry goods stores in Niagara County. Later, the Irishman relocated to Buffalo to become co-owner of a dry goods company with Herbert A. Meldrum, the son of one of the founders of AM&A's. Sweeney eventually served as president of the H.A. Meldrum Co.; however, he had grander plans.

Sweeney retained his share in the H.A. Meldrum Co. and opened his own store, Sweeney's, at 268 Main Street, in the former William Hengerer Company building. On September 28, 1904, the ambitious Irish immigrant opened the doors to the "Store of the People," which focused on providing the best deals for the middle class, not just wealthy patrons. With seventy-five departments under one roof, Sweeney maintained that the store could supply every household need.[31] The year he opened his new store, he had $1,000,000 of merchandise, and it took seven hundred employees to stock the store for opening day. The *Buffalo Times* called it the "most complete department store between New York and Chicago."[32] The building's seven floors included 200,000 square feet of floor space, seven elegant elevators, 387 electric arc lights, and 600 incandescent lights.[33] The store was stocked with every conceivable type of clothing, furniture, pottery, appliances, carpets, drapes, cigars, groceries, and wine. Sweeney, known for his dedication to pleasing his customers, added a tea room, a men's smoking room, an entertainment room, and a theater that could seat five hundred people.[34] Based on the enthusiastic newspaper articles about the store's opening, it undoubtedly offered one of Buffalo's most extraordinary retail experiences.

Active in the Catholic Church, Sweeney was remembered for his generosity to those who sought his assistance. His friends recalled his great sense of humor, optimism, and cheerfulness.[35] In his last few years, he spent considerable time in Ireland and other parts of Europe.[36] Before he died at age 58 in 1913, the Irish native was considered one of Buffalo's most prominent merchants and one of the first local merchants who opened a store with multiple departments.[37] His building still stands next to the Glenny Building on Main Street and, in 2016, the new owners renamed it The Sweeney Building to pay tribute to this pioneering Irish businessman.

Ruthless Businessmen—Daniel O'Day and William "Fingy" Conners

On the morning of October 15, 1906, in Manhattan, John D. Rockefeller and his son, John D. Rockefeller, Jr., served as pallbearers at a funeral service at the Church of the Blessed Sacrament on 71st Street near Broadway. Several other high-ranking Standard Oil officials also attended. Archbishop John Farley, the leader of the Roman Catholic Church for the New York Archdiocese, was present and said the benediction. Fifty boys and girls from the Roman Catholic orphanage in Kingsbridge, a neighborhood in the Bronx, sat quietly in the pews. All were present to pay their respects to an Irish immigrant from Western New York who rose from humble beginnings and became one of the masterminds behind Standard Oil's domination of the American oil market. His name was Daniel O'Day.

On February 6, 1844, in County Clare, Michael and Mary O'Day welcomed their new son, Daniel, to the world. The following year, the family emigrated to the United States at the start of the Great Famine, settling on a farm near Ellicottville, New York, fifty miles south of Buffalo. Young Daniel worked the family farm with his father and received a limited education for three months each winter. His life on the farm was filled with long, tiresome hours of hard labor. His parents were described as "plain, thoughtful, Christian people, who encouraged the study of good books and fireside discussion of topics of interest."[38] Later in his life, O'Day credited his business success to his father, who had created a rigorous educational program for him.

O'Day was restless with farm life, so, at age sixteen, he moved to booming Buffalo, attracted by the chance to become wealthy in business. He took a job handling freight in a warehouse. Working for New York Central Railroad, he was quickly promoted to messenger and later to clerk. In these roles, he developed a thorough understanding of the railroad business and the intricacies of moving freight efficiently. Later, he parlayed this knowledge into a fortune in the oil business.

Four months after the Civil War ended, O'Day moved to Titusville, Pennsylvania to partake in the oil boom. Gifted with an ability to solve complex logistical puzzles, O'Day improved the process of moving oil for two large railroad companies, solidifying his reputation for problem solving. His big break, however, came when the refiners started shipping petroleum by pipelines—a less expensive method than rail. The megalomaniac John D. Rockefeller, who was on his way to becoming the wealthiest man in American history, wanted ownership of all aspects of oil production—drilling, refining, and transportation, including pipelines. Around 1874, Rockefeller hired O'Day to lead the transportation side of his oil colossus, making him head of the American Transfer Company, one of Standard's subsidiaries. O'Day was tasked with quickly and efficiently installing a network of oil pipelines throughout western Pennsylvania so they could secure a monopoly. He executed this task with ruthless precision.

At that time, moving oil by pipelines was not a simple proposition; many others who tried it had failed. Before O'Day's era, pipelines had been used to transport oil for short distances, such as from wells to refineries. There were engineering limitations regarding how far you could transport the liquid using pipes. O'Day was one of the first to conceive that you could use powerful pumps to move oil from the Pennsylvania wells directly to the East Coast. This was a transformative innovation. As president of the National Transit Company, another shell company of Standard Oil, he led the construction of the first significant pipeline system in the United States, consisting of a six-inch pipe that went from Olean, New York to Bayonne, New Jersey. This ushered in the "era of mass movement of oil."[39] The new pipeline, which had to cross fourteen rivers and eighty mountain peaks, was an extremely complicated project, but O'Day succeeded.[40]

Standard also had to deal with angry railroad bosses, who feared losing lucrative oil transportation revenue. The railroad companies even hired agents to sabotage the pipelines. But O'Day and his army of workers, many of whom were fellow Irish Catholic immigrants, could lay the pipe faster than the saboteurs could destroy it. On an average day, he and his crew installed an astonishing one and a half miles of pipe and connected five wells to the Standard Oil network.[41] O'Day was so efficient in his efforts that he is credited with turning pipeline management into a science.[42] By 1876, thanks to O'Day's efforts, Standard Oil controlled half of the oil pipelines in the United States and, four years later, almost all of them.

O'Day was described as "one of the most colorful figures in Standard [Oil] history" and a "profane, two-fisted Irishman who tempered ruthless tactics with wit and charm."[43] O'Day used strong-arm, perhaps unethical, tactics to secure the lowest rates from the oil producers. He negotiated land rights and threatened to ruin them if they disagreed with his price. He threatened to navigate the pipeline around their land or prevent them from using Standard's storage tanks, which meant their oil would simply drain back into their land. To others, O'Day would lie and tell the landholder that their oil was too far from his pipeline, forcing the producers to drop their prices.

O'Day, who once received a scar on his forehead from a brawl during the Pennsylvania "Oil Wars" of the 1870s, was referred to as one of the "strong men" of Standard Oil.[44] In his letters to Rockefeller about a competitor, the Irish immigrant coldly stated, "I would have no mercy on them." Elsewhere, he said he would physically destroy this same competitor's infrastructure.[45] He threatened railroads that complained about the shipping prices he demanded. To one railroad company that serviced Olean to Buffalo and balked at his proposed rate, he threatened to run a pipeline between the two cities to put them out of business.[46]

Some oil producers had had enough of Standard's monopoly and O'Day's tactics and decided to fight back. A syndicate from Oil Creek, Pennsylvania devised a plan to pipe oil to a railroad company and send it via cars to Buffalo, bypassing Standard's network. Rockefeller directed O'Day to thwart this threat by any means. So, O'Day purchased the rail line to Buffalo, told the pipe manufacturers not to sell their product to this upstart competitor, and eventually disconnected his company's pipelines to the refiners associated with this new company. Today, these tactics would be illegal and considered highly unethical.

By 1877, O'Day had settled back in Buffalo with his wife, Louise (Newell) O'Day, eventually buying a home on Delaware Avenue with the other local industrialists. Around this time, O'Day, John D. Rockefeller, and seven other directors at Standard were indicted by a grand jury in Pennsylvania for conspiracy to monopolize the buying and selling of crude petroleum and for manipulating the price of oil.[48] Paranoid about being extradited and forced to testify, Rockefeller reduced the shipping rates for the producers, and the prosecutor dropped the charges; Standard, which lost this battle, ended up winning the war.

By 1884, O'Day, known for his business acumen, was at the forefront of the developing natural gas business. Natural gas was still a mysterious substance with safety concerns, but this challenge only energized the Irish immigrant. He engaged in a two-year campaign to determine how to transport natural gas safely. Once this was resolved, O'Day oversaw the construction of an 87-mile-long pipeline from McKean County, Pennsylvania, to Buffalo, which surpassed the previous longest line of twenty-five miles. This project convinced Rockefeller that volatile natural gas could be safely and efficiently shipped from western Pennsylvania to major cities nationwide.[49] Standard Oil engaged in an acquisition spree by buying nine natural gas companies in New York, Ohio, and Pennsylvania. O'Day's job was to incorporate all nine into Standard, so he served as a director at each company. At its peak, the National Transit Company was transporting most of the natural gas in the United States and 85 percent of the nation's oil.[50]

O'Day represented Standard Oil's interests in over two dozen companies across the country. Several of these were companies based in Buffalo, including Buffalo General Electric Company (he served as director and president); Buffalo Natural Gas Company (director and president); Buffalo Railway, Niagara Falls Power Company (director); the Crosstown Street Railway of Buffalo (director); and Snow Steam Pump Works of Buffalo (director). He also had large stakes in Buffalo companies associated with electric lighting, street railways, and grain elevators. He served as president of the People's Bank of Buffalo and was the vice president of National Transit Co., a subsidiary of Standard Oil.

The workaholic found time for socializing as a member of the Buffalo Club, where he served as vice president (1888). He most likely was the first Irish Catholic admitted to this elite social and business club, setting a precedent for future Irish members.[51] It was not until the 1920s that the club had a sizable Irish Catholic membership.

Following the death of his first wife in 1890, O'Day moved to New York City but retained business dealings and an extensive real estate portfolio in Buffalo. He continued serving as the president of the People's Bank of Buffalo and the Buffalo General Electric Company—the primary supplier of electricity that illuminated Buffalo's city streets and powered its commercial buildings. The same year he left for New York City, O'Day and John D. Rockefeller, Sr. built and co-owned an ornate seven-story building at 534 Main Street in Buffalo (on the site of the present-day Hyatt Regency Hotel). The Green and Wicks-designed building housed a carpet and drapery business.[52]

O'Day, who lived in a Manhattan mansion, built a palatial summer home in Deal Beach, New Jersey, on the Jersey Shore. Typical of the dwellings of industrialists of his day, his Tudor-style Jersey Shore mansion was excessively opulent. On eighty-five acres, the fifty-six-room estate had a three-story marble fireplace, a copper roof, stables, separate servants' quarters, greenhouses, tennis courts, a boat house, a polo field, and sunken Italian gardens.[53] It was said to be the pride of the New Jersey shore area. In homage to his Irish village in County Clare, he named his house "Kildysart."[54] The same year it was constructed, O'Day returned to Buffalo to host a party for several hundred guests at the humble O'Day family homestead near Ellicottville, where he grew up. The timing of the two events—the party in Ellicottville and the completion of his New Jersey mansion—was likely an effort to show the world that he had triumphed from lowly beginnings to lofty heights.

At his New Jersey summer home, he hosted a 2,000-person party with guests such as former President Grover Cleveland. He hired the 69th Regimental Band of New York to perform, leased special trains to take his guests from their homes in the city area to New Jersey, and rented forty carriages to transport them from the train station to his house. His decadence rivaled Jay Gatsby.

O'Day did not enjoy his new home for long. In 1906, 62-year-old Daniel O'Day died from a cerebral hemorrhage while visiting his daughter in France. Some speculated that the Irish immigrant may have worked himself to death. His *New York Times* obituary headline proclaimed, "Standard Oil's Traffic Pioneer, O'Day, is Dead." The subheading read, "He Always Fought to Win."[55] The paper acknowledged him as the mastermind behind the plan to monopolize the transportation side of Standard's business. At his death, he was one of the company's wealthiest executives, holding about $1.8 million in the company's stock (equivalent to about $52 million in 2020).

O'Day, often devious and forbidding during his lifetime, shocked his family in his will. He stipulated that if Eliza, his second wife, ever remarried, she would lose access to his twelve children from his first wife and all of her inherited assets. She would also lose her annual income of $325,000 (roughly $10 million a year in 2020), the $1 million country estate at Rye, New Jersey (worth about $30 million in today's dollars), her mansion in New York City, the yacht, the horses, and the automobiles.

For almost four decades, O'Day was an innovative energy pioneer. While he did not devise the idea of moving oil through pipelines, he solved the problem of transporting it over long distances. To this day, pipelines are still the primary method of transporting oil. He also demonstrated that natural gas could be safely moved through pipelines over long distances —a breakthrough that opened up this critical energy source to numerous American cities. O'Day's obituary declared that he fought the independent producers, crushed them all, and won the war. This Irish Catholic succeeded at penetrating Rockefeller's Protestant inner circle, rising to become one of his closest lieutenants.

After O'Day's death, public animosity toward Standard Oil exploded with Ida M. Tarbell's publication of *The History of the Standard Oil Company* (1904), which exposed the opaque oil colossus. In 1911, the United States Supreme Court officially broke Standard Oil up into several smaller companies, ending the monopoly that O'Day dedicated his life to creating. In 2016, O'Day's revolutionary pipeline from Olean to Bayonne, which was decommissioned in 1925, was cited by the Department of Environmental Conservation for potentially contaminating three hundred miles of groundwater, soil, and wetlands across New York State. Exxon-Mobil, one of the companies that spun off from Standard, is responsible for the massive remediation project.

Following O'Day's death, his beloved son and successor at Standard, Daniel, Jr., died of heart disease at age forty-six. His daughter, Grace, committed suicide. In 1935, his beloved summer mansion on the New Jersey shore burned to the ground. Even though he was one of the wealthiest and most influential citizens of his day, there are no traces of this business tycoon in Buffalo.

William "Fingy" Conners

In the early 1920s, when the state of Florida had neither the budget nor the expertise to build a fifty-three-mile-long paved road along the swampy edge of the Everglades, state officials turned to a Buffalo-born industrialist.[57] On July 4, 1924, in Okeechobee City, Florida, 15,000 people attended a celebration to open a new toll highway and honor the man who built it. Dignitaries compared this Buffalonian to the late President Andrew Jackson, developer Henry M. Flagler, and the railroad baron James J. Hill. One speaker likened him to both Saint Patrick and Charlemagne.[58]

The project's difficulty hinged on the fact that there was neither an existing road nor a railroad to transport the heavy equipment, stones, and hundreds of laborers needed to complete this undertaking. This privately-funded toll road was constructed at a personal cost to the builder of $2 million ($31 million in 2021), and it extended from West Palm Beach to Lake Okeechobee. It was the final link in an east-west highway from West Palm Beach to Tampa, shortening the trip to just six hours, and it was "hailed as an engineering marvel of the time."[59] Economically, it was significant because it opened up the area's bountiful vegetable, poultry, and sugar markets to the rest of the country. The Buffalo Irishman who completed this engineering marvel—on time and on budget—was William J. "Fingy" Conners.

On January 3, 1857, William Conners was born in Buffalo's First Ward to a pair of County Cork Irish immigrants. His father, Peter Conners, progressed from a lake sailor to the more skilled occupation of a stonecutter, which enabled him to save enough money to buy a saloon. Young William dropped out of school at age eleven or twelve to become a porter on steamboats on the Great Lakes, and later worked stacking cords of wood for the railroads.[60] At age seventeen, the blue-eyed, muscular Conners became a longshoreman on the docks. Because of his toughness and fighting ability, he became the leader of a small crew of workers.[61] The charismatic young man was a natural leader, but also ruthless. This trait would guide him, for better and for worse, throughout his future commercial and political endeavors.

Almost everyone had a nickname in Buffalo's First Ward, a primarily Irish, working-class neighborhood along the bustling Buffalo River. Some people claimed they did not know their neighbor's first name until death when the name appeared in their obituary. Conners acquired his nickname as a boy when he goaded one of his friends that he didn't have the nerve to cut off one of Conners' fingers. Conners underestimated his friend, who indeed sliced off one of Conners' fingers on his left hand. As the legend goes, Conners ran down the street with a bloody stump, yelling, "he cut off my fingy." From that moment, he was known as Fingy Conners.[62]

Tragedy would strike Fingy in his late teens when his only sister died in a house fire. At about age nineteen, he lost his mother from the grief of his sister's death, and his father died the following year. Fingy now depended on himself for survival. He inherited his father's First Ward saloon and rooming house and used the insurance money from his parents' and sister's deaths to expand his saloon operation. The moderate success of the saloon gave him a taste for making money, but he wasn't satisfied. Using his gifts of leadership, the inheritance money, and a keen sense for business, Fingy figured out a way to profit even further from the burgeoning commerce on the waterfront.

As the need for dockworkers in Buffalo exploded in the late nineteenth century, shipping companies lacked the resources to hire the longshoremen directly. So, they delegated this task to saloon owners, who would then control hiring workers to unload goods from the boats. For instance, a ship's captain would go to a saloon owner and ask for ten workers; the saloon owner, or "boss" in the terminology of the day, would then pick his ten favorite customers. Saloon bosses like Conners obviously preferred to hire unmarried men who would also be boarders and loyal bar patrons. For their pay, workers received a tab at the saloon, which further lined the pockets of the saloon boss.

Several saloon owners profited from this system, but Fingy envisioned creating a monopoly with him as the premier boss—a task he accomplished ruthlessly. As a reward for keeping costs low and running his operation efficiently, he was awarded a contract for all of the shipments on the Great Lakes for the Union Steamboat Company in 1885.[63] Fingy now controlled the operations of unloading goods from the lake vessels to the docks. Conners eventually owned the remaining operations: from the dock to the warehouse and the warehouse to the railcars. At only thirty-eight, he was reportedly the largest freight contractor in the United States, the owner of two major Buffalo newspapers, and the president of Magnus Brewery.[64]

While his system was highly profitable for himself and his cronies and efficient for the shipping companies, it was vehemently opposed by workers, neighborhood priests, and some in the press. Public criticism, however, did not derail Conners. Within a decade after he consolidated his freight handling of dry goods, he set his sights on controlling the lucrative grain handling business. Fingy eventually monopolized this business as he had the others and became known as "The Uncrowned King of the Docks."[65] As previously mentioned, Conners lost this title after the Great Strike of 1899.

In addition to Fingy's grain trade dealings, he acquired wealth from his interests in newspapers, street-paving companies, poultry farming, breweries, and real estate.[66] Conners left the south side of Buffalo and gained entrance into the elite Protestant enclave when he purchased a mansion on Delaware Avenue. Two years later, he was elected chairman of the Democratic State Committee, where he was influential in the 1908 U.S. Presidential election.

In 1916, at age 59, William J. Conner's fortunes brightened once again. The Panama Act, legislation enacted by the U.S. Congress, ended the railroad companies' monopoly on Great Lakes shipping. Forced to divest their Great Lakes shipping operations, the railroad companies urged their longtime friend Fingy Conners to consolidate their disparate lake freight lines into one company under his control. Fingy, a former cabin boy on the lakes, quickly bought their shipping lines and formed the Great Lakes Transit Corporation. He became Chairman of the Board of this new company and one of the most influential businessmen on the Great Lakes; the 33-vessel enterprise employed between 4,000 and 6,000 men weekly. At one point, Conners claimed that he was the largest individual employer of labor in the United States.[67] Eventually, he controlled a staggering 85% of the package freight on the Great Lakes.[68]

During the First World War, Conners offered the entire Great Lakes Transit fleet and his beloved yacht, the *Mary Alice*, to the U.S. government for whatever price they offered. The war department also hired him as a consultant to figure out logistical problems with transporting freight to French ports.[69] After the war, Conners split his time between Buffalo and West Palm Beach, Florida, where he purchased 4,000 acres near Lake Okeechobee and built homes. His real estate project at Okeechobee City townsite was reportedly the largest in the state's history. He had a massive farm, which he described as "the finest farm in the South" and claimed was the largest vegetable farm in the world.[70]

The state of Florida eventually purchased Conners' Florida toll road, and it became part of what is now Route 80 and U.S. Highway 98, which runs across Florida to the Alabama border. Conners also built the 3,330-foot-long Warren G. Harding Memorial Bridge over the Kissimmee River in Florida as part of his efforts to connect Florida's eastern and western coasts. About Conners' highway, the *Palm Beach Post* wrote, "the connecting link between the east and west coasts of Florida will stand as a monument to the builder [Conners] and proof of his vision."[71]

On October 5, 1929, less than three weeks before the 1929 stock market crash, Fingy Conners died of a heart attack. Some would argue that he exemplified the American Dream: an uneducated laborer with street smarts and unbridled ambition who became a nationally prominent multimillionaire. Others would say that the Buffalo business tycoon was a cruel and greedy businessman who lived his opulent lifestyle off the backs of poor laborers, especially the dock and grain workers in Buffalo. He remains a complicated figure. Many Buffalonians associate Conners and his family with the *Courier-Express* newspaper (which will be discussed later in the book), but that was only a small part of his massive enterprise.

His mansion on Delaware Avenue and the *Courier-Express* headquarters on Main Street, now the Diocese of Buffalo's Catholic Center, are the only traces of his controversial legacy.

Trailblazing Women

At the end of the nineteenth century in Buffalo, professional occupations for women were limited. Some of the most popular were public school teacher, nurse, florist, portrait painter, artist, skilled embroiderer, dressmaker, and language teacher.[72] It was difficult for women to break into male-dominated professions, but two pioneering Irish-American women succeeded. Born in the same year, one came from Quincy, Massachusetts, and the other from Paterson, New Jersey. Both settled in Buffalo because of their husband's jobs, and both became widows at a young age, forcing them to support their large families. The first was Emily McDonnell, a prominent businesswoman, and the second was Dr. Jane Carroll, a successful physician and lawyer.

On Sunday, April 8, 1894, Emily A. McDonnell, a 44-year-old housewife and mother of seven, lost her husband, John Quincy McDonnell, to a massive heart attack. John was 43 years old and president of the Buffalo branch of McDonnell & Sons, a national wholesaler and retailer of granite monuments and mausoleums.[73] His sudden death shattered Emily's tranquil, upper-middle-class existence at 440 Prospect Avenue on Buffalo's West Side.

Her husband John was the younger of two sons of Patrick McDonnell, an Irish immigrant from County Roscommon. Patrick settled in Quincy, Massachusetts in 1835 and founded a leading granite firm twenty years later. McDonnell's firm owned massive quarries in Quincy and Barre, Vermont, and sold polished blocks of granite to retailers who then sold finished monuments to consumers. When Patrick decided to retire, Emily's husband, John, and his older brother, Thomas, bought out their father's business. In 1884, John set up his retail operations in Buffalo, New York, where he purchased two lots at 858-860 Main Street near Virginia Street to build his headquarters and showroom. The Neo-Grec-style building had a storefront with a sculptor's studio and a sizable yard to display the firm's monuments. The two-story façade was decorated in polished gray granite so that the building itself became an advertisement for the firm's capabilities.

Wealthy Buffalo industrialist John Blocher, a manufacturer of boots and shoes, requested McDonnell & Sons to build a monument to honor his late son Nelson. The fabrication of this unique bell-shaped monument in Forest Lawn Cemetery was complicated because the bell had to be cut down from a single 60-ton piece to one piece weighing twenty-six tons. The crypt also contained life-sized marble carvings of each of the three family members and an angel, all protected by heavy plate glass imported from Paris. The McDonnell firm erected the monument in 1887. It soon had so many visitors that cemetery workers created a unique path to access it.

Legend says that Nelson Blocher fell in love with the household's Irish maid. To break off this forbidden love affair, the senior Blocher and his wife sent Nelson to Europe and promptly dismissed the young maid. When Nelson returned from Europe, he died of a "broken heart." He actually died of kidney disease, but the more romantic version of the story struck a nerve with Buffalonians and visitors from around the country. The grief-stricken and perhaps guilt-ridden Blochers spent a small fortune on their son's monument (over $3 million today). At the time, the Blocher Mausoleum was "probably the most widely known private cemetery memorial in America."[74] Visitors continue to be drawn to this impressive structure as much for the beauty of its granite design as the tragic love story surrounding it.

The commission to repair the Soldiers' and Sailors' monument in Lafayette Square was the second significant project that the company completed in Buffalo. Women from the Ladies' Union Memorial Association had raised money for a monument to honor Buffalo's Civil War veterans. They had selected a firm from Maine to construct it, with Irish-born George Keller as the architect. The towering monument, erected in 1884, was built to last "for the ages." However, six years later, it was crumbling and leaning to one side. After public outrage, the city hired McDonnell & Sons to repair the 85-foot-tall monument. It cost the city a small fortune, but McDonnell's Soldiers' and Sailors' monument is still standing 130 years later and is one of the most recognized public monuments in Erie County.

Though John McDonnell built the company, McDonnell & Sons prospered under the direction of his wife, Emily. Born in November 1848, Emily was the third child of Daniel and Mary Ann Dinegan. Daniel Dinegan, an Irish immigrant from County Longford, emigrated to Quincy, Massachusetts, in the early 1840s, where he worked as a bootmaker. After her studies, Emily worked as a schoolteacher in Quincy until she married John McDonnell in 1874.

Most women in Emily McDonnell's circumstances would have probably sold their husband's share of the company. She had no business experience but needed to provide for her seven children. As a woman in this male-dominated business, Emily would face obstacles that her husband could never have imagined. At the turn of the twentieth century, Buffalo women business owners of national firms were rare, so she had few role models. Yet, Emily decided to assume the role of president of the McDonnell & Sons' Buffalo branch.

A few years later, the enterprising Irish woman bought out her brother-in-law's share of the business and formed a partnership with her four sons: John, Thomas,

James, and Robert. She opened a state-of-the-art manufacturing plant in Barre, Vermont, which eventually became one of the world's largest and best-equipped granite finishing facilities. Under Emily's leadership, the company focused on craftsmanship and hired the industry's best designers and builders. While her company shipped monuments nationwide, some of their best work resides in Buffalo cemeteries. At the turn of the twentieth century, the McDonnells were annually erecting over fifty percent of all of the monuments in Buffalo.

At Forest Lawn Cemetery, McDonnell & Sons built the Red Jacket Monument, the Volunteer Firemen Memorial, the Philip Becker Monument, and the Blocher Mausoleum. The McDonnells provided the granite for the magnificent archway that welcomes visitors at the Main Street entrance. They provided monuments and mausoleums for the wealthiest citizens in Western New York, including Spencer Kellogg, Bronson Rumsey, George B. Matthews, and Jacob Dold. They designed stately monuments for families with names such as Sibley, Hengerer, Sattler, Bissell, Goodyear, Schoellkopf, Wendt, Meldrum, Jewett, Baird, McNulty, Wadsworth, Chapin, Statler, Flickinger, and Slee. Their monument for Mayor Philip Becker was the largest cut of granite in the US in its time—84 tons finished. Families spent small fortunes on the monuments and mausoleums in Forest Lawn, with some mausoleums costing over $1 million in today's dollars.

At Holy Cross Cemetery in Lackawanna, McDonnell monuments mark the graves of many prominent individuals and families from the south side of Buffalo: Father Nelson Baker, William J. "Fingy" Conners, Congressman William H. Ryan, Miss Ernestine Nardin, and William F. "Blue-Eyed Billy" Sheehan. Other prominent monuments from the firm in the Buffalo area include the Father Hennepin monument in Niagara Falls, the Commodore Oliver Hazard Perry Monument in Front Park, and the Laura Secord Monument in Queenston, Ontario.

McDonnell & Sons worked in every state in the continental US and had many commissions in Canada and in countries as far away as China. Their monuments stand in over five hundred cities and towns across America. Numerous prominent politicians and military figures employed the McDonnells to build their family monuments. Among them were New York Governor Samuel Tilden, US Vice President Charles Fairbanks, US Supreme Court Chief Justice Salmon P. Chase, and General George B. McClellan. Emily's company also built monuments for notable civilians, such as the Mormon leader Joseph Smith III, the family of Eugene V. Debs, and the Mead Johnson family.

Emily managed offices, plants, quarries, and agents nationwide, employing nearly three hundred people. She was president of the company for over three decades and was actively running the business as chairman of the board until her death in December 1926. At age seventy-seven, Emily died of complications from diabetes and was buried with her husband, John, under the tallest monument in Holy Cross Cemetery in Lackawanna.[75]

One obituary declared that "she came into national prominence" for her dedication to improving memorial standards. "She proved the power of womanhood to cope with big situations, and she must ever stand as an example of what lofty vision and indomitable courage can achieve." She built "one of the most successful business houses in the country, judged by the quality of its output and the volume of its business." The *Courier* newspaper claimed she was "one of Buffalo's most remarkable women," and she "was known coast to coast for her remarkable business ability."[76]

At the end of World War II, McDonnell & Sons left their handsome storefront at 858 Main Street, where they had been for sixty years, and moved to a smaller shop on Delaware Avenue. The company started to wind down around 1950, and the Memorial Art-Crawford firm purchased its assets.

The McDonnell & Sons headquarters building at 858 Main Street changed hands over the years. In 2006, First Amherst Development Group redeveloped this building as part of a larger project, Granite Works, named for the distinctive granite façade on the McDonnell building. It is now home to a retail shop and residential units in the heart of the medical campus. The McDonnells' work at Lafayette Square, Front Park, Forest Lawn, Holy Cross Cemetery, and hundreds of other sites throughout the United States and Canada will survive for generations. Emily McDonnell, a former schoolteacher and mother of seven, was the guiding force behind much of this granite legacy.

Jane (Wall) Carroll was a trailblazing Irish Catholic medical doctor and Emily McDonnell's contemporary. The *Courier* claimed Jane Carroll was "one of Buffalo's first active woman [medical] practitioners."[77] She was born in New Jersey in 1848 to an Irish-born father, Stephen Wall, an affluent dry goods merchant, and Emeline, a housewife.[78] Jane attended a Catholic convent school, where she excelled at music, literature, and the arts.

Jane married a native New Yorker, Peter Carroll, who moved the family to Buffalo in 1878 to enter the canal and lake transportation business. Like the McDonnells, the Carrolls resided on the West Side of Buffalo. Peter Carroll died at a young age, so Jane, like Emily McDonnell, had to support the family financially. Before his death, Jane Carroll had graduated from the University of Buffalo Medical School at age 43, the same year she gave birth to her tenth child. Her daughter, Evangeline Carroll, earned her medical degree the year after Jane.[79] Jane managed a thriving medical practice for twenty years. While she was not the first female doctor in Buffalo, she was a pioneer.

In 1906, at age 58, Dr. Jane Carroll graduated from the University of Buffalo Law School and was admitted to the New York State Bar two years later. Only two practicing female lawyers were in Buffalo when she entered law school, so she was likely the first Buffalo woman to have graduated from both medical and law school. As an aside, it is interesting to note that Carroll, both a physician and a lawyer, could not vote until the 19th Amendment passed in 1920.

Carroll lived on Buffalo's Ashland Avenue and participated in several social, civic, and religious organizations. She was the president and one of the founders of the Buffalo Physicians' League.[80] Carroll was also president of The Professional and Business Women's Club and a founding member of the Women's Union. On Sundays, she sang in the choir at St. Joseph's Cathedral as the leading soprano. Her friends remembered her as a talented musician and a gifted singer. In 1902, Carroll was vice president of the University of Buffalo Medical Department Alumni Association, the only woman serving with seven male officers. She was active in Buffalo's Irish Land League—an organization that agitated and raised funds so farmers in Ireland could purchase land from absentee English landowners.

For ten years, she was the first female physician to serve as the Supreme Medical Examiner for the Ladies' Catholic Benevolent Association, a national insurance organization. In this capacity, she supervised a thousand physicians across the country. At local conferences, Dr. Carroll often delivered papers on topics such as "Women in Medicine," "Diseases of Children," "The Microbe," "The Prevention of Tuberculosis," and "What We Eat and Why We Eat It." She also hosted conventions in Buffalo for women physicians, such as the Women's Medical Society convention at the Statler Hotel in May 1912. During these years, Carroll enjoyed spending her free time at her cottage in Waverly Beach, Ontario, and traveling with her daughters to Europe on summer holidays.

Carroll, a savvy businesswoman, was one of the largest stockholders of Rochester Gas and Electric Company and Mohawk Valley Company.[81] Her friend Robert M. Searle, the president of Rochester Gas and Electric, said that, unlike other physicians who charged patients a price by the minute, she supplemented the usual cures with inspirational visits and sincere friendship.[82] Her obituary described Carroll as "one of those lovable and kindly women whose every thought was the comfort and happiness of others."[83]

In 1913, Dr. Carroll returned to Paterson to manage her deceased mother's vast real estate holdings. With the help of her son, she designed her dream house in New Jersey, which became one of the show houses in Paterson. She furnished her home with rare paintings and fittings from her travels across the globe. In 1927, while vacationing with her daughters, Carroll died in Rome, Italy, at the age of 80.

One of her obituaries remarked that she did *not* have the backing and encouragement of her family and friends when she pursued her career.[84] "Of course, she received credit for her indomitable perseverance, but it was greatly outweighed by the burden of opposition she encountered. This was a penalty of pioneering."[85] Her hometown paper of Paterson proclaimed, "The Life of Dr. Jane W. Carroll was an inspiration in ambition, courage, and service."[86] The Buffalo Catholic newspaper claimed Dr. Carroll was "one of Buffalo's most ambitious and active women."[87]

Other Leading Business People

In 1873, in Chicago, Martin and Mary McNulty welcomed James H. McNulty into the world. James's paternal grandparents were born in Ireland, as was his mother. James started working at age eleven for a local paint and varnish company. At nineteen, he was employed by Pratt & Lambert, a New York City-based company, and three years later, he was promoted to manager of the Chicago plant. In 1902, the company moved its headquarters from New York City to Buffalo, the site of its largest manufacturing plant. McNulty transferred to the Queen City as the company's secretary and sales manager. He was promoted to treasurer and eventually elevated to president in 1917. Under his guidance, the company expanded beyond manufacturing wood varnishes into the lucrative exterior and interior paint market. McNulty, who gained a national reputation in his field, built Pratt & Lambert into one of Buffalo's largest manufacturers.

Aside from running one of Buffalo's best-known companies, McNulty was a tireless civic fundraiser, especially for the University of Buffalo (UB). At his death, the *Courier* declared him one of the "big men" of the city because of his success in commercial and civic affairs.[88] In 1915, as a member of the UB Council, McNulty chaired the committee that raised $600,000 to build a College of Arts and Sciences building at UB, which was instrumental in expanding the university beyond its limited professional degrees. A few years later, McNulty was one of the principal organizers of a campaign to raise funds to create an endowment for the university's professional and undergraduate schools. University of Buffalo Chancellor Samuel P. Capen declared, "His contribution to it [UB] in effort and in substance during the last six years was one of the most influential factors in bringing it to its present stage of development."[89] Capen added that McNulty was one of Buffalo's "foremost citizens."

During the First World War, McNulty also served as vice chairman of the Liberty Loan and Red Cross fundraising campaigns, exceeding each quota assigned to him. He also served as a director of the Marine Trust Company, the Buffalo Federal Reserve Bank, the Pierce-Arrow Motor Company, and a half dozen other industrial companies. In his spare time, he served as the president of the Buffalo Club and as a director of the Buffalo Athletic Club.

On a Saturday afternoon in October 1926, when McNulty was on his way to play golf just north of Buffalo, his car collided with another vehicle and rolled over three times. The next day, the fifty-three-year-old Buffalonian died at the hospital from head trauma and a fractured skull. His obituary claimed, "James H. McNulty was a man whose militant energy and superior talents were great and creative forces in community advancement and civic development and growth."[90] The year after his death, his wife donated a gift worth $2 million in today's dollars to UB for an endowed chair, "The James H. McNulty Professorship in English."[91] James McNulty's funeral monument at Forest Lawn Cemetery, built by McDonnell & Sons, is one of the cemetery's most noteworthy monuments.

From the 1870s until the 1920s, Buffalo was one of the largest livestock markets in the country because so many railroad lines had hubs or terminated their lines in the Queen City. Most of the livestock trade—stockyards, meatpacking plants, the stock exchange, and the commission houses—was located in East Buffalo, along and around William Street.[92] By 1902, Buffalo was ranked first worldwide for the number of lambs and sheep processed and was second to Chicago for cattle and hogs.[93] The New York Central Live Stockyards on William Street, just one of many companies in the area, could process an astounding 80,000 animals daily. While the Germans in Buffalo, with dealers such as Jacob Dold, Louis Fuhrmann, and Christian Klinck, dominated this industry, one Irishman became prominent as well.

John Hughes was born in County Kilkenny in 1842, and he emigrated to America at age ten, penniless and accompanied by a friend of the same age. After attending Bryant & Stratton school, he went into business with Edward Swope, a pioneer in the emerging livestock trade. The Swope & Hughes company prospered as livestock dealers, and in 1882, the expanding firm added Hiram Waltz and John Benstead as partners. The firm operated out of the Livestock Exchange Building in East Buffalo, specializing in hogs, cattle, and sheep. In 1887, Hughes was elected president of the East Buffalo Live Stock Association. Shortly after, he and Benstead opened up a livestock company in Cleveland, Ohio, with Hughes serving as president. Together, they also started Excelsior Farms in West Seneca, where they bred racehorses.[94]

Hughes, who lived in a stately house at 591 Niagara Street on the Irish West Side, also owned a large estate in West Seneca and a 54-acre farm in Hamburg. He had a chauffeur, servants, and a coachman on his estate. Hughes was also involved with many civic endeavors and, despite being Catholic, was accepted into civic organizations generally run by the Protestant elite. From 1898 to 1902, he served as the president of the Board of Park Commissioners, and in 1901, he replaced John J. Albright as a member of the Board of Directors of the Pan-American

Exposition. Hughes was the only Irish Catholic on the long list of officers, directors, and executive committee members of the Exposition, filled with the wealthiest and most powerful Buffalonians. He was also part of the small Buffalo delegation, which traveled to Washington, D.C., to personally invite President William McKinley to Buffalo for the Pan-American Exposition. Hughes was prominent in banking circles as a founder and a director of the People's Bank of Buffalo, where he served with Daniel O'Day. He was also a longtime director and the one-time president of the Irish-American Savings and Loan, which provided money for Irish Americans to purchase homes.

In April 1921, Hughes died while visiting his family in Phoenix. At his death, the *Buffalo Enquirer* declared, "Buffalo [lost] one of its sterling characters," who was "a genial, whole-souled, warm-hearted man" and "known in all of the country's great cattle marts."[95] The *Buffalo Times* claimed that "he was one of the most successful and best known and best-liked livestock men in the United States."[96]

The Modern-Day Business People

Maurice Courtney, who in 1911, lamented the fact that Buffalo Irish were "financially and commercially weak," would be contented to know that the Celts eventually succeeded as businesspeople. The list of prominent Buffalo Irish businessmen and women from the early twentieth century is too long to list. Some of the notable business people in that period include John J. Boland, the co-founder of the American Steamship Company; James Mooney, who started a successful real estate and insurance firm, which today is Walsh-Duffield; William H. Fitzpatrick, a prominent builder, and Irish-born Michael Beecher, the founder of Globe Belting. Some of these men and their families will be discussed further in other chapters.

In the modern era, Irish business leaders have populated the executive suites and boardrooms of many of Buffalo's leading companies. Irish American Robert Brady, a Buffalo native and M.I.T. graduate, was the longtime chief executive officer and chairman of Moog, Inc., the area's second-largest public company. In 2011, Irish-born and raised John Scannell succeeded Brady as Moog's CEO, and in 2023, Irish-born Patrick J. Roche replaced Scannell.

In recent years, Bernard J. Kennedy was the longtime chief executive officer for National Fuel Gas Co., Buffalo's third-largest public company. The late South Buffalo native Frank J. McGuire founded over thirty companies, including the engineering firm Industrial Power & Lighting and the McGuire Group, a healthcare conglomerate. John P. Courtney, a son of Irish immigrants, became head of Computer Task Group (CTG), one of Buffalo's top ten public firms. He is also the father of Kathy Hochul, New York's first female governor. The late John "Jack" Cullen founded Multisorb, a world leader in packaging solutions, sold his firm, and became one of Buffalo's most prominent philanthropists.

Buffalo's largest insurance firm, Lawley Insurance, was founded and is still run by an Irish-American family by the same name. Walsh-Duffield, another leader in the insurance industry, has been led by an Irish-American family for five generations. Mark Sullivan served as the president and chief executive officer of Catholic Health, the second-largest health system in Western New York. Irish American William McHugh co-founded Independent Health, the area's second-largest health care plan, and later served as CEO of Amerigroup, which he grew into a Fortune 500 Company.

Buffalo Irish women leaders are also prevalent. Maureen (O'Connell) Hurley was the executive vice president and chief administrative officer for Rich Products, Buffalo's largest private company. Dottie Gallagher was the president and chief executive officer of the Buffalo Niagara Partnership. South Buffalo-raised Patricia Farrell is the group vice president and managing director of Wilmington Trust, and Eva Hassett was the longtime executive director of the International Institute.

While many Irish had a knack for business, others earned a living and became famous performers on the stage and screen. Some even merged business and entertainment and created successful commercial enterprises. We turn to them now.

CHAPTER FIVE

Entertainers-The Early Years

The First Stars of the Stage

Buffalo launched the stage careers of two of America's most colorful and controversial nineteenth-century stars. Edwin Pearce Christy and George Harrington, both of Irish ancestry, dominated one of America's most popular forms of entertainment for that period: blackface minstrelsy. Today, such minstrelsy is considered appalling and racist. From the 1840s until the turn of the twentieth century, however, working-class northerners packed theaters night after night.

Edwin Pearce Christy, also known as E.P., arrived in Buffalo in the 1830s after being raised in Philadelphia. His Irish-born father, Robert F. Christy, worked in local government and was involved in Philadelphia's Democratic party.[1] E.P. Christy developed a talent for entertaining, and, in the early 1830s, he joined a circus group in New Orleans, where he performed as a blackface comedic singer.[2] While there, he would regularly go to Congo Square in the heart of the city to watch Black men and women sing, dance, and play music.[3] These performances strongly influenced the content of his future skits.

When he moved into Buffalo's seedy Canal District, Christy honed his comedic act while working for a few theaters. He befriended a Black singer from Buffalo, named "One-Legged" Harrison, who showed him some dance moves and shared some song lyrics, which Christy later used in his shows.[4] Christy also met Harriet E. Harrington, an illiterate daughter of Irish immigrants, who owned a boarding house, a dance hall, and at least four properties in the area. Harrington, who was a widow, had a son named George.

After Harriet Harrington and E.P. Christy became acquainted, he managed her rental properties, which tenants occasionally used for illicit liaisons. At one point in the mid-1830s, they were both charged with one count of running a house of ill-repute during Mayor Samuel Wilkeson's reign. Wilkeson, who pledged to reform the prostitute-filled District, reputedly coerced Christy to marry Harriet, believing that this formal union would put them on the straight and narrow.[5]

After their marriage, Christy adopted Harriet's son, George Harrington. George excelled in his studies and was a natural performer. One of his teachers remembered that he staged amateur theatrical shows with other students after class.[6] George also earned money by dancing in blackface for the sailors on Buffalo's docks.[7] In 1839, at age twelve, under the direction of Christy, George performed jig dances in the Eagle Theater in Buffalo. Around the same time, he also assumed the last name "Christy" to capitalize on his stepfather's well-known surname.

Together, the Christy duo traveled to canal towns across New York State, performing and refining their act. In 1842, at a hall on Water Street in Buffalo, E.P. Christy formally organized a troupe of minstrel entertainers who called themselves Christy's Minstrels (also sometimes referred to as the Christy Minstrels). After four years of performing in and around Buffalo, Christy decided that he and George should try their luck in New York City.

Before they departed, E.P. Christy secretly sold many of Harriet's assets, which he used to fund their venture in New York City. The Christys quickly found commercial success in their adopted city. In Manhattan, Christy engaged in a relationship with a prostitute named "Pretty Mary" Miller, despite still being married to Harriet.[8] In 1847, they started performing at Mechanics' Hall on Broadway in Manhattan, where their show ran for more than seven years in front of packed crowds. In total, they performed at that venue 2,792 times, claiming to turn away a thousand patrons on some nights.[9] They became *the* premier minstrel company in the United States, which allowed them to choose the best songs (plantation ballads and sentimental ditties) from upstart songwriters.[10] Their troupe achieved fame on both sides of the Atlantic Ocean after some members of E.P. Christy's original group broke away and moved to London. In fact, the word "Christys" became the British term for any generic minstrel group.[11]

E.P. Christy boasted that his ensemble was the first blackface minstrel troupe. Actually, they were probably the second after Dan Emmet founded his group in New York City. However, Christy left a lasting legacy by transforming the traditional program of disjointed solo acts into a structured three-act performance. This format eventually became the standard for most minstrel shows in the United States throughout the rest of the nineteenth century.[12] During the performances, Christy, dressed in a tuxedo but not blackface, served as a master of ceremonies; he introduced the blackface performers, who sat on stage in a semicircle with their musical instruments. He then presided over "a program of rapid-fire cross-talk—jokes, malapropisms, puns, songs—starring the semicircle's 'endmen'— grotesquely large-grinning Tambo and Bones, so named for the instruments they played [tambourine and rhythm bones]."[13] To make minstrel shows more family-friendly, Christy toned down the racier—but not racist—aspects of the show.[14] In fact, at some theaters, children under twelve could attend evening performances at half price.[15]

E.P. Christy not only launched the career of his stepson, George, but he also promoted entertainers such as Irish-born Richard M. Hooley, who performed in Buffalo as early as 1845 and later opened prominent theaters in New York City and Chicago. Irish descendant Stephen Foster, known as the "father of American music," wrote many of the most popular songs performed by Christy's Minstrels. Christy even put *his* name on some of Foster's songs, including the famous "Old Folks at Home," but let Foster keep the royalties.[16] Around 1850, Christy published *Christy's Plantation Melodies*, a catalog of his group's songs that sold well nationwide, and helped cement his fame.

Working-class Irish in northern cities were overrepresented in both the audience and on stage. In addition to E.P. and George Christy, and the previously mentioned Richard Hooley and Stephen Foster, some of the biggest stars and songwriters of nineteenth-century minstrel shows had Irish ancestry, including Dan Emmett, Dan Bryant, Billy Emerson, and Joel Walker Sweeney.[17] In addition to garnering fame and fortune, the popularity and success of the Irish minstrel performers "broadened and softened the negative images of the Irish" held by some Americans.[18]

Although E.P. Christy was a skilled manager and innovator, his stepson, George (Harrington) Christy, was the troupe's star. George was considered the "genre's best comic" and the "headlining member" of the company.[19] The younger Christy claimed he was the first performer to introduce the "negro wench" to the minstrel stage.[20] With black paint on his face and wearing women's clothing, he popularized a Black character named "Miss Lucy Long." For twelve years, E.P. and George Christy prospered in their partnership; however, George allegedly fell out with E.P. around 1850 over E.P.'s unwillingness to support Harriet.

George Christy subsequently partnered with Henry Wood and founded one of the best-known companies in the United States prior to the Civil War.[21] Christy was so famous that even though Wood's Theater in New York City could hold 1,300 people, they regularly turned away five hundred to a thousand people a night.[22] By this time, George had eclipsed the fame of his celebrated stepfather and was making a fortune at the box office. One of George's most famous skits was a parody called "Uncle Tom's Cabin," which made a mockery of Harriet Beecher Stowe's anti-slavery novel by the same name. In 1858, George Christy dissolved his partnership with Wood and, up until his death, toured with multiple companies as *the* star minstrel. Christy published his own collection of songs, jokes, and routines titled *Christy and White's Ethiopian Melodies*.

Neither George nor E.P. Christy enjoyed a happy ending to their lives. In 1854, at about age forty, E.P. retired a wealthy man after operating several Christy's Opera Houses; the year before his retirement alone, he reputedly made $1.7 million in today's dollars.[23] At the start of the Civil War, however, E.P. started to become paranoid that he would lose his fortune because of the conflict. His friends claimed that he quickly lost his mental faculties, and they considered him insane. In 1862, E.P. attempted suicide by jumping out of his Manhattan home's second-story window. Paralyzed and badly hurt, the forty-seven-year-old died within two weeks of the fall. About four days before he expired, E.P. hastily married "Pretty Mary" Miller and removed Harriet and George from his will.

For George Christy, his workaholic nature and life on the road contributed to his declining health.[24] Others speculated that it was his love of drink that led to his demise. In May 1868, at age forty, he experienced a neurological event that caused brain swelling and eventually killed him. Upon George Christy's death, his daughter described him as a lively character and a very generous man.[25] *The Brooklyn Daily Eagle* wrote that he was "a brilliant exponent of the better days of minstrelsy" and lived a "dazzling life as a star" despite suffering a sad end.[26]

Edward Rice, the great producer of minstrel shows, declared that George Christy was "one of the greatest performers that ever graced the minstrel stage."[27] The *Philadelphia Inquirer* claimed he was the "best delineator of negro character, its drolleries and comical stupidities."[28] Before his death, the *Gleason's Pictorial* claimed that George Christy's "versatility is unparalleled, his fame world-wide... there are few residents of New York, or casual visitors to the metropolis who have not witnessed and enjoyed the original genius of George Christy...."[29]

E.P. and George Christy profoundly influenced minstrelsy, the "first truly American form of popular entertainment."[30] From a twenty-first-century perspective, this form of entertainment is repulsive. Even in the heyday of minstrelsy, Frederick Douglass described its purveyors as "the filthy scum of white society, who have stolen from us a complexion denied to them by nature...to make money, and pander to the corrupt taste of their white fellow citizens."[31] The fact that the Buffalo Irish helped popularize blackface minstrelsy is noteworthy but not commendable.

Chauncey Olcott—The Irish Tenor

Another Buffalo Irishman from the Canal District started his career in minstrelsy but eventually soured on it. On July 21, 1860, Chauncey Olcott, one of the most recognized Irish-American singers and songwriters of all time and one of Buffalo's first national stars, was born on the second floor of his father's horse stable in

Buffalo.[32] Chauncey's father was Mellen Whitney Olcott, a Yankee Protestant who owned a saloon in Buffalo. Chauncey's mother, Margaret "Peggy" Doyle from Killeagh, County Cork, had grown up in a primitive cabin in an Irish shantytown in Lockport, New York.[33] She married Mellen Olcott, nicknamed "Handsome Jack," when she was just sixteen. Mellen objected to a Catholic baptism for Chauncey, so Peggy had to arrange a secret baptism for her son while her husband was away.[34]

Mellen Olcott's saloon at Canal and State Streets was in Buffalo's rough-and-tumble Canal District. Peggy managed the tavern for several years while Mellon was busy training horses and working as a horse dealer. Chauncey spent his earliest years in this dodgy district where his neighbors were saloonkeepers, cooks, prostitutes, and sailors. The family moved around often but stayed in the downtown area.

Chauncey spent his boyhood summers in Lockport with his mother's Irish immigrant family, the Doyles. They filled the boy's head with romantic stories and songs of the Emerald Isle, which cultivated his love for his ancestral homeland.[35] Olcott claimed that "he loved Ireland from the day he drew his first breath," but it was in his grandparents' cabin in Lockport where he formed a bond with his mother's ancestral home.[36]

Tragedy and loss marked Olcott's youth. When he was a young boy, his father abandoned the family, remarried, and moved to New York City, where he managed horse stables.[37] Chauncey's mother was forced to run the saloon to support the family. Two of Chauncey's brothers died in childhood, and his beloved grandfather Doyle drowned while working on the canal at Lockport.[38] Due to these misfortunes, Olcott became very attached to his mother, and the theme of motherhood was prominent in many of his plays and songs later in life.

Olcott finished his studies at age thirteen, and while he wasn't a remarkable student, he was a gifted singer. At age four, he sang an Irish ballad to a crowd at St. Michael's school, and the audience burst into wild cheers. Olcott's talent caught the attention of the Buffalo Public Schools' music supervisor, who encouraged Olcott's singing by allowing him to display his talents at building dedications or when dignitaries visited Buffalo.[39] On the Fourth of July in 1869, eleven-year-old Olcott was mentioned in the newspaper for singing in front of a large crowd at Franklin Square. By age seventeen, however, like many of his working-class counterparts, he was forced to "working on the lakes."

At this time, Olcott's enterprising mother, Peggy, owned a small tugboat business on Buffalo's waterfront. She urged her son to pursue a career in her tug business, promising that someday he would be captain of his own tug. Olcott half-heartedly worked on one of her vessels as a fireman until one day, while shoveling coal into its engine, his shirt caught on fire.[40] Interpreting this as a sign that he was supposed to do something else with his life, Olcott told his mother that he was finished with working on the waterfront and would pursue a career on stage.

Coming from the working class, Chauncey had limited options to break into the performing arts. Blackface minstrelsy was one path that many Irish-American entertainers pursued. One day in 1879, while Olcott was singing in a tavern, Billy Emerson, a prominent minstrel company owner, recognized Olcott's talents, and invited him to join Emerson's Minstrels in Chicago.[41] Chauncey's minstrel career took him from Chicago to London, where the Prince of Wales, later King Edward VII, was so impressed with Olcott's performance that he requested the Buffalo singer visit him in his private box.[42] Around this time, Olcott aspired to perform in a more "respectable theater."[43] But to make the move, he needed someone to discover him.

In 1886, leading lady Lillian Russell recognized his talent after watching one of his performances. Russell selected the blue-eyed Buffalo singer for the leading role of Pablo, opposite her in the comic opera *Pepita*, performed at the Union Square Theatre in New York City.[44] Although this could have launched his career on Broadway, Olcott was dismissed when Russell's husband, the opera's producer, found a note in Lillian's handwriting asking the handsome Olcott to join her for dinner. Another version of the story suggests that negative reviews of his awkward kissing scene with Russell forced him to resign.[45]

In 1890, Chauncey decided to pursue a career as an opera singer by taking voice lessons in Milan. Upon his dangerous sea voyage to Italy, he demanded to be let out in England, where he stayed and enrolled in voice lessons in London to improve his diction. There, he performed as a tenor in the comic opera *Miss Decima* at the Prince of Wales Theatre. It was in this comic role—as an Irish adventurer posing as a Spanish bullfighter trying to win the heart of a Spanish girl—that he finally found his calling. Olcott was equally suited to perform as a romantic Irish ballad singer and a comedic actor.

In 1893, Olcott caught another break when America's leading Irish tenor, William J. Scanlan, the star of the popular play *Mavourneen*, was forced to retire at age thirty-seven due to early-onset dementia. The producer of *Mavourneen* urged Olcott to take Scanlan's place, and within days, he proved to be an audience favorite.[46] Olcott's wife credited his success to the fact that when he sang his songs, "he put into his voice all the bitter history, the broken homes, the fairy memories of the Emerald Isle. Irish hearts in his American audiences wept in their exile."[47] President Grover Cleveland became a fan of Olcott and arranged for him to dine and sing at the White House.

Mavourneen launched Olcott's meteoric rise to fame. Over the next three decades, he played the lead role in at least twenty plays, establishing himself as the "reigning Irish tenor in the American theater."[48] Along the way, he expanded the kinds of roles played by Irish-American male actors. With the help of writers from Tin Pan Alley in New York City, Olcott changed the image of the stage Irishman by creating songs and plays with themes aligned with his vision. Before the 1890s, Irish male characters, often "Paddy," were stereotyped as drunk, pugilistic, mischievous, and ignorant. Increasingly, Irish-American theatergoers rejected these stereotypes and demanded something different.

In an interview in 1909, Olcott explained that his life's mission was "to help the world along with the genius of Ireland."[49] He detailed numerous accomplishments of the Irish in all aspects of life. In his opinion, negative stereotypes in theater held the Irish back from an equal place in America. He went on to outline how the Irish were not inferior to other groups:

The Irish gentleman is as fine an ideal as his British, French, or German counterpart; the belle of wealthy Irish society will compare with her sister in New York, London or Paris; the village priest is as interesting, benevolent, and devout as any of the clerical roles which have been drawn from other lands.

In 1897, he married theater enthusiast Margaret "Rita" O'Donovan from San Francisco, who collaborated with Chauncey on several plays and inspired one of his biggest hits: "My Wild Irish Rose." By 1900, Chauncey's career as a songwriter and actor was well-established. The year before, "My Wild Irish Rose," for which he had written the lyrics and music, reached number one on the Billboard charts and sold one million copies. His most famous song, "When Irish Eyes Are Smiling," came ten years later. But he had already become the "most renowned Irishman" of his time.

Olcott helped popularize the genre of Irish romantic comedies and sentimental operettas with Irish themes. His plays often took place before the Famine to avoid focusing on the humiliation of the Great Hunger and years after. One music historian claimed that Olcott's plays helped the Irish Americans build up a past of "dignity and respectability" and clothed "Ireland in more sentimental, sunnier aspects, without dwelling on such unpleasant details as eviction, famine, and revolution."[51] The playwright often cast the Irish hero opposite a British or Anglo-Irish character who was attempting to defraud him. The handsome and witty Irishman always triumphed and won over his blue-eyed colleen. Later in his career, Olcott starred in plays infused with a romantic longing to return to an idyllic Ireland.

As an actor, Olcott was considered good, not exceptional. As a singer, however, he was known in the United States and Europe as "*the* Irish Tenor." Newspaper writers and reviewers also referred to him as "the Irish Thrush" with a "silver tongue" or "golden voice." Not only did he write songs that touched his audiences emotionally, but his singing mesmerized them. At the same time, they were charmed by his comedic acting. After each performance, he often received multiple encores, often leaving his audience in tears, singing songs such as "Mother Machree."

Some of the plays in which he performed went on for exhausting two-year runs, touring to sixty-six cities across the United States and Canada. By 1909, it was estimated that Olcott had appeared in 3,000 stage performances and had entertained over seven million people. Buffalo and Lockport were regular stops on his theater tours, where he performed in front of sold-out crowds at Peter Cornell's Star Theater in Buffalo and the two thousand-seat Hodge Opera House in Lockport.

Chauncey wrote hit songs such as "My Wild Irish Rose" and "Mother Machree" and co-wrote the lyrics to "When Irish Eyes Are Smiling." He also introduced and made famous several classics of the Irish-American canon to the general public. Olcott was associated with songs such as "I Love the Name of Mary," "Where the River Shannon Flows," "A Little Bit of Heaven," and "'Tis An Irish Girl I Love."

Olcott's songs often reached number one on the music charts: "My Wild Irish Rose" (1899), "Mother Machree" (1911), "I Love the Name of Mary" (1911), "Too-Ra-Loo-Ra-Loo-Ra (1913)," and "When Irish Eyes Are Smiling" (1913). In 1913, "When Irish Eyes Are Smiling" was ranked the number-one song for the entire year.[52] And for the whole decade of the 1910s, his rendition of "My Wild Irish Rose" was ranked as the sixth biggest hit song. Olcott was so famous that his name appeared in the lyrics of the 1904 number-one hit song "Bedelia," written by William Jerome and Jean Schwartz.[53]

Bedelia, I want to steal ye,
Bedelia I love you so,
I'll be your Chauncey Olcott
If you'll be my Molly O'

Olcott amassed a fortune from his success at the box office and sales of his songs. A 1925 Buffalo Times article claimed he was "said to be the richest actor in the country."[54] He and Rita owned a beautiful townhouse in a tony section of Manhattan near the East River (worth about $8 million today) and a writing studio in New York City. The Olcotts eventually retired to their villa in Monte Carlo overlooking the Mediterranean, equipped with a Rolls Royce and a driver. They spent summers at their large estate in Saratoga Springs, New York, surrounded by beautiful gardens, including a replica of the Irish cottage where his mother was born. The Olcotts also accumulated an impressive collection of early American antiques and furniture, as well as medieval tapestries, ceramics, paintings, and a fine library.[55]

George M. Cohan, the great Irish composer, once wrote that he "adored" Olcott, describing him as "a very gentle and graceful gentleman."[56] During World War I, Olcott, known for his generosity, donated half of his earnings to the war effort and performed in charity benefits. He hosted an annual fundraiser in New York City to benefit the Franciscan friars and offered free concerts to raise funds for Holy Angels Church in Buffalo. The childless Olcotts adopted a young piano prodigy, Janet, whom they met at a Catholic girls' academy in Monte Carlo.[57]

On October 30, 1925, Olcott fell ill while playing his dream role of Sir Lucius O'Trigger in Richard Brinsley Sheridan's *The Rivals*. It was his final stage performance. Almost seven years later, at his villa in Monaco, Chauncey died in the early hours of March 18, 1932, when it was still St. Patrick's Day back in Buffalo and New York City. As the revelers made their way home, possibly humming Olcott's "When Irish Eyes Are Smiling" or "My Wild Irish Rose," no one yet knew that the Irish legend would be forever silent.

Olcott was buried from St. Patrick's Cathedral in New York with Irish luminaries such as Governor Al Smith, New York City Mayor James J. Walker, George M. Cohan, and John McCormack in attendance.[58] His *New York Times* obituary claimed Olcott was "perhaps as widely known as any player on the American stage" and credited him with a new stage style that included weaving Irish melodies into plays. The *Buffalo Courier* declared him the premier singer of Irish ballads, and *The Irish-American Advocate* claimed, "No Irish actor ever reached the pinnacle of popularity that he did, and no Irish singer (except John McCormack) ever had the heart-appeal of the Irish people as strongly as Olcott."[59]

In the 1930s, the legendary Irish tenor John McCormack brought Olcott's songs to a global audience. American singer and actor Bing Crosby kept Olcott's tunes alive during the 1940s on the radio and in movies. Crosby's recordings and performances of Olcott's songs, such as "When Irish Eyes Are Smiling," "My Wild Irish Rose," and "Mother Machree," cemented them into the mainstream of American popular culture. Rita Olcott wrote his biography, *A Song in His Heart*, which Warner Brothers turned into a 1947 Oscar-nominated film, *My Wild Irish Rose*, starring Dennis Morgan and Arlene Dahl.[60] Olcott is perhaps the only Buffalonian with a major Hollywood movie devoted entirely to his life.

In 1970, Olcott was posthumously inducted into the Songwriters Hall of Fame. The Recording Industry Association ranked Olcott's recording of "When Irish Eyes Are Smiling" as one of the greatest songs of all time, ahead of songs like Nat King Cole's "Mona Lisa" and Bob Dylan's "The Times They Are a-Changin'."

In Buffalo, he is commemorated with a granite plaque on Elmwood Avenue's
Buffalo Cultural Walk of Fame, and a wooden-carved statue of Chauncey Olcott
stands in front of the Irish Center in South Buffalo.

Generations to come will continue to enjoy Olcott's songs and melodies.
While this Buffalo native would be pleased that his songs continue to entertain
people, he would be more proud that he helped improve the image of the Irish—
both on the stage and off.

Kittie O'Neil—Dancing Star

Buffalo's first female Irish star, Kittie O'Neil, was born in the Canal District, in
the same neighborhood as Chauncey Olcott. Kittie (sometimes spelled Kitty) was
born in 1855 to William and Elizabeth (McKernan) O'Neil. Kittie's mother was
a native of Ireland, and her father, a machinist and saloon owner, was born in
New York City to Irish immigrants. By age three, O'Neil was a dancing prodigy
who performed publicly at the Academy of Music as a child. Recognizing her
talent, O'Neil's parents sent her to Rochester for dance lessons to complement
her repertoire of Irish jigs.[61] Kittie was a child star at age eight, and her mother
accompanied her as she performed in cities as far away as Pittsburgh and Chicago.
She regularly performed at Frank Wild's Theater at the corner of Terrace and
Commercial in the Canal District.[62]

Newspaper accounts described her as petite and graceful, with beautiful gray
eyes, black lashes, and a "pretty face, combining freckled sauciness and a certain
frank, good nature, which won the love of the lads."[63] As a performer, she was "a
dependable crowd-pleaser and the idol of the newsboys in the gallery."[64] In 1871,
news of her talent spread to New York City. Tony Pastor, considered the father
of American vaudeville, signed the fifteen-year-old Buffalo Irish girl to perform
at his variety theater in the Bowery, where she quickly charmed New York City
audiences. O'Neil excelled at many forms of dance, including the straight jig (a
dance developed by enslaved African-Americans and "characterized by syncopated
rhythm and eccentric movements"), the sand jig (similar to the straight jig but
with "shuffles and slides on a sand-strewn stage"), and clog dancing.[65] Throughout
the 1870s and '80s, O'Neil was the premier jig dancer against whom all others
were judged—all others were mere imitators.[66]

A few years after O'Neil's New York debut, a famous variety theater owner in
Boston hired her away from Pastor's theater, and her fame spread to New England.
Later, she returned to Broadway, performing at Ned Harrigan's theater, where
she had secured some minor acting and singing roles for his short plays. O'Neil
then toured across the Northeast and Midwest with a variety company. In 1882,

when she was at the height of her fame, a musician whose name has been lost to history composed a seven-part fiddler's piece in her honor titled "Kitty O'Neil's Champion Jig," which is the "most sophisticated sand jig that survives from the 19th-century variety tradition."[67] It is still performed today on both sides of the Atlantic Ocean, and recordings can be found online.[68]

O'Neil left New York City in April 1888 to tour throughout California, performing frequently in the Irish hotbed of San Francisco. In 1890, at age thirty-five, she returned to Buffalo because the physical demands of dancing began to take their toll. Two years later, she attempted a comeback at Shea's Theatre with a newspaper advertisement that read, "Kittie O'Neil: The Famous, The Great Champion Clog and Jig Dancer of the World."[69] However, critics harshly reviewed her physical appearance and performance. Her career now over, O'Neil turned her energy towards running the Alhambra Variety Theater on Commercial Street and managing her many rental properties in Buffalo.

Although O'Neil's professional career was a triumph, she suffered several personal tragedies. At eighteen, she had married a New York City saloon owner, who died three years later of tuberculosis. She then married the famous Irish-American comedian Harry Kernell, but he had a wandering eye, and O'Neil filed for divorce shortly after. After her return to Buffalo, O'Neil found a third husband, and she finally felt content. But her happiness was not to last long. In April 1893, at age thirty-eight, O'Neil, who had been suffering from kidney issues, went to the hospital for surgery for an unspecified female ailment; she died shortly after the operation from complications. O'Neil, who had been fiscally prudent throughout her career, left her husband, parents, and siblings financially comfortable.[70]

Throughout her career, O'Neil entertained tens of thousands of fans nationwide and helped popularize the jig, among other types of dance. One Vaudeville historian asserted that O'Neil was "probably the greatest sand jigger in all of vaudeville."[71] At her death, the *New York Times* and dozens of papers nationwide declared Kittie O'Neil the best female jig dancer in the world.[72]

Michael Shea—Impresario

The Irish American who contributed most to Buffalo's entertainment scene was raised in the neighborhood next to Kittie O'Neil. In April 1859, Mary (Griffin) Shea, wife of Daniel, gave birth to a son, Michael, who was probably born in St. Catharines, Ontario. Shortly after his birth, the family settled in Buffalo's First Ward.[73] The young Shea attended school in the Ward and, by age twelve, was working at Union Iron Works company.[74] Four years later, he labored as an ironworker, helping to build some of the era's most prominent railroad bridges in the United States.[75] He also worked along the waterfront docks, unloading goods and developing a reputation as a fighter. Shea, a handsome man who sported a trimmed mustache, was well-liked by everyone who interacted with him.

In 1884, twenty-five-year-old Shea owned a profitable saloon on Elk Street, which gave him the financial means to expand into other business ventures. Two years later, he and John Kreitner opened a saloon downtown on Clinton Street near Main Street. Their saloon was unique because it had a stage for musical concerts, which attracted top performers and large crowds. The following year, city officials enacted laws that prohibited saloon owners from hosting musical shows. Shea disobeyed the orders, temporarily losing his liquor license.

In 1890, Shea, who had not given up on providing musical performances for his patrons, opened Shea's Music Hall in James Mooney's Wonderland Building.[76] Music halls, which generally offered entertainment for the working class, had been popular in England for several decades, but this was one of the first of its kind in the United States. Shea hosted entertainers, who appeared for weeklong engagements, from as far as England and France.[77] In December 1893, an explosion in his establishment almost killed Shea, who was asleep in one of the building's apartments. After the disastrous incident, he opened Shea's Tivoli on Washington Street next to the stately Lafayette Hotel, where he refined his knack for finding top talent for his variety shows.

In 1898, Shea opened Buffalo's first vaudeville theater, Shea's Garden Theatre. The First Ward native was one of the first in the U.S. to start a vaudeville house, and he is credited with improving the reputation of this new form of entertainment, including banning smoking and alcohol consumption.[78] Two years later, Shea beautified his theater, striving to make it one of the premier vaudeville houses in the country.[79] In 1905, Shea expanded his empire and opened Shea's Vaudeville House on Court Street with a tagline: *Shea's—Devoted to the Highest Class of Exclusive Vaudeville Attractions.*[80] Shea often traveled to New York City to find the elite performers. He would entice them to perform in Buffalo by offering them more money than the going rate. Although genial, he had high standards and would pay close attention to each performer's opening night act. If the performance was subpar, he would promptly go to the dressing room, give them their weekly salary, and dismiss them.[81]

At age forty, Michael Shea settled down and married Josephine Carr, settling on the West Side. His business ventures continued to prosper, and by 1905, he had a chain of theaters throughout Buffalo. However, Shea's genius was understanding the changing entertainment tastes of the masses and shifting to meet these new demands. For instance, in 1914, he expanded into motion pictures when he opened Shea's Hippodrome on Main Street near Chippewa Street. At its opening, the Hippodrome, with its 2,800 seats and opulent interior, was regarded as the finest picture house between New York City and Chicago.[82] Shea provided a split billing of a vaudeville act followed by a feature film, which was a unique format. The indefatigable Shea opened movie theaters across Western New York, including Shea's North Park Theatre, Great Lakes Theatre, the Seneca, the Elmwood, the Century, the Community, the Park, the Bailey, and the Riviera in Tonawanda. In Niagara Falls, he owned Shea's Bellevue, and south of Buffalo, Shea's Lackawanna. The First Ward businessman even expanded his operations internationally to Toronto, Canada, where he owned two of the largest theaters in that city: Shea's Vaudeville and Shea's Hippodrome (in fact, the Hippodrome was the largest movie house in Canada in 1914).[83]

Despite these successes, Shea still had a vision for his crowning achievement—a "cathedral" dedicated to entertainment. Soliciting the help of the prominent Chicago architects C.W. and George L. Rapp, and with an initial budget of $1 million, Shea built and designed one of the most remarkable theaters in the United States at the time. His masterpiece, located on a prominent stretch of Main Street, was initially named The Buffalo and later called Shea's Buffalo. Shea wanted his masterpiece to rival other show houses in the major cities across the country and spared no expense; consequently, the building costs quickly escalated to $2 million. The Rapp brothers used the finest furnishing companies in Chicago and Buffalo to outfit the building, including The Victor Pearlman Company, Marshall Field and Company, Wm. Hengerer Co., and Wurlitzer Company. The terra cotta exterior, crystal chandeliers, and marble staircases built in the Baroque Revival style created a look of opulence; the theater was meant to resemble the elaborate opera houses of Europe from the sixteenth and seventeenth centuries.[84]

On January 16, 1926, the 4,000-seat theater opened with the kind of glitz and glamour you would expect from Buffalo's greatest showman: an estimated 7,000 exterior lights illuminated the theater on opening night. The theater was wildly successful and profitable for its first three years until the start of the Great Depression in 1929. During the Depression, Shea lost about $1 million a year on his vast enterprise but refused to lay off employees.[85] In 1930, despite the onset of the global economic disaster, Shea and his wife moved to the affluent Delaware Avenue neighborhood. Despite Shea's optimism that the economy would turn around, he would never enjoy his past financial success.

The famous Broadway producer George M. Cohan once said: "Shea made his house in Buffalo the finest show stop in America. He had an astonishing flair for picking what the public liked."[86] In its first twenty-five years of existence, Shea's Buffalo hosted world-famous performers such as W.C. Fields, Mae West, Will Rogers, George Burns and Gracie Allen, The Marx Brothers, Bob Hope, Red

Skelton, Duke Ellington, Benny Goodman, Jimmy Dorsey, Glenn Miller, and Bing Crosby. Michael Shea was also a good businessman who set admission prices that everyone could afford.[87]

Famous Vaudeville star Joe Laurie, Jr. once declared, "There never was a rougher, tougher, sweeter and nicer Irishman than Mike Shea!"[88] On Shea's fiftieth anniversary in show business, *Variety* magazine published an article claiming, "He [Shea] is the last of the Mohicans, the lone survivor of that colorful band of men who started from scratch in the 1880s and nursed vaudeville from a museum to the most popular form of entertainment of its time."[89] Michael Shea was known throughout the US, England, and France for his efforts at promoting and helping improve vaudeville's image.[90] Michael Shea passed away in May 1934 in the midst of the Depression, and his wife and daughter sold their shares in the entertainment enterprise shortly after he died. While only a few of his theaters still survive (Shea's Buffalo, North Park Theatre, Shea's Seneca, and the Riviera Theatre), Buffalo is richer today for what he built.

After Shea died in 1934, Shea's Buffalo, his downtown masterpiece, was sold to various movie companies, such as Paramount and Loew's Corporation. In the mid-1970s, the theater was closed, and there was a possibility that it would be demolished. A group called The Friends of the Buffalo Theatre stepped in and kept it operational. Irish-American George O'Connell, the city's comptroller, secured city funds to stabilize and update the space, ensuring it would survive. In 1980, the Shea's O'Connell Preservation Guild was established to manage the theater.[91] Over the years, more than $28 million has been invested to upgrade and preserve this iconic institution. The theater, now called Shea's Performing Arts Center, is one of America's most successful in terms of ticket sales for hosting big-name Broadway musicals. The theater also hosts opera, dance, musical concerts, and movies, entertaining 300,000 people annually.[92] In recent years, Irish Americans Michael Murphy and former Congressman Brian Higgins have served as president of Shea's Performing Arts Center.

Peggy O'Neil—International Star

Buffalo's first Irish female international star was born and raised in the Hydraulics neighborhood, just north of Michael Shea's childhood home. Margaret "Peggy" O'Neil (no relation to Kittie O'Neil) was born in June 1894 to Frederick O'Neil and Mary (Buckley) O'Neil. There has been much confusion about whether Peggy was born in Ireland or Buffalo, but her official government documents claim she was born in Buffalo.[93] Her father, whose family came from County Clare, moved from Auburn, New York to Buffalo to work as a railroad engineer. As a young girl living on Seneca Street, Peggy O'Neil attended St. Patrick's School on Emslie

Street, where she displayed a talent for performing in school plays. In 1897, tragedy struck O'Neil's family when her father was killed in a train accident outside of Buffalo. Peggy's mother died a decade later, so thirteen-year-old Peggy was raised by her aunt on Buffalo's West Side. In 1910, one of Peggy's uncles recognized her talent for performing and had her staged as a choir girl in the musical comedy, *The Sweetest Girl in Paris* in Chicago.

About a year later, O'Neil dropped out of Buffalo's Central High School in her junior year and boarded a train to New York City to seek her fame on Broadway. Soon after, she was cast in *The Bird of Paradise*, which was performed for long runs. But her big break came in 1913 in Chicago when she was chosen for the lead role of *Peg O' My Heart*, from over four hundred young women who auditioned. Audiences in Chicago fell in love with her during the show's twenty-six-week run.[94] Two years later, she returned to her hometown of Buffalo to perform as the lead in *Peg O' My Heart* at the Teck Theater. One reporter gushed that "she had come back a star—a star that gleamed with its own light."[95] Another claimed that O'Neil was made for the role as she is "that wonderful little specimen of real Irish girlhood that has endeared herself to the hearts of millions." The crowd was so excited that there was constant applause throughout the play, stopping the action several times and forcing O'Neil to bow dozens of times.[96] She soon returned to New York City, where she was cast in *Flame*, and was chosen for the lead in *Tumble In*, which ran for one year on Broadway.[97]

Peggy O'Neil, described as a blue-eyed beauty with coal-black curly hair and a bubbly personality, was an exceptional actor with a gift for comedy. In 1920, she moved to London to be the lead actress in *Paddy, the Next Best Thing* at the Savoy Theatre. The play received poor reviews, but the British audiences adored O'Neil, and she carried the show; it ran for 867 performances. The praise continued for her performance in *Love's a Terrible Thing*, when the *London Observer* critic called her "the darling of the gods."[98] London's theater newspaper, *The Play*, described O'Neil as "a young actress from America who is a comedienne of exceptional attraction and ability," hoping she would make London her permanent home. The following year, she relocated to London and stayed until the end of her life. In a 1921 interview, O'Neil told the interviewer she had an upcoming performance in Dublin, which she declared was "the dream of my life—to play in Dublin in an Irish role before a real Irish audience."[99] While in Ireland, she visited her father's homestead in County Clare and her mother's home in County Antrim.

Around 1920, at the height of her career, O'Neil was so famous that some of the greatest artists from all over the world painted her, and sculptors made bronze and marble busts of her.[100] While in London, she was invited to royal parties where she once danced with the Prince of Wales.[101] In 1921, Harry Pease wrote a hit song about her entitled "Peggy O'Neil," which was still popular at her death in 1960. The lyrics provide a fitting description of how her admirers perceived her on both sides of the Atlantic:

> *Peggy O'Neil is a girl who could steal any heart,*
> *Anywhere, any time*
> *If her eyes are blue as skies, that's Peggy O'Neil*
> *If she's smiling all the while, that's Peggy O'Neil*
> *If she walks like a sly little rogue*
> *If she talks with a cute little brogue*
> *Sweet personality full of rascality*
> *That's Peggy O'Neil*

Despite having many suitors and being engaged at least once, Peggy neither married nor had children. She once declared: "There's girls that were made for wives and mothers. And there's other girls that have other work to do in the world. I am one of those other girls."

O'Neil also worked in movies during the silent film era. She acted in over a dozen films between 1913 and 1926, including *The Battle of Shiloh* (1913), *The Penny Philanthropist* (1917), *Air Pockets* (1924), and *Non-Stop Flight* (1926), to name a few. In 1930, the Buffalo actress was reputedly the first person ever interviewed on television.[102]

Despite living life on her own terms, Peggy endured many hardships. In addition to losing her parents at a young age, she was targeted when an anonymous person tried to kill her by sending arsenic-laced chocolates to her dressing room in London. After ingesting one of them, she was in a stupor for several days, and doctors sent her to recuperate in Switzerland. Unfortunately, her dog also consumed one of the poisonous treats and died.[103] The culprit was never found. During the Great Depression, O'Neil lost her fortune due to poor investments and declared bankruptcy. She tried to make a comeback in the theater, to no avail. O'Neil also suffered debilitating arthritis that kept her in a wheelchair for her last twelve years.

At her death in 1960, the *New York Times* described Peggy O'Neil as "the red-haired, blue-eyed Irish beauty of the first two decades of the [twentieth] century who took New York and London by storm." The writer added, "She had the reputation of being one of the loveliest and gayest personalities ever to appear on the stage."[104] The headline for her obituary in London's *Guardian* newspaper simply proclaimed, "Peggy O'Neil: Heroine of the 20's." There was no money for a funeral at her death, so the Actors' Benevolent Fund paid for her service. It was a tragic end to one of Buffalo's first stars on the international stage.

Drawing on the tradition of their native Ireland, Irish immigrants brought entertainment and the arts to Buffalo. Notwithstanding their involvement in popularizing blackface minstrel shows, the early Irish entertainers in Buffalo contributed handsomely to the performing arts. Chauncey Olcott helped shine a positive light on the image of the Irish in his lyrics and plays. Kittie O'Neil introduced the world to the beauty and power of jigs and Irish dance. Michael Shea was a savvy businessman who built grand theaters and improved the reputation of vaudeville. And Peggy O'Neil enchanted theater audiences in Chicago, New York City, London, and beyond. Now, we turn to modern performers who shaped the local and national entertainment scene.

CHAPTER SIX

Entertainers-The Modern Era

Theater

The Irish are everywhere in Western New York's theater scene. But it was not always this way. Irish actors, such as Dublin-born John Collins, performed in Buffalo as early as 1850.[1] But he was more the exception. Collins, a former cook turned actor, entertained adoring crowds in New York City in the late 1840s. By 1850, he regularly appeared in Irish-themed plays at Buffalo's Eagle Street Theatre.[2] Collins brought successful Broadway plays, often from playwright John Brougham, to canal towns like Buffalo and performed in multi-night engagements. Almost all of his plays were comedies or farces where he acted in Irish stock character roles. Collins appeared as Terence O'Grady in *The Irish Post* and O'Hara in *The Irish Attorney*. Other plays he performed in Buffalo included *Happy Man*, *The Irish Fortune Hunter*, *Irish Engagement*, and *The Irish Ambassador*. The local newspapers, which rarely had anything positive to say about the Irish, praised his performances.

The Irish presence in local theater emerged only in the second half of the twentieth century. By 2020, men and women of Irish heritage managed many of Buffalo's premier theaters: Vincent O'Neill at the Irish Classical Theatre; Josephine Hogan at the Red Thread Theatre; Dan Shanahan at Torn Space Theatre; Mary Kate O'Connell at O'Connell & Company; Michael Murphy at Shea's Performing Arts Center; Richard Lambert at the New Phoenix Theatre; and Loraine O'Donnell at The Kavinoky Theatre. To pinpoint when the Irish takeover of Buffalo's theater scene started, you would have to return to 1964.

That was when Brother Augustine Towey (born Dennis Joseph Towey) arrived at Niagara University, twenty-two miles north of Buffalo, to teach literature and speech in the English department. Towey was born in 1937 on Long Island to Irish immigrants Patrick and Anna Towey. He graduated from St. John's University in Brooklyn, studied in England and France, and received his Ph.D. in theater studies from New York University.[3] He was ordained to the Vincentian religious order in 1961 and assigned to Niagara University three years later.

Soon after arriving, Towey envisioned transforming the university's nondescript theater program into a regional powerhouse. It was a twenty-year project, but he finally prevailed. Towey built Niagara University's program "into one of the most prestigious undergraduate theater programs in the United States."[4]

While at Niagara University, the Vincentian brother directed an astonishing 135 plays, as well as dozens of plays at other Western New York theaters. His Niagara University Players performed classics such as *Death of a Salesman*, *Waiting for Godot*, *Jesus Christ Superstar*, *King Lear*, and *West Side Story*. The humble Towey established close friendships with musical theater heavyweights such as Alan J. Lerner and Frederick Loewe (of *Camelot* fame), Fred Ebb, and John Kander (creators of *Chicago* and *Cabaret*). Towey—known by many simply as "Bro"— also developed a close friendship with Vincent O'Neill, a co-founder of the Irish Classical Theatre Company (ICTC). Towey directed ten plays at the ICTC and others with organizations such as Opera Sacra, the Buffalo Philharmonic Orchestra, and the Irish Repertory Theatre in New York City.[5] He was the founder and longtime director of the Artpark Repertory Theatre, where he offered a five-week summer program to help train area high school drama teachers.

Towey wrote twelve plays, including *Vincent in Heaven* about St. Vincent de Paul. He also wrote a play called *The Guardian*, about performers who are "born again" as they enact the Passion Play. It was performed in 1978 on NBC-TV to eight million viewers.[6] Towey was also an accomplished poet who published seven volumes of poetry. When asked what he would have done if he hadn't dedicated his life to theater, the Vincentian brother suggested he "might spend it teaching poetry or helping people to love poetry."[7] Regarding his poetry, his friend Vincent O'Neill said that Bro was "extraordinarily sensitive and [had] a beautiful feel for language and word magic."[8] To this day, thanks to the work of Brother Augustine Towey, Niagara University still houses an exceptional theater program that produces high-quality theater and talented graduates who perform locally and nationally.

The Irish Classical Theatre Company

In 1985, two brothers from Dublin, Chris and Vincent O'Neill, former members of the famed Abbey Theatre Company, were coming off of performing Samuel Beckett's *Waiting for Godot* in Dublin to much acclaim and looking for a stage in New York City. There was, however, an issue with the rights to the play being performed in Manhattan, so they rerouted to Rochester, New York, and staged Beckett's masterpiece at Nazareth College. Kevin Townsell, Irish-American owner of the Airways Hotel just outside of Buffalo, heard rave reviews about the brothers' performance, so he invited them to bring the play to his hotel. Although there was a blizzard on the evening of their Buffalo show, it was performed in the hotel's dining room to an enthusiastic audience who enjoyed the performance. Vincent recalled that they were paid with Guinness and chicken wings.[9] The talented brothers were encouraged by David Lamb, director of The Kavinoky Theatre, to relocate to Buffalo. Chris stayed; Vincent returned to Dublin.

The O'Neill brothers grew up in Sandycove, a Dublin suburb, with their sister and another brother. Their father, a dedicated civil servant, was the youngest of thirteen children born to a poor farmer from West Cork. Their mother (née Casey) was raised in inner city Dublin.[10] From 1972 to 1979, before he arrived in Buffalo, the older brother, Chris, was a regular, along with Gabriel Byrne, on the hit Irish TV drama *The Riordans*. Chris attended the Abbey School of Acting in Dublin and later started his own theater, the Oscar Theatre, in the suburbs of Dublin. He also served as one of Ireland's first theatrical agents, representing clients such as Gabriel Byrne.[11]

Chris's younger brother, Vincent, was sent to acting school at age eight because his parents hoped it could cure his shyness. Vincent graduated with honors from University College Dublin and Trinity College. Both brothers joined the Abbey Theatre company, traveling the world with their fellow actors. Vincent relocated to Paris to study mime with the world-renowned Marcel Morceau for three years. He then returned to Dublin to help run his brother's theater. Vincent and Chris opened the Oscar Mime Company, Ireland's first professional mime company, founded a theater school, and toured Ireland with a small troupe. After that, they shuffled off to Buffalo.

In the late 1980s, Chris was finally granted a US visa after many attempts. Not long after, Vincent was randomly selected for his visa. So, on December 29, 1989, Vincent and the accomplished actor Josephine Hogan, his wife and the third founder of the Irish Classical Theatre Company, moved to Buffalo for a six-month trial. After successfully performing at various venues around Buffalo, the O'Neills recognized the potential for a first-class Buffalo theater focused on Irish and classical plays. The following summer, the couple met on a patio off Elmwood Avenue to discuss their plans with Chris O'Neill and Dr. James "Jim" Warde, another Irish immigrant. That night, the four put $200 into a hat to fund a theater. Thus, with good timing, perseverance, and a little Irish luck, four Irish immigrants from Dublin founded one of Buffalo's premier theaters. They subsequently received assistance from Saul Elkin—an actor, director, and the University at Buffalo theater department chairman. Elkin lent them the Pfeifer Theatre on Main Street to stage an original collaboration between Vincent O'Neill and Irish writer Ulick O'Connor: a play about James Joyce called *Joyicity*. They staged Brian Friel's *Faith Healer* at the same theater to rave reviews, and the momentum kept building.[12]

Chris O'Neill's talent was unquestioned. He was gifted with an incredible memory for plays and Irish poetry. He excelled in theatrical roles, especially one-person plays that focused on his favorite poets and writers, such as Brendan Behan, W.B. Yeats, Patrick Kavanagh, Oscar Wilde, James Joyce, and Samuel Beckett. *Buffalo News* arts editor Terry Doran stated that O'Neill was "among the world's finest interpreters of the theater pieces of Samuel Beckett."[13] Doran described Chris as "tall, thin as a blade, with a head of unruly curly hair and a face with eyes so haunting and haunted that in appearance alone he was ideal for any of Beckett's…plays."[14] Buffalo theatergoers often used the word "genius" to describe O'Neill's performances. But Chris was a restless soul who was not destined to stay in Buffalo.

As the Irish Classical Theatre Company (ICTC) started becoming a formal entity, Chris O'Neill relocated to New York City. In 1993, he co-founded the award-winning Irish Bronx Theatre, which catered to an audience of Irish immigrants. O'Neill also had an eye for talent and gave Irish immigrants their first opportunity to work with a professional theater company.[15] He convinced an Irish immigrant bartender, Paul Ronan, to perform in his Bronx theater's first play, Hugh Leonard's *Da*.[16] Ronan brought his young daughter, Saoirse, to rehearsals, where she was first introduced to theater. Saoirse Ronan is now a four-time Oscar-nominated actor in movies *Lady Bird*, *Little Women*, and *Brooklyn*. According to Saoirse, "If it wasn't for Chris [O'Neill], neither of us [her father or herself] would be acting today."[17]

As Chris was off in New York, Vincent and Josephine were looking for a more permanent home for their theater. They were in luck, for Buffalo entrepreneur Mark Goldman, who had recently purchased a historic building on the derelict block of Chippewa Street, was establishing an arts café. Goldman had seen Vincent O'Neill's *Joyicity* performance and declared it "the most powerful theatrical performance" that he had ever seen in Buffalo.[18] As a result, in January 1992, Goldman invited Vincent and Josephine to stage an Irish play, *The Galway Girl*, for three Sunday afternoons at his arts café, the Calumet; the production was so popular that it ran for three months. One of the storefronts in Goldman's building became available, so he proposed that the fledgling Irish theater company open a permanent theater in his space. After a successful five-year run at the Calumet, the ICTC had outgrown the space and needed a new home.

Vincent became acquainted with developer Larry Quinn, who showed him a site on Main Street and declared, "This is where your theater is going to be."[19] Numerous leaders in the community, including Frank McGuire, helped raise $1.3 million to build a new facility. Peter Andrews—grandson of Buffalo Irish industrialist William "Fingy" Conners—and his wife Joan provided a sizable gift for the Andrews Theatre. The newly-built theater, the first in fifty years constructed from the ground up in Buffalo, opened in January 1999 with the same theater-in-the-round design as the Calumet.[20]

Josephine Hogan, founder of the ICTC with the O'Neill brothers, was equally instrumental in its success. Hogan and Vincent O'Neill met in Dublin when she was a twenty-two-year-old student in his mime class, and they eventually married and had two children. Over her years at the Irish Classical Theatre, Hogan acted in over sixty-eight shows and directed at least six ICTC plays. Hogan has been a star since arriving in Buffalo as an actor and director.[21] She performed several significant roles in Irish, British, and American plays and has one of the "highest batting averages of any artist at the ARTIE awards [the annual Buffalo theater awards]."[22] She has been nominated for twelve of these prestigious awards for ICTC productions and won four times. Hogan has also received numerous community awards, such as an Arts Council Award for artistic excellence.

Hogan claims the theater bug bit her at eleven when her grandmother took her to a play. After that, in her words, she knew her "fate was sealed."[23] She studied voice at the Abbey Theatre in Dublin, Ireland's National Theatre, and the Royal Shakespeare Company in London. Her most significant theater influence was an English theater and television director, Chloe Gibson, who taught her "everything about Shakespeare." Hogan toured in Shakespearean productions throughout Ireland under Gibson's direction.[24]

Hogan acknowledged that while she loves her adopted home of Buffalo, she misses Dublin. In addition to her family, she pines for "the kindly, mischievous spirit of my people, Dublin theatre, the cozy pubs, random walks in the pine forest and Dublin mountains."[25] Her favorite childhood memory is evenings sitting around the fire with her sister and four brothers, reading Enid Blyton books. Still, she established roots in Buffalo, co-founding the ICTC and co-founding Red Thread Theatre with actor/director Eileen Dugan in 2010. Their theater aims to improve the underrepresentation of female artists in Western New York.[26]

The fourth ICTC founder was Jim Warde, a physician who served as the deputy director of the Buffalo Psychiatric Center. In addition to providing financial assistance for the theater, he served as the company's first board treasurer and general manager of theater staff. Warde and his wife Lucy hosted the first Bloomsday celebration, now an annual celebration of James Joyce's novel, *Ulysses*. This yearly event of readings, song, and dance, which takes place on Bloomsday, June 16, has become an ever-expanding cultural event.

Since its founding, the ICTC has continued to thrive. Vincent O'Neill was the artistic director for the theater company while acting, directing, and serving as the chair of the University at Buffalo's Theatre and Dance program. Sadly, at the peak of his career in 1997, Chris O'Neill, the catalyst and guiding spirit of the theater, died at fifty. Just a few months before he died in Florida, he directed Samuel Beckett's *Happy Days* in Buffalo to widespread acclaim. During his years in the United States, he also appeared in minor roles in nearly ten films. But his legacy is felt most in Buffalo and the Bronx.

In September 2017, the Theatre District of Main Street, which spans the 600 block (Tupper Street to Chippewa Street), was renamed "Chris O'Neill Way." On September 12, 2022, Vincent O'Neill was inducted into the Theatre District's Plaza of Stars, and the nearby section of Main Street was renamed "The Brothers O'Neill Way." Vincent O'Neill received the Lifetime Achievement award at the Spark Awards two years prior. This honor was in addition to numerous ARTIE awards for Outstanding Actor, Outstanding Director, and Outstanding Artistic Playwright.

Over the years, Vincent O'Neill has publicly thanked the Buffalo Irish-American community for warmly embracing the ICTC since its inception. In addition to the previously mentioned local donors with Irish heritage, such as Peter Andrews, Frank McGuire, and Larry Quinn, others such as Joe Crowley, Paul Hartigan, John Collins, John Donovan, Kevin Quinn, Kevin Brady, and Chris O'Brien have all raised funds or served in leadership positions on the board of trustees. O'Neill has given back to the Irish community by doing free readings and fundraisers throughout the city, including the annual Bloomsday celebration.

Throughout its thirty-year run, the company has won more awards for plays than any other theater company in Western New York. Along the way, it has launched acting and directing careers for dozens of talented Buffalonians. The ICTC brought numerous luminaries to Buffalo, including Marcel Marceau and Irish directors and actors such as Peter Sheridan, Bryan Delaney, Milo O'Shea, and Shay Linehan. The company has also collaborated with numerous cultural entities in Buffalo, including the Buffalo Philharmonic Orchestra (twelve times).

Buffalo is one of a handful of cities in the country with a theater dedicated to performing Irish and classical plays. Through their company, Vincent O'Neill, Josephine Hogan, and the rest of the ICTC troupe have done much to enhance and promote Irish culture in Buffalo. Since 1990, ICTC has staged over seventy of the greatest Irish and Irish-American plays ever written—not to mention another one hundred classic and contemporary plays from outside of Ireland. Following in the footsteps of Chauncey Olcott, who wanted to share the "genius of the Irish" with the world, ICTC has exposed Buffalonians to Ireland's tradition of storytelling, as well as the wit and wisdom of her people. In 2023, the theater hired the talented Irish-American dancer, actor, and director Keelie Sheridan as artistic director.

Female Leaders in Theater

About five years after the O'Neills started their theater, an Irish-American actor from Buffalo created her own. In 1995, Mary Kate O'Connell launched O'Connell & Company. She began acting in the 1970s with companies such as the Lancaster Opera House, Artpark, and Theatre of Youth. In the 1990s, she was the executive director of Summerfare Musical Theatre (now called MusicalFare Theatre). Along the way, the talented vocalist appeared with the Buffalo Philharmonic Orchestra, directed plays, and served as the director of performing arts at Mount St. Mary Academy. But O'Connell envisioned a new theater to fill a gap in the local theater scene. Namely, she wanted to create a company that would produce plays by women and feature women.

O'Connell was the sixth of seven children born to Beatrice and George D. O'Connell, former comptroller for Buffalo. She grew up in a close-knit Irish Catholic family in North Buffalo, graduated from Holy Angels Academy, and acted during her time at Rosary Hill College (now Daemen College). Her maternal grandmother (Gormley) was from County Tyrone in Ireland and would often speak of the hardships back on the Emerald Isle—including a story of six people having to share a piece of bread.[29] Her Irish grandmother was also a singer, and that may be where O'Connell acquired her talent as a vocalist. Besides her Irish grandmother, O'Connell was surrounded by resilient Irish women, among them her mother, Beatrice. When O'Connell was growing up, Irish actor Maureen O'Hara, who starred in *The Quiet Man*, was one of her favorite performers. O'Connell is passionate about her Irish ancestry. During a talk at the Buffalo Irish Center in 2018, O'Connell told the mostly Irish crowd that the Irish should treasure their heritage and culture. It is one of the reasons she cherishes the Buffalo Irish Center, where she has helped with fundraising.[30]

O'Connell founded O'Connell and Company with the belief that theater should make a difference in people's lives, not just provide entertainment.[31] Her hit cabaret, *Diva by Diva*, is the longest-running cabaret in Western New York. Inspired by her mother, she ensures that the show is newly scripted for each performance, filled with poems, songs, and humorous stories meant to enlighten patrons about strong women. Proceeds from her usually sold-out shows are donated to women's and children's charities. O'Connell has been producing Diva by Diva for twenty-two years, and over 350 women from the community have performed with her company.

O'Connell also stages an annual performance, *Women's Little Christmas*, based on an Irish tradition whereby the men serve the women for one night. She has also presented a successful all-female cast of *1776: The Musical*, a play

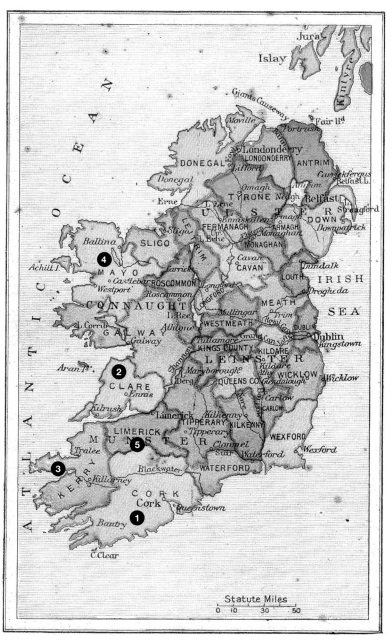

1

The Buffalo Irish predominantly came from the south and west of Ireland, the areas most devastated by the Great Famine. In one sample of Buffalo Irish residents, roughly 60% came from counties Cork (1), Clare (2), Kerry (3), Mayo (4), and Limerick (5).

2

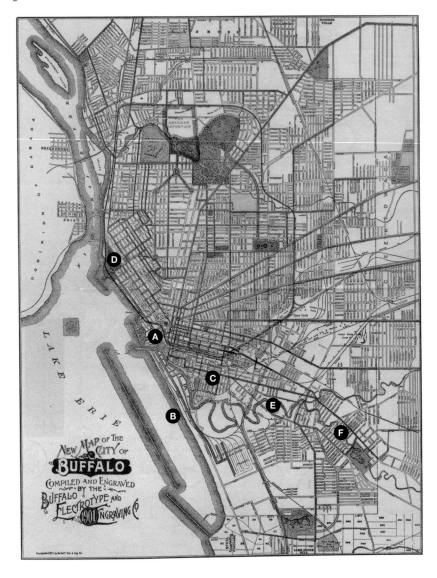

A Buffalo map labeled with some of the largest Irish settlements in the 19th century: Canal District (A), Beachers (B), First Ward (C), West Side (D), The Valley (E), and South Buffalo (F). In the 21st century, some of the largest Irish-American centers in the Buffalo area by percentage of the total population are South Buffalo, Hamburg, Blasdell, West Seneca, Orchard Park, and Clarence.

3

4

Samuel Wilkeson, son of immigrants from Northern Ireland, built the first artificial harbor on the Great Lakes and was instrumental in Buffalo's selection as the western terminus of the Erie Canal.

Mary Lynch O'Rourke and her family arrived in Buffalo in 1815 and were most likely the first Irish Catholic family in the city. She owned a boarding house and was generous to Catholic charities.

5

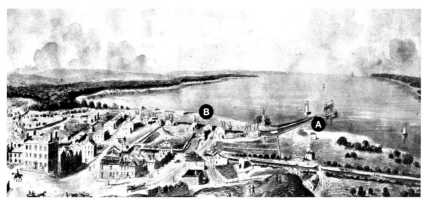

A view of the Buffalo harbor from the Exchange Building, September 1829, four years after the opening of the Erie Canal. Samuel Wilkeson's pier and harbor (A), and the Erie Canal's western terminus and Commercial Slip (B). Without Wilkeson's efforts, Buffalo's development may have turned out differently.

Hundreds of Irish laborers blasted miles of solid rock in Lockport to build one of the most difficult portions of the Erie Canal. Injuries and deaths were common among the Irish workers.

Thousands of Irish workers played an important role in Buffalo's grain transshipment trade. In this photo, Dakota Elevator workers in the First Ward, some of whom are Irish, take a break for a photo.

Sister Hieronymo (Veronica) O'Brien was one of the founders of Sisters of Charity Hospital in Buffalo and the founder of St. Mary's Hospital in Rochester.

The Sisters of Charity, many of them Irish, founded Buffalo's first hospital in 1848. Their timing was fortuitous because Buffalo suffered from several cholera outbreaks shortly after.

10

11

William Glenny, an immigrant from Northern Ireland, founded a prominent national retail company in Buffalo. He was the first of many successful Irish retailers.

Standard Oil executive Daniel O'Day was one of John D. Rockefeller's most trusted advisors and became one of Buffalo's wealthiest citizens.

12

13

William J. "Fingy" Conners was a business tycoon and publisher of the *Courier-Express* newspaper.

James Mooney was the co-founder of the Mooney-Brisbane building and an ardent Irish nationalist.

14

Emily McDonnell was a pioneering businesswoman who ran a Buffalo granite monument company with plants and offices across the country.

15

Dr. Jane Carroll was perhaps the first woman in Buffalo to work as both a medical doctor and a lawyer.

16

17

Msgr. Nelson Baker, who was Irish on his mother's side, built Our Lady of Victory Basilica and founded several important charitable organizations.

Sister Mary Mechtilde O'Connor was the founder of Kenmore Mercy Hospital and a longtime hospital administrator.

18

19

Bishop Joseph Burke was the first Buffalo-born bishop of the Buffalo diocese.

Sister Denise Roche transformed D'Youville College into one of Western New York's most successful educational institutions and an anchor on Buffalo's West Side.

20

Thomas V. O'Connor was
president of the International
Longshoremen's Association
and one of several Buffalo
Irish labor leaders.

21

Judge John Curtin ruled on
some of Buffalo's most important
court cases in the second half of
the twentieth century.

22

Buffalo's Kittie O'Neil, who became famous in New York City and Boston, was one of the best Irish dancers of her era.

23

24

Chauncey Olcott, a singer and actor, was a national star who wrote some of the most famous Irish-American songs.

Peggy O'Neil, daughter of Irish immigrants, became a star on the stage in New York and London but died penniless.

Joe Conley, a native South Buffalonian, was a Hollywood star who appeared as Ike Godsey in the hit television show *The Waltons*.

Tom Shannon, a Buffalo native, was a nationally known disc jockey and radio broadcaster.

South Buffalo-born Sean Cullen was a popular television and Broadway star who has appeared with stars such as Al Pacino and George Clooney.

Dublin-born Vincent O'Neill (left) and his brother Chris O'Neill (right) were two of the founders of Buffalo's Irish Classical Theatre Company, which has produced dozens of award-winning Irish and modern classical plays.

Erin Lynch (left), Fiona Dargan (center), and Kevinah Dargan (right) are Irish dance champions from Buffalo who have performed as professional Irish dancers on the international stage.

While growing up in Buffalo, F. Scott Fitzgerald witnessed how the rich lived differently than everyone else. It would be a prominent theme throughout his novels.

Charles Brady was a prolific author and a favorite English professor at Canisius College. Brady was also a long-time literary critic for the *Buffalo News*.

Buffalo-born Joseph Hassett (center) was a lawyer, author, and philanthropist. The Hassett family has brought prominent Irish writers to Buffalo to speak to the public and students at Canisius College. Hassett shares a laugh with Nobel-prize winner Seamus Heaney (right) and Father James Pribek (left).

Buffalo-born Brigid Hughes
once served as the executive
editor of *The Paris Review*
and later founded the literary
magazine *A Public Space*.

Stephan Talty is a *New York
Times* bestselling author who
co-wrote *A Captain's Duty*, which
was turned into the blockbuster
movie *Captain Phillips*, starring
Tom Hanks.

An etching of prominent Buffalo graphic artist and printmaker Kevin O'Callahan by his friend Robert Blair. O'Callahan was one of the founding members of the Buffalo Print Club.

36

Artist Philip Burke (right) and business owner Rory Allen (left) holding up one of Burke's paintings of the Goo Goo Dolls.

Billy Kelly of the *Courier-Express* was the first of Buffalo's long list of Irish-American sports columnists and editors.

Jack O'Brian, a First Ward native, was a famous national newspaper columnist and ardent anti-Communist.

William J. Conners, Jr. (right) and William J. Conners, III (left) both served as publishers of the *Courier-Express* newspaper.

about the founders of the United States. In March 2021, she hosted a Diva by Diva performance entitled *The Purple Wave* on International Women's Day "to commemorate our extraordinary women leaders, from the Suffragists to our current Vice President, who have shattered glass ceilings and shaped future journeys for women." Mary Kate O'Connell's company enlightens Western New Yorkers about the accomplishments of women while raising thousands of dollars for worthy women's charities along the way.

Loraine O'Donnell, the former executive artistic director of The Kavinoky Theatre, is another Irish female theater leader. Her mother, Donna O'Donnell, studied music, played the piano, and performed in community theater, undoubtedly shaping her daughter Loraine's interest in the arts. Loraine O'Donnell's father, Thomas, whose ancestors were from County Kerry, owned a bookstore in Boonville, New York.

At age fifteen, Loraine O'Donnell appeared in high school musicals and continued performing at SUNY Morrisville, where she majored in broadcast journalism. One of her theater professors suggested she had the talent to make a living in theater, so she studied at the American Musical and Dramatic Academy in New York City for two years in the mid-1980s. Buffalo's Alleyway Theatre signed her to a one-year contract, and O'Donnell planned to return to New York City after her term expired. Her first play at the Alleyway was the hit *Holy Ghosts*, for which she received enthusiastic reviews for her singing and piano playing. Along the way, she fell in love with Buffalo and its people—and decided to stay.

In addition to the Alleyway, Loraine worked for MusicalFare during her early Buffalo years. Like Mary Kate O'Connell, she was concerned with the lack of women in theater. In 1993, she and fellow Irish American actor Maureen Porter formed the Women in Theatre company, hiring women for most roles and successfully co-producing Tennessee Williams' *A Cat on a Hot Tin Roof.* O'Donnell also worked in local radio and television, producing and directing a morning show for WECK-AM radio. In 2011, *Buffalo Spree* magazine awarded her its "Best Voice in Radio Award." At WKBW-TV, she co-hosted the popular television shows *AM Buffalo, PM Buffalo*, and *Off Beat Cinema*.

In 2016, she was hired as the managing director of The Kavinoky Theatre, which was losing money and in danger of closing. When the theater's artistic director resigned, she was offered a position as artistic director and managing director. She transformed the theater by producing a more eclectic mix of shows while modernizing and updating the interior of the theater.[33]

In 2012, O'Donnell was honored with the New York State "Women of Distinction" award for her work in theater and the community.[34] In a 2021 interview, O'Donnell claimed that if she hadn't found a career in theater, she would have become a homicide detective or worked for the FBI.[35] Buffalo theatergoers and numerous charities in the community are glad she found a home in the arts.

Another talented Irish female thespian is South Buffalo native Meg Quinn, the long-time artistic director of the Theatre of Youth (TOY). As a student at Rosary Hill College in 1972, Quinn was one of five founders of Buffalo's first theater dedicated to children's plays. After four years there, she moved to New York City and later to Rochester, where she continued acting. However, she returned to Buffalo in 1988 and was hired as the marketing director for TOY. Five years later, she was promoted to Artistic Director. In 1999, she oversaw TOY's move to its permanent home, the Allendale Theatre on Allen Street.

As the company's leader for over twenty years, Quinn claimed that one of her most significant challenges was showing that children's theater belongs in the professional theater realm.[36] When selecting plays, she chose stories that teach children that "some of life's difficult decisions take courage and can change the world."[37] She wanted to help young people think about these issues. Each performance also has a "talk back" session where the children can ask questions and comment on what they just watched.[38] Like Michael Shea at his theater, Quinn kept ticket prices low at TOY to ensure the theater was available to more people in the community. Quinn challenged the notion that the primary purpose of children's theater is to create the theatergoers of tomorrow. Instead, she believed theater should speak to children about issues that concern them.[39]

Other Irish Theater Professionals

Richard Lambert, a New York City native, opened a theater that, in contrast to the Theatre of Youth, focused on edgy plays for adults. After graduating from Brooklyn College, Lambert moved to Buffalo, where he received his M.F.A. in Theatre/Theatre Arts Management at the University of Buffalo. The following year, in 1996, he opened The New Phoenix Theatre in a former lecture hall at 95 Johnson Park, aiming to create a theater that performed bold and challenging contemporary, as well as classical, plays. Lambert produced provocative plays by the new generation of Irish playwrights, such as Conor McPherson and Martin McDonagh. Lambert's brother Thomas, a local lawyer, served on the theater's board and was also a leader on New York's Ancient Order of Hibernians State Board.

Another theater leader who enjoys pushing boundaries is Daniel Shanahan, an Irish American raised in the city of Tonawanda. He and his wife, Melissa Meola, founded Torn Space Theater on Fillmore Avenue, focusing on contemporary avant-garde productions. In the 1990s, Shanahan was attracted to independent music and cinema experience, profoundly shaping his theater's mission. A Buffalo State graduate, he is primarily self-taught in theater. After watching some Samuel Beckett short plays performed by the Irish Classical Theatre Company, Shanahan became intrigued by the Irish Nobel Prize-winning playwright. In the early years, Torn Space produced some of Beckett's short plays, and Beckett's minimalistic style has shaped Shanahan's productions.[40]

Shanahan eventually moved away from classical plays to produce original works by national or international playwrights. His company has also staged performances that use film, light, sound, and virtual reality (Oculus goggles handed out to patrons), offering theatergoers an entirely new way to experience theater. The theater, located in a Polish cultural center on Buffalo's East Side, has become an anchor in a neighborhood slowly experiencing a rebirth. Torn Space has also staged performances at Rick Smith's Silo City, a cultural campus situated among massive grain elevators along the Buffalo River in the First Ward. These performances have garnered both national and international recognition. Each year, Shanahan and his colleagues stage a performance that responds to a significant global theme relevant to that year, further using theater to explore new ideas.[41]

Movies, Television, and Radio

While most Irish entertainers found success as performers, a few excelled on the business side of the profession. One such person was Patrick Anthony Powers, who was "a pioneer in the motion-picture industry and an Irish immigrant who rose from blacksmith to a multimillionaire."[42] Born in County Waterford in 1869, Powers and his family emigrated to Buffalo in the 1880s. Not much is known about his mother, Mary (Shea) Powers, or his father, John Powers, who raised Patrick on the West Side and downtown area of Buffalo. After initially working as a blacksmith and then serving as a police officer, Patrick Powers had a work history that resembled those of many other immigrants from the Emerald Isle. But Powers was a hustler who sought fame and fortune. In 1898, he was a bicycle dealer on West Huron Street, and two years later, he was selling phonographs for the Edison Phonograph Company on Main Street. Eventually, he went from owning a single store to managing forty Edison stores throughout the eastern United States.[43] In 1907, he and a business partner, Joseph Schubert, created the Buffalo Film Exchange, which purchased films and sold them to nickelodeons (early movie theaters that generally charged a nickel for admission).

In 1910, Powers co-owned the Temple Theater, a moving picture show house in Buffalo. He was suspected of financial misconduct, and a Buffalo judge ordered him to hand over his financial records.[44] When Powers refused, the

judge issued a contempt of court notice. Powers left Buffalo for New York City
to form the Powers Motion Picture Company. In July 1912, his film company
merged with five other companies, creating the Universal Film Manufacturing
Company—later Universal Picture Company, and eventually Universal Pictures.
Carl Laemmle, president while Powers served as treasurer, eventually bought out
all of his partners, including Powers, and moved the company from New York to
Hollywood. As a result, Powers became a very wealthy man.

In 1914, when Powers returned to Buffalo to serve as a witness in a trial against
Eastman Kodak Company, the *Buffalo Morning Express* noted that he had left
Buffalo a few years earlier as an "inconspicuous businessman" and now returned as
one of the leaders of the motion picture industry.[45] In 1917, when the New York
State legislature considered taxing motion pictures, Patrick Powers was the first
witness they called to testify. He argued against the proposed tax, contending that
owners took considerable risks to produce movies while movie stars, who took no
risk, made all the money.[46] By 1918, Powers had expanded his media company by
becoming a dealer for numerous Victor Talking Machine stores nationwide.

In the early 1920s, during the silent film era, Powers was an investor and
former head of the Film Booking Offices of America (FBO).[47] Board member
Joseph P. Kennedy, father of the future president of the United States, eventually
purchased the company and formed RKO Pictures—one of the top five studios
during Hollywood's Golden Age, leaving Powers to move on to another venture.
Although Powers was experiencing great success, newspapers often wrote about
his unscrupulous business activities, including a 1920 accusation of stock fraud by
Powers Film Company's shareholders. Yet he always seemed to escape charges.

In 1928, he formed Powers Cinephone, a sound equipment manufacturing firm
that produced one of the first sound devices used in motion pictures. Animator
Walt Disney purchased one of Powers' devices to create sound cartoons such as
Mickey Mouse's *Steamboat Willie* (1928), the first Mickey Mouse movie ever
distributed. Disney couldn't find a distributor for his sound cartoons, so he turned
to the Irish immigrant from Buffalo. Powers distributed *Steamboat Willie* through
his Celebrity Pictures and was the first to distribute Disney's *Silly Symphony* series
of popular cartoons.[48] In a short time, Disney and Powers had a falling out over
the terms of their contract, and Powers hired away Disney's top animator, Ub
Iwerks, forever terminating his relationship with Walt Disney. During the silent
movie era, Powers produced over three hundred films—many of them shorts; *The
Wedding March* (1928) was the most notable.

The successful entrepreneur also established the Powers Film Products
Company in Rochester, producing stereographic films that created or enhanced
the illusion of depth in an image. Amassing a fortune from his ventures, he had
homes in Manhattan and Westport, CT, and often traveled to Europe.[49] In 1938,

his wife, Pearl Lapey Powers, discovered he was having an affair with Renee Thornton, an Italian duchess and famous opera singer. Pearl demanded a $1 million settlement from the multimillionaire movie man (about $18 million in 2020), but it is unknown how much he paid.[50] In 1948, the former blacksmith from Buffalo died after suffering a heart attack while dining at the distinguished Metropolitan Club in New York City. Private funeral services were held in Buffalo, where he was buried next to his mother at Holy Cross Cemetery in Lackawanna. To this day, Powers' role in creating Universal Pictures and his pioneering work with Disney's Mickey Mouse cartoons are generally unknown.

Joe Conley and The Waltons

Outside of Patrick Powers producing silent films and Chauncey Olcott and Peggy O'Neil performing in silent films, few of the Buffalo Irish found success on screen. That changed in the 1950s when Buffalo native Joe Conley appeared in several minor roles on television and film. It wasn't until 1972, however, that Conley became a household name for playing Ike Godsey, postmaster and general store owner in the American hit television series *The Waltons*.

Joseph H. Conley, born in Buffalo in 1928, was the son of Joseph H. Conley, Sr. and Mary (McMahon) Conley. The Conleys raised their family at 110 Whitfield Avenue in the Irish stronghold of South Buffalo. Joseph Sr., grandson of Irish immigrants, worked as a painter and later for Buffalo's Department of Public Works. His wife Mary McMahon, born in New Jersey, had been raised in a family of entertainers.

Mary's father, "Snake Oil Johnny" McMahon, a Brooklyn-born son of Irish immigrants, settled in Buffalo while performing in a traveling vaudeville show. Although his official occupation in the 1920 census was listed as "Toilet Articles," McMahon made a living by entertaining people as a medicine man. While McMahon was the main attraction, his show featured musicians, including his daughter Mary, who played the piano. There were also comedy sketches and banjo playing, and, at the end of each performance, Snake Oil Johnny sold his tonics— which were touted to "cure any ailment"—as popular souvenirs.[51] When a lice outbreak hit Buffalo's Riverside neighborhood, he sold a white soap guaranteed to "kill any kind of vermin in your kid's head."[52] Mary McMahon eventually left her father's troupe to perform in her own vaudeville act.

Joe Conley, Jr. attended Holy Family Elementary School as a child, occasionally appearing on "Buffalo Bob" Smith's radio show. At South Park High School, he became known as "Hollywood Joe."[53] Around 1945, his parents separated, and his mother, who aspired to become a full-time performer in California, brought young Joe with her when she moved there. In his autobiography, Conley explained that he had a choice to live with either parent. Still, he was closer to his mother, who always encouraged him "to accomplish and aim high" and regaled him with stories about his colorful grandfather, Snake Oil Johnny McMahon.[54]

While Conley was attending Loyola University in California, where he performed in the college's theater, his parents reconciled, and his mother moved back to Buffalo. Young Joe Conley stayed on the sunny West Coast and, after college, served as a second lieutenant in the United States Army during the Korean War. Wounded in battle, he earned a Silver Star for "conspicuous gallantry and intrepidity in action against the enemy."[55] While in a military hospital, Conley enjoyed performing for the troops so much that he vowed to allow himself three years to become a self-supporting actor.

When he returned from Korea, he quickly became a prolific television actor, appearing in minor roles in shows such as *Big Town* (1955), *Casey Jones* (1957), and *Alfred Hitchcock Presents* (1958). He also appeared in film noir drama, *Crime of Passion*, starring Barbara Stanwyck. In the 1960s, he appeared in dozens of hit television shows including *Green Acres, Mister Ed, Dragnet, Lassie, Gunsmoke*, and *The Beverly Hillbillies.*[56] But his role as the genial, bow tie-wearing store owner in The Waltons—which ran for 172 episodes over nine seasons (1972-1981)— cemented his legacy. From that point forward, he would be known to millions worldwide as "Ike Godsey." Conley recalled that people would walk up to him and "call me Ike and carry on a conversation like we're old friends. I have to remember that for ten years I did visit their home every week. To them, I am an old friend or a member of the family."[57]

After *The Waltons*, he performed in a few television commercials (such as a comical Wendy's commercial) and had a small part in *Cast Away* (2000) with Tom Hanks. Despite his success in television, Conley's wealth came from founding a real estate firm in California's San Fernando Valley. In 2001, when Conley attended a South Buffalo reunion while researching a screenplay he was working on about his colorful vaudevillian grandfather, Snake Oil Johnny, he said he had fond memories of growing up on Whitfield Avenue in South Buffalo. He was also surprised that the side streets of his old neighborhood hadn't changed much in the sixty years since he left.[58] While there are no remnants of Conley in his hometown of Buffalo, you can visit Ike Godsey's general store at the Walton's Mountain Museum in Schuyler, Virginia. In 2013, "Hollywood Joe" Conley died in California from complications of dementia.

Sean Cullen

South Buffalonian Sean Cullen found his love for theater at St. Martin of Tours Elementary School, where he performed in the musical *Godspell* in 1974.[59] He continued performing at Bishop Timon High School while playing for the school's baseball team (which won the city championship in 1978). He directed and performed in plays as a student at St. Bonaventure University.

Sean was the son of John F. Cullen, a teamster whose family roots were in County Wicklow, while Sean's mother, Mary (Healy) Cullen, was the daughter of a Buffalo businessman from County Cork who leased gas stations. While later years of Sean Cullen's youth were spent in West Seneca, he claimed that much of his world revolved around South Buffalo.[60] At age twenty-three, he relocated to New York City, like many other Buffalo Irish stars (E.P. and George Christy, Kittie O'Neil, and Chauncey Olcott). After four attempts at admission, he was accepted at the prestigious Yale School of Drama, where he performed in thirty-six plays in just twenty-eight months. Graduating at thirty, he struggled professionally for ten years but successfully directed Henrik Ibsen's *The Wild Duck* in Manhattan.

Cullen's most significant break came at age forty when he was cast as an understudy for Christopher Walken in *James Joyce's The Dead* on Broadway. Walken, playing the main character, Gabriel Conroy, had to leave town for the Sundance Film Festival. Cullen received glowing reviews in his Broadway debut, and when the show moved to Boston and San Francisco, he replaced Walken. In a later interview, Cullen declared that he loved acting in *The Dead* because it put him "in touch with my Irish heritage that I knew growing up in South Buffalo."[61] His 2008 performance as Commodore William Harbison in the Tony Award-winning revival of Rodgers & Hammerstein's *South Pacific* ran for two and half years at Lincoln Center in New York City, with Cullen acting in 1,000 performances.

Cullen also found prominent roles in movies and television. The hit television show *Law and Order* cast him in various roles, including a serial killer. The handsome and charismatic Buffalo actor also appeared on the soap opera *One Life to Live*. Other memorable performances include his role as FBI Director William Webster in Netflix's hit show *Mindhunters*; gangster Carl Billings in *Boardwalk Empire*; and a prison warden in *Suits*. He acted with Al Pacino in HBO's *Paterno* and the science fiction movie *Simone*. He was cast in *Revolutionary Road* with Leonardo DiCaprio, and played the police captain in *Cop Out* with Bruce Willis and Tracy Morgan. In 2022, he appeared with Carrie Mulligan in *She Said*. His favorite film experience, however, was playing Gene Clayton, brother of George Clooney's character in *Michael Clayton*.

Cullen wrote a play, *Safe Home*, which the Interart Theatre in New York City performed in 2010. A *New York Times* theater critic described it as a "lovely little one-act drama," describing Cullen as "a master of the dialogue of rapidly changing emotions."[62] Buffalo's Road Less Traveled Productions also staged a reading of this semi-autobiographical play about a family living on Cumberland Avenue in South Buffalo, the street where Cullen's father grew up. The play revolves around Sean's uncle, Jimmy Cullen, who died at nineteen in the Korean War, just three weeks before the conflict ended.

Unlike some other stars, Cullen has stayed close to his hometown. In 2011, his high school, Bishop Timon-St. Jude, awarded him its first Timon Center for Media & the Arts Distinguished Alumnus Award. In 2020, he performed the lead role in Annie Baker's play *Antipodes* at Road Less Traveled Productions (RLTP), where he was named American Theater Master. Three years later, at the same theater, Cullen played the lead role of Joe Keller in Arthur Miller's *All My Sons*. Sean Cullen also founded the American National Theatre (the ANT), which aims to advance and celebrate new American plays.

Another connection between the Buffalo Irish and Hollywood involves a Roman Catholic priest. Father William O'Malley was born in Buffalo in 1931, attended Canisius High School and Fordham University, and entered the Jesuit order in 1951. He taught English and theology for twenty-two years while directing the theater program at McQuaid Jesuit High School in Rochester, New York. Father O'Malley later taught at Fordham Preparatory School in the Bronx before leaving to teach at Seattle University. Over the years, he directed 99 plays and musicals—for student productions and community theaters—and wrote thirty-seven books on Catholic themes.

In 1973, O'Malley, a "strikingly handsome man looking more like a movie star than most movie stars," was cast as Father Joe Dyer in William Peter Blatty's *The Exorcist*. The Buffalo-born priest also used his knowledge of the Church to serve as an advisor for the film. More than twenty-five years after his performance in *The Exorcist*, O'Malley stated that he was still very proud of the movie because it "stripped the glamour from evil." He was the first Catholic priest to play a priest in a major motion picture.

Michael Healy and Disney

After Patrick Powers, Michael Healy is the Irish Buffalonian with the most impressive career as a media executive. Healy was born in Buffalo in 1948 to Edward G. Healy, a physician and major in the U.S. Army during the Second

World War, and Elvira (Rogers) Healy, a nurse. The Healy family grew up on the border of Buffalo on Burke Drive in Cheektowaga. In 1970, Michael Healy graduated from Canisius College with an English degree and then studied at Harvard for two years, where he received a master's degree in English Language and Literature.

Returning to Buffalo in 1972, Healy worked as a columnist for the *Courier-Express* and wrote the screenplay for *Vamping* (1984), a movie filmed in Buffalo about a down-and-out Buffalo saxophone player, starring Patrick Duffy. After the *Courier* closed, Healy moved to Colorado, where he worked as a film critic for the *Denver Post*. In 1987, he relocated to California to write for the *Los Angeles Daily News*. While he was in the Golden State, a friend from his Canisius College days recruited him for an executive position as director of development at Warner Brothers Television. Healy moved around to a few media companies, including the CBS Corporation, where he worked as director of motion pictures-for-television on fifty films. Five years later, he left CBS for the Disney Channel, where he became vice president for original movies and had a hand in producing more than ninety movies.

Working for the Disney Channel, Healy rejected most movie scripts until 2005, when Peter Barsocchini proposed a story about a star high school basketball player who dreamed of becoming a musical star. Healy enthusiastically endorsed the script and agreed to produce this modern-day *Romeo and Juliet*. Casting Zac Efron and Vanessa Hudgens, *High School Musical* was an overnight success. While others sought a stronger singer, Healy insisted on Efron; today, Efron and Hudgens are household names.

More than 200 million people in about a hundred countries have seen the original movie's coming-of-age story with its catchy tunes and thrilling dance numbers.[65] It was so successful that Disney launched two sequels and created a popular video game called *High School Musical: Sing It!*. In 2006, the soundtrack became the year's biggest-selling album and was certified quadruple platinum by the Recording Industry Association of America. Meanwhile, the DVD became the fastest-selling disc of a television film in history.[66] The *High School Musical* franchise—encompassing many Disney platforms—became a billion-dollar enterprise, helping to solidify the Buffalo boy as one of the giants in the business.

For sixteen years, Healy developed original feature films at the Disney Channel. Besides *High School Musical*, he also supervised movies such as *The Luck of the Irish* and *Camp Rock*. For the latter, he wisely signed the Jonas Brothers just as their careers were about to take off. Even though it had not been written for the Jonas Brothers, Healy and his team quickly rewrote the script to capitalize on the band's rising popularity.[67] He also signed the brothers for a show called *J.O.N.A.S.*, where the trio of teen siblings played young spies. In 2009, Healy's team released the hit movie *Princess Protection Program*, which paired two teen stars, Demi Lovato and Selena Gomez. When it aired in June 2009, 8.5 million viewers watched it, making it that year's most-watched scripted program on cable. Healy, who knew it would be successful, was pleased that "it did better than we had hoped."[68]

By the time Healy left the Disney Channel, he had helped turn it into a powerhouse. For eleven consecutive years, Disney Channel was the number one cable television telecast for original movies in the tween audience segment (nine to fourteen-year-old viewers), and, for six out of seven years, it was the number one scripted cable television telecast for total viewers.[69] When Healy left, the president of Disney Channels Worldwide said, "Michael's contributions to Disney Channel have been enormous, and we will definitely miss his wit, wisdom and his remarkable story-telling ability."[70] Award-winning producer and director Stuart Gillard, who worked with Healy, described him as "a brilliant storyteller" whose films "always had some philosophical point to them."[71] Since 2013, Healy has worked as an independent television producer and writer, hoping others will take a chance on his work.

More Entertainers

In addition to stage and film, the Buffalo Irish have excelled in radio. Thomas "Tom" Shannon, born in 1938 and raised on Lockwood Avenue in South Buffalo, was the son of Francis Shannon, an engineer with the Buffalo Public Schools, whose father was born in Ireland. Tom's mother, Melvina Boutet, worked as a telephone operator for Western Union. Tom, the eldest of three boys, graduated from South Buffalo's Holy Family grammar school and later moved to Buffalo's East Side, near Schiller Park, where he attended Bishop Ryan High School. Nicknamed "Irish" in the 1956 Bishop Ryan yearbook, Shannon worked on the radio and was a glee club member.[72] The same yearbook has a photo of him with a priest looking over his shoulder as he recites the rosary over the school intercom system. His broadcasting career would take him far afield of rosary recitals.

At age fifteen, he started as a newsman with WXRA radio (now WUFO). In 1958, while attending Buffalo State, Shannon began working at WKBW-AM 1520, a powerful 50,000-watt radio station, where he and radio stars Joey Reynolds and Danny Neaverth played Top 40 rock songs for audiences across the East Coast.[73] Shannon, described as a "breaker of hearts and as smooth a disc jockey as Buffalo, Detroit, Denver, LA, or anywhere else has ever known," helped WKBW become the dominant Buffalo radio station, with a 50% market share— no station has ever come close.[74]

Shannon's fame spread in 1963 when the theme song of his radio show, *Wild Weekend*, which he co-wrote with the late Phil Todaro, became a national hit. That year, a Buffalo band called the Rockin' Rebels recorded the song, which rose to No. 8 on the Billboard Hot 100 and No. 22 on Billboard magazine's Top 100 singles in the same year, generating royalty checks until the end of Shannon's life.[75] Around the same time, Buffalo's Channel 7 hired him to host the wildly popular *Buffalo Bandstand*, and later, Channel 2 hired him for their program *Hit or Miss*. With Hollywood good looks, Shannon became a local celebrity, featured shirtless in a bathing suit for a print advertisement for sparkling beverage maker Queen-O.

In 1964, Shannon accepted an offer to work for Detroit's rock 'n' roll powerhouse CKLW-AM, where he quickly became the reigning disc jockey in the Detroit area, spreading his reputation throughout the Midwestern United States and Canada. One reporter claimed, "Shannon has always been radio royalty, living in a world of prime-time slotting and big salaries."[76] In 1968, he won the prestigious Bill Gavin Award, which honors the nation's top disc jockey. Three years later, he hosted the Motor City's *Morning Show* on Channel 7, going on to run a radio and television show in Denver.

Shannon, a nationally known disc jockey during the rock 'n' roll era, rubbed elbows with countless stars, including Frank Sinatra and Elvis Presley. After working in various cities throughout the United States and Canada, Shannon finally returned to Buffalo in the 1990s to host an afternoon radio show on Oldies 104. In 2005, after working fifty years as a disc jockey, Shannon retired. Despite his frequent moves throughout the country, his daughter, Catherine Shannon, claimed her father "loved Buffalo and was proud to be from there."[77]

In 2001, Shannon was inducted into the Buffalo Broadcasting Hall of Fame, where he was described as a "Buffalo heartthrob" who became "one of America's best-known rock jocks via KB's near-total East Coast penetration at night."[78] He was also inducted into the Buffalo Music Hall of Fame three years later.

Tom Shannon is remembered for being "a gentleman and a loyal friend," an "astute businessman," and "the epitome of cool."[79] Local radio legend Danny Neaverth claimed that the Irish boy from South Buffalo was "one of the most admired disc jockeys in Western New York history."[80] Others wrote, "[h]is smooth on-air delivery, coupled with his boyish good looks make him as popular, especially with teen girls, as the rock stars of the day."[81] Like other Irish stars from South Buffalo, he remained humble despite his fame. "Tom never let his ego get in the way of his talent...he always remained grounded."[82]

Billy Sheehan—Legendary Musician

Billy Sheehan, one of Western New York's most talented musicians, grew up in the Buffalo suburb of Kenmore, graduated from Blessed Sacrament Elementary School, and attended Kenmore East High School. In 1972, Sheehan, who played bass, founded the band Talas, which played 3,500 engagements over twelve years. Receiving more radio air time on the West Coast than in his hometown, Sheehan and his bandmates moved to Los Angeles in 1985, where they signed a multi-record deal, quickly becoming a fan favorite on the Los Angeles concert scene.

The Buffalo native caught the attention of David Lee Roth, with whom he toured internationally and appeared in numerous MTV videos. Roth said, "The man the guitar magazines call the premiere rock-bass player of this century... Sheehan performed nightly miracles on four strings in front of literally millions of wide and often bloodshot eyes."[83] Sheehan, an international star, has been named five times as *Guitar Magazine's* "Best Rock Bassist."[84]

During the late 1980s, Sheehan formed the band Mr. Big, which produced the 1991 number-one Billboard hit "To Be With You" from their gold record album *Lean Into It*.[85] When Billy Sheehan returned to Buffalo that same year for a charity benefit, 10,000 Buffalonians came out to cheer him on. *Buffalo News* music critic Jeff Miers wrote, "Buffalo is associated with some major names in the world of popular music—Ani DiFranco, the Goo Goo Dolls, moe., and Rick James among them. But in terms of musical virtuosity, one name stands above the others—Billy Sheehan."[86]

Sheehan, whose paternal ancestors were from the Emerald Isle, is proud of his Irish heritage. At a July 4, 2018, concert in Dublin, Billy Sheehan issued a thank you message to his "Irish friends for a warm and wonderful welcome back to my family's roots and heritage."[87]

Irish Dancers

Kittie O'Neil, who graced the dance halls of New York City and Boston in the 1870s and '80s, was the first prominent Irish dancer from Buffalo, but not the last. While Irish dancing was performed in the Queen City throughout the nineteenth and twentieth centuries, it wasn't until the twenty-first century that Buffalo produced professional Irish dancers. Unlike in O'Neil's time, Irish dance was no longer performed in smoky variety halls, but rather in a variety of community venues, as well as professional theaters and performing arts centers. In recent years, three Western New York women have gained international reputations as professional Irish dancers: Kevinah Dargan (world champion), Erin Lynch (national champion), and Fiona Dargan (world champion).

Kevinah Dargan hails from a family rich in the tradition of Irish dancing. Her grandmothers, several aunts and cousins in Ireland, and her mother, Tracy Dargan, were all dancers. As mentioned, her sister, Fiona, is also a dancing champion. Their mother, Tracy, was raised in Western New York by two Irish immigrants, Aby and Anne (Kavanagh) Marks. The Dublin-born Markses, who settled in Buffalo in 1959, were involved with several Irish cultural organizations and were among the co-founders of the Buffalo Irish Festival. Kevinah and Fiona's father, Kevin Dargan, were born in Derry, Northern Ireland, and raised in Dublin. He is one of the principal owners of the Banshee Irish Pub, a popular Irish bar in Buffalo.

At age four, Kevinah started dancing at Mary Kay Heneghan's Rince Na Tiarna school in South Buffalo. Here, seventeen years of training at the school led to a terrific career in Irish dance. In 2002, at age eight, Kevinah won the National Solo Champion finals in Boston against dancers from all over the United States, England, Canada, and Ireland, being the first dancer from Western New York to win a national championship. The following year, she won the competition again.[88] In 2005, Kevinah won at the World Irish Dancing Championships in Ennis, Ireland, and was the youngest North American to win a world championship. She has been a repeat World Champion, an All-Ireland Champion, and an eight-time North American Champion.

In 2015, Kevinah auditioned for and won the lead role of Saoirse opposite Michael Flatley in *Lord of the Dance: Dangerous Games*, a dance and musical performance centered around Celtic lore. Flatley, the star of the original *Riverdance* in 1994, is credited with popularizing Irish dance across the globe. This role took Kevinah to the Dominion Theatre in London's West End, where she performed for a six-month engagement. Later that year, Dargan joined Flatley as he made his Broadway debut at the famed Lyric Theatre in New York City. After her residency there, she auditioned against five hundred other dancers for one of two available slots in *Riverdance*. She was selected and joined her Buffalo friend Erin Lynch on a thirty-six-city tour of China.

Dargan returned and performed for *Riverdance* in Dublin for five months at the Gaiety Theatre and in Killarney, Ireland, where fans treated her like a rock star.[89] Along the way, in addition to performing to packed crowds in London, New York City, Dublin, and Shanghai, she appeared on the *Graham Norton Show* and *Britain's Got Talent*. Her success also led to numerous invitations to perform with artists and bands such as Eileen Ivers, the Chieftains, Cherish the Ladies, and Black 47.

Erin Lynch, who started dancing at Rince Na Tiarna at age four, is also an accomplished professional dancer. She has competed on the national and world stage, qualifying for the World Championships eleven times and winning national championship awards in team contests. At age nineteen, Lynch was chosen for

Lord of the Dance: Dangerous Games while studying at a dance school in Dublin. For eight months, the Buffalo dancer performed on London's West End at the Dominion Theatre and then, with Kevinah, joined Michael Flatley on Broadway in New York and danced in *Titanic Dance* and *Magic of the Dance*.[90] In 2016, as mentioned, she performed with *Riverdance* on their Chinese and North American tour, where audiences from Mexico, France, England, Germany, Ireland, and Scotland witnessed Lynch's graceful dancing.

Fiona Dargan inherited the same championship dancing gene as her sister. In 2008, she competed against almost two hundred dancers and won the gold medal at the All-Ireland Dance Championships in Killarney for her age group.[91] That same year, she competed in Belfast for the World Irish Dance Championship for ten to eleven-year-olds; she also won that competition, making her the best Irish dancer in the world for her age. On August 25, 2018, Kevinah, her sister, Fiona Dargan, and dozens of cast members from *Riverdance* were invited to perform in Dublin at Croke Park Stadium for Pope Francis at the World Meeting of Families. Fiona described it as one of the most memorable experiences of her life as Pope Francis and 90,000 people enthusiastically applauded at the conclusion of the performance.[92] In March 2022, the Dargan sisters performed for a national audience on *The Tonight Show Starring Jimmy Fallon*.

In early 2020, Erin Lynch, Kevinah Dargan, and Fiona Dargan were selected to be part of a small group of thirteen dancers for *Riverdance: The New 25th Anniversary Show*, taking them to Montreal, Toronto, New York City, and their hometown of Buffalo.[93] After the tour was launched in New York City at Radio Music Hall in March 2020, the coronavirus pandemic hit the United States, leading to the cancellation of the multi-city tour. When the *Riverdance* tour resumed in April 2022, all three dancers performed as special guests at Shea's Theatre in their hometown of Buffalo.

As performers, the Buffalo Irish have left an enormous legacy here and nationwide. They have also contributed as poets, writers, and artists to the local and national arts and cultural scene. We will now learn about them.

CHAPTER SEVEN

Literary Figures and Artists

F. Scott Fitzgerald—Poet Laureate of the Jazz Age

F. Scott Fitzgerald, the great American novelist, is associated with several residences: New York City, Paris, and the French Riviera. Few people know that Fitzgerald spent much of his youth in Buffalo, where he showed signs of superior intelligence, a gift for writing, and a love of literature. Buffalo is also where he experienced a family financial disaster that helped shape his thoughts on the illusion of the American Dream.

Much of Fitzgerald's biography is well known: his Princeton education; a tumultuous relationship with his wife Zelda; a chronicler of Jazz Age New York; his acceptance by the literary types in Paris and the French Riviera; and his tragic descent into an alcoholic-fueled death spiral. But his upbringing in St. Paul and Buffalo made him who he was.

Francis Scott Key Fitzgerald was born in 1896 in St. Paul to Edward Fitzgerald and Mary "Mollie" (McQuillan) Fitzgerald. Scott's father, born in Maryland, came from old English and Irish stock. Edward's relative Francis Scott Key wrote the "Star-Spangled Banner." Scott's devout Catholic mother, Mollie—a social climber—was the daughter of Philip McQuillan, an Irish Catholic immigrant from County Fermanagh, who made a fortune in the wholesale grocery business in St. Paul. Scott learned about being a self-made man from his Irish maternal grandfather and referred to his mother's family as "straight 1850 potato-famine Irish." In a letter to author John O'Hara, he referred to being "half black-Irish" because of his McQuillan ancestors.[1] One biographer suggested, "His [Fitzgerald's] Irish roots were mercantile and unglamorous."[2]

When Scott was one and a half, his family moved to Buffalo after his father's wicker manufacturing business failed. In the Queen City, the senior Fitzgerald found a job as a salesman for Procter & Gamble. The family moved into the fashionable Lenox apartments, later a hotel. They then moved to an apartment at Elmwood Avenue and Summer Street. During their years in Buffalo, money from Fitzgerald's mother's family enabled the family to live an upper-middle-class lifestyle, including attending the finest Catholic schools.[3]

After a short interlude in Syracuse, the family moved back to Buffalo in 1903, settling at 29 Irving Place. Fitzgerald attended Holy Angels' school and Miss Nardin's Academy. At Holy Angels, Fitzgerald was said to have "fallen under the spell" of Father Michael Fallon.[4] During this same time, Fitzgerald's father introduced his son to poets such as Poe and Byron and writers such as Sir Walter Scott.

In Buffalo, Fitzgerald's friend Hamilton Wende introduced him to the theater. Together they attended performances at the Teck Theatre, and returned home to re-enact plays for the neighborhood children.[5] Around this time, Scott realized he had a gift for writing, which provided him with a way to win the admiration of his peers—something that he craved.[6] Fitzgerald won awards for essays on George Washington and Ignatius of Loyola. He even started a history of America and a detective story. Sadly, none of his early Buffalo writings were preserved.[7]

While the Fitzgeralds lived among the upper-middle class, they were always considered outsiders. In addition to being Irish and Catholic, they didn't have the financial means to be members of Buffalo's elite. They were invited to country clubs and social clubs, such as the Park Club and the Twentieth Century Club, but never gained membership to any of these prestigious clubs. Scott attended charity balls and parties with his wealthy friends, including wealthy Buffalonians such as Dorothy Knox, Seymour Knox's sister, and Harriet Mack, the daughter of the *Buffalo Times* owner.[8] While he was a charming young man who befriended Buffalo's most affluent elites, Fitzgerald was still an outsider.[9]

In Buffalo, Fitzgerald learned about class distinctions and how the rich were indeed different. The bright young man also started to realize how hard it was for ordinary folks to join the upper class. Later in his life, he wrote, "I have never been able to forgive the rich for being rich, and it has colored my entire life and works."[10] He would use these experiences to write about the American aspiration to chase after a higher social class and status. This idea was central to his masterpiece *The Great Gatsby*, arguably the Great American Novel.

Another central theme in Fitzgerald's writing is failure and loss, which he experienced firsthand during his time in Buffalo. In 1908, Scott watched his father get fired from his Procter & Gamble sales job. Twenty-eight years after the event, Fitzgerald wrote the following:

> That morning he had gone out a comparatively young man, a man full of strength, full of confidence. He came home that evening, an old man, a completely broken man. He had lost his essential drive, his immaculateness of purpose. He was a failure the rest of his days.[11]

Fitzgerald was not unscathed by his father losing his job. He worried that disaster would destroy his family and prayed they would be spared the poorhouse. The Fitzgeralds were forced to move back to St. Paul to be financially supported by Scott's grandfather.

Fitzgerald, well-known for his novels *This Side of Paradise* (1920) and *The Great Gatsby* (1925), started writing *Tender is the Night* amid the Roaring Twenties. It was the Irish-American author's "intended masterpiece" and "his favorite among his books."[12] He thought it would surpass the fame of *The Great Gatsby*. His friend Ernest Hemingway agreed that it was his best work. But the novel was published in 1934, during the Great Depression, and readers were uninterested in a story about the wealthy luxuriating on the beaches of the French Riviera. Sales of the book were underwhelming, and it never attained the acclaim Fitzgerald had hoped.

Fitzgerald borrowed material from his own life for *Tender is the Night*, as he had with his other fiction. He chose Buffalo as the place from which the main character, Dick Diver, springs and where he returns later in the story. The fictional Dick Diver has a lot of F. Scott Fitzgerald in him. In addition to being raised in Buffalo, Diver is the son of a financially strapped father. Like Fitzgerald, Dick Diver admired his father and learned honor, courage, and decency from him.[13]

The ambitious Dick Diver leaves Buffalo and graduates from some of the most prestigious universities in the world: Yale, Oxford, and Johns Hopkins. But his middle-class background makes him an outsider in the world of the wealthy upper class. Dick completed his training in psychiatry, working with the world's brilliant minds in Vienna and Switzerland. Diver strives to be a great psychiatrist, perhaps the greatest ever known. Fitzgerald uses Diver's career ambition, not the mere accumulation of wealth, to define the main character's idea of the American Dream.

Diver blames his mentally ill wife, Nicole, for his lack of success. Meanwhile, Nicole, born into money, recovers from her illness and thrives. In Fitzgerald's mind, the rich always thrive, while tragic characters like Dick Diver (Fitzgerald) must row against the current in their quest for the American Dream. Toward the end of the novel, Diver and Nicole separate, and he leaves Europe to return to Buffalo. Diver eventually leaves Buffalo for smaller and smaller towns in Western New York and the Finger Lakes, which Fitzgerald uses to illustrate the protagonist's decline from the time he lived in Vienna and the French Riviera. Buffalo, the city where Fitzgerald's own father struggled financially, is the site for Dick Diver's disillusionment with the American Dream.

F. Scott Fitzgerald was a keen observer of American life. From the rise of consumerism, to embedded class distinctions, to the illusion of the American Dream, these themes came out of his time in Buffalo. These formative experiences shaped the characters and themes in his greatest novels. As we see in his hoped-for masterpiece, *Tender is the Night*, his time spent in Buffalo left an indelible impression on him and his writing.

James Nicoll Johnston—Buffalo's Dean of Poets

Buffalo's first poet of note, James Nicoll Johnston, lived less than a mile away from F. Scott Fitzgerald's home on Irving Place. Johnston was born in Donegal, Ireland, in 1832, and when he was fifteen, his parents, Girard, a carpenter, and Jane Johnston brought him and his siblings to the bustling city of Buffalo. Knowledge of Johnston's life in Ireland is limited, besides the fact that he received a good education in Donegal. Although he was a Protestant, James Johnston was an ardent Home Ruler (the political movement associated with self-government for Ireland). But he also advocated for peace and did not want any divisions between the north and south of Ireland.[14]

After finishing his schooling in Buffalo, Johnston worked as an agent for William Pryor Letchworth, a wealthy owner of an iron manufacturing company. The poet's knowledge of the German and French languages was invaluable to Mr. Letchworth.[15] In addition to their business relationship, Johnston and Letchworth became close friends. At age thirty-six, Johnston retired from business to devote himself full-time to writing, a rare occupation at the time.

Starting in 1858, Johnston was an active member of Buffalo's Nameless Club, a literary club for prominent Buffalonians, including William Letchworth, William Bryant, David Gray Sr., James O. Putnam, and J.N. Larned.[16] This progressive club, which numbered about a dozen members, also included at least four women. During his two decades as a member, Johnston wrote one of his most well-known poems about President Abraham Lincoln, titled "Abraham Lincoln: Lying in State in Buffalo April 27, 1865."[17]

Johnston, noted for his intellectual gifts, was referred to as the "Dean of Buffalo's Poets" and "Buffalo's Poet Laureate."[18] He had the look of an "aristocrat" and the manners of a "gentleman."[19] A lifelong bachelor, he lived at 383 Pennsylvania Street with his younger sister. He led a quiet life dedicated to his poetry and his friends, who remembered his quick wit and gift for conversation. Johnston was praised for diligently promoting Buffalo writers.[20]

Johnston's greatest gift to Buffalo was his anthology of Buffalo poetry. His book, *Poets and Poetry of Buffalo*, published in 1904, took several years to complete. He compiled poems from more than a hundred local writers—men and women—in a book that was close to five hundred pages. The real hero of the project was Johnston's talented mother, Jane Nicoll Johnston. For decades, she had maintained scrapbooks of poems that were published in local newspapers.[21] These scrapbooks provided the bulk of the poems for his anthology, which he supplemented with other unpublished works. Johnston's sister Margaret also assisted in the project. Buffalo's library superintendent claimed, "It can be said safely that no other city in this country has anything of local anthology to compare, in completeness and historical value...."[22] The voices from Buffalo's literary past would have been lost to history, if not for the efforts of the Johnston family.

The anthology contained over one hundred Buffalo writers, a handful of whom were Irish. Johnston included Thomas D'Arcy McGee, a Buffalo journalist, and Father Patrick Cronin, a Catholic newspaper editor. Other Irish surnames in the anthology included Glenny, MacManus, McKenna, Mahany, O'Connor, and Shea.[23]

In 1909, Johnston, then 76 years old, published a book of his work called *Donegal Memories*. His poems capture the wild and picturesque Donegal landscape, as remembered from his childhood. One book reviewer commended Johnston for his "rhythm and melody" and remarked that he wrote verses of "rare charm."[24] Another praised it as a gem and perfect in every detail.[25] A local newspaper noted that even though Johnston had lived in Buffalo for fifty years, "he has retained all his love and veneration for dear Ireland, the land of his birth...."[26] Another reviewer declared, "When he sings of the ocean roar around Sheep Haven Bay, or the leads and the daisies, the sweet hawthorn hedges of the land of Tyrconnell, his readers are one with the boy standing on the Bridge of Cloon."[27]

In one poem, Johnston wrote of his love for his homeland:

> For there's life on the hills and life by the sea,
> And Voices forever are calling to me
> From the Wilds of Donegal!"

Similarly, in another poem:

> Your sons' and daughters' new lives have planned
> Away in a kind and generous land;
> Yet ofttimes they long for the mountain air,
> Old joys, and a day at the Creeslough Fair.

In 1916, Johnston was hit by a car while walking along Bidwell Parkway. After the accident, his health deteriorated, and he died at 87. At his death, he was one of Buffalo's oldest residents and an essential link from the city's pioneer past to the modern metropolis it had become. His obituaries praised him as one of the "best known" and "most liked" Buffalonians. He was a "high-souled representative of idealism in an age too much devoted to material affairs."[28] At his death, libraries throughout the United States, Canada, Ireland, and Great Britain held copies of both of Johnston's books. Today, the University at Buffalo offers an academic scholarship in James Nicoll Johnston's honor.

Charles A. Brady—Buffalo's Man of Letters

On April 14, 1912, as the *Titanic* sank, one of Buffalo's most remarkable men of letters was born. His name was Charles Andrew Brady. He corresponded with some of the leading writers of his generation, wrote a handful of historical novels, educated thousands of students, and wrote hundreds of newspaper and literary articles. Shortly after Brady's death, Congressman John J. LaFalce referred to him as one of the country's brightest intellectual beacons.[29]

Charles Brady was born to Andrew Brady and Belinda (Dowd) Brady. Andrew Brady, a bright and ambitious immigrant from Cavan County, Ireland, arrived in the United States in about 1870. After working in the white pine lumber trade, he settled in Buffalo in 1878.[30] Andrew Brady and his brother, Peter, formed Brady Brothers, a lumber firm in North Tonawanda that prospered throughout Buffalo's construction boom. Charles's mother, Belinda, a schoolteacher, was a daughter of Irish immigrants who had settled in Black Rock.

Charles Brady enjoyed a comfortable childhood in his home on Humboldt Parkway in Buffalo—allegedly, many homes along the parkway were built using his father's lumber. He remembered his childhood home being filled with conversations about the Irish and Wilsonian Democratic politics.[31] When Charles was thirteen, tragedy struck; his father passed away unexpectedly.

Charles not only suffered the loss of his father, but also contracted rheumatic fever, confining him to a bed and wheelchair for two years.[32] During his recovery, he immersed himself in the classics provided to him by his mother.[33] At Canisius High School, he published his first poem, and he continued his Jesuit education at Canisius College, graduating in 1933. There he read and admired the works of G.K. Chesterton, Evelyn Waugh, Graham Greene, and Charles Dickens. In 1930, at age eighteen, Brady earned an opportunity to interview Chesterton, one of his literary heroes, who had come to speak in Buffalo.

Brady, a gifted student, had an opportunity to go to Harvard for graduate school. His widowed mother, however, lost a large portion of the family's savings in the stock market crash. The Jesuits offered the talented Brady a deal. They would pay his $1,000 tuition to Harvard, if he agreed to return to Canisius College to teach for five years.[34] He accepted, and stayed at Canisius for forty-two years. While at Harvard, he studied Old Irish and Old Norse sagas, which shaped the content of his future novels. Years before going to Harvard, Brady met his future wife, Mary Eileen Larson, who graduated from Cornell with a degree in dairy science. They married in Boston, moved back to Buffalo, and raised six children, several of whom had their own successful writing careers.

Brady had an accomplished career as an English professor at his alma mater, serving as department chair for half of his academic career. But Brady's prowess as a lecturer and teacher had the most lasting impact. In 1970, he wrote the centennial history of Canisius College, and the selection of the school's mascot, the Griffin, came from a poem he wrote as a student. Brady loved Canisius College, and the students loved him back, dedicating the school's yearbook to him twice. The Canisius Alumni Association presented him with the Peter Canisius Medal for his "scholarly brilliance and teaching excellence that inspired legions of Canisius students."[35]

When Brady was not teaching, he was writing scores of poems, short stories, essays in scholarly publications, book reviews, and novels, all while corresponding with internationally famous authors. In 1968, the Poetry Society of America awarded him first prize for his poem "Keeper of the Western Gate."[36] One of his most noteworthy achievements was his correspondence with C.S. Lewis. In his letters to Lewis, the famous British author declared, "You [Brady] are the first of my critics so far who has really read and understood all of my books and 'made up' the subject in a way that makes you an authority." Lewis continued, "I have always been haunted by the fear that all of our studies of the dead authors (who can't up and protest when we go wrong) may, in spite of careful documentation etc., be quite wide of the mark: on the whole you set that at rest."[37] Lewis urged Brady to visit him and his friends at Oxford. However, the meeting never happened. The Brady-Lewis letters now reside in the Bodleian Library at Oxford University. Besides being an American authority on C.S. Lewis, Brady was also an expert on J.R.R. Tolkien and Sigrid Undset, the Norwegian winner of the Nobel Prize for Literature in 1928, with whom he also corresponded.

When Brady wasn't writing literary criticism, he found time to write historical novels, citing Willa Cather's *Death Comes for An Archbishop* as his influence.[38] His seminal work, *Stage of Fools*, was published in 1953; it is also his best-known book and was on the best-seller list for a short time. His novel, which predated by several years Robert Bolt's classic play *A Man For All Seasons*, examines the tumultuous last years of Sir Thomas More's life, with flashbacks to More's earlier life. Brady's *Stage of Fools* received laudatory critical reviews.[39] "[Thomas]More's great faith and his sense of justice are always in evidence, and the saint's marvelous wit and forbearance shine throughout these pages."[40]

Three years later, Brady wrote a loosely autobiographical novel called *Viking Summer* (1956) set in his home in Kenmore and a summer home in Crescent Beach, Canada, with characters that mirror his own family members.[41] Blending his Irish heritage and his wife's Norwegian ancestry, he wrote a historical novel, *This Land Fulfilled* (1958), about the Leif Ericson voyage to Vinland, or coastal North America. The story's narrator is a Norseman who, by the end of the story, has become a priest in Ireland. *The New York Times* gave it a favorable review.

Brady's last novel, the *Crown of Grass* (1964), is a detective novel about Rene Chateaubriand, the nineteenth-century French ambassador to the Vatican States. Brady also wrote four children's books and edited *A Catholic Reader*, an anthology of works by thirty-five Catholic poets.

Brady served as the chief book critic for the *Buffalo Evening News*, later the *Buffalo News*, for fifty years, and thousands of Western New Yorkers have been familiar with his Saturday book reviews. Brady was perhaps the only American book reviewer who illustrated his reviews with a caricature, drawn by himself, of the featured author.[42] In 1986, the Burchfield Penney Art Center exhibited the talented artist's drawings in a one-man show.[43] In addition, Brady wrote reviews for the *New York Times*, the *New York Herald Tribune*, *America* magazine, and other periodicals.

Congressman Richard "Max" McCarthy, a friend of forty years, claimed, "I do not believe that Buffalo has ever produced a more brilliant or erudite Man of Letters."[44] Dr. Richard J. Thompson, a Canisius professor and colleague of Brady, remembered him as "the most gifted man he ever met," and remarked that Brady was a polymath with a photographic memory and an expert on any kind of literature.[45] The Jesuits' $1,000 investment in Brady's education paid out handsomely for Canisius College, and for Buffalo.

Other Canisius College Writers

As Brady was stirring the lecture halls of Canisius College, the English department hired another gifted writer. Roger Burke Dooley was born in 1920 to Roger J. Dooley and May (Riordan) Dooley and grew up in South Buffalo. His father, Roger, whose parents were born in Ireland, was a well-respected waterfront patrolman whose beat was the Buffalo River and harbor. Tragically, Roger J. Dooley passed away at age 40, when Roger was only five. May Dooley, the daughter of an Irish mother and raised in the First Ward, supported the family as a public school teacher. May provided young Roger with details about life in the First Ward—the subject of the early part of his trilogy on the Buffalo Irish.

As a student at School 27, Dooley won the prestigious Jesse Ketchum Gold Medal award for outstanding scholarship.[46] At South Park High School, Dooley was inspired to write a book about the Irish in Buffalo. In his words, he "conceived the grand ambition of trying to record in fiction the world in which I was growing up, the complex network of families, most of them Irish, known to each other for generations, since their early years in Buffalo's colorful old First Ward."[47]

His debut novel, *Less Than Angels* (1946), published when he was only twenty-six, was well received. It was not the Buffalo Irish novel he aspired to write; that would come next. Scores of public libraries across the country added it to their shelves in 1946. The *Boston Globe* reviewer commented that all the characters in the book are Catholic, and if it weren't for the "clerical motif," the book would have become a bestseller.[48]

After the success of *Less than Angels*, Dooley launched his Buffalo Irish-American trilogy. *Days Beyond Recall* (1949) is about the fictional Shanahan family, a large Irish Catholic family in Buffalo's First Ward at the turn of the twentieth century. One book critic wrote that Dooley "has the gift of the true storyteller" and complimented his "galloping prose."[49] *The House of Shanahan* (1952) takes place during the Roaring '20s, following Rose (Shanahan) Crowley and her extended family as their way of life in the Irish First Ward started to unravel. About *Gone Tomorrow* (1960), the final book in the trilogy, one reviewer remarked that "the events of this Buffalo-Irish family grip the interest of the readers, [and] the tumultuous tale of this family steeped in tradition and Irish pride make this book a memorable one."[50]

When Dooley was not writing, he was teaching at Canisius College, until he left in 1952. He moved to New York City, completed his Ph.D. in literature at Catholic University, and taught in New York City. In 1964, Dooley became the Dean of Humanities at Manhattan Community College, teaching film and literature until 1985.[51] In 1981, he published *From Scarface to Scarlett: American Films in the 1930s*, the definitive book on Hollywood movies from that era, arguing that the 1930s was the golden age of American film. Dooley served as president of the Shakespeare Club of New York and was a member of the prestigious PEN America organization.

In 1963, Joseph M. Hassett, a Canisius College student in Buffalo, won the St. Patrick's Scholarship to attend summer school in Ireland, which took place at University College Dublin (UCD) and the Yeats International Summer School in Sligo. While in Ireland, this young man acquired a passion for Irish literature, especially William Butler Yeats. Decades later, this experience led to one of the most important cultural exchanges between Buffalo and Ireland.

Hassett is a third-generation Irish American; all his great-grandparents emigrated from counties Clare and Cork. His mother's family, the Meegans, settled in the First Ward, while his father's family settled east of Buffalo.[52] Hassett was raised in North Buffalo and attended Canisius College, where Professor Charles Brady introduced him to Irish literature. But it was Hassett's summer school trip to Sligo that ignited his passion for W.B. Yeats. Hassett graduated from Harvard Law School and became a successful corporate and securities lawyer in Washington, D.C., all the while nurturing his love for Irish literature. In 1981, during a work sabbatical, Hassett received an M.A. in Anglo-Irish Literature from University College Dublin; four years later, he earned a Ph.D. in the same subject from the same university.

In 1986, Hassett published *Yeats and the Poetics of Hate*, an account of how Yeats used hate, especially ancestral hatred, as a source of creativity. He followed up with his acclaimed *W.B. Yeats and the Muses* (2010), making the case that nine dynamic women inspired Yeats's poetry. In *Yeats Now: Echoing Into Life* (2021), Hassett provides the reader with "a guide to living" focusing on the poet's themes of friendship, love, anger, and politics.[53] Hassett's *The Ulysses Trials: Beauty and Truth Meet the Law* (2016) focused on the controversy surrounding the publication of James Joyce's novel, *Ulysses*.

Hassett not only wrote about Yeats, he also collected memorabilia and rare books related to the poet. He wanted to "recover these bits of the visible past" to share them with future generations.[54] In 2013, Hassett donated his large Yeats collection to his alma mater, University College Dublin (UCD). The *Joseph Hassett Collection* at UCD contains a significant collection of 20th and 21st-century Irish poetry, numerous signed copies of W.B. Yeats's first-edition books of poetry, and essential manuscripts related to the women who inspired Yeats. The same year, UCD curated an exhibit, "W.B. Yeats and His Muses," incorporating many pieces from Hassett's donated collection. Hassett also supports an annual Yeats lecture at the National Library of Ireland in Dublin to commemorate Yeats's birthday.

The Buffalo native has been recognized for his significant financial contributions toward restoring Thoor Ballylee, a 14th-century tower in County Galway that had fallen into disrepair. This Hiberno-Norman tower, sometimes called Yeats' Tower, is where the Nobel prize-winning poet spent twelve years writing some of his most important poems. Irish poet Seamus Heaney once referred to Thoor Ballylee as the most important building in Ireland due to its association with Yeats. Thanks to Joseph Hassett and other benefactors, the site is a thriving cultural center.

In Buffalo, Hassett and his family created the first Hassett Family Reading series at Canisius College in 2003. In the inaugural year of the series, Irish-American author William Kennedy entertained a crowd of Buffalo literary enthusiasts. Since then, sixteen Irish-American and Irish authors and poets have spoken to packed audiences at the Montante Cultural Center in Buffalo. Literary giants such as Nobel Prize-winner Seamus Heaney, Oxford historian Roy Foster, novelist Alice McDermott, Man Booker Prize-winner Anne Enright, and Colm Tóibín have inspired countless Buffalonians (for the complete list of speakers, see Appendix C). It has become one of the most important annual Irish literary reading series in the United States because it continues the "tradition of intellectual exchange between Ireland and the United States."[55]

Hassett also created the Mel Schroeder Memorial Scholarship, which sends two Canisius College students each year to the Yeats International Summer School in Sligo. With the Irish Classical Theatre Company (ICTC), Hassett collaborated on a performance called *The Yeats Project*. He also created a CD of Yeats's poetry with the ICTC's then-artistic director Vincent O'Neill and singer Mary Ramsey.

Hassett has been praised on both sides of the Atlantic for his legal and literary work. He was one of ten recipients of Ireland's 2022 Presidential Distinguished Service Award for the Irish Abroad. The *Irish Voice* newspaper regularly selects Hassett as one of the 100 best Irish-American lawyers. Irish Professor Roy Foster declared, "Joe Hassett possesses a rare ability to bring a close, meticulous, and inspirational focus on the reading of literary texts, notably the poems of W.B. Yeats; in a series of original and elegant books, his insights have explored the ways that modern Irish writing clarifies and illuminates the national mind."[56] Irish poet Theo Dorgan added: "What may not be so apparent, to those who have not the pleasure of knowing him, is that Joe is the epitome of decency, a witty, large-hearted and generous man, possessed of a wise and discerning mind, a copiously stocked memory and an unquenchable enthusiasm for doing good."[57]

South Buffalo Writers—Stephan Talty and Richard Blake

Stephan Talty is one the most prolific Buffalo-born writers who is relatively unknown in his hometown. As a *New York Times* best-selling author of a dozen nonfiction books and several works of detective fiction, Talty's acclaim grows each year. He was the ghostwriter for *A Captain's Duty* (2011), about the story of the *Maersk Alabama* container ship hijacked by Somali pirates. Tom Hanks starred in the award-winning film, *Captain Phillips* (2013), which was based on Talty's book. The movie rights to another Talty book, *The Black Hand*, have been purchased by Leonardo DiCaprio. The novel is a page-turning tale about one Italian police officer's courageous efforts to stop the Black Hand Society, a vicious criminal enterprise.

Talty's parents, immigrants from County Clare, arrived in the United States in the 1950s. Vincent Talty, Stephan's father, a construction tradesman, worked on the massive St. Lawrence Seaway project. The senior Talty later met his future wife, Brigid (O'Neill) Talty, at an Irish dance; they married and settled off Seneca Street in South Buffalo.[58] His immigrant parents felt at home in South Buffalo because, as Talty notes, "it was an Irish place," with "a connection to the old country in the faces and the names and the music."[59]

After earning degrees from Bishop Timon High School and Amherst College, Talty started his writing career as a newspaper reporter for the *Miami Herald*. As a freelance writer, the Buffalo native wrote articles that have appeared in *The New York Times*, *The Irish Times*, *GQ*, and the *Chicago Review*. Talty's literary inspirations in high school were F. Scott Fitzgerald and J.D. Salinger.[60] But as time passed, he discovered a love for narrative nonfiction books, such as Erik Larson's *Devil in the White City*. Talty emulates authors like Larson, who have a gift for writing gripping narratives.

Talty's *Empire of Blue Water* (2007) is an enthralling tale about Henry Morgan, the swashbuckling 17th-century Caribbean pirate who changed the course of the English and Spanish empires. Twentieth Century Fox purchased the movie rights to his book *Saving Bravo: The Greatest Rescue Mission in Navy Seal History* (2018), about a Navy Seal who goes behind enemy lines to rescue a captured pilot during the Vietnam War. His recent book, *The Good Assassin* (2020), shares the thrilling 1965 mission of a small group of Mossad agents who tracked down and assassinated the "Butcher of Latvia." Talty claims the unifying theme in his books is "one individual or small group of individuals who go up against larger forces and change history."[61]

Stephan Talty described his hometown of South Buffalo as a "two-fisted, sharp-witted working-class neighborhood" and "an intense, colorful, memorable space."[62] Those memories from his youth provided material for his thrilling detective novel, *Black Irish* (2013), whose protagonist, Abbie Kearney, is a misfit detective investigating a serial killer with ties to South Buffalo. Talty portrays Buffalo in a dark light and South Buffalo as clannish and closed to outsiders. Talty is currently the most prominent Buffalo Irish-American writer on the national stage.

Richard Blake, also from South Buffalo, has enjoyed considerable success writing about Western New York topics. Blake graduated from Canisius High School and earned a degree in journalism at St. Bonaventure University. He is a freelance financial journalist in New York City. Blake's Irish roots are from County Clare, and his father played an integral role in preserving the Buffalo Irish Center. Blake's most recent book, *Slats: The Legend and Life of Jimmy Slattery* (2015), is a page-turning biography of a Buffalo boxing legend. Blake also wrote a local favorite, *Talking Proud* (2005), about the 1980 Buffalo Bills' electrifying season and its uplifting impact on a downtrodden city.

Other Irish writers associated with Buffalo include Paul Horgan and Robert Creeley. Paul George Vincent O'Shaughnessy Horgan was born in Buffalo to an affluent Irish Catholic father and a mother of German descent. Like F. Scott Fitzgerald, Horgan attended Nardin Academy until age twelve, when the family moved to Albuquerque, New Mexico. A prolific writer of historical fiction and history focused on the Southwest, he published forty books. Horgan twice won the Pulitzer Prize for History: first, in 1955, with *Great River: The Rio Grande in North American History*, and second, in 1976, with *Lamy of Santa Fe*. The *New York Times* described him as a polymath, an accomplished painter and musician, and fluent in several languages. While some critics considered him one of America's top-ranked twentieth-century writers, others argue that he focused too narrowly on the Southwest and Catholic subjects.[63] Horgan received a papal knighthood from Pope Pius XII for his work with the Catholic Church.

Robert Creeley was born in Arlington, Massachusetts and lost his father at a young age. A bright student, he attended Harvard, where the school magazine published his first poem. In 1954, noted poet Charles Olson invited Creeley to join the faculty at Black Mountain College in North Carolina and edit the *Black Mountain Review*. Creeley was also associated with literary giants such as Allen Ginsberg and Robert Duncan. The University of Buffalo's English department hired him to teach poetry in 1967, and he remained there for thirty-seven years. Creeley published more than sixty books of poetry, winning several prestigious prizes, such as the Bollingen Prize. He was the New York State Poet Laureate from 1989 until 1991. In his poem, "Theresa's Friends," he reveals his excitement when his mother informed him, when he was twenty-one, that Creeley was an Irish name. His poems have appeared in several Irish-American anthologies, such as *The Book of Irish American Poetry* (2007). Creeley founded the University at Buffalo's Program in Poetics, and scholars consider him one of the most influential poets of the second half of the twentieth century. For a list of additional Buffalo Irish authors, see Appendix D.

Brigid Hughes—Literary Editor

In literature, literary magazines are indispensable for uncovering new voices and stories. One of the national stars in this realm is Buffalo-born Irish-American Brigid Hughes. She is the daughter of Patrick Hughes, a well-respected Buffalo neurologist, and Patricia Hughes, a research nurse. Brigid's father, a lover of poetry, was born and raised in Athlone, Ireland. Brigid grew up in "a family of readers and a house full of books."[64] She graduated from Nichols High School and earned an English degree from Northwestern University in Chicago. In 1995, at 22, she became an intern at *The Paris Review*, regarded by some as the most famous American literary magazine, and was later promoted to an editorial role. In January 2004, shortly after the death of legendary editor George Plimpton, 31-year-old Hughes succeeded him as the magazine's editor. She became the first female editor-in-chief of *The Paris Review* in its 51-year history.[65] After assuming the top position, her goal for the magazine was "to publish good writing, whatever form that takes."[66]

In 2006, after a decade at *The Paris Review*, Hughes left to become the founding editor of *A Public Space* in Brooklyn, New York. She chose Brooklyn because of its multitude of writers with fresh voices. Her magazine focuses on emerging writers from all over the world. Hughes has been described "as a discerning editor, a champion of unheard voices, and an advocate for international and boundary-breaking writing...."[67] Hughes and her team read thousands of manuscripts from writers who are unknown or yet to be discovered. They also publish established writers who want to take a risk that would not be possible with a commercial publishing house.[68] In Hughes's words, "The writers working away from the mainstream are often the most exciting ones."[69]

In her career, she has discovered or nurtured dozens of writers and launched at least two literary stars: Yiyun Li and Jesmyn Ward. *A Public Space* has also discovered or nurtured the careers of other award-winning writers, including Leslie Jamison, Amy Leach, and Dorthe Nors. She has published emerging writers such as Roxane Gay and Teju Cole. *A Public Space* also has a publishing arm under the same name. The book division recently brought out the critically-acclaimed *Calm Sea* and *Prosperous Voyage* (2019) by Bette Howland.

In 2018, *A Public Space* won the inaugural Whiting Literary Magazine Prize. "It stands as a paradigm of what literary magazines can be: a gorgeously curated collection we experience as a cabinet of wonders."[70] Hughes herself received the PEN/Nora Magid Award for Magazine Editing. Although based in Brooklyn, Hughes has not forgotten her hometown. With journalist Ed Park, she co-edited a popular book of short stories, titled *Buffalo Noir*, by Western New York authors. She also returns to speak at schools and universities. Undoubtedly, Brigid Hughes will continue to uncover and nurture new writers for years to come.

Kevin O'Callahan and Philip Burke—Artists

Irish artists, much like writers, were in short supply in nineteenth-century Buffalo. Buffalo's first renowned artist was a well-off son of a medical doctor. Kevin B. O'Callahan was born to William H. O'Callahan, a Dublin-born physician who settled in Buffalo in 1890, and Patronella O'Callahan, a housewife and watercolorist. The O'Callahans lived on Niagara Street on Buffalo's West Side with a cluster of other upper-middle-class Irish families. After graduating from Technical High School, Kevin O'Callahan attended Carnegie Institute of Technology in Pittsburgh to pursue an engineering degree. After two years, he realized he wanted to become a commercial artist, so he moved to New York City.[71] There, he experimented with fantasy watercolors infused with ideas from Irish mythology and Oriental motifs.[72] After several years in New York, the budding artist returned to Buffalo to live with his mother. Like the poet James N. Johnston, who was discussed earlier, O'Callahan was a lifelong bachelor who dedicated his life to his art. Around 1930, O'Callahan discovered a passion for printmaking. Primarily self-taught, he was obsessed with the process of producing high-quality prints. Within a few years, his work attracted national acclaim from experts who appreciated the quality of detail in his art.[73] O'Callahan's primary subject was industrial scenes, ubiquitous in Buffalo.

O'Callahan's wood engravings of grain elevators and Buffalo River industrial scenes are highly valued. His *Lakeport Landscape* (1936) was chosen for the "Exhibition of Contemporary American Art" at the 1939 New York World's Fair.[74] This engraving exemplifies his complete mastery of recreating a complex industrial scene. The image contains railroad cars, concrete cylindrical grain storage bins, brick office buildings, wooden shacks, industrial cranes, and a wooden dock. His masterful engraving transports a contemporary viewer to Buffalo's industrial age. Shortly after the World's Fair, O'Callahan's *Lakeport Landscape* was exhibited at the Paris Exposition in France.

The Buffalo artist was not limited to industrial scenes. O'Callahan's etchings of Buffalo backyards and streetscapes are particularly evocative. He also recreated scenes from rural Western New York with images of barns and bridges. However, he is most remembered for his 1930s and '40s shipbuilding engravings. His maritime engravings of the complex geometric forms of the hulls of ships, with shadows of light and darkness, exemplified that he was in an elite company of artists. O'Callahan completed a series of prints that traced the shipbuilding process from beginning to end, which one expert claimed was "unlike any other American industrial art."[75] The *American Prize Prints of the Twentieth Century* included one of his prints. O'Callahan once shared his passion for shipbuilding engravings. "It offers excellent possibilities for interesting patterns and more so, because it is something which is constructive. I do not like much of the present-day interest in destruction and decay."[76]

By the end of the 1930s, O'Callahan's prints dominated the Western New York art scene. He won prestigious art prizes, and museums and print clubs across the country featured his work.[77] Often, O'Callahan's prints glorified Buffalo's industrial strength. He and his contemporary Charles Burchfield both appreciated the beauty of the machine age.[78] O'Callahan refrained from using his art to make social commentary, with one exception. He used the title and subject matter of his 1936 print, *Pride and Prejudice*, to highlight the extravagant expense of the then-recently completed Buffalo City Hall building. The Art Deco-style building, built during the Great Depression, was one of the costliest city hall buildings in the nation. His engraving features the stately building juxtaposed with dilapidated homes in the foreground. The artist wanted city leaders to feel ashamed at such an extravagant expense when the urban poor suffered.[79]

O'Callahan's contribution to the Buffalo art scene went beyond his prints. In 1931, he was the primary organizer and founding president of the Buffalo Print Club.[80] The club aimed to share ideas and offer fellowship for those interested in printmaking. The Albright Art Gallery allowed the members to use its basement for gatherings and facilitated the shared use of printmaking equipment. Members of the club included some of Buffalo's best artists of the era: Niels Anderson, Rixford Jennings, Robert Blair, Catherine Catanzaro Koenig, and William Schwanekamp. O'Callahan remained the club's guiding force and president for twenty years.

In the 1950s, O'Callahan accepted a teaching position at the University of Buffalo's Engineering School. He also volunteered his time on radio and in print to educate the broader public about printmaking. About a decade later, his mother, Patronella, passed away, and he gave up his beloved printmaking craft. The Buffalo Print Club, which met in his home at 620 Niagara Street, also folded.

Andrew Wyeth, the well-known American artist, was a close friend and neighbor of O'Callahan when he summered in Thomaston, Maine. When Wyeth and his wife came to East Aurora to visit her family, the two artists found time to paint together. In a letter, Wyeth urged his friend O'Callahan to continue his art. "I consider your drawing the very best in the country."[81] But the encouraging sentiments were not enough to change O'Callahan's mind. O'Callahan retired from teaching in 1968 and lived as a recluse for his last ten years, dying in 1977.

Kevin B. O'Callahan's Buffalo Print Club helped foster the struggling local art community during and after the Great Depression. Nancy Weekly, a Burchfield Penney Art Center curator, claimed that O'Callahan was "perhaps the finest printmaker" in the Buffalo Print Club.[82] He was also considered "Buffalo's best-known graphic artist."[83] The quality of his prints stands the test of time. His shipbuilding prints are some of the highest quality of the American Precisionist movement.[84] Thanks to his work, current and future generations have a visual connection to Buffalo's industrial heyday. As one biographer commented, "O'Callahan presents a superb portrait of Western New York at the height of its industrial age."[85]

In 1988, the Burchfield Art Center published a book, *Kevin B. O'Callahan and the Buffalo Print Club*. It revived interest in this essential but forgotten artist. Around the same time that Kevin O'Callahan withdrew from Buffalo's art scene, another Buffalo artist was just getting started. His subject matter was nothing like O'Callahan's, and he would soar to even greater heights.

Philip Burke's work is widely recognized nationwide, but many don't know him by name. His portraits have appeared in dozens of major newspapers and magazines for four decades. Burke doesn't live in hip New York City or glitzy Los Angeles but resides in his working-class hometown of Western New York. Burke was born in 1956 in Tonawanda, just outside of Buffalo. His parents were Howard Burke, a lawyer, and Mary Burke, a mother of eleven children and a community and church volunteer. Philip Burke's great-grandfather, Joseph S. Burke, emigrated to Buffalo from County Mayo, arriving in the United States in 1868. Philip's great uncle, Joseph A. Burke, was the first and only native Buffalonian to serve as the Roman Catholic Bishop of Buffalo.

Burke lacked formal art training but, at a young age, had a gift for drawing. At age fifteen, while Philip was attending Calasanctius Preparatory School for gifted students, his father gave him a book of caricatures by the famous artist David Levine. Young Burke was immediately captivated. "When I was a teen, I wanted to be a rock star, but I couldn't play any instruments, and I was too shy to sing. So, I put my dream into painting and drawing rock stars."[86] His tireless efforts have paid off. One writer declared that Burke is now "a rock star among painters."[87] Another stated, "For rock music, Philip has been a sort of visual historian in a sense."[88]

During his teen years, Burke learned that cartooning was a way to express his frustrations.[89] As a student at the University of Toronto, he studied the experts of his craft, including Ralph Steadman and David Levine. Later, he studied fine artists such as Van Gogh and Matisse. It was Picasso, though, who "knocked his socks off." Burke lists the Spanish artist as one of his heroes, and one can see some of Picasso's style in the Buffalo artist's work.

Burke's first job was at the *Buffalo Courier-Express*, where he contributed a weekly cartoon. After a short stint at the *Courier*, in 1977, he headed to New York City to attend art school. But a fortuitous meeting with David Levine changed his plans. Levine convinced him to skip art school, and go right to work.[90] Burke agreed. Slowly, Burke received requests for his drawings from the *Village Voice* and the *New York Times*. He initially drew his caricatures in black and white but experimented with color sketches. In 1982, the Buffalo artist took a leap—painting with oil. Around this time, Burke ran into Andy Warhol, who told him he admired his work. Burke asked if he could paint the legendary Pop artist. Warhol agreed. It took Burke a few years to complete the painting, but it is one of his finest works.

Burke's big break came when *Vanity Fair* magazine offered him a multi-year contract. *Vanity*'s executives granted him the freedom to experiment with his work.[91] This experience allowed him to hone his distinctive style. One critic characterized Burke's early style as an "acerbic, expressionistic style of cartooning, which at times is hilariously funny while always confrontational."[92] He noted, "I used to want to scare people, I wanted to give them a start by being as grotesque as possible." Burke's drawing style was "violent, his imagery was shocking, and his wrath was deep-seeded and forceful."[93] He wanted to elicit a reaction from people. But this style of art was not what he wanted to produce. So, instead of focusing on his subject's external appearances, he tried to reveal their internal persona or soul. Revealing the complexities of the individuals he painted became his new mission. "Caricature is dealing with masks. I'm now showing what's behind the mask."[94]

With a steady income from *Vanity Fair*, Burke returned to Buffalo, married and started a family.[95] Around this time, he turned to Buddhism, which he claimed improved his drawing process. Buddhism gave him "a sense of freedom and confidence that I didn't have before with so many things."[96] His chanting technique allowed him to turn anger into joy, positively impacting his work. In 1989, *Rolling Stone* magazine hired Burke as a featured artist, where he flourished for seven years. Burke painted or drew many of the famous musicians of the time: Bono, Madonna, Miles Davis, Jerry Garcia, Mick Jagger, Ray Charles, and David Bowie, to name a few. He is often associated with rock & roll from his time at *Rolling Stone*, but his scope is much broader.

Burke's work has appeared in many of the nation's major newspapers and magazines, such as *Time, Newsweek, The New Yorker, GQ, Sports Illustrated* and *The New York Times*.[97] In addition to rock stars, he has painted politicians, movie stars, athletes, literary icons, and other celebrities. Burke rarely painted his subjects live. Instead, he used more than a dozen photos, taken from different angles, of a given subject to find the expression he wanted to transfer to the canvas.

Prominent art galleries across the country, from Beverly Hills, California, to Baltimore, have exhibited Burke's work. In 2006, Cleveland's Rock & Roll Hall of Fame displayed a collection called *The Color of Rock: The Art of Philip Burke*. The show then traveled across the country, further broadening interest in the Buffalo artist.

For Burke, one of his most important exhibitions was in Buffalo. In 2015, the Burchfield Penney Art Center curated a massive exhibit of his work called *The Likeness of Being: Portraits by Philip Burke*. The museum displayed more than seventy-five of his most well-known works. Giant canvases of Princess Diana, Senator Hillary Clinton, President George W. Bush, Kurt Cobain, Bob Marley, The Beatles, Muhammad Ali, Bill Murray, and Audrey Hepburn covered the museum's walls.

The show was also a catalyst for his involvement in the local arts scene, where Burke met local musician Robby Takac of the Goo Goo Dolls, who put him in touch with the local music scene.[98] Burke started a live painting event at music concerts at Artpark in Lewiston, New York—stationing himself a few feet from the stage, painting the musicians as they performed in front of packed crowds.

Burke raffled off some of his artwork to raise funds for the park. In 2019, he partnered with Zoom, a local printing company, to brighten up a commercial district in North Buffalo. Burke's painting of the Goo Goo Dolls was adapted into a massive 24 x 48-foot mural on the side of a building at the corner of Hertel Avenue and Lovering Avenue. A few years later, Burke added murals of Snoop Dogg and Patti Smith on a Main Street music venue.

Burke's art has made an impact both locally and globally. He has allowed people throughout the world to see our cultural icons and politicians, famous and infamous, in a new light. His work encourages the viewer to get past the façade and see his subjects' complexities, helping us better understand the world around us.

CHAPTER EIGHT

Journalism and Media Stars

When it comes to the news business in the modern era, Irish Americans have left their mark. But this was not the case in earlier times. In the mid-nineteenth century, most Buffalo newspaper publishers disliked the Irish and viewed them as a ragtag lot. And opportunities for the Irish to work as reporters and editors were limited. It wasn't until the end of the nineteenth century that the Irish secured senior leadership positions in local newspapers. Even then, it was rare. By the second half of the twentieth century, however, the Buffalo Irish had a disproportionate influence in the field of journalism. As native English speakers, they had an advantage over some other immigrant groups, and they descended from a Celtic tradition that valued storytelling. Like politics, journalism gave them the power to address societal ills.

Early Irish Catholic Newspapers

When Bishop John Timon arrived in Buffalo in 1847, he understood that he could not change the editorial bias of the nativist Protestant newspapers. So he started his own newspaper. In 1852, Timon lured Thomas D'Arcy McGee to Buffalo from Boston, where McGee was the editor of the *American Celt*. Timon and a few dozen priests pooled their money to launch this new Buffalo paper, and in return, they wanted editorial control over church issues. McGee acquiesced and changed the paper's name to the *American Celt and Catholic Citizen*.

Before McGee emigrated to the United States, he was a prominent leader in the 1848 Young Irelander Rebellion in his native land. After the failed uprising, which sought the repeal of the union between Ireland and the United Kingdom, the British authorities issued his arrest warrant for high treason. Disguised as a priest, McGee escaped from his native land and arrived in the United States later that year. The Famine profoundly influenced him. In an 1848 speech in Dublin, he explained, "My heart is sick at the daily scenes of misery. I cannot endure this state of society longer. The towns have become one universal poorhouse and fever shed, the country one great graveyard."[1] After arriving in the United States, McGee was shocked to see people from this once-proud Celtic race relegated to "waiters at hotels...shovelers of earth-works, carriers of mortar-spades and axes, tools and tackle, for other men's uses."[2]

From his office on Washington Street in downtown Buffalo, he attacked the English and the bigoted American nativists. He saved much of his venom for the *Commercial Advertiser*, which often disparaged the Irish. McGee set out to show that the Celtic people were not inferior to the Anglo-Saxons. McGee partnered with Bishop Timon to enhance the Irish intellectual life in Buffalo. Both men spent tireless hours writing articles and giving lectures, encouraging the Irish to improve themselves through education. In 1852, with the help of some other prominent Buffalo Catholics, McGee founded the Catholic Institute.[3] It housed a library and a meeting space for lectures where members were encouraged to debate the issues of the day. He helped launch a local chapter of the Irish Archaeological Society to promote the illustrious history and culture of the Irish.[4]

Over time, McGee grew impatient with how long it took for news to travel from Europe and the Eastern United States to Buffalo.[5] So, in 1853, he moved to New York City. He eventually became disillusioned with the United States and moved to Montreal, where he became one of Canada's Fathers of Confederation, or founders of Canada. Thomas D'Arcy McGee, one of the most eminent Irishmen ever to reside in Buffalo, accomplished much in his short time here.

In 1872, Timon's successor, Bishop Stephen V. Ryan, launched a new diocesan paper, the *Catholic Union*—later called the *Catholic Union and Times*. Diocesan newspapers played a dual role: countering bigoted attacks from the secular press and teaching Catholics their doctrine and dogma. Ryan selected a gifted communicator, Father Patrick Cronin, as the paper's editor. Cronin used the paper to advocate for Irish issues, particularly independence from the English. Born in 1835 in County Limerick and a survivor of the Famine, Cronin studied in Adare, Ireland, before emigrating to the United States with his father. In 1862, he was ordained a priest in St. Louis, and eight years later, he became the chair of Latin at the College and Seminary of Our Lady of Angels, later called Niagara University.

Cronin was fiery and full of blistering attacks toward bigoted writers and anti-Irish Catholic perpetrators. Even though he was courteous and cheerful, "he could utter sarcasm that stung; sharp words that wounded deep—when he thought himself justified."[6] Nationally, Cronin gained a reputation as a brilliant prose writer and an accomplished poet. A gifted orator, Father Cronin was remembered for his eloquent sermons and memorable speeches.[7] In 1880, he hired Katherine Eleanor Conway, an Irish Catholic woman, as the assistant editor of the Catholic Union. Conway advocated for women's education but not women's suffrage. She was almost certainly the first Irish Catholic female editor of a Buffalo newspaper.

When Cronin died in 1905, after thirty-two years as editor, he was remembered as a "many-sided genius."[8] His newspaper's board of directors wrote, "The *Irish* people at home and abroad [lost] one of their most illustrious and zealous advocates."[9] Buffalo Bishop Charles H. Colton said, "The Rev. Patrick Cronin was a great man. He was a power in the church, not only in his own diocese...."[10] The *Catholic Union and Times* building was draped in mourning for thirty days.

After Cronin's death, his newspaper became a monthly publication, and the paper's importance diminished because Catholics were more accepted in Buffalo society. The Irish also started securing positions as reporters and editors at local newspapers.

Irish Newspaper Owners

The first Buffalo publisher with Irish heritage was Edward H. Butler, Sr. He was born in Le Roy, New York, to Dennis Butler and Lucy M. (Chaney) Butler, a Dublin-born immigrant. His father, who died when Edward was only six, co-founded the first Roman Catholic congregation in Le Roy. Edward and his three siblings were raised by their Irish mother, who worked as a laundress. Butler worked as an apprentice at the *Le Roy Gazette* and later as a reporter at the *Scranton Times*. He met and married Mary Elizabeth Barber, a descendant of wealthy Protestants. He converted to her Presbyterian faith and used his wife's family fortune to fund his future newspaper endeavors.[11] After moving to Buffalo, Butler successfully founded the *Buffalo Sunday News* in 1873. Seven years later, he transformed it into a daily paper and renamed it the *Buffalo Evening News*. By 1897, it boasted the largest sales of any newspaper in Buffalo.

Under Butler, the *News* became known "as a crusader on behalf of the city's underclass."[12] In 1874, the *News* was one of the first papers in the nation with a regular column focused on labor issues, and one of the only local papers that supported the workers during the Great Railroad Strike of 1877. Butler's paper also advocated for seamstresses who suffered from poor working conditions and low pay. While other local papers dismissed the Polish immigrants as lazy, Butler urged the government to assist these new arrivals, some starving and destitute.[13] Butler also advocated for closing the Hamburg Canal—a festering source of cholera and other diseases among the working class in the Canal District. By 1887, however, Butler had joined the Republican Party. After that, Edward Butler opposed the railroad strikers in 1892 and suppressed union initiatives in his newspaper.[14] From then on, the *Buffalo News* editors actively engaged in local and national Republican politics until the late 1970s.

In 1892, Buffalo Irish businessman William J. "Fingy" Conners purchased the *Enquirer*. Five years later, he bought the *Courier* and now owned two of the six major English daily Buffalo papers. In 1900, Conners hired Charles Bennett Smith as the *Courier*'s editor; this made Smith one of Buffalo's first Irish top editors. Conners, a Democrat, was elected chairman of the State Democratic Committee (1906-1910), and his paper's editorials leaned toward the interests of the Irish working class.

Conners eventually purchased the *Express*, his archrival, and merged it with the *Courier*, leaving the *Buffalo Times* as the only local English daily newspaper not owned by an Irishman.

Conners filled his newspaper management team with fellow Hibernians. His Irish general managers included William S. Bennett (1926-1937), Belfast native Eugene C. Murphy (1937-1942), Frank J. Clancy (1942-1956), A. Gordon Bennett (1956-1971), and Richard C. Lyons (1971-1974). Fingy Conners, his son (William Jr.), and his grandson (William III) all took turns as publisher and president. The *Courier-Express* also hired countless Irish-American journalists and editors.

Jack O'Brian—National Columnist

Only a few Buffalo Irish Americans have achieved national fame in journalism. John "Jack" O'Brian's *New York Times* obituary called him the "Columnist of the Entertainment World."[15] Jack O'Brian was born in Buffalo's First Ward in 1914 to Charles J. O'Brian and Josephine Loretta Kelleher. His grandfather, John Kelleher, came from County Cork to Buffalo "on the run" from the British, with "a price on his head."[16]

Like other famous First Ward men, young Jack was quickly introduced to the hardships of working on Buffalo's waterfront. After attending Our Lady of Perpetual Help, O'Brian dropped out of school at age 13. Later, he said, "he was too busy getting an education to go to school."[17] In addition to working dozens of day labor construction jobs, he also worked as a sailor and even a gravedigger. He once loaded one-hundred and two-hundred-pound bags of limestone into railway cars for ten hours a day.[18] "From the time I was a lad, I don't remember a job I ever held—except journalism—that didn't involve sweat and muscle, and pick and shovel."[19]

His father, an alcoholic, was a New York Central railroad conductor. His mother died when he was a teenager. "I was pretty much on my own, a teenager out of work more than not. I didn't even know I was homeless—I just knew I often for months was dead broke and I actually fainted three times, at least, from hunger."[20] Both of O'Brian's grandfathers were saloon owners in the Ward, so he was no stranger to the inside of a tavern.[21] O'Brian saw himself as a "barstool Irishman, and friend of First Ward cops and saloon waiters."[22]

At age seventeen, O'Brian started writing for the *South Buffalo News* and the *Catholic Union and Times*. Later, he excelled at writing for the *Bugle*, a newspaper that covered prominent Buffalo divorces. At the *Courier-Express*, he was nominated for a Pulitzer Prize for a story in which he uncovered a large-scale fraud with food rationing coupons during World War II. O'Brian relocated to New York City to work for the *Associated Press* and became one of the nation's leading critics of theater, movies, and radio.[23] His "Broadway" column was carried by 1,400 newspapers across the country. However, he wanted to be "the voice of the common folk, champion of decency, and fighter against soft-on-Communism liberals."[24]

In 1950, O'Brian started a column called "On the Air," where he became one of the nation's leading critics of television shows, actors, and news reporters. He was highly critical of many famous journalists and entertainers, including Steve Allen, Ed Sullivan, Danny Kaye, and Jackie Gleason.[25] O'Brian had many detractors who loathed his vitriolic style. The famous TV personality Steve Allen wrote that O'Brian "is the only TV critic in the nation who is rude, inaccurate, unchristian and vengeful," describing him as the "neighborhood bully" and "shockingly vulgar."[26] But O'Brian's readers loved it.

O'Brian helped expose the scandal on the NBC quiz show *Twenty-One*, leading to a Congressional hearing based on his reporting. The contestant in question, Charles Van Doren, admitted in the hearings that the show was fixed. O'Brian is, however, most remembered for his controversial anti-communist columns and even more controversial support of the Wisconsin senator Joe McCarthy and his chief counsel Roy Cohn. O'Brian made it his mission to expose reporters, actors, and other entertainers if he suspected they had communist sympathies. The CBS reporter Don Hollenbeck, renowned for his reporting during the McCarthy hearings, was one of O'Brian's primary targets. One author claimed that O'Brian was responsible for Hollenbeck's suicide.[27]

Jack O'Brian's unlikely rise from the saloons of Buffalo to being a nationally syndicated columnist was quite remarkable. While O'Brian was the first Buffalo Irish journalist on the national stage, he was not the last.

Tim Russert—Media Celebrity

"Florida, Florida, Florida." Those are probably the three most memorable words from the contentious 2000 US Presidential contest between Governor George W. Bush and Vice President Al Gore. Days before the election, *Meet the Press* moderator Tim Russert correctly predicted that the state of Florida would decide the election. On election night, as other networks used complicated graphics to explain how each candidate could reach 270 electoral votes, Tim Russert used a dry-erase board and simplified it for the viewers. As each state was called for a candidate, he would simply cross it out and show the remaining states in play and who needed which states to win. Finally, he wrote, "Florida, Florida, Florida." The winner of this contentious election would come down to the Sunshine State, as he predicted. Viewers were glued to Russert's coverage, and they later showered the network with compliments on how he had made the complex simple.[28] Russert later recalled that he was just channeling his father, a South Buffalo working-class guy, who used a legal pad to simplify the family budget.[29] But no one, not even Russert, could have predicted the hanging chad chaos that would ensue or the need for the US Supreme Court to decide the winner. For thirty-five days after the contested election, Russert captivated national viewers on NBC's *Today Show* with his political commentary and analysis. If Americans didn't already know Russert from *Meet the Press* fame, they knew him now.

Timothy John Russert was born in Buffalo on May 7, 1950. His hero was his father, Timothy Russert Sr., or "Big Russ." Big Russ dropped out of school in the tenth grade to fight in the Second World War, almost perishing in a horrific plane crash. He recovered and came home to Buffalo but never finished high school. For thirty-seven years, the senior Russert worked two jobs—as a truck driver and a sanitation worker—to put his four children through Catholic schools while Russert's mother stayed home and raised the children. Russert learned the values of hard work and integrity—attributes he was later renowned for—from his South Buffalo family and Catholic school education.

He had fond memories of South Buffalo, where he was surrounded by the descendants of the Irish immigrants who built the canals and railroads. He described South Buffalo as "a warm and tightly knit neighborhood where most people were Irish Catholics, and everyone seemed to know one another and each other's relatives."[30]

In an interview with *Irish America* magazine, Russert shared the importance of his Irish ancestry. Six of his eight great-grandparents were from Ireland, and the legendary Cork hurler, Nicholas "Christy" Ring, was a relative. His surname, Russert, is Alsatian—the small part of his heritage that was not Irish.[31] Ring and Gilhooley were among his Irish ancestors' surnames. In the interview, Russert teared up talking about the Famine-immigrant struggles and the difficult journeys that Irish Americans, like his family, endured.[32] When Russert was thirteen, one of his heroes, President John F. Kennedy, was assassinated. The Kennedy presidency was so important to Russert and Irish Catholics. Nothing seemed impossible anymore; the limits placed on the Irish were a thing of the past.[33]

When Russert was in the seventh grade at St. Bonaventure school, one of his teachers chose him to be the school newspaper editor.[34] It was his first experience in journalism. Later, Russert graduated from Canisius High School where he learned Latin, discipline, and the virtue of hard work. After high school, he worked as a sanitation worker and threw newspapers off the back of a *Buffalo News* truck. Russert was the first in his family to graduate from college and then law school. Eventually attracted to politics, he worked for Buffalo Comptroller George D. O'Connell, who ran a powerful political machine. Russert told the *Irish America* interviewer that not all aspects of political machines were corrupt, especially when they provided—like O'Connell did—for the needs of their constituents.[35]

In 1976, Russert's big break in politics arrived when Joe Crangle, Buffalo's Democratic boss, dispatched him to Manhattan to help Daniel Patrick Moynihan's fledgling campaign for the United States Senate. Crangle, who possessed astute political instincts, believed that the other Democratic candidates were too liberal, and that Moynihan had the greatest chance of winning in the general election. Russert recalled feeling intimidated by Moynihan's Ivy League staff and worried he might not fit in. Moynihan reassured his Buffalo staffer, "What they know, you can learn; but what you know, they will never learn. Remember, none of these guys has ever worked on a garbage truck." The future senator recognized that Russert had an understanding of people and a sense of decency for others that came from his South Buffalo upbringing.[36] These qualities would later serve him well in journalism.

After winning the election, Moynihan was so impressed with Russert that he named him head of his Buffalo office. Two years later, the senator promoted the 29-year-old South Buffalo lawyer to chief of staff—at that time, the youngest chief of staff in the Senate. In this role, Russert visited Ireland in 1980, meeting Irish Prime Minister Charles Haughey and John Hume, one of Northern Ireland's leading nationalist politicians. While there, he witnessed some of the horrors of the Troubles in Northern Ireland. Russert also played a pivotal role as a liaison between Moynihan and Buffalo mayors Stanley Makowski and James D. Griffin on issues from the Blizzard of 1977 to local redevelopment efforts. In 1983, Russert left Moynihan to work as a top aide to New York State Governor Mario Cuomo.

The following year, *NBC News* hired Russert for a position in their Washington news bureau; five years later, they promoted him to bureau chief. In December 1991, the Buffalo Irishman took over the reins as moderator of *Meet the Press*. Russert transformed the talk show into the most-watched Sunday news program, and the most quoted news show in the world.[37] As an innovator, Russert interspersed graphics, charts, and newspaper clippings into his interviews, making the program more interactive with his audience. Along the way, he set the gold standard for

Sunday political shows and became one of the country's most trusted interviewers and journalists. The *New York Times* claimed that Russert transformed the show "from a sleepy encounter between reporters and Washington newsmakers into an issue-dense program, with Mr. Russert taking on the week's newsmaker."[38] Former House Speaker Newt Gingrich said Russert "made *Meet the Press* probably the most important single policy hour in television in America."[39]

Russert appealed to ordinary Americans for several reasons. Many commented on his calm demeanor and unbiased cross-examination of both Republicans and Democrats. His love of politics and lawyerly obsession with getting at the truth appealed to viewers. His son, Luke Russert, has a few theories on America's love for his father. First, people perceived Tim Russert as an everyman, someone they could relate to and want to have a drink with. Second, he was able to make the most complex issues of the day simple enough that everyone could understand them. Third, he held politicians accountable, making sure they did not get away with lies or deception.[40]

Over the years, Russert interviewed hundreds of powerful politicians. Some of his memorable interviews included David Duke, a former Ku Klux Klan leader and candidate for Governor of Louisiana, whom Russert exposed as not qualified to govern his state; Ross Perot, candidate for US President, whose campaign derailed after Russert's questions on Perot's budget; and President George W. Bush, whom he questioned about whether the decision to invade Iraq was a "war of choice" or a "war of necessity." Howard Fineman coined the term the "Tim Russert Test," a grilling that aspiring politicians had to survive in order to seek higher office.[41] Not everyone, like David Duke or Ross Perot, survived it. Others found it akin to torture. After an excruciating Russert cross-examination, Senator John McCain proclaimed, "I hadn't had so much fun since my last interrogation in prison camp." At the end of every program, no matter how heated the debates, Russert, with his big Irish smile, would sign off, "That's all for today. We'll be back next week. If it's Sunday, it's *Meet the Press.*"

Russert won an Emmy Award, the Edward R. Murrow Award for excellence in television journalism, the Annenberg Center's Walter Cronkite Award, and the David Brinkley Award for Excellence in Communications. *Reader's Digest* chose him as America's best interviewer. In 2001, *Washingtonian* magazine called him the most influential journalist in Washington. In 2008, *Time* magazine named him one of the 100 most influential people in the world.

Russert loved Buffalo, and Buffalo loved him back. There was a hometown pride knowing that one of your own moderated the leading Sunday political show. Russert's best-selling memoir, *Big Russ & Me: Father and Son: Lessons of Life* (2004), focused on his Buffalo upbringing. He praised the teachers, friends, and mentors who nurtured him. But, of course, much of the focus was on "Big Russ" and the values he imparted to his son Tim. Although Russert's career sent him to Washington and Albany, he never forgot Buffalo. He believed that no matter where life takes you, you shouldn't be disloyal to your hometown. When he worked for Senator Moynihan, he observed that the New York City staffers lacked respect for Buffalo. Russert thought, "you aren't better than us," and argued that they shouldn't look down on the second-largest city in the state. That sentiment never left him.[43] He was also a loyal Buffalo Bills booster. An unabashed hometown fan, in good times and bad, Russert would sign off every *Meet the Press* national broadcast during football season with "Go, Bills!"

Russert was also generous to his hometown. He helped fund a park, not far from the public library he used to visit, on land that had been a derelict city lot.[44] The park contains a wooden statue of the famed journalist with a sign that reads, "Tim Russert's Children's Garden." Other memorials to Russert include a "Tim Russert Way" sign in South Buffalo at Woodside Avenue and McKinley Parkway, where he grew up. In 2008, President George W. Bush renamed a portion of Route 20 A outside of Buffalo—near the Buffalo Bills stadium—as Timothy J. Russert Highway. In West Seneca, on the border of South Buffalo along Indian Church Road, the town named its municipal park Tim Russert Park. In 2014, the Buffalo History Museum acquired Russert's NBC office from the Newseum in Washington, DC. Visitors in his hometown were able to view his desk, library, and Buffalo memorabilia, and it was one of the leading attractions at the museum.

When Russert died at the young age of 58, he was treated like a national hero. His sixteen years as host of *Meet the Press*, the longest ever, made him a fixture in many American homes, where as many as five million viewers tuned in to watch him weekly. Former television journalist Tom Brokaw praised his former friend, noting that from "the humblest of beginnings, he rose to one of the most powerful positions in journalism, always asking the questions the country wanted to ask and getting the answers the country deserved to know."[45] Bob Schieffer of *Face the Nation*, Russert's principal competitor on Sunday, claimed, "Tim was the best of the best, the best of our profession..."[46] Before his death, *New York Times* columnist Maureen Dowd heaped on the praise. "He [Russert] is absolutely the best, he does the most homework. In an era where everybody in the media is ahistorical and nobody knows anything, he knows everything. He's very Irish in the sense that he has no pretensions."[47]

Tim Russert was one of the most recognized Western New Yorkers of his time and will rank as one of the most prominent Buffalo Irish Americans ever. Of the political commentators in his era, especially on the Sunday news shows, Russert was unrivaled. At university commencement speeches, he reminded graduates that in America, success was not reserved solely for the Ivy League-educated or the wealthy, but rather open to the sons and daughters of working people and immigrants. With genuine joy and awe, he added, "What a country!" He did Buffalo proud.

The Irish Invasion of the Buffalo News

As with the *Courier-Express*, the *Buffalo News* started to hire Irish Americans to fill editorial positions at the start of the twentieth century. One of the first was Ed Scanlon, a family friend of the Butlers from Le Roy and the son of an Irish immigrant. Around 1900, Butler made Scanlon his Albany correspondent and liaison with the governor of New York and later promoted him to Western New York editor. By 1915, William O'Connell, a son of Irish immigrants, was the *News*' city editor, and Edward P. Hartnett was assistant city editor. Hartnett was born in the First Ward to an Irish immigrant father from County Cork. He was a star football player at St. Joseph's Collegiate Institute, where he played with the future World War I hero, William J. Donovan. Hartnett later became the executive city editor, a position he held until 1946. At a tribute before his death, civic leaders referred to him as "the king of newspapermen," and another paper reminded its readers, "There will only be one Eddie Hartnett, he has no equal, he has no peer."

The *Buffalo News* named their first Irish Catholic executive editor of the *Buffalo News* in 1966. His name was Paul Neville, and he spent his childhood in Ware, Massachusetts, not far from Springfield. Just before the American Civil War, all four of Neville's grandparents, survivors of the Famine, had emigrated to Ware from Ireland, three from County Limerick. None of them could read or write, but they found work in Ware's bustling cotton mills. Paul Neville graduated from the University of Notre Dame in 1942 and served in the Ninth Air Force in Europe during World War II. After the War, he worked as the chief political reporter at the *South Bend Tribune* and eventually became its managing editor.

The *Buffalo News* recruited him in 1957 to serve as the assistant to the editor, and the following year he was promoted to managing editor. In 1966, Neville replaced Alfred H. Kirchhofer—one of the most prominent twentieth-century Buffalo newspapermen—as executive editor. The two men couldn't have been more different. Kirchhofer, the son of a German immigrant, was a fastidious and austere man who was deeply involved in local and national Republican Party politics. Unsurprisingly, during Kirchofer's nearly four decades as an editor, the *News* endorsed only Republican presidential candidates.[48] Conversely, Neville was a charismatic and affable Irishman who stayed out of party politics. But on a trip to Ireland, he endeared himself to local residents by distributing a bag full of Kennedy half dollars.

Besides being a brilliant newsman, Neville was also a Buffalo booster and was active in bringing a professional football team to Buffalo. In 1959, through a mutual friend, Neville was introduced to Detroit businessman Ralph Wilson, who was reluctantly interested in starting an American Football League franchise in Buffalo. During their meeting, which included a visit to War Memorial Stadium, Neville promised his full personal and civic support for a team. Wilson remembered Neville as an enthusiastic football fan who delivered a solid and convincing sales pitch of how the city would support a new team. In a 2009 *Sports Illustrated* article, Wilson explained that when he met with Neville, Wilson asked for the *News'* support if he brought a team to Buffalo. Wilson recalled, "I told him [Neville] I'd give the city a franchise for three years if he promised he'd write about us every day. He said yes, and that was it."[49] Citing Neville's efforts at helping to secure the Buffalo Bills, *News* columnist Bob Curran made the case in 1998 that Paul Neville belongs on the Bills' Wall of Fame.[50]

In his short time at the helm of the *Buffalo News*, Neville was also instrumental in adding a lively arts page to the paper and improving the coverage of Buffalo's Black community. Believing that a newspaper should be an instrument to help citizens get things done, he created a column called "NewsPower" to assist people who were struggling to resolve consumer complaints with companies.[51] This successful column, which ran for twenty-four years, resolved countless problems for readers. After Neville's death of a stroke in 1969, at age 50, his legacy continued. There is an annual scholarship in his name at the University of Notre Dame: *The Paul Neville Award for Excellence in Journalism*. And in 1985, his son, John P. Neville, was hired by the *Buffalo News*. The younger Neville was hired as a copy editor, promoted to assistant managing editor of the news desk, and later promoted to editorial page editor.

While Paul Neville was editor, three South Buffalo Irish Americans, born three years apart, were climbing the management ranks at the *News*. South Buffalo native William J. Malley, a gifted newspaper editor, became a copy editor at the *News* in 1966, and, within a few years, he was elevated to assistant news editor. In 1977, Malley became the first editor of *The News* Sunday magazine.

Malley, described as a perfectionist, was tasked with several significant innovations at the paper, in addition to the Sunday magazine. In 1980, he became assistant managing editor and later supervised the rollout of the Sunrise edition—a new morning paper to fill the void after the closing of the *Courier-Express*. In 1987, he was promoted to deputy managing editor and was given a more challenging task: a complete redesign of the newspaper. Malley's boss credited him with guiding the paper into the twenty-first century. He was responsible for several new ideas such as the suburban edition and the 'Spotlight' page.[52]

Edward L. Cuddihy, close in age to Malley, was hired as a reporter at the *News* in 1962 and, over four decades, worked his way up to managing editor. Cuddihy also wrote a colorful book about the Jaeckle Fleischmann law firm called *The Merging of Titans* (2008) and co-authored *On the Canal* (2004) about the Battle of Guadalcanal. At his retirement, he was remembered for his integrity, respect, and fairness over his four decades at the *News*.[53]

The third Irish American under Neville was John Patrick Quinn, Jr., the son of South Buffalo New York State Assemblyman John P. Quinn, Sr. After graduating from Canisius College, Quinn Jr. worked briefly at the *Courier-Express* and, in 1967, became a reporter at the *Buffalo News*. For almost thirty years, Jack Quinn worked at the *News*, where he was eventually promoted to night city editor. As a reporter, he was a finalist for a Pulitzer Prize for a series developed after he was embedded undercover with the Buffalo Police Department. The paper's editor, Margaret Sullivan, described Quinn "as the classic city editor with a sometimes gruff and sardonic manner balanced by his strong sense for a good story, and a core of true kindness."[54]

Pioneering Female Editor

Margaret Sullivan is a trailblazing Buffalo Irish-American woman and one of the most remarkable journalists, Irish or otherwise, to spring from Western New York. She was born to John J. Sullivan Jr. and Elaine Saab and grew up in Lackawanna, New York. Sullivan graduated from Nardin Academy and credited Joanne Langan, her English instructor, as the person who encouraged her to get involved with the student newspaper.[55] After graduating from Georgetown University, she added a master's degree from the prestigious Northwestern University's Medill School of Journalism. She was then offered internships at both the *Courier-Express* and the *Buffalo News*. Her father suggested she choose the *News* because it was the city's dominant paper. The *Courier* folded two years later, in 1982.

Margaret Sullivan has a mix of Irish and Lebanese heritage. Her Irish roots in Buffalo go back to at least the mid-nineteenth century and her great-grandfather, Cornelius Sullivan. Both her father and grandfather were prominent local attorneys. About her Irish heritage, Sullivan said she believes that her father's "literary sensibility, verbal gifts, quick wit and quiet spirituality came from that source [his Irish heritage]. And I hope that I have inherited some small measure of these through him—or at least an abiding appreciation of them."[56]

In 1980, after Sullivan's internship at the *Buffalo News*, she was hired as a full-time reporter. She was promoted to assistant city editor and elevated to assistant managing editor of the *Lifestyles* and *Features* sections in 1989. Murray Light, the executive editor of the *News*, said at the time that Margaret Sullivan rose to senior editor faster than anyone in the history of the paper. In January 1998, she became the *News'* first female managing editor. On the day of the announcement, she received a standing ovation from her fellow journalists and remembered it as "one of the great thrills and honors" of her life.[57]

The following year, Sullivan was named the first female top editor of the *News* in the paper's 120-year history. At age forty-two, she was the youngest female editor of a major daily in the nation.[58] Two years later, she was named the paper's first female vice president, a job she held for thirteen years. In the top spot at the *Buffalo News*, Sullivan focused the paper's reporting on poverty, economic development, and public education. She also focused on creating a more diverse staff and promoting minority journalists.[59] In addition, Sullivan established the paper's first investigative team and helped develop its successful website.[60]

In 2012, Sullivan left the *News* to become the first female public editor of the *New York Times*. In this position, reporting directly to the publisher, Arthur Sulzberger, Jr., she served as an independent watchdog for the newspaper. The Buffalo native ensured that the *Times'* reporters were ethical and followed the highest journalistic standards. Her job was to advocate for the *Times'* readers while sometimes being critical of its journalists. In 2016, at her departure from the *New York Times*, Sulzberger heaped praise on Sullivan and wrote that she had "ushered the position [public editor] into a new age."[61]

Sullivan left the *Times* to work directly for the publisher of the *Washington Post*, Marty Baron. As the *Post's* media columnist, she wrote about media trends, like the shifting of news to platforms such as Facebook and the collapse of local news departments. Sullivan left the *Post* to become a media and politics columnist for *The Guardian* and, as of 2024, was the executive director of Columbia University's Center for Journalism Ethics and Security.

While Sullivan lives in Manhattan, she returns to her family cottage south of Buffalo each summer. In 2020, she authored a well-reviewed book, *Ghosting the News: Local Journalism and the Crisis of American Democracy*. The book captures the decline of the newspaper business, especially local news reporting, and explains how the rise of the internet and digital media led to massive cuts in journalists and loss of advertising revenues. Sullivan often draws on her years as the editor of the *Buffalo News*, noting that there are now half the number of journalists at her former paper compared to when she took the reins.[62] Journalists, however, are not the only victims. Nationally, there are two thousand fewer newspapers than there were in 2004. The long-term prospects for most newspapers, in her opinion, are tenuous without new sources of revenue. Sullivan argued that with fewer newspapers, there are negative consequences to our democracy, including corruption and abuse of power. Her book outlined several solutions to the decline in newsrooms, including experimental models such as Buffalo's non-profit *Investigative Post*.

Sullivan has received several local and national awards. In 2006, *Buffalo Spree* magazine listed her as one of the top ten most powerful Western New York women.[63] The following year, she was inducted into the Western New York Women's Hall of Fame. Her alma mater, the University of Northwestern University's Medill School of Journalism, inducted her into its Hall of Achievement, and the prestigious Pulitzer Prize Board invited her to be a member. In 2017, at the annual Buffalo Nite in Washington, DC, Sullivan was awarded the celebrated "Charging Buffalo" Award. This award goes to someone whose career connects Buffalo to the nation's capital. She is in good company with previous winners, such as Wolf Blitzer and the late Tim Russert.

After Sullivan departed from the *News* in 2012, the tradition of having an Irish American as top editor continued. Sullivan was replaced by Michael K. Connelly, an Iowa native, who came from the *Sarasota Herald-Tribune*, where he led the paper to a Pulitzer Prize. Connelly's focus has been on local news, and his general philosophy about news reporting is "Good news organizations help people make sense of the world. Tell them things they don't know that matter to them." He believes journalists should "reach up into that ocean of information washing over all of us and flush out the eight, ten, or twelve things that add up to something important in our community and our lives."[64]

Prominent Buffalo News Columnists

Margaret Sullivan wasn't the only trailblazing Irish American female journalist. Karen Brady learned the craft of writing from her father, Charles A. Brady, Canisius professor and chief book critic for the *News*. At age fourteen, after watching an episode of *Superman*, she declared that she wanted to be Jimmy Olsen.[65] The ambitious young girl called the *News* asking for an interview with the then editor, Alfred H. Kirchhofer, and he obliged. At 17, she began as a copy kid at the *News*, working summers, weekends, and holidays while also attending Rosary Hill College (now Daemen College), where she majored in English literature and was editor of the school paper. In 1960, she was one of three local college students selected to participate in the inaugural St. Patrick's Scholarship exchange to study Irish history and culture at University College Dublin. Later, she continued on her own to the first Yeats International Summer School on the West Coast of Ireland, sending stories of her overseas adventures via telegram to the *News*.

Years later, Brady was accepted to the country's leading journalism school, the Columbia University Graduate School of Journalism—she was one of a small group of women admitted into a mainly male program. After graduating, she spent three years as an assistant editor at a Manhattan-area publishing house before returning to Buffalo and the *News* as a general assignment reporter. Two years later, Congressman Richard "Max" McCarthy recruited her as his press secretary in Washington, DC. After only one year in Washington, the *News* called her back home.

This time, Brady was given her own weekly column, "From This Side of 30," and—two years later—her own full-time general subject column, the award-winning "Karen's Korner." She was the first woman given such a column at the *Buffalo News*; Margaret Sullivan was the second. Brady's columns focused on women's rights, Buffalo history, the cultural scene and working motherhood (she is the mother of three daughters). Her colleagues of the time included Irish Americans Terry Doran, the arts editor and guiding force for the Gusto section, and John Dwyer, the talented and much-loved classical music critic. She also covered social justice issues. After she wrote about a local group associated with California labor leader Cesar Chavez, editor Paul Neville suggested to Brady that "you are a champion of the underdog." In Brady's words, she "made it something of a mission in 'Karen's Korner' to take the road less traveled, go to the places we didn't usually go, and interview the people we didn't often stop to talk to."[66]

Her reporting on Buffalo's Black community led to an exclusive interview with Rosa Parks, which she says was her most memorable interview.[67] Incidentally, Brady's sister, Kristin, worked as a copygirl for the *News* before she became an internationally-known scholar of Victorian literature. After meeting with *News* publisher Kate Robinson Butler, Kristin Brady was instrumental in getting the paper to include Black brides on the wedding page, where they had been excluded.

Karen Brady's articles on women's rights focused on married women who, at the time, were still forced to take their husbands' surnames and were stigmatized if they worked, particularly after bearing children. Murray Light, the longtime *Buffalo News* editor, singled out Brady for "having paved the way" for future female reporters, and having a "fine career as a reporter and many years as a popular columnist..."[68] After over forty years at the *News*, Brady retired in 2002 but wrote book reviews until late 2017. Throughout her career as a journalist, she dignified those who were often overlooked.

In 1967, Paul Neville recruited a reporter who became one of the *Buffalo News'* most beloved columnists. His name was Bob Curran. For thirty-two years, Curran wrote a column for the *News* called "Curran's Corner." According to John Neville, the former *News* editor, Curran occasionally wrote about famous or well-connected people, but more often than not, he wrote about ordinary people in Western New York, many of whom volunteered their time to improve the lives of others.[69]

Robert "Bob" Curran was the son of Irish immigrants who settled in Boston. Curran graduated from the prestigious Boston Latin school, where he excelled on the debate team and the football field. He attended Cornell, where he also played football, before enlisting in the Army during World War II. As a platoon sergeant in the Army Rangers, Curran fought valiantly throughout France, Belgium, and Germany. General George S. Patton recognized his heroism and awarded him the prestigious Combat Infantryman Badge.[70] Wounded twice, Curran also earned two Silver Stars, two Bronze Stars, and a Purple Heart.

After the War, Curran finished his degree at Cornell and then worked for an advertising agency in New York City. Before coming to Buffalo, he was a syndicated columnist. In 1961, he made national news by uncovering the Australian man who had rescued John F. Kennedy during the PT-109 disaster in World War II. Curran tracked down Reginald Evans, the Australian coast watcher, and coordinated a White House visit so Kennedy could formally thank his rescuer. At the event, the press took a photo of President Kennedy, Curran, and Evans, and it appeared in countless papers across the country.[71]

The previous year, Curran made national news with a story about an American war hero with tax troubles. In his article, "The Desertion of Sgt. York," he reported that the US government was pursuing Sergeant Alvin York, a World War I Medal of Honor recipient, for back taxes. Meanwhile, the government gave a tax break to an unnamed wealthy athlete. Curran ran an article about this injustice, galvanizing President John F. Kennedy and Speaker of the House of Representatives Sam Rayburn to rectify the situation. Later, Curran received a handwritten note of gratitude from the war hero.[72]

When Curran wasn't working as a journalist, he was writing books. He wrote seven of them, including *The Kennedy Women* (1964), which profiled eight of the most influential women in the famous Boston clan. Curran also wrote *Spiro Agnew: Spokesman for America* (1970), a glowing biography of Richard Nixon's vice president, arguing that he should lead America. Agnew, of course, resigned three years after the publication of Curran's book, the result of an investigation into kickbacks he received as Governor of Maryland.

Shortly after Curran arrived in Buffalo, he fell in love with the Queen City and became one of its biggest boosters. He was also a popular speaker at civic and fraternal organizations across Western New York, which further endeared him to the public. In addition to writing about the ordinary people in Western New York who improved our community, Curran also wrote passionately about veterans' issues. In his articles, he often added the phrases "say a prayer for our guys Over There" and "hang tough." He also enjoyed writing lighter columns for St. Patrick's Day.

When Curran died at age 80 in 2003, *News* editor Margaret Sullivan exclaimed, "Bob Curran was an institution in this community and one of the best-loved and best-read writers in *The News*' history."[73] For more than three decades, he shared inspiring stories that helped us better understand ourselves and our community.

Labor, Politics, Religion, and Irish Issues

In the middle of the twentieth century, tens of thousands of Western New Yorkers who toiled in steel mills, automobile plants, grain and flour mills, and other industries belonged to labor unions. J. Edmund Kelly—Ed Kelly, to most—started reporting on labor issues for the *News* in 1949 and, for over forty years, had a front-row seat to the rise and fall of unions. The son of a local attorney and grandson of an Irish immigrant, Kelly graduated from St. Joseph's Collegiate Institute and Canisius College and received a Master of Science degree from the Columbia University Graduate School of Journalism. After college, he started working at the *News* covering state politics in the newspaper's Albany bureau.

Kelly's column, "Labor Comment," was "a must-read for Western New York's hundreds of thousands of working men and women who counted on Mr. Kelly to cover the labor beat and report on how it affected their lives."[74] Margaret Sullivan, then editor of the *News*, described Kelly as "an old-fashioned, hard-working, shoe-leather reporter who was scrupulously fair and even-handed." Sullivan cited the fact that he was respected by people on both sides of labor issues as a testament to his journalistic ability.[75] His big Irish smile, warm personality, and passion for reporting on labor issues contributed to his success.

As Kelly's career with labor ended in 1983, another Irish American was just getting started. Robert J. McCarthy owned the political beat at the *Buffalo News* for almost three decades after replacing George Borrelli in 1992. McCarthy had roots in Schenectady and Auburn, New York where his parents worked for the American Locomotive Company. Four of his grandparents emigrated from Ireland. His paternal grandfather, John McCarthy, arrived in Troy, New York, from County Cork—and was killed in a workplace railroad accident in the same city. McCarthy's maternal ancestors came from County Tyrone in Northern Ireland. So green and orange were the colors in his house.[76]

Like many other local media professionals, McCarthy graduated with a journalism degree from St. Bonaventure University. After writing for the college newspaper, he accepted a position at the *Olean Times-Herald* and stayed there for five years. In 1982, the *Buffalo News* hired McCarthy as a general assignment reporter. His first assignment was writing "cops and robbers" stories. Early in McCarthy's career at the *News*, he worked with another McCarthy, Richard "Max" McCarthy, who covered politics as the Washington bureau chief.

At a public lecture, McCarthy recalled his early memories working at the *News*. The newsroom was a noisy place the size of a football field, with a cloud of smoke and endlessly ringing telephones. "There was nothing like it, and I am glad I experienced it." In terms of local politicians, McCarthy thought former Congressman Jack Quinn was the best of all of the politicians he covered on the campaign trail.[77] He also praised Kathy (Courtney) Hochul as a talented campaigner. When asked about the late Mayor James D. Griffin, he replied, "What a beauty!" McCarthy added that he liked Griffin, but because of his association with Borrelli—whom Griffin hated—the mayor treated him with suspicion.[78] Throughout his career, McCarthy stayed true to one of his guiding principles when writing his column: keeping politicians honest.

The *News* often hired Irish Catholics to report on religious matters. Richard J. Burke, born in 1915, grew up on Buffalo's West Side when it was still a predominantly Irish neighborhood. His Irish heritage, which he traced back to County Kilkenny, was important to him throughout his life.[79] After the Second World War, Burke became the news director for WBEN-Radio and WBEN-TV. Later, Burke switched from the *Buffalo News'* radio and television division to their newspaper. There, he worked as a religion reporter covering Vatican II in Rome and Pope Paul VI's address at the United Nations in 1965. He also wrote a weekly nature column. Burke won a New York State Associated Press award in 1972 for a series of articles on bicycling in Western New York. After his 1977 retirement from the News, he carved Irish walking sticks and wrote poems and one-act plays. His grandson claimed he "was forever trying to understand what it meant to be Irish-American."[80]

Another popular writer on the religion beat was David Condren. His paternal great-grandparents came from Ireland, and his grandfather made a living as a farmer in Niagara County. Condren, who grew up in Newfane, studied to be a priest but dropped out after three years. His newspaper career started in 1960 at the *Lockport Union Sun and Journal,* but he wound up at the *Courier-Express* three years later. At that paper, he covered the ill-fated domed stadium in Lancaster, New York, and the plans for the Metro Rail system.[81] He also reported on the explosive growth of the towns of Amherst and Clarence.

After the *Courier* closed, the *Buffalo News* hired him, and he worked there for twenty years, mainly as the religion writer. He primarily focused on issues of the Roman Catholic Church, including the trips of Pope John Paul II to the United States and the conferences of the US Catholic bishops. The Catholic Diocese of Buffalo presented him with the St. Paul Award for his reporting on the local church. Condren stayed connected to his Irish heritage as a member of the Ancient Order of Hibernians. Known for his extraordinary wit, Condren wrote his own obituary with a note attached to it that stated, "Hi. Here is an outline for my obit. Don't screw it up too badly."[82]

Unsurprisingly, the *News* often assigned Irish reporters, such as Anne Neville and Barbara O'Brien, to cover stories in the Irish hotbeds of South Buffalo and the Southtowns. Anne Neville, originally from Albany, came to Western New York with her husband and former *News* editor, John Neville. Anne Neville has a predominately Irish heritage, including that of her mother, who was part of the Haggerty family; her maternal ancestors emigrated from County Mayo. Her other Irish ancestors included the Brennans and Byrneses. Raised "culturally Irish," she became involved with Irish causes at 17. A priest inspired her to join the James Connolly Irish Republican Club in the Albany area. The club was named for the former union advocate and leader of the 1916 Easter Rising. Neville was part of a group that secured a commemorative plaque at Connelly's former home in Troy, New York, where he lived briefly before returning to Ireland.

Neville became president of the Connelly Club and was involved with Irish republican clubs throughout the United States, leading a tour for other clubs to Belfast during the Troubles. Over the years, she supported efforts to improve civil rights for Catholics in Northern Ireland. At the *News*, Neville wrote Irish-themed articles on topics such as the disputed date of the inaugural Buffalo St. Patrick's Day parade and reports on new Irish immigrants in Buffalo. In recent years, she and her husband generously donated a sizable collection of Irish republican newspapers, pamphlets, and posters, as well as photos, letters, and membership cards to the Glucksman Ireland House in New York City. Part of their collection was a gift to the State University of New York at Albany. Locally, the Irish-American couple helped in the planning and building of the Irish Famine Memorial on Buffalo's waterfront.

The Legendary Billy Kelly

There is a strong tradition of Buffalo Irish sports journalists, starting with Billy Kelly. William J. "Billy" Kelly was born on July 4, 1879 in Bergen, New York, a one-hour drive east of Buffalo. His father, William H. Kelly, was an electrician, and his mother, Anna (Kirk) Kelly, was the daughter of two Irish immigrants. When Billy was six, the Kelly family moved to Buffalo. After graduating from St. Joseph's Collegiate Institute, Kelly worked as a Western Union messenger boy and then, in 1900, the *Courier* hired him. He covered the assassination of President William McKinley and the trial of Leon Czolgosz. In 1902, he penned his first sports column, and he was hooked.

Billy Kelly became a force in the world of sports. His "Before and After" column in the *Courier* was a must-read. His columns were well-written, noted for their breezy style and loaded with news hot off the press. Even the great Yankees manager, Joe McCarthy, who won seven World Series, asked Kelly to break the story of his retirement from baseball. But Kelly didn't just write about sports; he immersed himself in them. Horse racing was his favorite sport, and he was a longtime placing judge at Fort Erie Race Track, just over the Canadian border; he even had a Kentucky yearling named after him.[84] In 1918, this horse was rated the top two-year-old gelding in America.[85] It was favored to win the 1919 Kentucky Derby but finished second to Sir Barton, who went on to win the Triple Crown.[86] Kelly, who attended the Derby, was thrilled to hear his name called out at Churchill Downs, but even more delighted when his $1,500 bet paid out.

If horse racing was closest to his heart, boxing was where he made his money and fame. Kelly helped bring legalized boxing to Western New York.[87] In the 1920s and '30s, Kelly was president of the Queensberry Athletic Club (Q.A.C.), a local private boxing club promoting major fights in Buffalo. In the 1920s, prizefighting was illegal in New York, so investors formed private clubs with dues-paying members to skirt the law.[88] In 1918, Kelly took a gamble by inviting the relatively unknown Jack Dempsey to fight at Buffalo's Broadway Auditorium. Kelly pitted Dempsey against a massively built boxer named Carl Morris, who was favored to win. Dempsey dominated his worthy opponent, and Kelly implored other promoters on the East Coast to sign Dempsey.

The following year, Dempsey won the World Heavyweight Boxing Championship and remained champion until 1926. Dempsey returned to Buffalo several times to fight for Queensberry-sponsored bouts, including defending his heavyweight title on July 24, 1922. The champ, a lifelong friend of Kelly for supporting him in 1918, gave the Q.A.C. boxing club the rights to the films of his fights, and he returned to Buffalo for numerous charity events. Covering almost all of Dempsey's title fights, Kelly built a national reputation. Wire services often published Kelly's well-written columns over his competitors' because Kelly's always came in first.[89]

Jimmy Slattery, a local favorite boxing champion, was also fortunate to have Kelly as his promoter. When Slattery was eighteen years old, Kelly wrote a column predicting that Slattery would be a future champion. Over the years, he wrote glowing articles about this Irish-American boxing upstart, trying to protect Slattery from the gossip about his drinking. Kelly's Q.A.C. co-sponsored Slattery's fights, such as the sold-out February 10, 1930 slugfest against Lou Scozza, which some have called Buffalo's "Greatest Fight of the Century."[90] Slattery won the bout, and Kelly and his partner split 25 percent of the ticket sales.[91]

Kelly traveled with the Buffalo Baseball Club for nine seasons. In the summer, when Kelly wasn't writing, he was golfing. He helped organize Buffalo's Newspaper Men's Golf Association, which he led for fifteen years, winning the championship tournament three times. A regular vacationer in Florida, Kelly started Buffalo Day at the Biltmore Country Club in Miami, which annually attracted 150 Buffalonians. Kelly also brought roller derby to Buffalo after seeing it first in Miami.

For fifty years (1904-1954), Kelly was a larger-than-life sports editor for the *Courier* and *Courier-Express*. During those years, he covered many national championship boxing matches, sixteen World Series, and most Kentucky Derby races. He promoted a host of sports and brought major boxing bouts to the area. He also furthered the careers of two boxing champions—Dempsey and Slattery—neither of whom ever forgot Kelly. It is unlikely that Buffalo will ever see another sports editor the likes of Billy Kelly.

The Other Sports Writers

Columnist Jim Kelley was five when Billy Kelly retired. But he likely heard of the legendary *Courier* columnist whose last name was so close to his own. Jim Kelley grew up in South Buffalo and attended Bishop Timon High School, where one of his teachers allegedly told his father, a Buffalo fireman, that his son was not college material. Kelley proved him wrong by graduating from Canisius College with an English degree. Prior to college, Kelley worked at the *Buffalo News* as a copy boy, where he used to refer to himself as a "kid from South Buffalo," proud to write for his hometown paper.[92]

Like fellow South Buffalonian Tim Russert, Kelley was relatable and well-liked. Out-of-town hockey general managers even shared confidential information with him.[93] "Jim Kelley could talk to anyone. Hockey executives, arena workers, players and the guy at the end of the bar...."[94] Another sports writer said, "Kelley had a gift of finding the essence of the contest and bringing it home to the reader."[95] At the peak of his career, Kelley's readers patiently waited for his Sunday column to get the latest sporting news.

Kelley became a legendary hockey writer. Starting in 1981, he covered the National Hockey League and the Buffalo Sabres, including twenty-three Stanley Cup Finals series for the *News*. Kelley also wrote for *Sports Illustrated* and ESPN. com. He also found success in radio, becoming one of the preeminent hockey voices of his era. In 2002, *Hockey News* proclaimed him one of the "100 People of Power and Influence in Hockey."[96] ESPN named him one of the top five hockey writers in North America. In 2004, Kelley was inducted into the Hockey Hall of Fame.

Kelley died of pancreatic cancer at the young age of 61. In 2011, the Buffalo Common Council renamed a section of Washington Street, between the *Buffalo News* building and the then First Niagara Center (the Sabres' arena), as Jim Kelley Way. Fellow Irish American columnist Mike Harrington, who took over Kelley's column, declared, "This is forever Kelley's space. He created this column. I'm just its current keeper."[97]

In recent years, the *Buffalo News* hired several other Irish Americans to write sports, including Jerry Sullivan, Michael Harrington, Bucky Gleason, Mark Gaughan, Keith McShea, Ryan O'Halloran, and Katherine Fitzgerald. Jerry Sullivan—known as Sully to some—started at the *News* in 1989. His Irish great-grandfather, a laborer from County Kerry, settled in Newport, Rhode Island in about 1890. Sullivan's father was a fireman, and his grandfather was a policeman.

Growing up listening to his beloved Boston Red Sox on the radio, Sullivan aspired to be a sports broadcaster.[98] After college, he worked for several newspapers, including New York's *Newsday*. Next, Sullivan decided to try Buffalo. He worked as the backup columnist to Larry Felser and, within a few years, was a regular on local sports radio station WGR 550, hosting a weekly one-hour radio show for two decades.[99] In 2001, after cultivating a loyal readership, he became the *News'* Buffalo Bills columnist—one of only thirty-two lead NFL columnists in the country. For many of Sullivan's years covering the Bills, the team was terrible or mediocre at best. His columns were highly critical of the owners, executives, and some of the players. Some felt his criticism was too biting, but many fans were glad someone held the team's leadership accountable. After three decades, he left the *News* for another opportunity.

The sports writer from Buffalo with the largest national following, however, is probably Erik Brady, brother of the aforementioned *News* writer Karen Brady. Erik Brady worked for the *Courier-Express* and, at age twenty-six, was the youngest lead sports columnist in Buffalo. When the *Courier* closed in 1982, he found a job at the fledgling *USA Today* and relocated to the Washington, DC area. He worked at *USA Today* as an enterprise sports writer until 2019. That year, Brady was the last of the founding members of that paper to retire. After retirement, he wrote a regular column for the *Buffalo News* from his home in Northern Virginia. Brady has retained his love for Buffalo. When once asked why Buffalonians, like him and Tim Russert, are so proud of their hometown, he replied, "Buffalo isn't where I'm from. It's who I am."[100]

The list of other Irish-American reporters and editors is too long to include, but they shouldn't be forgotten, so they can be found in Appendix E.

Television Journalists

The Western New York Educational Television network, known as WNED-TV, was created in March 1959. In the early years, Irish American J. Michael Collins was the publicity manager, and he eventually became the station's manager. Over the course of his forty-year WNED career, the pioneering broadcaster spent thirty-one years as the chief executive officer, leaving a lasting imprint on the station. He was a masterful fundraiser and marketer who appeared on countless pledge drives. Collins also presided over the station's move to its current headquarters at Horizons Plaza—"a monument to his ability to get things done," according to *News'* media columnist Alan Pergament.[101]

A visionary, Collins expanded programming to attract Canadian viewers in Southern Ontario. By 1988, forty percent of the $5 million in public contributions came from Canadians.[102] Collins expanded the organization from one television station to a conglomerate of two television stations and three radio stations. He also presided over two nationally syndicated programs: *The Mark Russell Comedy Specials* and *Reading Rainbow*.[103] At the time of his retirement, he was the longest-serving CEO at a single station in Buffalo. Thanks to Collins's efforts and those of his team, more than 1.5 million people in Western New York and Southern Ontario tuned in to enjoy WNED programs each week.

Kevin O'Connell started his career in journalism about a decade after Collins joined WNED. O'Connell comes from a prominent local Irish-American family: his late father George was the former Buffalo Comptroller and an important local Democratic politician, and his sister, Mary Kate O'Connell, founded O'Connell & Company. After graduating from Buffalo State in the mid-1960s, Kevin O'Connell started working in radio before transitioning to television at WBEN in the 1970s. In 1982, he moved to Los Angeles to work as a newscaster and a game show host, for which he won several awards. But after eight years, Buffalo pulled him back.

In 1990, WIVB-TV hired O'Connell for its noon broadcast with Jacquie Walker and, within a year, it attained the highest rating of any news show in Buffalo history.[104] WGRZ-TV lured him away, and he worked as their chief weather anchor for twenty-five years, always showing up with his giant Irish smile, rain or shine. WGRZ's general manager praised the Buffalo Irishman: "His broadcasting talents and body of work are among the best Buffalo has seen." He added that O'Connell was a prominent reason that the news station went from last place to the top spot.[105] According to *News* columnist Alan Pergament, O'Connell's popularity with viewers is due to his likable personality and his generosity—he has volunteered countless hours helping raise over $19 million for local charities.[106] O'Connell will be remembered as one of Buffalo's most popular and beloved weather forecasters.

Buffalo was home to several other noteworthy Irish-American television journalists. Pete Gallivan started as a reporter for WGRZ-Channel 2 in 1996. For nearly three decades, the award-winning television journalist was a mainstay at that station, serving as the weekend anchor and a co-anchor of the acclaimed "Daybreak" show, Buffalo's number one morning program. At the same station, Kevin O'Neill, a Buffalo native, has worked as a meteorologist and reporter for nearly two decades. Prior to that, O'Neill was an admired reporter known as the "Why Guy" on Channel 4's early morning *Wake Up!* program.

While not a recognized face on local newscasts, South Buffalo's Kevin Cusick had a successful national television career. Cusick, a Buffalo State College graduate, was a longtime producer for ESPN. The seven-time Emmy award winner made a name for himself with his coverage of the Olympics and the Tour de France. He also produced hundreds of sports telecasts for many of the major networks and a documentary, *The History of the African American Athlete*.[107]

South Buffalo was also home to MaryLynn Ryan, who helped shape one of the largest online news networks. Ryan, the daughter of Tom and Marjorie Ryan, graduated from Canisius College and worked for local television news stations. In 1995, CNN hired Ryan to produce a successful program called *CNN TalkBack Live*. In 2002, she became managing editor of CNN/USA, responsible for the daily editorial decisions. Two years later, she became the Southeast regional bureau chief for CNN, managing the coverage of news stories such as Hurricane Katrina, the Deepwater Horizon oil spill, and the shooting of Trayvon Martin. After twenty-five years at CNN, Ryan left to become the Vice President of News for Georgia Public Broadcasting.

Radio Journalists

Irish Americans were also prominent on local radio. John Murphy, who had one of the most recognized voices in Western New York, was the longtime announcer for the Buffalo Bills Radio Network. Tens of thousands of fans were captivated by his game-day announcing during the highs and lows of the Bills for four decades. He also worked as a sports anchor on local network television and as the play-by-play voice of the Buffalo Bisons. National audiences may recognize Murphy from his appearance in the 2003 movie *Bruce Almighty*, starring Jim Carrey.

John Murphy was raised in a prominent family in Lockport, New York. His paternal ancestors came from County Mayo and settled in Lockport in the 1890s.[108] His father, Matthew Murphy Jr., was a beloved New York State Assemblyman, referred to as a "gentle giant" and described as a "big-smiling Irishman." Constituents remembered him for his tireless support for people in need and local Niagara County causes, including the Lockport Community Soup Kitchen.[109] The assemblyman played a significant role in launching the "I Love NY" tourism campaign and was instrumental in establishing the 400-mile Seaway

Trail. He also spearheaded a monument in Lockport dedicated to the forgotten Irish canal workers. The city of Lockport recognized him by naming one of the bridges over the Erie Canal "Matt Murphy Way."

Matt's son John Murphy started a career in radio after majoring in broadcast journalism at Syracuse University. In 1982, he hosted a successful radio show with two colorful Buffalo Bills, Fred Smerlas and Jim Haslett. Two years later, he was named the sports director for WBEN-AM and, in the same year, became the color commentator for the Bills, working side by side with announcer Van Miller. In 2004, Murphy became the Buffalo Bills play-by-play announcer after Miller's retirement. Local television producers recognized his talent and hired him for their newscasts. WKBW-TV Channel 7 promoted him to sports director, but rival WIVB-TV Channel 4 lured him away. In 2012, he left for a full-time position with the Buffalo Bills. The Buffalo Broadcasters Association inducted John Murphy into their Hall of Fame, declaring, "John Murphy is a name that needs almost no explanation—he is synonymous with Buffalo sports, especially WNY's pride and joy, the Buffalo Bills."[110]

Mike Desmond was another Irish American who had a successful radio career. Desmond's Irish paternal ancestors arrived in Buffalo before the Civil War.[111] Desmond's father, Edward, was one of the lead lawyers in the legendary *Tewksbury* legal case, and his uncle, Charles S. Desmond, was the Chief Judge for New York State. After starting his career at the *Courier-Express* in the 1970s, Mike Desmond became a reporter with WBFO radio, where he worked for more than three decades. Desmond, one of the most recognized voices on local radio, covered thousands of stories about science, business, the environment, and education.[112]

Digital and Other Media

Local Irish journalists have also left their mark on regional and national financial reporting. James "Jimmy" Collins, Mike McKeating, and Bill Flynn each served a stint as financial editor of the *Buffalo News*.[113] Jack Connors, raised in South Buffalo, was the founding editor of *Business First*, Buffalo's premier business journal. His paternal ancestors came from Counties Cork and Kerry and settled in Scranton, Pennsylvania. Like many other Irish immigrants and their descendants, his grandfather and great-grandfather were coal miners. His father's family eventually came to Western New York from the Scranton area to work at the Lackawanna Steel plant, later Bethlehem Steel.

To put himself through Canisius College, Connors worked for one of the local steel companies. At the *Courier-Express*, he became assistant city editor before the paper folded in 1982. After a two-year stint as the *Niagara Gazette*'s news editor, Connors was hired by *Business First*, a start-up business newspaper, in 1984.

Within two years, the paper named him publisher and president. *Business First* thrived and expanded under Connors' leadership with the acquisition of the *Buffalo Law Journal* and its successful transition to digital publishing. Connors considers himself a Buffalo booster and is pleased that his paper contributed to Buffalo's recent renaissance.[114] After forty-five years in the news business, including thirty-three at *Business First*, Jack Connors retired in 2017.

Jim Heaney, a former *Buffalo News* award-winning investigative reporter, has Irish roots from Northern Ireland.[115] After graduating from Medaille College, he went to work at the *Orlando Sentinel*. Returning to Buffalo, Heaney founded a small neighborhood newspaper before becoming a reporter for the *News*. In 1993, he was a finalist for a Pulitzer Prize for reporting on slum housing.[116] Heaney also wrote a five-part series on the state of all seventy-two Buffalo schools, which was one of the most comprehensive series in the history of the paper.[117] While at the *News*, he was also a leader of the Buffalo Newspaper Guild, advocating for journalists and media workers.

In 2012, after twenty-five years at the *News*, Heaney launched a successful media company called *Investigative Post*. Margaret Sullivan, his former boss at the *Buffalo News*, recently wrote that Heaney's unit is "a small but impressive news organization that concentrates on holding public officials accountable."[118] With colleagues like Geoff Kelly, the former editor at *The Public* and *Artvoice*, the *Investigative Post* has exposed important civic matters such as corruption in government contracts, the most serious of which was the bid-rigging scheme linked to the "Buffalo Billion" economic development program. Heaney uncovered that the contract was structured in a way that intentionally favored one of Governor Andrew Cuomo's most prominent donors. As a result of his reporting, several people were convicted and sentenced to prison. Throughout his career, Heaney has advocated for the poor and the voiceless and has held people in power to account for corruption and misdeeds.

Local Irish-American journalists sought to help those in need, uplifting the downtrodden and working to improve their communities. Their thirst for justice likely stemmed from the less-than-warm welcome their immigrant ancestors received when they came to Western New York. Bigotry and prejudice against the Irish, fueled by nativist newspaper publishers, led to grave injustices on their forebears. These talented writers and reporters rose to positions of power and influence locally and nationally. Using their natural gift for language and love of storytelling, they have often wielded this power to improve the lot of those who are voiceless or marginalized.

CHAPTER NINE

Policticans

The Irish and Politics

More than any previous immigrant group, the Irish mastered the political system and used politics to improve their condition. One historian explained that although the transition from rural farm communities in Ireland to urban areas in America was difficult, the Irish were remarkably quick to reorganize themselves:

> Within a generation they translated their numbers into control of the Democratic Party in the major cities and turned municipal patronage into an immediate and pragmatic method for softening the ravages of boom-and-bust capitalism.[1]

> They [Irish Americans] used the Democratic Party the way they used the Catholic Church, as a rallying point and redoubt, a place in which they gained the resources and discipline to recover from the shattering dislocation endured in their mass exodus from the ancient, familiar patterns of rural life to the freewheeling, winner-take-all environment of urban America."[2]

Unlike other ethnic groups who were content being members of the Democratic Party, the Irish grabbed hold of the party leadership and never let go. The Irish were "given to politics," and no other ethnic group made the same contribution to the building of urban machines.[3] By the 1890s, the Irish were so proficient at the political game that they controlled most Democratic Party organizations in Northern and Midwestern cities.[4] Buffalo was no exception.

Former US Congressman Richard "Max" McCarthy from Buffalo suggested that "the political life seemed to come naturally to the Irish. They seemed to have a built-in faculty for shaking hands, speech-making, and for rallying people to a cause."[5] The fact that most spoke English gave them an advantage over non-English speaking fellow immigrants such as the Germans, Poles, and Italians.[6]

In Buffalo, the Democratic Party doled out civil service jobs, so if you were Irish and not independently wealthy, you stayed loyal to the Party. But the clever Irish built political machines for both major political parties, ready to grab patronage jobs and monies, regardless of which party was in power.

The Scoundrels—The Sheehan Brothers

In 1843, Buffalo's First Ward voters elected Irishmen Patrick Smith as their alderman and Patrick Milton as First Ward Democratic chairman. This election marked the start of Irish dominance in this district. Decades later, in this same First Ward neighborhood, John and William Sheehan, two sons of Irish immigrants, built Buffalo's first political machine. Their parents, William and Hanora Sheehan, from County Cork, settled on Elk Street in the First Ward. William Sr. was a railroad contractor and engineer who lost considerable money during the Civil War and was forced to become a day laborer.

John C. Sheehan, born in 1848, secured a clerical position at a local railroad office after his schooling. Later, John studied law and opened a practice on Franklin Street. But politics—and the power that came with it—was his real ambition. John, with the help of his younger brother, William, would shape Democratic politics across New York State for several decades.

John was tall, somewhat slender, and handsome. One biographer described him as having a "gentlemanly character, which readily disarms opponents and wins him hosts of friends."[7] In the autumn of 1877, at age 29, John was elected as the city's comptroller. Four years later, he lost his position because a neophyte politician, Grover Cleveland, decided to run for mayor to fight the corruption in city politics. But Cleveland refused to run on the Democratic ticket with Sheehan.

[After considerable urging for him to] reconsider, Cleveland sent word that he might—not definitely, just might—run if the devious and corrupt Democratic "boss" John C. Sheehan, who was seeking the second-spot office of comptroller, was bounced from the ticket. This posed a problem: Sheehan was the boss of the voter-heavy First Ward, a primarily working-class Irish constituency. Besides, he was the ringmaster of that year's nominating circus.[8]

John Sheehan was so confident that Cleveland would lose and that the reform movement would fail that Sheehan removed himself from the ticket.[9] The Sheehan machine encouraged Timothy J. Mahoney, a loyal friend, to run for comptroller in John's place on the Cleveland ticket. Meanwhile, the Sheehan brothers were quietly trying to derail Cleveland's candidacy by encouraging the Irish to vote for his Republican opponent, Milton Beebe. Despite the machine's efforts, the Irish overwhelmingly voted for Cleveland, and he defeated Beebe.

Timothy Mahoney won the comptroller job and quickly discovered that his friend John Sheehan had left office with money that belonged to the city.[10] After a series of missteps to cover up his embezzlement of city monies, and with overly complicated efforts to repay it, John Sheehan began to realize that he needed a fresh start. So in 1885, he moved to New York City and immersed himself in Tammany Hall politics, which was the primary engine for political advancement for Irishmen in New York City.[11] This former First Warder quickly rose in the Tammany leadership and was selected as Police Commissioner of New York City in 1892, even though many knew of his financial scandal in Buffalo. The unscrupulous Sheehan also drew a substantial salary at a law firm, even though he never tried a case in court. He also served as a partner for a contracting firm that obtained massive contracts for building projects in Long Island City.[12]

In 1892, the same year he became police commissioner, Sheehan founded a Tammany Hall political-social organization called the Pequod Club in New York City's Tenderloin District.[13] As president of the club, Sheehan explained that the club's purpose was to increase the political participation of club members. In actuality, it was a front for Sheehan and his friends to fleece members. For instance, Sheehan coerced neighborhood saloon owners to donate to his annual fundraiser. In return, he instructed his police captains to ignore drinking establishments that operated illegally on Sundays.[14] In testimony, Sheehan admitted that pool hall owners paid police for protection, but claimed he had no idea what happened to the money. Eventually, these shenanigans led to the 1894 Lexow Committee, which investigated Sheehan and others suspected of police corruption. When Sheehan refused to hand over the club's financial documents and list of members, the committee indicted him, threatening him with a one-year imprisonment.[15]

As in Buffalo, the authorities in New York City accused Sheehan of fraudulent election practices. While under investigation, he ordered the ballot clerks in his district to give out amended ballots with only *his* preferred candidates listed on them. Sheehan claimed that the clerks were permitted to hand out the entire ballot if someone requested it.[16]

At the start of the investigation, Richard Croker, the head of Tammany Hall, who became a multimillionaire from receiving bribes from prostitution, gambling, and saloon profits, fled New York City to his vacation home in Ireland. He stayed for three years until the inquiry concluded. While Croker was away, Tammany needed a new chief, so they selected former Buffalonian John C. Sheehan, despite the corruption investigation.

After Croker returned to New York City, Sheehan stepped down as leader. In 1899, Sheehan tried to pry the reins of Tammany back from Richard Croker, but was defeated.[17] With the help of his younger and more astute brother, William, however, he continued to shape New York politics for years to come.

John's younger brother, William "Blue-Eyed Billy" Sheehan, was born in 1859. After he clerked at his brother's law firm, Buffalo voters elected him to the New York State Assembly in 1885, at the age of twenty-six. Billy was described as dashing and attractive with a winning personality.[18] He once shared what motivated him to serve in elected office: "No man is fully equipped for great public service whose heart does not cry out against wrong and oppression, and whose soul does not dwell in the midst of struggling humanity wherever it is found."[19] Six years later, Sheehan's colleagues elected him to the powerful position of speaker of that body. He "was a born parliamentarian, a well-equipped debater, an earnest and vigorous speaker, and an uncompromising partisan."[20] While in the Assembly, Sheehan secured funds for Buffalo's harbor and doled out patronage jobs, endearing him to his constituents.

In 1892, at age 33, Sheehan became the youngest lieutenant governor of New York in its history. The same year, his Democratic colleagues considered him for US senator from New York, a position then appointed by the state legislature. The *New York Times* described Sheehan as "young, ambitious, aggressive, and [he is] proud of the victory the party won under his management."[21] Although he was an exciting candidate, it wasn't his time.

In 1911, when a new opportunity emerged to select a US senator from New York, "Blue-Eyed Billy" Sheehan had positioned himself as the inevitable candidate. He was the leading candidate in the caucuses and the choice of Tammany's boss, Charles F. Murphy. The *Times* stated, "The consensus of opinion expressed at the Capitol is that Mr. Sheehan has a better chance than any other candidate now in the field."[22] It was now Sheehan's time. But a young and aggressive New York state legislator, wanting to reform the Democratic Party, successfully blocked "Blue-Eyed Billy" Sheehan's candidacy.[23] That state legislator was Franklin Delano Roosevelt.

Roosevelt objected to the fact that William Sheehan was the candidate endorsed by corrupt Tammany Hall and demanded a reform candidate. After Roosevelt rallied twenty-one Democratic legislators to oppose Sheehan, the Buffalo Irishman resorted to threats and political rallies to silence the opposition. Roosevelt, however, was not intimidated and held his caucus together, and Sheehan eventually withdrew his name from consideration.

Sheehan returned to his prosperous law career in New York City and purported multimillion-dollar fortune earned primarily from his law practice (and perhaps a little graft). Another Buffalo lawyer explained that "[Sheehan] was looked upon as a man who made a fortune as a lawyer from his political connections."[24] After political office, Sheehan represented some of the largest corporations in New York City; he earned a handsome sum serving as a board member of the Albany Southern Railway, the Edison Illuminating Company, and the Continental Rubber Company.[25]

While working in the private sector, Sheehan never abandoned politics and was the unofficial leader of the "Gold Standard" Democrats. In 1896, he opposed the nomination of William Jennings Bryan and correctly predicted he would be defeated. In 1904, at the Democratic Convention, Sheehan, executive chairman of the Democratic National Committee, swayed enough delegates to block the nomination of fellow Buffalonian Grover Cleveland and William Randolph Hearst for the Democratic presidential nomination. He encouraged those same delegates to support his future law partner and friend, Judge Alton B. Parker.[26] The Democratic delegates chose Parker, proving that Sheehan still had sufficient political power to shape the US presidential election. Unfortunately for Sheehan, President Theodore Roosevelt defeated Alton B. Parker in the general election.

In February 1916, at the age of sixty-seven, John C. Sheehan, who was leading a prosperous life as a lawyer, collapsed in his office in New York City and later died.[27] On March 14, 1917, only a year after the death of John, William "Blue-Eyed Billy" Sheehan succumbed to kidney disease while residing in Manhattan. William Sheehan's body was returned to Buffalo for burial in Holy Cross Cemetery in Lackawanna, New York. New York State Judge John Woodward, Sheehan's friend, claimed that after Presidents Millard Fillmore and Grover Cleveland, Sheehan was Buffalo's "most notable contribution to public life."[28] After Sheehan's funeral, the *Buffalo Times* wrote, "No nobler tribute was ever paid to the memory of a distinguished citizen than that in which Buffalo rendered funeral honors to William F. Sheehan."[29]

Another Scoundrel—Jack White

In 1877, John "Jack" White, a former ship carpenter, was elected as a Republican alderman (council member) in the heavily Democratic First Ward. White's motivation to become a Republican is uncertain, but he was probably a pragmatist. The Republicans and Democrats equally ruled Buffalo politics for much of the late nineteenth and early twentieth centuries. White, from County Cork, was astute enough to realize that, as the Republican leader of the First Ward, he would benefit when the Republicans ruled the city. By aligning with the Republicans, he could dole out patronage jobs, which would increase his power in his district.

Regarding lucrative patronage jobs, White desired quantity over quality. A *New York Times* article claimed that White preferred to trade his vote in the Buffalo Common Council for twenty bridge tender jobs at $2 a day, compared to one $1,500 yearly canal section boss.[30] He was also friends with owners of railroad, steamboat, and grain elevator companies. In exchange for his vote in the Common Council, he could also place people in private-sector jobs, as well. Sometimes, legislative votes in the Buffalo Common Council ended in a tie, and White's vote was the tiebreaker, giving him even more power.

"Jack White put more Irish policemen and schoolteachers to work than anyone in the city's history."[31] In 1880, a newspaper reporter claimed that by colluding with the Democrats, White had a gift for getting his way regarding municipal committee appointments. By appointing these key figures, he could obtain steady employment for his constituents in departments like sewers, streets, schools, and fire.[32] The same reporter complained that White had appointed four Irish members to the streets committee from his district (the First Ward), which had "scarcely a paved street on it."[33] White's reign as Republican alderman from the Ward lasted almost a quarter-century.

Jack White fought fiercely with the ruling William Sheehan machine throughout his career. In 1892, Sheehan and White had a significant falling out, and tensions boiled over the next year, during White's re-election campaign. William Sheehan decided it was time for White to be defeated, so he ran his cousin, John Sheehan (not to be confused with his brother John Sheehan), to oppose him. "Blue-Eyed Billy" Sheehan was the lieutenant governor at the time, but his web of control over Buffalo's politics was still extensive. Sheehan loyalists were responsible for the election campaign in the First Ward's second and fourth districts. Sheehan also controlled the loyalties of the police department and the comptroller's and assessor's offices in Buffalo, which allowed him free reign to employ his dirty tactics to elect his cousin John.

Sheehan's multi-pronged attack on White's campaign started in July of 1893 when Sheehan's government cronies held up issuing liquor licenses to saloon keepers who were allied with White. Without a liquor license, saloon keepers could not serve alcohol and consequently would lose any influence over their customers' voting preferences.[34] However, the most flagrant abuses by the Sheehans came on Election Day. In the fourth district of the Ward, Sheehan's man, James Kennedy, hired three thugs—all former boxers—to intimidate voters at the polling places. In the meantime, another Sheehan loyalist handpicked deputy sheriffs to "keep order" at the polling places. More ruffians loyal to Sheehan, armed with fake deputy badges, intimidated voters at polling places.

On Election Day, there were even allegations that Police Captain Michael Regan looked the other way as the Sheehan loyalists started throwing White's poll watchers out of the polling area, preventing White's supporters from casting their ballots.[35] Sheehan's plan worked, and his cousin won. An embittered Jack White contested the election. After an investigation, his claims of fraud were proven legitimate.[36] One year after the debacle in Buffalo, the New York State Constitutional Convention enacted statewide controls to prevent such corruption in the future.

Jack White's political influence in Buffalo extended for several decades. In his later years, White, who had amassed a fortune from all of the favors owed to him over the years, moved to a fashionable home, fit for a business tycoon, on Richmond Avenue. His *Buffalo Times* obituary described Jack White as "the first of the great Republican bosses."

United States Senator James Mead

While Buffalo's William Sheehan was denied a US Senate seat (twice), another Buffalo Irishman was more successful. James "Jim" Mead was born on December 27, 1885, in a "crude hut" adjacent to the Lackawanna Railroad tracks in Mount Morris, New York.[39] He was one of eight children born to Thomas Mead, an Irish immigrant who worked as a railroad engineer, and Jane (Kelley) Mead, a restaurant worker at a railroad station. When young Jim was five, the Meads moved to Buffalo, settling on the city's east side. At age twelve, Mead quit grammar school and started working as a water boy at the Lackawanna Railroad company.[40] Later, he progressed from a lamplighter to a switchman.[42] His years working for the railroad awakened his interest in labor issues.

Mead played semi-professional baseball in Buffalo and even considered a professional career. But in 1910, he accepted a position with the United States Capitol Police in Washington, DC. While there, the former railroad water boy predicted to his fellow police officers that he would return to the nation's capital in ten years as a congressman—Mead did it in eight. But first, he returned to Buffalo to work for the Erie Railroad, where he became the Switchmen's Union president. The following year, Mead's meteoric rise commenced when the voters elected him to the Erie County Board of Supervisors (now called the Erie County Legislature). The year after, he won his election as a New York State Assemblyman, focusing on labor issues. One of his chief accomplishments was steering the passage of the Railroad Full-Crew Bill, which specified a set number of workers per train to improve employee and passenger safety. He also championed legislation to reduce working hours for women and children in the cannery industry and pushed for workers' compensation legislation.[43]

During his first term in Albany, Mead married Alice Dillon, who would play a crucial role in his seventeen political campaigns. In 1918, Mead ran as a Democrat for a congressional seat against an incumbent in a heavily Republican district and won. For the next ten years, despite repeated Republican landslides throughout the 1920s, he continued to win with larger and larger pluralities in each subsequent election. All the while, the ambitious congressman enrolled in classes at Canisius College and Georgetown University.

Possessing a pleasant manner and a quick wit, Mead made friends easily. At 6'2" and weighing two hundred pounds, he had an imposing presence and was a skillful orator. As a lifelong athlete, Mead was considered Congress's finest baseball and softball player. Concerned about many of his fellow legislators' health ailments, he helped establish the congressional gym.

In Congress, Mead joined the United States House Committee on Post Office and Post Roads and was elevated to chairman. Within a few years, he became the nation's leading expert on postal affairs.[44] The former union chief authored bills to shorten the postal carriers' work week to 44 hours, eventually reducing it by four more hours. He also passed a bill to improve the condition of carriers in rural areas. Legislation he championed improved the working lives of tens of thousands of Americans. In a show of gratitude, the Buffalo-area letter carriers named their local union after him. A public library in Buffalo's Lovejoy neighborhood also bears his name.

Mead's noteworthy accomplishments went beyond improving the postal employees' working conditions. In 1939, at the end of the Depression, he co-sponsored the Mead-Barry HOLC (Home Owners' Loan Corporation) Bill, which extended mortgages from fifteen to twenty-five years, and helped hundreds of thousands of borrowers struggling to make payments. He also supported legislation to reform rampant abuses within the federal civil service. At the same time, he sponsored bills to expand the number of people who could qualify for the civil service, including older adults.

The economic devastation of the Great Depression galvanized Mead to take action on behalf of the poor. On the street where he grew up in East Buffalo, two-thirds of the families were on relief, and his former railroad company faced bankruptcy. It was no surprise that Mead supported President Franklin D. Roosevelt's New Deal. The president's advisors frequently invited the Buffalo politician to the White House to share his opinions on various policies. On some issues, he was even more sympathetic to the laboring class than the president, as when he fought the Roosevelt Administration's efforts to reduce the pay for federal custodial workers and cleaners. Mead's progressive efforts did not go unnoticed. The *New York Times* referred to him as one of the outstanding exponents of the New Deal since its inception in 1933.[45]

In 1938, the death of US Senator Royal S. Copeland advanced Mead's political career when he was appointed to take over the remaining two years of

Copeland's senate term. After two years, he ran for another six-year term in the Senate, winning convincingly. James Mead is still the only Buffalo native ever to hold this office. In May 1941, Senator Mead was appointed to the Special Committee to Investigate the National Defense Program, which was chaired by Senator Harry S. Truman. As a committee member, Mead traveled to combat zones worldwide, meeting with political dignitaries, military leaders, and ordinary soldiers. After returning home, the Buffalo senator wrote a best-selling book, *Tell the Folks Back Home,* documenting his experiences; he donated the book proceeds to the American Red Cross and the American Legion.[46] When Truman was nominated as Roosevelt's vice president, the capable Mead replaced him as the chairman of this high-profile defense committee, where he served until 1946. The national news regularly profiled his efforts in exposing workforce fraud and waste of military supplies. In 1946, Mead ran for governor of New York but lost to Thomas E. Dewey, the popular Republican incumbent.

In 1949, President Harry Truman appointed Mead to the Federal Trade Commission (FTC), and the following year, Mead became the chairman of this powerful agency. As the leader of the FTC, he enforced antitrust laws and consumer protections. In his words, he delivered "some more good licks for the little guy."[47] In 1956, Mead retired from public service after more than two decades in Congress. The hardworking public servant from Buffalo left Washington and relocated with his wife to a home—complete with an orange grove—twenty miles west of Orlando, Florida.

James Mead once declared, "We should declare a war against poverty, against ignorance, against persecution, against prejudice, against inequality, against exploitation."[48] Born to a poor Irish family, raised in a shack next to railroad tracks, and shaped by physical labor, James Mead, "New York's Great Liberal," tirelessly advocated for the underdog throughout his four decades in public office.[49]

The Congressmen

In 1895, Buffalo voters elected Rowland B. Mahany, the first congressman of Irish heritage. A Harvard-educated lawyer and the son of Protestant Irish immigrants, Mahany worked on behalf of the Irish workers in Buffalo's Great Strike of 1899. He also held numerous federal government positions, including Acting Secretary of Labor in 1920 and ambassador to Ecuador.

In 1899, William H. Ryan, a First Ward resident, defeated Mahany and became Buffalo's first Irish Catholic congressman. After working as a shoemaker, Ryan, a son of Irish immigrants, entered politics in 1894, eventually becoming chairman of the board of supervisors of Erie County.[50] After his election to Congress in 1899, he served five consecutive two-year terms. In 1909, Irishman Daniel Driscoll, the son of an undertaker from County Cork, was elected to fill Ryan's seat and served until 1917. Driscoll also served as Buffalo's postmaster and the Phoenix Brewing Corporation president.[51] After Daniel Driscoll's term, James Mead served as a congressman in that district until he became a US Senator in 1938.

Several decades later, one of Buffalo's most colorful Irish members of Congress came on the scene.

Richard Dean "Max" McCarthy

Richard "Max" McCarthy was born in Buffalo in 1927 to an Irish family with roots mainly from County Cork. His father, Ignatius D. McCarthy, was a lawyer, and his mother, Kathleen (Walsh) McCarthy, raised their family in Buffalo's University Heights neighborhood. Max's paternal grandfather, Charles McCarthy, came to Buffalo from Bantry Bay, County Cork, in 1888, while Max's mother's Irish ancestors arrived in the Buffalo area before the Famine. In about 1960, Max penned a family history with detailed information about his McCarthy and Walsh ancestors, which shed light on the early years of the Buffalo Irish.

McCarthy's maternal Irish great-great-grandfather Walsh (first name is unknown) and his wife arrived in Black Rock in 1822, where he worked as an engineer on the Erie Canal.[52] They had a son, Peter B. Walsh, born three years later, who became a successful shipbuilder and First Ward alderman in 1859. Richard McCarthy's great-grandfather, Cornelius Sullivan, was a First Ward pioneer, building his homestead on Kentucky Street in 1861. Sullivan and his wife had nine children, but only one—the last one—lived to adulthood. Sullivan labored in a backbreaking job unloading iron-ore ships with a shovel, and to numb the pain, he and his fellow laborers purportedly consumed two quarts of whiskey a day.[54]

Max McCarthy's First Ward-born father, Ignatius McCarthy, worked twelve-hour days, seven days a week, for the railroads. Later, Ignatius graduated from the University of Buffalo's law school and became interested in the Irish independence movement. In 1921, he served as the youngest delegate to the Chicago convention of the American Association for the Recognition of the Irish Republic.[55]

Max McCarthy acquired a passion for Irish history from his father, including an interest in the famed 1866 Fenian Invasion. On June 2, 1966, to commemorate the 100th anniversary of the Irish invasion of Canada, Max McCarthy and a handful of Buffalo lawyers tried to lay a wreath on the Canadian shore near Frenchman's Creek. But Canadian park police put a stop to this well-meaning gesture.[56]

McCarthy graduated from Canisius High School and was drafted into the Navy during World War II. He then graduated from Canisius College in 1950 and served in the Army during the Korean War. After the war, the *Buffalo Evening News* hired him as a reporter, and National Gypsum hired him as their public relations director. Throughout his business career, however, he always dabbled in politics. In 1964, at age thirty-six, McCarthy, a scrappy 5'8," 150-pound Irishman, ran as a Democrat in a heavily Republican district controlled by six-term Congressman John Pillion, a conservative Republican—and McCarthy won. At the time, his wife, Gail (Coughlin) McCarthy, described her husband as unassuming. She said people often underestimated him—as John Pillion did—but "they soon discover he's a dynamo." She added that her husband's zest for politics was contagious.

During the campaign, one of McCarthy's chief policy issues had been addressing the pollution in Lake Erie.[58] As a pioneer environmentalist, he became one of the House's leaders on pollution-related matters. McCarthy's mother was passionate about these issues and co-founded the Housewives to End Pollution in Buffalo.[59] Ahead of his time, Max also sounded the alarm about the harmful effects that costly political campaigns had on democracy. He wrote a book on the topic, *Elections for Sale* (1972), in which he offered solutions for campaign reform. But the issue he will be most remembered for is uncovering the Pentagon's massive secret stockpile of chemical and biological weapons (CBW). He accomplished this partly thanks to his wife, Gail McCarthy.

Gail, an Irish former South Buffalo resident, had watched a 1969 television documentary on chemical weapons and was appalled to learn about the US military's chemical weapons program. When she asked her husband what he knew about this program, Max admitted he didn't know much but agreed to look into it. Pentagon officials were reluctant to reveal details, but McCarthy kept pushing for answers. Eventually, after a Congressional investigation, the Pentagon admitted that there was a massive lethal gas and biological program to which only a few people in government were privy. While many were shocked at the revelation, some, including House Republican leader Gerald Ford, blasted McCarthy. Ford even implied that the Buffalo congressman was part of a plot to unilaterally force the United States government to discontinue this strategic program. McCarthy replied that if there was a plot, his only co-conspirator was his wife, Gail. As a result of the hearings, McCarthy put pressure on President Richard Nixon to adhere to the Geneva Protocol on germ warfare and demanded that Defense Secretary Melvin Laird stop dumping poisonous gas into the sea until the government reviewed its potential harm to the water supply.[60] He also forced the Pentagon to admit that they spent $350 million annually on chemical and biological weapons.[61] Now, every household knew the name of Congressman Max McCarthy.

A headline in the *Boston Globe* read, "Another McCarthy Explodes on the National Scene."[62] In April 1969, the *New York Times* referred to the chemical defoliants used in the Vietnam War as "a dark corner of the defense department's many-sided enterprise." The reporter added, "Now, because of the courageous initiative of Representative Richard D. McCarthy of upstate New York, more light is shining into this dark corner."[63] Despite much initial resistance to McCarthy's efforts, on November 25, 1969, President Nixon announced an end to the United States' offensive biological weapons programs. The president also implemented a no-first-use policy for chemical weapons. The Buffalo congressman had won an epic battle against powerful government officials.

Fresh off his triumph, McCarthy wrote *The Ultimate Folly: War by Pestilence, Asphyxiation and Defoliation* (1969), detailing the Pentagon's CBW program. McCarthy also railed against the government's unsafe storage and transportation of chemical agents domestically and on foreign soil.[64] In 1970, the year after he published his book, the rising star from Buffalo was encouraged to run for one of New York's US Senate seats. But a senate run meant leaving his safe congressional job. The fearless McCarthy charged into the race, campaigning on his recent success with the biological weapons program. But, for Democratic primary voters, that single issue was not enough to merit their vote. McCarthy placed fourth on the primary election evening, with only 11% of the vote. In later years, Karen Brady, a former McCarthy press secretary on Capitol Hill, claimed the loss "sent his personal political career on a downward spiral."[65] Jack Kemp, a Republican and the former star quarterback for the Buffalo Bills, won McCarthy's congressional seat.

While McCarthy's political career was over, he was still sought after for various offices and posts. Harvard University's Institute of Politics named him a fellow, and he was a visiting professor at Canisius College and Niagara University. In 1973, Buffalo's Mayor Stanley Makowski hired him to develop the city's human resource department. President Gerald Ford appointed him press attaché at the US embassy in Iran the following year. He also worked in legislative affairs for the Carter administration. In 1978, McCarthy returned to the *Buffalo News*, eventually becoming the Washington Bureau chief. Even after retirement, he wrote a weekly column for the paper.[66]

McCarthy helped co-found the Greater Buffalo Development Foundation and served as its vice president for eight years. In 1993, this foundation merged with the Buffalo Chamber of Commerce and became what is now known as the Buffalo Niagara Partnership. In his free time, McCarthy enjoyed opera, fine literature, and Irish history. In 1995, at age sixty-seven, McCarthy died in his home in Arlington, Virginia, after a long battle with amyotrophic lateral sclerosis (ALS), also known as Lou Gehrig's disease. The *Buffalo News* described Max as "an outstanding citizen of Buffalo, outstanding patriot, and a fine newspaperman."[67] The progressive McCarthy was also remembered for his pioneering work on environmental issues—especially for highlighting the urgent need to clean up

America's waterways. The Buffalo politician's advocacy for campaign reform was also progressive for his era. His most profound achievement, however, was exposing the US military's stockpile of chemical and biological weapons, which would have never happened without his wife, Gail.

Other influential Irish congressmen followed Richard "Max" McCarthy, such as Jack Quinn, Kathy Hochul, and Brian Higgins, who will be introduced later.

James T. Molloy

James "Jim" Molloy, a second-generation Irishman who served as the doorkeeper of the House of Representatives in Washington, DC, was one of Buffalo's most beloved native sons. Molloy, born in 1936, was the son of Matthew Molloy, a First Ward fireman, longshoreman, and active union member. His mother, Catherine Hayden, was a homemaker. The Molloy family, part of an exodus from Scranton, Pennsylvania, relocated to Buffalo. After graduating from Bishop Timon High School, young Jimmy worked in the waterfront grain elevators and for the Buffalo Fire Department to put himself through Canisius College. But politics was his passion, and he even once described himself as "a political creature."[68] Like his father, Molloy was interested in labor issues and served as a union representative in the fire department. At the age of twenty-seven, Molloy was elected as the youngest ward boss in Buffalo's history.[69] After Molloy served a stint in the Erie County district attorney's office, Democratic chairman Joseph Crangle offered the affable and witty young man a job in the nation's capital.[70]

In Washington, Molloy worked as a supervisor in the House Finance Office and befriended powerful congressmen like Thomas "Tip" O'Neill from Boston. As part of his job, Molloy "organized luncheons, softball games, and social hours for staff," which helped him build a name for himself. In 1974, the well-liked, thirty-eight-year-old South Buffalonian was encouraged to run against the incumbent doorkeeper of the House of Representatives, William "Fishbait" Miller. Molloy won and became responsible for four hundred employees and an $8 million budget. His office also published all House documents and the representatives' newsletters. One of Molloy's most important duties was handling arrangements for prominent visiting dignitaries, like Pope John Paul II, Queen Elizabeth II, the Dalai Lama, and the Prime Minister of Ireland. In this role, he also became close friends with President Ronald Reagan and Congressman Hugh L. Carey, who later became Governor of New York.

Fellow Buffalonian Tim Russert said: "He [Molloy] was a good man who knew everybody and was proud of taking care of his own."[71] Molloy went out of his way to help scores of Buffalonians secure internships in the House of Representatives or other government positions in Washington. Many Western New Yorkers also enjoyed watching Molloy at the beginning of each nationally televised State of the Union speech. Every year, for two decades, he declared with his distinct South Buffalo accent, "Mister Speaker, the president of the United States." On more than one occasion, while covering the national event, NBC's Tom Brokaw would share that Molloy was "the pride of South Buffalo." Molloy also helped promote Buffalo with his work as "an early organizer" of the annual Buffalo Nite in the nation's capital.[72]

In an interview, Molloy remarked that, over his twenty-five years in Washington, he witnessed the transformation of old ward politics in Congress to its members' obsession with image and PAC money.[73] In 1994, the doorkeeper position, which had been around since the Continental Congress in 1789, was eliminated by Congressman Newt Gingrich. Molloy told a reporter that he had "the greatest job in the world. There are very few people who have spent as much time as I have on the floor…I love politics, and I love being that close to politics."[74] In retirement, the gifted Irish storyteller became a great ambassador for Buffalo as he received invitations to speak across the country. In 2011, at age seventy-five, Jim Molloy died from complications of diabetes. Before Molloy's death, the US Congress named a South Buffalo post office after him.

Irish Party Chairmen

During the nineteenth and twentieth centuries, political party chairmen—often called party bosses—ruled their organizations like autocrats. They controlled the party's finances, vetted judicial candidates, filled vacant political offices, and distributed numerous patronage jobs. They also had the final word over who could run in local elections. For more than a century, the Buffalo Irish dominated the leadership of the local Democratic party. As we will see, they also shaped state and national affairs.

As previously detailed, John and William Sheehan ruled as the unofficial Democratic bosses in Buffalo in the 1880s and '90s. While neither held the title of party chairman, they often pulled the strings behind the scenes, using their proxies. One such Sheehan man was John Cunneen. Born in 1848 in County Clare, Cunneen came to the United States alone at age thirteen and worked on his cousin's farm outside of Buffalo. Although his schooling was limited, he possessed a keen intellect and taught himself law in the evenings. After clerking in a law office, the former farmhand became a lawyer at twenty-seven. In 1888, Cunneen entered a law practice with William F. Sheehan and became involved with Democratic politics. He rose to Erie County Democratic Chairman at the turn of the twentieth century, and the party thrived under his leadership.[75] By 1902, his reputation had spread, and he won a statewide election as New York State's attorney general. Cunneen relinquished his position as party boss, and he was replaced by another Buffalo Irishman, who, with the help of his son, controlled local Democratic politics for almost half a century.

The Fitzpatricks

William H. "Fitz" Fitzpatrick was born in Buffalo to Irish immigrant parents in 1865, just a few months after the conclusion of the Civil War. His father, Jeremiah, was in the wholesale milk trade at their family farm at Seneca Street and Bailey Avenue. William joined the family business, delivering milk to South Buffalo homes, after a few years of schooling. At a young age, he became involved in Democratic politics. After allying with party powerhouses William Sheehan and William J. Conners, he was elected Democratic party chairman in 1903. As chair, "Fitz," as he was widely known, was recognized for his prominent role in electing Democratic Mayors James N. Adam (1906) and Louis Fuhrmann (1910).[76] Fitz, however, had larger ambitions outside of Buffalo. Immediately after becoming chairman, he endeared himself to New York City's Tammany Hall boss, Charles F. Murphy. After Murphy died in 1924, Fitzpatrick became the de facto Democratic boss of New York State.

Fitzpatrick played a crucial role in the 1932 Democratic presidential primary, where he was one of the strongest advocates for former Governor Al Smith to become the Democratic nominee. The Smith supporters thought he deserved another chance at running after his 1928 blowout defeat to Herbert Hoover. Furthermore, the Democrats had a strong chance of winning the presidency because of the economic depression gripping the nation—so the stakes were high. But Governor Franklin D. Roosevelt also desired the top office. Fitzpatrick not only believed Smith was the better candidate, he also despised Roosevelt. This animosity stemmed from Roosevelt's blocking of Buffalo Irishman William Sheehan from a US Senate seat twenty years earlier. Fitz never forgot nor forgave the blue blood from Hyde Park.

During the first week of January 1932, Fitzpatrick went to New York City to help secure the nomination for Al Smith. While there, Fitz suffered a massive heart attack at the Hotel Pennsylvania and died the next day. With his death, the enthusiasm for Smith's candidacy waned, and Roosevelt won the nomination. In Fitzpatrick's obituary, the *Brooklyn Daily Eagle* wrote that from the beginning of the twentieth century until 1931, he "was the dominant figure in Democratic politics in Buffalo and Erie County."[77] His death did not end the Fitzpatricks' influence on New York state politics.

William Fitzpatrick's son, Paul Fitzpatrick, was born in Buffalo in 1897, grew up in South Buffalo, and was president of South Park High School's first graduating class. After serving in the US Naval Air Corps during World War I, he returned to obtain a civil engineering degree from Cornell University. At an early age, he became a partner in his father's real estate and construction business and became involved in politics as a district committeeman.[78]

Paul Fitzpatrick served as the Erie County Democratic Chairman from 1939 to 1942. Between his father's party leadership and his own, other Irishmen such as Daniel J. Riordan, John Patrick (J.P.) Sullivan, and Frank J. Carr led the local party. The tall, handsome Fitzpatrick used his charm to build a loyal following across the state.[79] In 1944, he was elected Democratic Chairman for New York State, serving for eight years. Fitzpatrick was the second Irishman from Buffalo to lead the state party; the first was industrialist William J. Conners (1906-1910). Despite the bad blood between Franklin D. Roosevelt and Fitzpatrick's father, in 1944, the younger Fitzpatrick fully supported Roosevelt's desire to run for a fourth term as president. As the New York State Chairman, he overruled a cabal of Democrats, including the previous chairman James Farley, who opposed another four years for the incumbent president. Thanks to the Buffalo chairman, Roosevelt secured the nomination and defeated Governor Thomas E. Dewey in the general election.

Fitzpatrick became a close friend of Roosevelt's successor, Vice President Harry S. Truman. In 1948, when state Democratic leaders were uncertain about supporting Truman's candidacy for president, Paul Fitzpatrick and Ed Flynn, the head of the Bronx Democratic party, enthusiastically backed Truman. Their efforts were instrumental in securing Truman's nomination.[80] After Truman's upset victory over Republican Governor Thomas Dewey, the newly-elected president flew seven of his closest political confidantes to his winter retreat in Key West, Florida—and Paul Fitzpatrick was on the plane.[81] As a reward for Fitzpatrick's loyalty, the administration granted him dozens of patronage jobs to disperse to his constituents.[82]

In 1952, after eight and a half years running the Democratic Party in New York, Fitzpatrick stepped down after his party suffered heavy losses in state elections, which were less about his efforts and more about the popularity of General Dwight D. Eisenhower, who was on the ballot for president. After his political career ended, Fitzpatrick devoted more of his time to his business ventures. He served as chairman of American Lubricants, Inc., and president of the Fitzpatrick Building Company and the Fitzpatrick-Danahy insurance firm. In partnership with the *Courier-Express* newspaper, he co-owned the radio station WEBR, and he was a director of several banks. The tireless executive owned a cattle ranch in Florida and farms in the Sunshine State and Ireland. Former *Buffalo News* journalist Richard "Max" McCarthy argued that Paul Fitzpatrick "was one of the most dynamic and energetic political and business leaders ever born on the Niagara Frontier."[83]

In 1958, in honor of their father, Paul Fitzpatrick and his brother Walter founded the William H. Fitzpatrick Chair of Political Science at Canisius College. They later endowed the William H. Fitzpatrick Institute of Public Affairs at the same Jesuit institution. In 1962, the Institute held the first Fitzpatrick Lecture series with former President Harry S. Truman as the inaugural speaker.[84] For over fifty years, this Buffalo institute has hosted prominent politicians, journalists, and government officials, including former President Jimmy Carter, Robert F. Kennedy, Jr., US Supreme Court Justice William J. Brennan, Jr., Theodore C. Sorenson, Carl Bernstein, and Diane Sawyer. With their endowment, the Fitzpatrick family has continued to shape the political debate in Western New York.

Crotty, Crangle, Lawley, and Lenihan

Irish Americans continued their domination of the Buffalo Democratic party into the second half of the twentieth century. One of the larger-than-life chairpersons was Peter J. Crotty. The son of Irish immigrants, Crotty was born in Buffalo in 1910. His father worked as a longshoreman, and his mother cared for their five children. After graduating from Canisius College and the University of Buffalo Law School, Crotty worked for the National Labor Relations Board during President Franklin D. Roosevelt's administration. In 1947, the well-liked Crotty was elected president of the Buffalo City Council. After Buffalo Irishman William B. Mahoney served as Democratic Party chairman from 1947 to 1954, Crotty led the Party from 1954 to 1965.[85] During that time, he lost elections for mayor of Buffalo and attorney general of New York. It seems Crotty was better at getting others elected than himself.[86]

Some of the "others" Crotty helped elect included John F. and Robert Kennedy. During the 1960 presidential primary, the New York State Democratic delegation had not coalesced around John F. Kennedy as their preferred candidate. Prominent figures such as Eleanor Roosevelt and former governor Herbert Lehman led a faction that tried to thwart Kennedy's nomination.[87] At the convention, support for both Adlai Stevenson and Lyndon B. Johnson was strong with New York delegates. But Crotty, with the help of Bronx boss Charley Buckley, made a passionate case for Kennedy, eventually swaying the delegation in his favor. The importance of Kennedy winning New York on his road to the White House cannot be understated. The result may have been vastly different without Crotty's efforts.

President-elect Kennedy was so grateful to Crotty that he convened a meeting at his Georgetown residence with New York state Democratic leaders. He demanded that Crotty be named the official state boss, but the state party leaders refused.[88] Still, because of Crotty's connection to the Kennedys, some considered him the unofficial boss of Democratic politics in New York State during the Camelot years.[89] Later, Ted Kennedy fondly remembered how Peter Crotty was the first Democratic leader in the nation to support his brother John's presidential campaign.[90] In 1964, Crotty paved the way for Robert F. Kennedy to run for the United States Senate seat in New York.

The other reform-minded, liberal Democrats across the state did not always support Crotty, which probably explains his defeat running for New York state attorney general. Daniel Patrick Moynihan thought the criticism of the Buffalo chief was unfair. Moynihan described Crotty as "a man of intellect, a diligent student of Catholic social theory, a formidable labor lawyer and a passionate believer in racial equality."[91] The *Buffalo News* claimed that the Buffalo boss elevated power in politics to an art form.[92] The *New York Times* obituary described Crotty as an "erudite king-maker who dominated western NY politics," and bridged the old boss rule and the new reform movement that emerged in the 1960s.[93] Today, Crotty is honored in his hometown with his name adorning the pavilion in Cazenovia Park in South Buffalo.

Only a few Buffalonians can claim to be advisors and confidants to accomplished national politicians such as Robert F. Kennedy, Edward M. Kennedy, Hubert Humphrey, and Daniel Patrick Moynihan.[94] But Joseph F. Crangle was such a person. Joe Crangle was the son of County Down immigrants Edward and Marguerita (McNutt) Crangle. After emigrating from Ireland, Edward Crangle settled in Buffalo and worked as a clerk for the New York Central Railroad. The Crangles raised their seven children near Hertel Avenue and later in the Kensington-Bailey neighborhood. Born in 1932, young Joe took three buses each way to attend Bishop Timon High School; he was in the school's first graduating class in 1950. He then attended Canisius College, where he was president of the student council, and later received his law degree from the University of Buffalo Law School.

Shortly after law school, Crangle joined Chairman Peter Crotty's staff at Democratic headquarters. He rose to become the chairman's first assistant, and in 1965, when Crotty decided to pursue elected office, Crangle was picked as his replacement. After Crotty lost the race, however, he wanted his chairman position back, but Crangle refused to step aside, and the two Irish politicians became adversaries.

Crangle, who served as Democratic chairman for twenty-three years, became the longest-serving party chairman—of any party—in Erie County's history. He wielded immense power, doling out countless patronage jobs, approving all judicial nominations, and having the last word on the state legislature and congressional candidates.[95] Crangle's success was derived from several factors. According to his son Joe, one of his favorite expressions was, "Small things matter." Crangle was obsessed with the minor details of a political operation, such as the number of mailers and telephone reminders sent out to make sure party members turned out to vote. He would also tirelessly campaign for a candidate, even if the individual had no chance of winning, to improve the turnout for the other candidates on the ticket.

Crangle had great instincts when assessing future stars in the party. He contributed to the careers of Henry Nowak, John LaFalce, Anthony Masiello, Byron Brown, Dennis Gorski, Richard "Dick" Keane, Bill Hoyt, David Swarts, Paul Tokasz and countless other politicians who dominated local politics for decades.[98] Crangle also found success at the state level. In 1971, like William J. Conners and Paul Fitzpatrick before him, the Buffalo politician served as the Chairman of the New York State Democratic Committee. Three years later, he successfully led the effort to elect fellow Irish American Hugh Carey as governor of the Empire State. That same year, under Crangle's leadership, the Democrats gained control of the State Assembly—for the first time in decades.[99]

National candidates took note of Crangle's talent. In the 1968 presidential campaign, Robert F. Kennedy chose him to chair his operations in Michigan. After Kennedy was assassinated in Los Angeles later that year, his family requested that Crangle be an honorary pallbearer. The Buffalo chairman and his wife, Rita, accompanied the Kennedy family on the funeral train from New York City to Washington, DC, and then to Arlington National Cemetery. In 1980, during his presidential primary campaign against President Jimmy Carter, Edward "Ted" Kennedy also picked the Buffalo politician, whom he called "a family friend," to run his Michigan operations and be the national director for party affairs. Crangle helped Kennedy defeat Jimmy Carter in Michigan, but Kennedy lost the national primary race to Carter. Crangle also served on the Democratic National Committee for twenty years, and, in 1968, he was one vote away from becoming the national party boss.

While Crangle was close with the Kennedy clan, he also admired Vice President Hubert Humphrey.[100] In 1976, Crangle tried, unsuccessfully, to draft Humphrey for president. Humphrey once declared, "If I'd had the good sense to have Joe Crangle run my campaign in 1968, we'd be having this meeting in the East Room of the White House."[101] One of Crangle's proudest achievements was Daniel Patrick Moynihan's election in 1976 as United States Senator from New York. Crangle, who drafted Moynihan, convinced him he could win the race. Moynihan once reminded the public, "If it was not for Joe Crangle, I would not be a United States senator today."[102] As an aside, when candidate Moynihan requested a driver for his Buffalo campaign stops, Crangle offered him one of his top staffers. That man was Tim Russert. As noted in a previous chapter, Russert eventually became Moynihan's chief of staff and a nationally known television journalist.

After his retirement as chairman, Crangle devoted much of his time to providing legal counsel for Western New York Native American tribes in their negotiations with New York state officials. His son Joe Jr. recalled that his father's desire to help the tribes was influenced, in part, by the hardships the Irish faced in earlier years.[103] For two decades, Crangle also appeared as a political analyst for WIVB-TV (Channel 4).

His son also disclosed that the senior Crangle cherished his Irish heritage and often became teary-eyed when he would sing Chauncey Olcott's "When Irish Eyes Are Smiling."[104] As someone who witnessed his parents' financial struggles, the senior Crangle also valued the Catholic Church and the Democratic Party for their commitment to helping others. In January 2021, Joe Crangle, aged 88, succumbed to complications from Covid-19. At the time, Len Lenihan, one of his successors as Democratic chairman, declared, "Erie County Democrats mourn the loss of the party's greatest chair. He was a historic figure who truly made history."[105] *Buffalo News* politics columnist Robert McCarthy wrote that "maybe more than anyone in history, he dominated Democratic politics around here."[106] Local politics will not see another like him.

In 2002, when the Democratic Party in Erie County was struggling after Steven Pigeon's tenure as chairman, they turned to a popular Irish American known as a consensus builder. Len Lenihan was born in 1948 in Lackawanna, New York, and raised in Kenmore. His paternal grandfather came from a farm in County Kerry and settled in Buffalo's First Ward. Both Len's father and grandfather worked as pressmen at the *Courier-Express* newspaper.

On September 28, 1960, Lenihan attended a campaign visit by then-presidential candidate John F. Kennedy, who spoke at Buffalo's Memorial Auditorium. He was one of the lucky ones who had a ticket to get inside the auditorium—in total, over 33,000 people showed up for an arena that held half that number. It was a fateful day for the twelve-year-old Lenihan because that was when the political bug bit him, shaping the rest of his life.[107] Sixty years later, he still remembered the end of Kennedy's speech, when the then-candidate quoted Abraham Lincoln, "I know there is a God and that he hates injustice, I see the storm coming, and I know that his hand is in it, but he has a place for me, I believe I am ready."

After graduating with a master's degree in public administration from the State University of New York at Albany, Lenihan entered elective office in 1977 when he was appointed to fill a vacant seat in the Erie County Legislature. Reelected ten times, Lenihan served until 1996, including stints as the Majority Leader (1988-1993) and chairman of the legislature (1993-1996). During Western

New York's bleakest economic days, Lenihan helped save the Niagara Frontier Transportation Authority's Rapid Transit System. He also played a significant role in reducing Erie County's massive budget deficit in the 1980s and provided financial assistance to the Buffalo and Erie County Public Library system.[108]

But by the 1990s, the Democrats in Erie County had lost several county-wide elections to Republicans, including a congressional seat to Jack Quinn, the county executive office to Joel Giambra, and almost all of the contested Supreme Court races. At the 2002 party convention, the Democrats were clearly in disarray and needed a new leader. Len Lenihan, who initially did not seek the job, was asked by some party leaders to be a compromise candidate to end the years-long divisions in the Party.[109] He beat James Keane and Ken Kruly to become the Erie County Democratic Party leader. Within a few years, under Lenihan's leadership, the party fielded stronger candidates, including Brian Higgins, who won a close race against Nancy Naples for an open congressional seat. During Lenihan's tenure as chairman, Kathy Hochul was elected County Clerk, then Congresswoman, and Mark Poloncarz became the Erie County Comptroller, then Erie County Executive. The Democrats won fourteen of eighteen Supreme Court seats. As of 2023, Higgins remains a popular congressman, Hochul is the Governor of New York State, and Poloncarz is the Erie County Executive. Lenihan left quite a legacy.

It is not surprising that the Irish dominated the leadership of the local Democratic Party. But they occasionally took control of the Republican Party as well. As previously discussed, First Ward Irish politician Jack White was a prominent Republican boss for decades. Buffalo's General William "Wild Bill" Donovan was an unsuccessful Republican candidate for New York state governor. Aside from those few noteworthy men, Irish men rarely ascended the ranks of the party of President Lincoln. Thomas W. Ryan, however, was one Irish Buffalonian who climbed to the top of the GOP. Tom Ryan grew up in the First Ward, the son of John Ryan, a shoe merchant, and Mary Ryan, a housewife. The younger Ryan served as an inspector in the police force. Later, in 1946, Governor Thomas Dewey appointed Tom Ryan as Director of the New York State Division of Safety, a new department created to improve traffic safety.

After his career in public safety, Ryan became president of the Niagara Frontier Transit System and later worked as an advertising executive. A political novice, he was elected the Republican chairman of Erie County in 1965. Eight years later, he was elected Erie County Sheriff. Ryan and his wife Elizabeth (Hogan) had four children, including Pamela (Ryan) Jacobs. In 2020, Pam's son, Chris Jacobs, was elected the Republican congressman for the 27th Congressional District representing Western New York.

James "Ray" Lawley, a one-time amateur boxer from the First Ward, replaced Thomas Ryan as chair of the Republican Party in Erie County—an incredible accomplishment for an Irishman from the Democratic south side of Buffalo. The 6'1" Lawley, son of a fireman whose family roots went back to County Cork, attended St. Bridget's School and St. Joseph's Collegiate Institute. In 1925, after graduating from the University of Buffalo Law School, he worked as a clerk for the firm Kenefick, Cooke, Mitchell, and Bass. The former First Warder dabbled in Wall Street, eventually losing everything during the Depression.[110] While his family members and neighbors were all Democrats, Lawley realized that if he wanted to enter into politics, his way forward would have to be as a Republican, as there were too many other Democrats in front of him. His son Bill Lawley explained that, in those days, the country was not as polarized, and the philosophical differences between the two parties were not as significant as they are today.[111] After all, Lawley's best friend was Peter Crotty, the Democratic Party Chairman with whom he played cards once a week, despite the fact that they were in opposing parties.

As a Republican committeeman in South Buffalo, Lawley made inroads in the Democratic base of his neighborhood. In the mid-1930s, Republican chairman Edwin F. Jaeckle recognized Lawley's talents and became his mentor, eventually appointing Lawley secretary of the county committee.[112] From Jaeckle, Lawley learned the art of politics, but he also possessed the natural gifts needed to succeed. His son, Bill Lawley, claimed that his father was a character and always entertained those he met with a good story or a sharp one-liner.[113] Lawley often helped people get jobs regardless of political affiliation. These traits helped him when he eventually became Erie County Republican Chairman.

In 1967, Governor Nelson Rockefeller came to Buffalo to honor Lawley for his diligent efforts in helping Republican candidates win that year's election. Rockefeller said Lawley personified the qualities of "integrity, honesty and devotion" and added that the county chairman had devoted "his life to caring, to action, to good government."[114] While working in politics, Ray and his wife Edna started an insurance business to supplement the family's finances. As of 2023, this seventy-seven-year-old business is the largest insurance firm in Western New York.[115]

The Mayors

Although Irish Buffalonians have held the office of mayor, they have not dominated this office. As mentioned earlier, in 1836, Samuel Wilkeson, son of Northern Irish Protestants, became Buffalo's fifth mayor. Five years later, Isaac Harrington, apparently of Irish Protestant ancestry, was elected mayor of the Queen City. In

1883, John B. Manning, born in Albany to an Irish Protestant father, was elected mayor of Buffalo. But it wasn't until 1941 that Buffalonians elected their first Irish Catholic mayor. Other cities with sizable Irish Catholic populations produced such mayors much earlier, i.e., Boston (1884), New York City (1885), and Chicago (1893).

While the Irish controlled the leadership of the Democratic Party, the Germans were the largest ethnic group. So the Irish never obtained a majority of the electorate. From the 1870s until the 1930s, the Germans controlled the mayoral office for many years. Furthermore, Buffalo residents elected Republican mayors as often as they did Democrats, so the primarily Democratic-affiliated Irish weren't competitive in many mayoral races.

In 1941, Buffalo residents finally elected their first Irish Catholic mayor. Joseph J. Kelly, the grandson of four Irish immigrants, was born in Buffalo in 1897. His father, James W. Kelly, a Democratic politician and successful businessman, co-owned the American Body Company. This large automobile parts company supplied companies such as E.R. Thomas and Pierce-Arrow Motor Car Company. After graduating from the University of Buffalo Law School in 1921, Joe Kelly served as Erie County Assistant District Attorney and City Court judge.

Kelly's term as mayor was unremarkable; he served at the height of the Second World War when resources for city services were scarce. When his term ended at the end of the war in 1945, he praised Buffalonians for their patience during the city's lean fiscal years. He recommended to his successor that repairs to city infrastructure and building projects should commence.[116] Kelly also presided over one of the worst winter storms in Buffalo's history, which started in December 1944 and continued until February 1, 1945. Over fifty inches of snow fell in January alone, paralyzing industries like the railroads.

After Kelly's single term, voters handed the reins over to Buffalo's second Irish Catholic mayor, Bernard J. "Bernie" Dowd. Born in 1891 and raised in Black Rock, Dowd was the son of a Buffalo fireman. Bernie served as a sergeant in the Army as part of the 78th Infantry Division during the First World War. In a battle in France, he was gassed but survived.[117] Dowd returned to Buffalo, graduated from the University of Buffalo Pharmacy School, and operated a pharmacy on the West Side for twenty-five years. Before being elected mayor, he had already served in various political positions, including committeeman and supervisor for the 22nd Ward.

As a Republican, Dowd was known for being fiscally conservative and was committed to running a more efficient government. One of his first acts in office was to prohibit city hall department heads from holding two jobs. He also demanded that every open position be cleared through him, preventing department heads from picking whomever they wanted. In 1947, he managed a citywide teacher strike for higher pay. On May 14, 1948, Dowd and Edward H. Butler, the publisher of the *Buffalo News*, ushered in Buffalo's first television broadcast on WBEN-TV.

Joe Kelly and Bernie Dowd paved the way for Jimmy Griffin, the third Irish Catholic and longest-serving Buffalo mayor in history (until Mayor Byron Brown broke the record in 2021)—more about Griffin in the last chapter.

New York State Legislators

For over a century, the Irish have represented Buffalo in the New York State Assembly and Senate. As previously mentioned, at a young age, William "Blue-eyed Billy" Sheehan was the leader of the Democrats in the New York State Assembly. In the following century, from 1936 to 1964, Buffalo's Walter J. Mahoney became one of the most powerful Republicans in New York State.[118] The grandson of four Irish immigrants and the son of a Buffalo fireman who died in the line of duty, Mahoney graduated from Canisius College and the University of Buffalo Law School. The political gene ran in the Mahoney family. While Walter was the Republican leader in the senate, his brother William served as the chairman of the Erie County Democratic Party.

Walter Mahoney possessed good looks, an outgoing personality, an "Irish tongue," and a gift for remembering the first name of everyone he met.[119] As an assemblyman, Mahoney shaped many of Buffalo's most important public institutions. He helped to transform the University of Buffalo by supporting its merger with the State University system, and later, he secured the commitment and the seed money to build the $500 million Amherst campus. The Buffalo Irish-American politician also wrestled funds from the legislature to expand Roswell Park and Buffalo State College and modernize the city's antiquated transit facilities. As his obituary declared, Mahoney oversaw Buffalo's "Golden Era."

In 1958, Mahoney ran for the Republican nomination for governor of New York State but finished second to Nelson Rockefeller, who also won the general election. Mahoney often clashed with more-liberal Republicans of the state, favoring more conservative positions, such as blocking Governor Thomas Dewey's tax increase proposals.[120] The Buffalo politician was also the majority leader of the Republicans in the New York State Senate for the last ten years of his career.[121] When his career in the legislature ended, he served as a New York Supreme Court justice. In his honor, a prominent government building on Court Street in downtown Buffalo was named the Walter J. Mahoney State Office Building.

Over the years, other well-known state legislators included Assemblyman Richard "Dick" Keane, Jr., the South Buffalo Irishman who was once the chairman of the Erie County Legislature and served in the Assembly for twenty-one years.

Congressman Brian Higgins described Keane as "a neighborhood politician" deeply connected to the South Buffalo community.[122] With his late friend Thomas V. Blake, Keane founded the annual St. Patrick's Day Luncheon at the Buffalo Irish Center—one of the essential Buffalo political gatherings of the year. As of 2023, some of the Buffalo Irish-American legislatures include State Senator Patrick M. Gallivan, who also served as Erie County Sheriff, Senator Sean M. Ryan, Assemblyman Patrick B. Burke, and Senator Timothy M. Kennedy.

Senator Timothy M. Kennedy

Senator Tim Kennedy, born in 1976 and one of five children of Marty and Mary Kennedy, was raised in South Buffalo. Marty Kennedy, whose family roots are from County Tipperary, worked as Buffalo's commissioner of assessment and taxation. Mary Kennedy was a cardiopulmonary nurse and a nursing instructor. After graduating from St. Joseph's Collegiate Institute, Tim Kennedy earned his master's in occupational therapy and worked in that field for eleven years. But all the while, he felt drawn to a life in politics.

In 1996, Kennedy started volunteering for South Buffalo Democratic politicians such as Brian Higgins.[123] In 2004, at age twenty-eight, he was elected to the Erie County Legislature. Seven years later, he became a New York State senator after defeating incumbent Bill Stachowski and Jack Quinn III in a competitive race. In March 2019, his Democratic colleagues chose the Buffalo politician as chairman of the powerful Senate Transportation Committee. After Kennedy's selection as chair, the *Buffalo News* stated, "Kennedy has become an overnight power broker in not only Western New York, but in regions stretching to central New York and beyond."[124] In fact, he has become one of Buffalo's most powerful state senators in decades.

As the committee leader, Kennedy successfully advocated for Western New York, including securing $100 million for the Niagara Frontier Transportation Authority (NFTA) for a five-year capital plan for Metro Rail maintenance and improvements. He also sponsored legislation that improved traffic safety across the state, including allowing municipalities to install cameras on school buses to capture drivers who break the law. Outside of transportation issues, Kennedy has advocated for the vulnerable by spearheading stiffer penalties for repeat child abusers and introducing a bill to protect victims of domestic violence from GPS stalking. He also supported a plan to designate $5 million from the Buffalo Billion fund to preserve Buffalo's architecturally historic Central Terminal.

Kennedy has been a strong advocate for all things Irish. His love of his Irish heritage was nurtured in South Buffalo and passed down from generations of his

Kennedy, O'Brien, McHugh, McCarthy, and Flynn families.[125] In 2008, Kennedy marched with Sinn Fein President Gerry Adams in the St. Patrick's Day parade in Buffalo's First Ward. Along the parade route, Adams tutored Kennedy about the 1866 Fenian invasion of Canada, launched from Buffalo by Irish Civil War veterans. After the parade, Kennedy worked with a task force to create a monument commemorating this historically significant international event.

Throughout his political career, Kennedy has worked to forge closer ties between Buffalo and the Emerald Isle. In Buffalo, Kennedy has hosted numerous prominent Irish leaders such as the former Lord Mayor of Belfast, the Lord Mayor of Dublin, the Irish Ambassador to the United States, an Irish senator, and several New York City Irish consuls general. These visits have increased awareness of Buffalo's rich Irish heritage in Ireland.

As a senator, Kennedy has honored dozens of Western New York Irish Americans at the annual *Irish Echo* awards event, which takes place in Manhattan.[126] Kennedy convinced the sponsors to host the national event in Buffalo in 2023, bringing more attention to the Queen City. After he served as a co-chair for the American Irish Legislators Society Annual Fundraising Dinner in Albany, the society honored Kennedy with their prestigious Daniel O'Connell Award in 2012. The South Buffalo politician was also one of a handful of founders of the National American Irish Legislators Society.

Kennedy has been outspoken about creating a world-class facility to house the University at Buffalo's priceless James Joyce Collection. In 2023, with the help of Governor Kathy Hochul, he helped secure millions of dollars to fund the project. Kennedy was also active in the New York-New Belfast Conference, which promoted commercial partnerships between New York and the capital city of Northern Ireland. With politicians such as Tim Kennedy, Buffalo's rich Irish heritage will continue to be shared with people across the globe. In 2024, Kennedy replaced Brian Higgins in the United States House of Representatives, giving him even more power to shape Western New York.

A Trailblazing Female Politician

On August 24, 2021, Kathleen "Kathy" (Courtney) Hochul was sworn in as governor of New York State, succeeding Andrew Cuomo, who resigned due to sexual harassment claims. Hochul was the first governor of the Empire State from Buffalo since Grover Cleveland (1883-1885) and the first Irish American since Hugh Carey (1975-1982). It was the first time in New York State's two hundred and forty-four-year history that a woman was the leader of the executive branch. In November 2022, Hochul was elected to the same office, defeating

Republican congressman Lee Zeldin. She had accomplished what other Buffalo Irish Americans such as William J. Donovan, James M. Mead, and Walter B. Mahoney had all failed to do.

Kathy Hochul was born in 1958 and grew up in a blue-collar Irish Catholic family in South Buffalo and Hamburg, New York. Her father, John "Jack" Courtney, ascended from a steel plant laborer to become president of Computer Task Group (CTG), one of Buffalo's largest companies. Kathy's mother, Patricia "Pat" (Rochford) Courtney, earned a social work degree and worked with domestic abuse victims.[127] Her parents, who opposed the Vietnam War and battled for civil rights, instilled in their six children a desire to be civically engaged.

Kathy's paternal grandparents, Jack and Mary Courtney, were born in the same village in County Kerry, Ireland, but met in Chicago. When a Buffalo steel company recruited the senior Jack Courtney, they married and moved from Chicago to the Queen City. While there, the Courtneys helped build the Buffalo Irish Center, and Kathy's grandfather and father played Gaelic football in Western New York. Her father, Jack, was even good enough to make the United States national squad.[128]

Irish culture shaped Hochul's formative years. So, too, did her Catholic faith. She credits both with inspiring her to serve others. She once recalled seeing a portrait of Jesus Christ next to President John F. Kennedy on the wall of her grandparents' house as a young girl. She said: "Those two pictures showed me that compassionate service to others, which my religious beliefs call for, can be accomplished through political leadership. I've often felt a moral obligation to ensure that we lift everyone up, and that no one is left behind, and have had to find a path to enact policies to make that happen."[129]

As an undergraduate at Syracuse University, Hochul served as the vice president of her class. After earning a law degree at Catholic University in Washington, DC, Hochul entered politics after meeting with fellow Buffalonian Tim Russert, then an adviser to Senator Daniel Patrick Moynihan.[130] Hochul began her career as an aide and legal counsel for Representative John J. LaFalce and later for Senator Moynihan, where she assisted the senator in efforts to help the poor. In 1994, the Hamburg Town Board appointed Hochul to fill a vacant board seat. Almost ten years later, she was appointed the Deputy Erie County Clerk, and then promoted to county clerk four years later. In 2011, after Congressman Christopher Lee resigned, she ran for his open seat as a Democrat in a Republican district and won. New York Governor Andrew Cuomo chose her to be lieutenant governor in 2014, and she succeeded him as governor in August 2021.

In a 2021 *Irish Echo* article, Hochul explained how her Irish heritage shaped her leadership style:

Like all Irishmen and Irishwomen, I'm willing to fight the good fight especially if it's for the people of my beloved state [New York]. We [the Irish] certainly have poetry in our hearts, but we are scrappy…we know how to survive adversity, and we never back down from a battle for what is right, even against all odds. We love the underdog, because the Irish have been underestimated and persecuted throughout our history.[131]

As a state leader, she has honored her Irish heritage, working hard to strengthen ties between New York and Ireland. She collaborated with the Irish Consul General to expand bilateral commerce opportunities between New York and Ireland.[132] As lieutenant governor, she gave a speech in New York during the 100th-anniversary commemoration of the 1916 Easter Rising, in which she connected Ireland's struggle for independence to America's: "An unbreakable bond [exists] between our two nations."[133]

When she assumed her role as governor of New York State, the *Buffalo News* Washington bureau chief claimed she was the most powerful female governor in US history and added, "Hochul wields extraordinary power and influence thanks to the state's constitution and New York's outsized place in the American story."[134] Her power stems from New York being the country's financial center and having the fourth-largest population.

After Hochul became governor, she said, "I want to make sure that people know that when I'm done with my administration…that they'll say: yes, women can lead, they can achieve greatness, they can do good for the people of their state, leave a strong legacy of accomplishment, but get it done in a way that's so different than we've seen before."[135]

As of 2023, Buffalo Irish men and women are in every area of politics in Western New York. At local ribbon cuttings, Irish politicians seem to dominate: Governor Kathy Hochul, Congressman Brian Higgins, New York state senators Tim Kennedy and Sean Ryan, New York State Assemblyman Patrick Burke, and Councilman Chris Scanlon, to name a few. Politicians with Irish heritage have shaped Buffalo for nearly two centuries. That trend shows no signs of diminishing.

Perhaps the two most consequential Western New York politicians in the last fifty years, Irish or otherwise, are Mayor James D. Griffin and Congressman Brian Higgins. We will profile their accomplishments later in the book.

CHAPTER TEN

Athletes

Jimmy Collins—Baseball Hall of Famer

Sports championships have been elusive for Buffalo sports teams, yet many championship athletes call Buffalo home. Boston fans can thank a Buffalo Irishman for leading them to their first championship in 1903, when the Boston Americans (later the Boston Red Sox) defeated the Pittsburgh Pirates in the first World Series.

James "Jimmy" Collins, born in 1870, was one of three children born to Irish immigrants. He went on to become one of the finest third basemen in Major League Baseball history. His father, Anthony Collins, who lived through the Irish Famine, moved to Buffalo in 1862, settling in the First Ward, where he worked as a laborer on the docks. Anthony and Alice (O'Hara) Collins lived in Niagara Falls at one point, and Jimmy was born there. The Collins family moved back to Buffalo from Niagara Falls when Anthony started work as a patrolman in the newly formed Buffalo Police Department. Jimmy attended St. Joseph's Collegiate Institute, where classmates remembered him as a natural athlete who could play every sport and finished first in all his classes.

The 1870s and 1880s have been referred to as professional baseball's "Emerald Years" because nearly forty percent of the players were Irish American. Collins most likely watched the Buffalo Bisons teams that were loaded with future Hall of Fame Irishmen.[1] More about them later. At age nineteen, Collins played for the Socials, an amateur team of Irish-American players from the Second Ward. Collins made his professional debut on May 25, 1893, with the Buffalo Bisons, unofficially called the Hibernians.[2] In his second year with the Buffalo club, Collins led the team with a .352 average, placing him in the top ten hitters in the Eastern League.[3]

In 1894, the manager of the National League Boston Beaneaters coveted Jimmy Collins and made him an offer he couldn't refuse. The Western New York native struggled his first year in Boston, but by the following year, Collins was the fan favorite. He enjoyed several winning seasons playing for the Beaneaters, where he redefined the third base position. With excellent arm strength and a fantastic eye, he played closer to the plate than most third basemen, allowing him to be more aggressive and make more plays. This style of play eventually became the norm for other third basemen.

In 1900, when investors formed a new American League to compete with the National League, Buffalo was slated to join, and Collins was interested in returning home. However, Buffalo's bid for a team fell through, and the American League added another club in Boston to compete with the successful Beaneaters. Charles Somers, the owner of the new Boston Americans team, desperately wanted Collins to join his team.

Collins accepted Somers' offer the following year and joined the new Boston team, where he was the team's star third baseman, captain, and manager. Moving to a new league was a gamble, but he signed a guaranteed three-year deal that included a share of the team's profits.[4] As a manager, Collins recruited talented players from his former league, such as future Hall of Fame pitcher Cy Young. Collins' team won the American League pennant in 1903 and faced off against the Pittsburgh Pirates in the first World Series. It was a thrilling series in which Boston came from behind to win the last four games, winning the series five games to three.

In 1904, the Collins-led team won the American League again. But the owner of the New York Giants, the winner of the National League, refused to play Boston, so there was no 1904 World Series. The owner of the Giants claimed that the new league was inferior, but more likely, he was afraid of losing to Boston. Collins continued to have success with Boston, but he was traded during the 1907 season and bounced around to a few different clubs until he retired from the Providence Grays a few years later. He played an impressive 2,201 games during his professional career.

Wages from professional baseball were paltry, so the forward-thinking Collins prepared for a future after baseball by building houses in South Buffalo off of Seneca Street, capitalizing on Irish migration to that area. Within a few years, the enterprising Collins used his earnings from baseball to acquire a substantial real estate portfolio in South Buffalo. Many sports writers wrote about his real estate business, with one reporter at the *Sporting News* writing, "It was business not sentiment that held him [Collins] in the sport of baseball and that he was out for the dough."[5]

In 1907, Collins, a longtime bachelor, married Sarah "Sadie" Murphy from Boston, and after he retired, they moved to South Buffalo, where they lived off the monthly income from his rental properties. In 1922, Collins became the president of the Buffalo Municipal Baseball Association (MUNY), an amateur baseball league consisting of eighty-eight teams and 1,100 players.[6] At that time, a local newspaper claimed Buffalo's MUNY was the largest amateur baseball circuit in the world.[7] Collins, president for twenty-one years, excelled in the role, inspiring thousands of young men, including future Hall of Famer Warren Spahn.

Although the MUNY League was going well, Collins' financial situation was deteriorating. In the 1920s, just before the Great Depression, the local housing market started crumbling, forcing Collins to sell properties. Eventually, he lost his real estate holdings. In 1933, Jimmy was forced to work for the Buffalo Parks Department to make ends meet. On a winter day in 1943, seventy-three-year-old Collins slipped on some ice, developed pneumonia, and died shortly after.

Throughout his career, writers often used superlatives like "greatest" to describe Jimmy Collins' play. In 1899, a Boston sportswriter declared that Collins was the greatest third baseman the game had ever produced.[8] In 1923, more than a decade after the Boston star retired, baseball historian and sportswriter Fred Leib said: "Jimmy Collins was the greatest third baseman of all time. That is a statement which few will contradict."[9] Twenty years after the end of Collins' professional career, another writer claimed: "No hard task confronts an expert called to pick the greatest third baseman of all time. Merely write down the name of Jimmy Collins, and nobody disputes the choice. It was almost impossible to hit a ball through Collins."[10] In later years, a Buffalo columnist wrote, "He (Collins) revolutionized the art of playing third base. Old time writers said day in and out he gave a grand opera performance in the field."[11] Despite this praise, Collins was left out of the Hall of Fame until New York Yankees manager Joe McCarthy and US Senator James M. Mead advocated on Collins' behalf.[12] Finally, in 1945, Collins was the *first* third baseman elected into the Hall of Fame, with his plaque declaring:

> Considered by Many the Game's Greatest Third Baseman. He Revolutionized Style of Play at that Bag. Led Boston Red Sox to First World Championship in 1903. A Consistent Batter, His Defensive Play Thrilled Fans of Both Major Leagues.[13]

Collins' biographer, Charlie Bevis, claims that Collins' legacy was not his play at third base (although he still holds the major league record for most putouts in a season and is second behind Brooks Robinson for most career putouts).[14] Instead, it is what Collins did for the Red Sox franchise. Not only was he the star third baseman and manager, but he was also the public face of the franchise that united a divided city, helping to restore it to national prominence.[15] Collins helped build the dynasty we now know as the Boston Red Sox by forging a championship team in three seasons and winning the World Series. Bevis wrote:

> Collins ensured that the Boston ballclub in the American League would always be number one among baseball fans in Boston. Without Collins' efforts, the Boston Red Sox would not be the iconic ballclub that it is today. Jimmy Collins truly is the patron saint of Red Sox Nation.[16]

Seventy years after Collins' death, the Dropkick Murphys, a Boston Celtic-rock band, produced a hit song called "Jimmy Collins' Wake," which pays tribute to the Buffalo native.

Jimmy Collins, who helped inspire thousands of young baseball players, was one of Buffalo's most accomplished professional athletes. In 1946, the Buffalo Common Council passed a bill to create the Jimmy Collins Memorial Fountain in Delaware Park to honor the hero. Irish-American mayor Bernard Dowd vetoed the bill because he thought the limited city funds for such projects should honor the local World War II soldiers who lost their lives. Jimmy Collins' hometown never built a fountain or memorial in his honor. Collins is buried in Lackawanna's Holy Cross Cemetery with a simple headstone that reads "Collins" and is adorned with a Gaelic cross.[17]

The Irish Buffalo Bisons

In the 1880s, at Olympic Park, located at Richmond Avenue and Summer Street, a young Jimmy Collins almost certainly watched a handful of Irish-American baseball stars who played for the Buffalo Bisons. During that decade, Buffalo fielded a National League team loaded with talent, with three Irish players later becoming Hall of Famers: James "Pud" Galvin, James O'Rourke, and Dennis "Big Dan" Brouthers.

In 1878, Buffalo signed Jim "Pud" Galvin, a son of Irish immigrants, who led the Bisons to an International Association pennant win in his first year. That season, he pitched a remarkable 96 complete games in a 116-game season, winning 72 contests (in this era, most teams had only a two-person pitching rotation).[18] Galvin, who played for Buffalo for eight seasons, finished his career in Pittsburgh, retiring with several baseball records, including most wins, most innings pitched, most shutouts, and most games started. He was also the first MLB pitcher to win 300 games. Thanks to efforts spearheaded by Bisons' historian Joe Overfield, who

referred to the Irish pitcher as "Buffalo's First Superstar," Galvin was elected into
the MLB Hall of Fame in 1965.[19] In 1902, despite his storied career, he died a
poor man at age forty-five.

In 1881, the Bisons were struggling financially, so the team's owner hired James
O'Rourke, son of Irish-born immigrants, as a player-manager to turn the team
around. O'Rourke led the team in hitting within a few years, and he had a talent
for managing. In a short time, the team was competitive, and Bisons' fans enjoyed
four straight winning seasons. In addition to Jim Galvin, O'Rourke added other
Irishmen such as Irish-born Hugh Daily, Tom Dolan, and Charlie "Curry" Foley.[20]
But O'Rourke's most important acquisition was first baseman Dennis Brouthers.

Dennis "Big Dan" Brouthers, a son of Irish Catholic immigrants, was a six-
foot-two-inch first baseman. After coming to Buffalo in 1881, Brouthers won the
National League batting title the following two years. While in Buffalo, the power
hitter twice led the league in slugging percentage and hits. In 1883, he set a major
league record with 97 RBI. To this day, Brouthers, who played for twenty-three
seasons and in 1,999 games, still ranks among baseball's all-time greats. He is in
the top ten for his .342 hitting average and 205 triples. O'Rourke and Brouthers
were elected to the Hall of Fame in 1945.

Irish players continued to lead the Bisons in the early twentieth century. In
1915, Irish-American owner and president Joseph Lannin hired Cork-born
Patrick "Patsy" Donovan, a former star outfielder in the major leagues, as his
manager. Donovan led the Bisons to the International League pennant in his
first two years. During that era, Irish-American Frank Gilhooley led the team
in hitting.

Even in the 1920s, the Bisons had a strong Irish presence, with the team's
1925 season referred to as the "Year of the Irish."[21] That year, Buffalo player Jimmy
Walsh won the International League's batting title with a .357 hitting average; the
Irish-born player won it again the following year. He was the first Bison to win
back-to-back titles since Irishman Dan Brouthers did it in 1882 and 1883.[22] In
1925, Irish American Billy Kelly, a Syracuse native and Walsh's teammate, led the
league in RBIs. The following year, Kelly, the Bisons' home run king of the 1920s,
led the nation with 44 home runs.[23] Billy Kelly is on the Bisons' top five all-time
list for almost every hitting category (home runs, RBI, hits, and triples).[24]

One former Bisons player of this era became one of the greatest managers in
Major League Baseball history. Joseph Vincent McCarthy, described as "stocky...
with a strong Irish face," played infielder for Buffalo for one season.[25] While
playing for the Bisons, McCarthy met his future wife, Buffalo native Elizabeth
McCave. McCarthy became the manager of the Chicago Cubs, leading the team
to a pennant in 1929. Two years later, the New York Yankees hired him away
from Chicago, and as manager, he led the Yankees to seven World Series titles in

sixteen years. His teams included legends such as Babe Ruth, Lou Gehrig, and Joe DiMaggio. He was the first manager to win a pennant in both the National and American Leagues, and his winning percentages in the regular season (.615) and the postseason (.698) are still the highest of any major league manager in history.

After he retired from baseball, McCarthy and his wife relocated to a 61-acre farm outside of Buffalo, where he lived for the last twenty-eight years of his life. A *New York Times* reporter wrote that as the skipper of the Yankees, McCarthy witnessed many of the most dramatic moments in sports history. As managers, Joe McCarthy and Casey Stengel share the record for winning the most World Series championships (seven).

Of the eight former Buffalo Bisons in the MLB Hall of Fame in Cooperstown to play at least one hundred games for the team, six were Irish or Irish-American: Jimmy Collins, James O'Rourke, Dennis Brouthers, Joe McCarthy, James Galvin, and Connie Mack.

Rowing

Although baseball and football were gaining popularity, rowing was the premier sport for young Irish men between the 1870s and 1890s.[26] Most men lived within walking distance of the Buffalo River or the Niagara River, and rowing was inexpensive. Irishmen dominated several of the most successful clubs, including the Hibernian Rowing Club, the Celtic Club, the Mutual Rowing Club, and the Lighthouse Rowing Club. These rowing associations also served as important Irish-American social clubs, with prominent members including William J. Donovan, Michael Shea, John Sheehan, William "Blue-Eyed Billy" Sheehan, and William "Fingy" Conners.

Michael J. Broderick, born in 1879 in Cork, Ireland, was a towering figure in Buffalo's rowing scene. After emigrating to Buffalo in 1899, Broderick was one of the founders of the West Side Rowing Club and, for thirty-six years, its president. In 1936, the US Olympic Rowing Team chose the Irishman as one of their team managers for the Berlin Olympics. The following year, Broderick secured the national rowing regatta for Buffalo, steering the club to national prominence. Years later, he served as vice president of the National Amateur Rowing Association and was inducted into the National Rowing Hall of Fame in 1982. The *Buffalo News* referred to Broderick as the "father of amateur rowing in Buffalo," and its sports editor wrote that he was "the grandest figure in sports in our grand city."[27] The West Side Rowing Club's original headquarters was located at the southern tip of Unity Island until it burned down in 1975. After Broderick's death, the city named a park at that site in his honor.

Edward J. "Algie" McGuire, a Buffalo police officer born in the First Ward, was one of the city's most accomplished rowers. On August 4, 1923, Algie McGuire, who rowed for the Mutual Rowing Club, shocked the rowing world with his victory in Baltimore at the National Single Scull Championship. In this match, the Buffalo rower defeated the two favorites, Hilton Belyea, the 1922 Canadian champion, and Paul Costello, a two-time Olympic gold medal winner, by jumping out with an early lead. McGuire beat the former champion Costello by eight lengths.

In describing the upset, *Time* magazine declared that "McGuire unexpectedly diverted rowing history from its chartered course."[28] On August 5, 1923, the front cover of the *Buffalo Courier* had a massive headline: "Ed McGuire Wins National Rowing Title."[29] Another article claimed all of the residents of the city's south side were celebrating, and plans were in place to have thousands of south side residents meet the rower when he returned home.

The following year, McGuire was invited to compete in Philadelphia for an opportunity to represent the United States in the single scull in the 1924 Paris Olympics. Before McGuire left for the qualifying event, a parade was organized in the First Ward to give him a proper sendoff. An enthusiastic crowd of several thousand lined the streets of the First Ward while Frank O'Brien, the president of the Mutuals, led a procession with McGuire in a car followed by hundreds of marchers. A large crowd gathered at the New York Central train station to cheer on McGuire.[30]

Three weeks later, on June 14, 1924, McGuire competed against E. Garrett Gilmore of Philadelphia for the open spot on the US Olympic team. For the first mile, the two rowers were neck and neck, but suddenly, McGuire, who had trained intensely for three straight weeks, suffered muscle cramps in his arms. Gilmore cruised to victory and later won an Olympic silver medal in the single-scull race in Paris. McGuire's hope for an Olympic medal was dashed, but he was still a hero back in Buffalo. While an Olympic medal eluded McGuire in 1924, another Western New Yorker of Irish descent brought one home almost a hundred years later.

Emily Regan—Gold Medal Winner

Emily Regan grew up in Williamsville, New York, in an Irish-American family that traces its roots to County Cork. Michael Regan, her paternal great-great-grandfather, served as Buffalo's police chief in the early twentieth century, and his son, Dave Regan, was one of Buffalo's best competitive rowers before the First World War. Born in 1988, Emily was a three-sport athlete at Nichols who had tried rowing in the fifth grade but did not enjoy it.[31] When Emily was a freshman at Michigan State University, her mother suggested that her six-foot-two-inch daughter try out for the school's crew team. Emily agreed and found success immediately as a walk-on athlete. Regan was a first-team All-American in women's rowing by her senior year.

After college, Regan spent a decade on the US women's rowing team, racing worldwide.[32] In Belarus, she won gold in the women's rowing eight (a boat with eight rowers and a coxswain) in the 2010 Under-23 World Championships. In Slovenia at the World Rowing Championships the following year, Regan and her teammates won gold in the women's four events, where four rowers are in a boat with no coxswain. In 2013, she and her teammates won gold in the women's eight World Championships in South Korea. In 2016, the twenty-eight-year-old qualified to represent the US on the women's eight rowing team in the 2016 Rio de Janeiro Olympics. Starting in the Rodrigo de Freitas Lagoon, the US women's team was in third place at the halfway mark. However, the US team found their rhythm, finishing two seconds ahead of Great Britain to win gold.[33] Regan, a four-time world champion, became the first Buffalonian to win an Olympic gold medal in rowing.[34]

In 2019, Regan was ranked the number two rower in the world, but after a battle with COVID-19, she did not qualify for the 2020 Tokyo Olympics, and her competitive rowing career was over. Two years later, Emily was hired as an assistant coach for the Boston University rowing team, where she is inspiring the next generation of champion rowers.

Golden Era of Boxing—Jimmy Slattery and Jimmy Goodrich

During the 1920s, two Irishmen from the south side of Buffalo became champion boxers. James Patrick "Jimmy" Slattery was born on August 25, 1904, on Fulton Street in the First Ward. He was the son of John Slattery, a fireman, and Mary (Hickey) Slattery, a housewife. Slattery's first fight was with a neighborhood bully who stole a box of chocolates from Slattery.[35] Witnesses say that close to two hundred people from the neighborhood gathered and watched Slattery, the budding pugilist, crush his much larger opponent.[36] John Slattery recognized his son's gifts, so he set up backyard boxing matches and took him to a local boxing club where Slattery's meteoric rise to national fame began.

At sixteen, the 128-pound Slattery, who acquired the nickname "Slats," started his pro career with an impressive thirty-five straight wins. He wore green trunks to honor his Irish heritage for every career fight. The young fighter won a six-round decision against the future world light heavyweight champion Jack Delaney at Madison Square Garden in New York City on October 3, 1924. People outside of Buffalo were now taking notice. A few months later, in February 1925, Slats fought the 4-to-1 favorite Jack Delaney in a regulation match at the Garden. Dancing on his toes with one of the most effective left punches in the sport, 5'11" Slattery stunned the boxing world by once again beating Delaney, moving Slattery to the world stage of boxing. After a 17-1 record the following year, the Buffalo boxer put himself into contention for the National Boxing Association title. After fifteen rounds, Slats finally defeated "Slapsie" Maxie Rosenbloom in Hartford, Connecticut, to win the 1927 World Light Heavyweight championship and sit on top of the world.

Boxing experts, sports writers, and fellow boxers nationwide could not contain their praise for Slattery. He was the favorite boxer of the *New York Daily News* sports editor and another New York sportswriter who referred to Slattery as a "darling of the gods."[37] The champion James Braddock, also known as the "Cinderella Man," proclaimed that "the greatest boxer in my time was Jimmy Slattery."[38] He added, "Joe Louis was a fine boxer, but Jim Slattery was far better." Boxing great Jim Corbett once said, "Slattery is the most perfect fighting machine I ever saw."[39] Even years after Slattery's death, in 1992, *Boxing Illustrated* ranked him as the seventh slickest boxer of all time, behind greats such as Sugar Ray Robinson, Muhammad Ali, and Sugar Ray Leonard. He was a darling of the press and his fellow boxers. Fans also loved him. Slats regularly fought in front of sold-out crowds in Madison Square Garden and Yankee Stadium in the Bronx. With Slattery's increasing success in the ring came a desire for women and alcohol. His lifelong battle with alcohol would eventually lead to his downfall.

While basking in the glory of national recognition, Slats never forgot his roots in Buffalo. There are countless stories of his generosity, from buying the bar drinks at his favorite taverns to giving his cars away to people in need. He donated a new altar for his church, bought books for a neighborhood elementary school, and paid for fans' medical bills, coal for heating homes, and funeral expenses.[40] However, between his charitable acts and expensive lifestyle, Jimmy squandered $400,000 in earnings, equivalent to over $6.0 million in 2022 dollars. By 1931, Slats was penniless.

After losing the title to Tom Loughran, Slattery attempted a comeback. Slats was in contention to win a second title in 1930 if he could beat Buffalo's West Side Italian legend Lou Scozza. In front of a sold-out crowd at Broadway Auditorium in Buffalo on February 10, 1930, Slats defeated Scozza in the fifteenth round. Slattery was on top of the world, having won the World Light Heavyweight title again.

However, Slattery lost his title only four months after regaining it, when Maxie Rosenbloom defeated him at Buffalo's Offermann Stadium. Reportedly, Slats was out drinking at the Palais Royale on Main Street in his hometown until 2:30 a.m. the night before the fight.[41] He retired from boxing in 1934, and his run-ins with alcohol and the law accelerated. In June 1935, he was put on probation for charges related to drinking, and a month later, he crashed his car. His legal problems mounted, with accusations ranging from robbery to assaulting a police officer.[42] During the Great Depression, Slattery was arrested at least ten times for crimes that involved alcohol, fighting, or both.

In 1942, Slattery was diagnosed with pulmonary tuberculosis, the same disease that killed his father and brother. He was lucky to have friends who paid for his recuperation in Arizona and assisted him in obtaining a city job in the Buffalo Parks Department, where he tended to flower beds at Delaware Park, a long way from the chanting crowds that had filled Madison Square Garden to see him fight. Slattery's marriage eventually fell apart, forcing him to sell his house. One night in late August of 1960, on one of the hottest nights of the year, Slats collapsed at his favorite bar, House O' Quinn, and he was taken to his flat close by. The following day, the hotel manager found his lifeless body on the floor of the boarding house where Slats lived.[43] The Shakespearean tragedy ended with him so poor at his death that his family buried him in an unmarked grave in Holy Cross Cemetery. Despite his demons, Jimmy Slattery will always be remembered as one of Buffalo's first athletic celebrities.[44]

Jimmy Goodrich, whose birth name was James Moran, was born in Scranton, Pennsylvania, to an Irish Catholic father, who died when Jimmy was young. As a teenager, Jimmy moved to Buffalo with his mother and stepfather, for whom Jimmy changed his last name from Moran to Goodrich. Jimmy's family was part of a larger Irish community that moved from Scranton to Buffalo to work at the Lackawanna Steel Company. As a young man, Jimmy worked as a laborer at the steel plant during the day and spent evenings boxing to supplement his wages.[45] In 1917, he teamed up with Paul "Red" Carr, Jimmy Slattery's manager, to pursue a professional career. Carr recognized Goodrich's talent and work ethic and appreciated that Goodrich, unlike Slattery, did not drink.[46]

From his first professional match in 1921, 5'4" Goodrich impressed fans and boxing experts who predicted that the "little Irishman" would win a championship. In 1925, New York City boxing officials hosted a five-month tournament to fill the vacant world lightweight title vacated by Benny Leonard. In the tournament's final bout, Jimmy Goodrich beat Chilean fighter Stanley Loayza to win the lightweight title at Queensboro Stadium in Queens, New York. After the fight, a newspaperman described the Buffalo boxer as a plodding fighter without inspiration who wins from persistence and perseverance.[47] Although Goodrich lost the world championship title five months later to Rocky Kansas, he continued to fight top world contenders for the next five years. Out of 182 professional matches, the Buffalo Irish boxer wasn't knocked out once.[48]

In 1931, after a decade of fighting, Jimmy "Champ" Goodrich retired from boxing. He owned several restaurants and taverns around Western New York and accumulated enough money to retire in Fort Myers Beach, Florida. After twenty years in the Sunshine State, where he worked as a popular bartender, Goodrich died after a long illness in 1982. Other notable Buffalo Irish boxers include Bobby Scanlon, Jackie Donovan, and Jackie Donnelly. But nothing compared to the 1920s when Buffalo had two light heavyweight champions living in the same city, both with connections to the Old First Ward.

Pro Football Advocate—Pat McGroder Jr.

On the Wall of Fame at Highmark Stadium in Orchard Park, New York, home of the Buffalo Bills, there are many familiar names: Jim Kelly, Bruce Smith, and Thurman Thomas. However, one name on the wall is unfamiliar to most people: Pat McGroder. While McGroder never played professional football, the Bills may have come to Buffalo only due to his tireless efforts.

Pat McGroder was born on St. Patrick's Day in 1904 to Patrick McGroder Sr., an Irish immigrant from County Monaghan, and Alice McGroder, also born in Ireland. The senior McGroder settled in Buffalo around 1887 and ran a successful grocery store on the West Side of Buffalo. The younger McGroder, 6'2" and 220 lbs., played football at Buffalo's Hutchinson High School and the University of Chattanooga in Tennessee. After college, McGroder entered the liquor business in Buffalo, later owning a profitable wholesale business.

McGroder also held several vital civic positions in the 1950s, including chairman of the board of the Buffalo Municipal Auditorium, Parks Commissioner, and director of the Buffalo Convention and Tourist Bureau. He was also one of the most passionate proponents of bringing professional football back to Buffalo after the city lost its team in 1949. In February 1957, city officials chose McGroder to present the city's case, about adding an expansion team in the Queen City, to the National Football League. At the time, the NFL considered expanding from twelve to fourteen teams, and the league's commissioner, Bert Bell, confided in McGroder that he supported Buffalo's expansion bid. McGroder was also close friends with NFL owners George Halas (Chicago Bears) and Art Rooney (Pittsburgh Steelers), which would help Buffalo's bid. The NFL owners, however, passed on adding a Buffalo franchise and chose Dallas instead.[49] Still, the Buffalo Irishman left an impression on league officials and became Buffalo's designated point person for future negotiations.

Two years later, after Buffalo's failed expansion bid, Ralph Wilson, a wealthy Detroit businessman, wanted to start a football club in the newly formed AFL. His first choice was to locate a franchise in Miami. Wilson passed, however, when he couldn't obtain the rights to play at the Orange Bowl Stadium. Meanwhile, Lamar Hunt, founder of the AFL, urged Pat McGroder to form a Buffalo club, which he declined, informing Hunt that Buffalo was waiting for an NFL franchise.[50] Spurned by Miami, Wilson warmed to the idea of a team in Buffalo. McGroder met with Wilson, who was impressed with his sales pitch. Wilson negotiated a favorable lease arrangement ($5,000 a year) for Buffalo's Civic Stadium (later renamed War Memorial Stadium), which was run down and needed repairs. Wilson also requested that the team receive three years of positive coverage from the local newspaper. Several years later, Wilson joked that the coverage during those first three years was the only positive coverage the *Buffalo News* ever gave his team.

After over a decade of trying to bring professional football to Buffalo, McGroder finally realized his dream and that of thousands of Buffalo fans. Wilson hired the Irish American to be the vice president of the club and a minority owner. McGroder, who was financially well-off, accepted a salary of $1 a year. For the next few decades, the Buffalo businessman was also the point person who negotiated the team's stadium lease and was instrumental in keeping the Bills in Buffalo.[51]

In 1959, Wilson and McGroder hired Richard "Dick" Gallagher, an assistant coach for the Cleveland Browns, to be the team's first general manager. Gallagher, an Irish American raised in Ohio, was the football architect who built Buffalo's championship football team in the 1960s. Within a few years, the new Buffalo team won back-to-back American Football League championships in 1964 and '65. They lost the 1966 AFL championship game to the Kansas City Chiefs, missing out on the opportunity to play the NFL's Green Bay Packers in the first Super Bowl. Gallagher left Buffalo and eventually became the director of the Pro Football Hall of Fame in Canton, Ohio.

In 1983, McGroder served as executive vice president and interim general manager of the Buffalo Bills. The following two years, the club had back-to-back 2-14 seasons. In 1985, at a ceremony to add McGroder's name to the stadium's Wall of Fame, the fans booed Ralph Wilson for the team's performance. When McGroder tried to defend Wilson, the crowd booed him, too. But McGroder was convinced that the Bills were on the verge of turning things around. The following year, quarterback Jim Kelly arrived in Buffalo, and the Bills became competitive. McGroder died in January 1986, eight months before Kelly threw his first pass for the Bills.

Upon McGroder's death, one of the former Buffalo Bills said that McGroder had been "a father figure to us all. He could be tough but, at the same time, gentle. He always had a big Irish grin and a good word for everyone…He was a great man who can never really be replaced."[52] Owner Ralph Wilson added, "Patrick McGroder and the Buffalo Bills will forever be synonymous. He was my closest and dearest friend."[53] Although McGroder was gone, it wasn't the end for influential Irish executives within the Bills organization because McGroder had groomed one of the legendary general managers of all time, who, like himself, was the son of an Irish immigrant. Within a few years of his arrival, this team executive would turn the Bills into one of the most celebrated teams in NFL history.[54]

Bill Polian—Builder of an NFL Dynasty

William (Bill) Patrick Polian Jr. was born in 1942 to William Sr. and Bernice (McLaughlin) Polian. The senior William Polian immigrated to New York City from County Westmeath, Ireland, six months before the Wall Street Crash of 1929. As with many Irish immigrants, the 22-year-old Polian had to leave Ireland because there wasn't enough land to divide among his siblings. He worked for New York's Brooklyn Edison, which later became Con Edison. After marrying Bernice, he settled in her family's neighborhood in the Bronx, where young Bill grew up.

Young Bill Polian grew up playing football at Mount Saint Michael Academy in the Bronx and later for a club team at New York University. His father preferred Irish hurling to American football, but father and son listened to Notre Dame football on the radio every Saturday.[55] When asked about Ireland, the senior Polian spoke sparingly about his native land. Instead, he fully embraced being a United States citizen. When teased about his thick Irish brogue, he would remind the jesters that he fought for the United States in the Second World War.[56] From his Irish father, young Bill learned the value of hard work and the belief that America was a land of opportunity where immigrants could succeed based on their merits. Polian once shared how his Irish heritage impacted how he treated other people, explaining that the Irish people's suffering under British rule had conditioned him to always look out for underdogs.[57]

Bill Polian's football career started in the fall of 1975. He was an unknown scout, issuing reports on American players to the coach of the Montreal Alouettes, a Canadian Football League (CFL) team. The coach asked a staff member if he could meet this mystery scout. The coach in question was Marv Levy.[58] This was the beginning of the duo that would rebuild the Buffalo Bills.

In 1978, Polian followed Marv Levy to the Kansas City Chiefs, where he worked on Levy's staff evaluating players. In 1984, the Buffalo Bills hired Polian as their pro personnel director. Pat McGroder, vice president of the Buffalo Bills, mentored Polian. In Polian's words, McGroder "kind of adopted" him and always sought ways to promote him. Looking back, Polian acknowledged how their shared Irish ancestry helped forge their close relationship.[59] But McGroder had also recognized that Polian had an excellent head for football.

Polian's first opportunity for advancement in Buffalo came in 1985 when Bills General Manager Terry Bledsoe suffered a health issue. McGroder persuaded Ralph Wilson to promote the diligent Polian to fill in for Bledsoe. Wilson agreed. Polian's honeymoon with the Bills didn't last long. He immediately faced the difficult task of signing first-round draft pick Bruce Smith. At the time, the USFL Baltimore Stars were wooing the future Hall of Famer with a lucrative contract. The struggling Bills were not exactly a tempting option for college stars—two years prior, the Bills had lost their first-round pick, Jim Kelly, to the USFL. But Polian convinced Smith, a Virginia native, that signing with the NFL over an upstart league was in his best interest. Smith became one of the greatest defensive players in NFL history and was crucial for the team's Super Bowl years. McGroder convinced Wilson to hire Polian full-time as the team's general manager.

Polian quickly made his mark rebuilding the team. One of his gifts was evaluating and acquiring talented players. After successfully signing Bruce Smith, he faced "a watershed moment," in his words.[60] The Bills still owned the rights to Jim Kelly, who had become a star in the USFL. In 1986, with that league folding, the Bills had to sign him within a year, or they would lose him. Years earlier, Kelly had made it clear that he didn't want to come to Buffalo. For Polian, the stakes had never been higher. If Kelly decided to sit out a year to sign somewhere else, Polian would lose his job as the team's general manager. After some tense negotiations, however, the two feisty Irishmen finally agreed to terms. The rest is history.

Later, Jim Kelly recalled what it was like to negotiate with Polian. "With Polian, that Irish temper of his, the sound coming from behind the closed door of any negotiation usually resembles an erupting volcano."[61] Despite the heated contract discussions, Polian and Kelly developed a close relationship. They used to joke about their Irish heritage. When Polian got angry about something, Kelly told him to calm down. Polian would respond, "We are both Irish; you know how it is."[62] In Kelly's autobiography, he wrote, "I knew I was going to like Polian from the very first time we met…besides being Irish, Polian was also a hard-nosed son of a gun who didn't take shit from anybody. He was a lot like me."[63]

Bill Polian quickly surrounded Kelly with talented players. He brought in veterans like Kent Hull, James Lofton, and Kenny Davis. Polian added Andre Reed, Will Wolford, Howard Ballard, Shane Conlan, Nate Odoms, Keith McKeller, Thurman Thomas, Don Beebe, and Phil Hansen through the draft. All of them played vital roles during the team's AFC Championship years. He also drafted quarterback Frank Reich. Polian said he "stood on the table" to get Reich, screaming, "We have to get this guy!"[64] Reich became a dependable backup quarterback when Kelly was hurt. Polian also masterminded one of the biggest trades in NFL history when the Bills acquired linebacker Cornelius Bennett. According to sports writer Chuck Pollock, Polian's most significant decision was replacing head coach Hank Bullough with Marv Levy in November 1986.[65] Polian, who owed his career to Marv Levy, now repaid the favor. Levy's low-key style was a perfect fit for the talented young team.

Polian's Bills quickly became one of the most dominant teams in the NFL, reaching the playoffs within two years of his arrival. The team he built won four consecutive AFC championships and appeared in four straight Super Bowls, an NFL record. Unfortunately for Bills fans, the team came up short all four years. Despite the team's success, Polian, known for his passion and Irish temper, wore out his welcome with owner Ralph Wilson. On February 4, 1993, four days after the Bills lost their third consecutive Super Bowl, Wilson fired Polian. Looking at Polian's accomplishments with his next two teams, it may have been one of Wilson's worst decisions.

In 1995, Polian became general manager of the new expansion team, the Carolina Panthers, and in just the second year of the franchise's history, the team played in the NFC Championship game. In 1998, Polian left the Panthers to become general manager of the Indianapolis Colts, a team in "rebuild" mode. His first major decision was to select Peyton Manning as the first pick in the 1998 NFL draft. Manning led the Colts to the postseason eleven times in thirteen years; the Colts won the division eight times, going on to two Super Bowls, and winning Super Bowl XLI against the Chicago Bears.[66] Polian finally received a Super Bowl ring, which had eluded him in Buffalo. Polian's three clubs (the Bills, Panthers, and Colts) appeared in eight championship games.

After Bill Polian's thirty-two seasons in professional football, critics agreed that he was one of the best general managers in professional football history. "Bill Polian's football teams are a reflection of the man: gritty, intelligent, and incredibly resilient."[67] Polian was the only executive named "NFL Executive of the Year" six times by *The Sporting News*. Bill Polian reached the pinnacle of his career when he was inducted into the Pro Football Hall of Fame in Canton, Ohio on August 9, 2015. When asked what it takes to get to the Hall of Fame (HOF), the humble Bronx native replied, "Jim Kelly, Marv Levy, Peyton Manning, and Tony Dungy."[68] Polian began his HOF speech by giving thanks to his family and appreciating his Irish heritage: "A journey that began on a boat from Ireland led to Canton."[69] Polian thanked Marv Levy and Ralph Wilson, who helped create a "team for the ages" and "one of the most memorable teams in league history." He referred to the Bills players as "Buffalo's boys of autumn," adding, "They brought a team, a talent, and a dream together like few others in NFL history."[70]

In interviews, Bill Polian regularly recognized his Irish-American wife, Eileen, for his success, noting that while he was chasing championships, she was home raising their four children.[71] Their three sons, Brian, Dennis, and Chris, have all been involved in college and professional football, while their daughter, Lynn, is a teacher. Polian still has good friends in Buffalo and fond memories of Western New York.[72] His near-decade in Buffalo included the most remarkable years of professional football in the city's history. Polian was one of the most distinguished sports executives to call Buffalo home. Those thrilling championship years were critical in disproving negative stereotypes about Buffalo and improving the city's image. Buffalo was a better sports town thanks to this feisty Irish American from the Bronx who, for a time, called the Queen City his home.

Jim Kelly—Hall of Fame Quarterback

While traveling outside Western New York during the 1980s and 1990s, if you mentioned that you were from Buffalo, chances are people would ask you about the Buffalo Bills. Decades later, people worldwide still knew about Buffalo from those four Super Bowl appearances. Off the field, much of the credit goes to Bill Polian. But on the field, it was the efforts of quarterback Jim Kelly, undoubtedly the greatest quarterback to play for the Bills. Some would argue he was the best Buffalo Bill of all time.

James (Jim) Edward Kelly grew up fewer than four hours south of Buffalo, in East Brady, Pennsylvania, a close-knit town of 800 people. It was a Catholic, working-class town of Irish, Italians, and Poles where many worked in the mills, while kids helped their parents make ends meet.[73] Kelly's Irish heritage comes from his mother, Alice (McGinn) Kelly. Alice's father, Patrick McGinn, born in County Down, was put in prison in the 1920s by the Black and Tans, who accused him of activities against the British.[74] The authorities also arrested six of Patrick McGinn's brothers for the same charge. Family legend suggests that they all escaped prison when one propped the door open with a Bible after the warden delivered their dinner. Shortly after this incident, Jim Kelly's grandfather, Patrick McGinn, fled Ireland and settled in Pittsburgh, where he worked as a bagman for the Pennsylvania Railroad. He was a tall man for his time, almost 6'2", and he passed his height on to his 6'3" grandson, Jim Kelly. McGinn married Amelia Woods, whose father was also from Ireland, and their eldest child, Alice, was Jim Kelly's mother.

Jim Kelly's father, Joseph Kelly, lost his parents at age two and was raised by nuns in a Catholic orphanage, and details about his heritage are scarce. We know that while Joe Kelly steered his son Jim into sports, he never played sports himself. Growing up in an orphanage meant constant work around the facility.[75] At age seventeen, Joe Kelly joined the Navy and returned to Pennsylvania to work as a machinist at a steel mill, where he married Alice McGinn and had six sons: Daniel, Patrick, Kevin, Edward, James, and Ray.

As a young boy, Jim Kelly remembered his parents listening to Irish music and talking about Ireland.[76] The Kellys were a very close family, and each brother looked out for the others. Even when Kelly became a sports celebrity, uncles, aunts, and cousins traveled to home games together in a Winnebago.[77] In a 1992 interview, Kelly shared his thoughts about his Irish heritage. "I am always very proud to say that I'm Irish."[78] When asked what it means to be a "true Irishman," he said it required loyalty and having a personality. During his football days, Kelly said he had a plaque on his wall that read, "God made the Irish number one." Kelly added, "To me, the greatest thing is to be Irish, and I've always lived by that, and I always will."[79]

Starting when his sons were in elementary school, Joe Kelly put them through strict workout regimens. Young Jim spent hours throwing and punting the football over and over again, never thinking he would make it into professional sports. No one from East Brady had ever made it. But that didn't deter Kelly. Kelly was a star player in high school, and he dreamed of attending Penn State. However, the school's coach, Joe Paterno, wanted Kelly to play linebacker, and Kelly wanted to be a quarterback. So, Kelly signed with the University of Miami, where he could play the position he wanted. In a few years, Kelly transformed Miami's lackluster squad into a competitive club and became one of the most coveted quarterbacks of the historic 1983 draft class, which included future Hall of Famers Dan Marino and John Elway.

The Bills drafted the star from the University of Miami, but Kelly didn't want to play in Buffalo. The fledgling United States Football League (USFL) needed star players, so the Houston Gamblers offered Kelly a chance to play in sunny Texas. Kelly jumped at their offer and abandoned the NFL. In Houston, Kelly quickly confirmed that he was a superstar, leading the league in passing yards and touchdowns. After three seasons, the USFL suspended operations, and Kelly had to make a decision. The Bills still owned Kelly's NFL rights, so he would have to sit out for a season to play somewhere else or play for the Bills that year.

After heated negotiations between Kelly and Bill Polian (mentioned earlier), Kelly signed with the Bills and became the highest-paid player in the NFL. Having previously snubbed Buffalo, Kelly was unsure of his reception in the Queen City. But the championship-starved Buffalo fans quickly forgave his earlier reluctance, and when Kelly arrived at the Buffalo airport, they welcomed him like a rock star. When Kelly was heading to the Hilton Hotel for a press conference, Buffalo fans lined the streets with banners exclaiming, "We Love You, Jim."[80] It was 1986, and Buffalo had caught "Kelly Fever."[81]

Kelly's signing with the Bills did more than boost a struggling professional football team—a franchise with back-to-back 2-14 seasons and wavering support from fans. Buffalonians, in general, had a gloomy outlook for the city. During the

1970s and '80s, Buffalo lost many manufacturing jobs, including thousands in the steel industry. News coverage of the Buffalo blizzards of 1977 and 1985 added to the negative perception of this once-great city. Upon Kelly's arrival, however, reporters streamed into Buffalo from all over the nation and across the globe, writing story after story about "the Kelly Phenomenon."[82] Fans in Buffalo and nationwide soon discovered that the Kelly hype was real.

Jim Kelly's boyhood dream to play in the NFL was realized on September 7, 1986. A packed stadium of desperate Buffalo fans enthusiastically cheered him on for his debut. Although he was energized by the electrified crowd, Kelly wasn't pleased with a massive painted sign on the stadium wall, "Kelly is God."[83] While a competitive player, he didn't like being referred to as 'savior' and 'messiah.' He wanted to play football, not be saddled with saving a city.[84]

With Kelly, the Bills earned respect quickly, and in his third year, he led the team to the playoffs. In eleven seasons, he led the Bills to the playoffs eight times. Under his leadership, the team won four straight AFC Championship titles, which no team had ever done. While the Bills went to the Super Bowl four consecutive times, losing each time, Kelly's Bills thrilled and excited fans for eleven straight seasons. Those who lived in Buffalo at that time always remember how rooting for the Bills united Western New Yorkers.

In 1997, after suffering a concussion, Kelly retired. Just like that, the glory days of the Buffalo Bills came to an end. After eleven seasons, the Irish American from East Brady was the team's all-time leader in pass attempts, completions, yards, touchdown passes, and completion percentage. For the NFL record books, Kelly was the eighth all-time in completions, tenth in yards, twelfth in touchdown passes, and thirteenth in attempts. He boasted the fifth-best completion percentage in NFL history and ranked fifth all-time in passing efficiency.[85] Kelly accomplished all this despite losing two years of his football career playing in the USFL.

Sportswriters regularly commented on Kelly's toughness and resilience. You could knock him down, but he just got back up. You could beat him in a Super Bowl, and he would return stronger the following year. But no one could have foreseen the challenges he and his wife, Jill, would face after he retired. Jim and Jill Kelly's only son, Hunter, was diagnosed with a rare but severe disease called Krabbe. This insidious disease destroys the protective coating of nerves in the brain and central nervous system. Because of their son's condition, the Kellys founded the Hunter's Hope Foundation, a non-profit organization that funds research and supports families caring for a child with Krabbe disease. In 2004, the Kellys also helped found the Hunter James Kelly Research Institute (HJKRI) at the University at Buffalo, which researches therapies for diseases like Krabbe.

In 2006, thanks to the Kellys' advocacy, New York State added Krabbe disease to its newborn screening protocols. Since then, other states have also added it, potentially helping hundreds of families. Jim Kelly also suffered his own health trials, including surviving three severe bouts with oral cancer. Along the way, Kelly has helped increase cancer awareness locally and nationally.

Jim Kelly endured many challenges and setbacks throughout his life. Growing up in a small town, he struggled financially. In his senior year of high school, he tore his shoulder so severely that doctors suggested he would never play again. He was drafted by the hapless Buffalo Bills, and then his team lost the Super Bowl four years in a row. His beloved son Hunter's tragic death at age eight was followed by Kelly's lengthy battle with cancer. Kelly inspired people with how he handled himself on the football field, but he inspired them even more with how he dealt with all of these personal trials and tribulations. His life modeled resilience and perseverance, which is partly why Western New Yorkers admire him.

For Kelly, charitable work is "the thing that gives me the most pride and pleasure...."[86] At the 2018 ESPY Awards, where Kelly was honored with the *Jimmy V. Award for Perseverance*, he told a national audience, "Make a difference today for someone who's fighting for their tomorrow." Kelly implemented this philosophy as soon as he arrived in Buffalo by establishing the Kelly For Kids Foundation, which has helped thousands of disabled or disadvantaged Western New York children. Since its inception, the foundation has donated over $5 million to dozens of local organizations that help children. Cradle Beach Camp, which serves youngsters with special needs and those in need, has been one of the biggest beneficiaries.

Jim Kelly has hosted an annual celebrity golf tournament for thirty-five years, raising millions for his charities. NFL stars like Dan Marino, John Elway, and Joe Namath have participated. Kelly has also hosted summer football camps for children aged ten to eighteen who are interested in learning more about football. Over the years, Kelly has helped thousands of kids learn the game of football and hone life skills. Kelly doesn't just show up for a photo opportunity but stays at the camp every day from sunrise to sunset.[87]

In 2002, just five years after his retirement, Kelly was inducted into the Pro Football Hall of Fame. There was never any doubt this would happen. Bobby Beathard, former general manager of the Washington Redskins, claimed, "When you think of Jim Kelly, I always think of one of the great, great quarterbacks of our time." Beathard added, "Jim's certainly as tough as they come and one of the great leaders of all time."[88] Former *Buffalo News* columnist Jerry Sullivan perfectly summed up Kelly's impact on Buffalo.

> Now his career is over, and we'll never see another like it. It has become a cliché in this town, but Western New Yorkers need to remind themselves what it was like before Kelly arrived, when the Bills were 2-14. The team was

a joke, an embarrassment in America's most popular pro sport at a time when the city's own self-esteem was at an all-time low. It's hard to believe that a pro football team can be a city's most significant link to the outside world, but that's the sort of culture we live in. Kelly's mission was to lift the city's profile, to put it back on the sporting map. He certainly did that. He made Buffalo relevant again in the nation's eyes.[89]

This Irish American from a tiny town in Pennsylvania made Buffalo his home. He won Buffalonians over and gave generously to the city on and off the field.

Buffalo's Connection to the Pro Football Hall of Fame

Joe Horrigan grew up in South Buffalo, the second-oldest of ten children, graduated from Frontier High School, and served in the Air Force for four years. His Irish-American father, John "Jack" Horrigan, was a noted sports writer for the *Buffalo Evening News* and then public relations director for the American Football League in the 1960s.[90] Jack Horrigan co-authored *The Other League: The Fabulous Story of the American Football League*, drawing on his experiences with the AFL. Jack later served as vice president of public relations for the Buffalo Bills (1966-1973). The Pro Football Writers of America created the annual *Jack Horrigan Award* to honor league or club officials who help pro football writers do their jobs.

Young Joe Horrigan's first involvement with football was at thirteen when the American Football League (AFL) held its annual draft in New York City. Jack Horrigan enlisted his son Joe to run cards with the draft picks of AFL teams to the media.[91] After graduating from the University of Akron in 1977, Joe Horrigan accepted a job as a curator at the fledgling Pro Football Hall of Fame (HOF) in Canton, Ohio. Starting with only three filing cabinets of historical documents, he organized the growing collection of memorabilia, and, over time, the South Buffalo Irishman became the point person for historical questions about the sport.[92] Horrigan was eventually promoted to vice president of communications and exhibits, and he traveled across the country to acquire historical documents and memorabilia from retired players and their families.[93]

Throughout the four decades Horrigan worked in Canton, the HOF museum expanded to four times its original space and welcomed more than ten million visitors. The Hall, located on a 100-acre campus, with several hundred employees and volunteers, now has ten times the exhibit space that it did when Horrigan joined, including six million photographs and 40,000,000 documents.[94] After being promoted to executive vice president of museums, Horrigan became the Hall of Fame's executive director in 2017. Along the way, he wrote a popular book about the league, *NFL Century: The One-Hundred-Year Rise of America's Greatest Sports League* (2019). His father, Jack, had written the definitive history of the AFL, and Joe wrote the history of the NFL.[95]

This unofficial historian of the NFL has been praised for his work. One HOF selector explained, "There has been and will only be one gatekeeper to Canton—that's Joe Horrigan. He is to the game's history what Jim Brown is to the game itself. There is no greater authority." In retirement, Horrigan continued to work as a senior advisor to the HOF and continued his work on the Black College Hall of Fame exhibition space in Canton. In 2022, the Pro Football Writers of America changed the name of the prestigious *Jack Horrigan Award* to the *Horrigan Award* to honor both father and son.

Basketball

On April 30, 1956, in New York City, the Rochester Royals selected South Buffalonian John McCarthy, a son of Irish immigrants, in the fourth round of the NBA draft. McCarthy, the twenty-fourth pick overall that year, graduated from Bishop Timon High School and later played for Canisius College, where he steered the team to some of the school's most memorable basketball seasons during the team's glory years in the mid-1950s. The six-foot one-inch guard scored 1,160 points in 61 games in his college career and led Canisius to back-to-back Elite Eight games at the NCAA tournament in 1955 and '56.[97] In 1956, when McCarthy was captain in his senior year, the Canisius team defeated North Carolina State, the second-ranked team in the nation, in a stunning four-overtime NCAA tournament game.

After a year playing for Rochester in the NBA, McCarthy joined the St. Louis Hawks. With the Hawks, he led the team in assists in the 1960 and '61 seasons, although the Hawks lost both years to the Boston Celtics in the NBA championship finals. The South Buffalo native joined the Bill Russell-led Celtics for the 1963 season and won a championship ring. During his first playoff game in 1960, he was the first of only four NBA players in history to score a triple-double (double-digit points, assists, and rebounds).[98]

After seven NBA seasons, McCarthy coached the NBA Buffalo Braves in 1971, and then three years later, he returned to coach at his alma mater, Canisius College. His son John told the *Buffalo News* that his father "remained a humble person, his whole life" and added that his father "never thought he was bigger or better than anybody else."[99] Former Canisius College president John Hurley said, "John McCarthy was clearly one of the best, if not the best, basketball players to come through Canisius College."[100] More than that, he was among the best athletes to come out of Western New York.

Five years after McCarthy, another future NBA-bound basketball player was born in the same South Buffalo neighborhood. Ronald Barry "Whitey" Martin, born in 1939, was raised on Woodside Avenue in Buffalo, deriving his nickname from his light blond hair. His mother, Anna (Barry) Martin, was the daughter of Irish immigrants from County Cork. As a Bishop Timon High School freshman, the 5'5" Martin was cut from the varsity basketball team. But the following year, he grew five inches and was the team's starting point guard.[101] Like McCarthy, Martin led his basketball team at Bishop Timon High School and was the most valuable player in the Catholic League.

In college, Martin led the St. Bonaventure team to their first NCAA tournament appearance in 1961, and in front of a sold-out crowd at Madison Square Garden, the Bonnies won their first-round match against Rhode Island. Their second-round game was in Charlotte, North Carolina, where they lost their contest to Wake Forest after the referees made controversial calls that favored the North Carolina team. In the 1961 NBA draft, the New York Knicks picked Martin in the second round with the fifteenth overall pick. Martin played sixty-six games for the Knicks in the 1961-62 season but was cut the following year. After his NBA career, Whitey Martin played semi-professional basketball.

Swimming

Another son of South Buffalo, George Breen, grandson of Irish immigrants, set records in swimming. Breen, born in 1935, was a champion rower at Bishop Timon High School. He swam at Cortland State University in Central New York and quickly dominated, winning his first national championship in 1955 and setting world records in the 1500 meters, the one-mile freestyle, the 800 meters, and the 880-yard freestyle the following year.[102]

Breen represented the United States in the 1956 Olympics in Melbourne, Australia, where he set another world record in the 1500-meter preliminary round. However, he fell short of his historic time in the Olympic finals for the same event and earned a bronze medal instead of gold. The South Buffalonian also earned a bronze in the 400-meter freestyle and a silver in the 800-meter freestyle. Four years later, at the Olympics in Rome, he won another bronze in the 1500-meter freestyle. In addition to four Olympic medals and six world records, Breen won 22 US National Championship competitions.[103] Throughout the 1960s and '70s, the star athlete coached the US Olympic team and is still one of the most decorated swimmers from Western New York.

Susan "Sue" Walsh, born in 1962 and raised in Hamburg, New York, has Irish ancestry on her father's side and German heritage on her mother's. She graduated from Mount Mercy Academy in South Buffalo, where she was one of the top female swimmers in the nation. The University of North Carolina women's swim team recruited her, and she dominated all four of her years at Chapel Hill, setting American records and winning two medals in the 1982 World Aquatics Championships.

Walsh qualified to represent the United States in the 1980 Olympics in Moscow, and experts predicted she would win a gold medal in the 200-meter backstroke. However, President Jimmy Carter boycotted the Olympics because Russia had invaded Afghanistan. While this devastated Walsh, she continued to win medals in the United States and abroad. In 1984, she was still the top 200-meter backstroke racer in the United States, but, during the qualifiers for the Olympics that year, she suffered an infection and missed qualifying by one one-hundredth of a second. Walsh won eleven NCAA swimming titles in her collegiate career and set NCAA records in the 50-, 100- and 200-yard backstroke races.[104]

Sue Walsh won the prestigious NCAA Top Five award, presented to the country's top five male and female college athletes. It is the NCAA's highest student-athlete honor, and she was the first UNC Tar Heel to win the prize. In her 40s, Walsh returned to the pool, dominating her age group again. In 2007, at forty-five, she established six world records at the US Masters Swimming Championships.[105] Between the ages of 45 and 49, Walsh was the best female swimmer in the world. At age 52, she set a world record in the 50-meter freestyle for her age group.

In a poll of *Buffalo News* sports staffers, Walsh was ranked the seventh-best female athlete in Western New York history.[106] Sue Walsh, a swimming legend, is still among UNC-Chapel Hill's most decorated athletes. In 2021, the College Swimming and Diving Coaches Association (CSCAA) chose her as one of the past century's top 100 swimmers and divers.

Running

Mary Robertson Wittenberg, who grew up in South Buffalo and West Seneca, was the oldest of seven children raised in an Irish Catholic family. Mary Robertson started running in her senior year at Canisius College and continued running competitively at Notre Dame Law School. In 1987, she won the Marine Corps Marathon and qualified for the 1988 Olympic trials in the same event.

After working several years as a partner at a corporate law firm, she resigned in 1998 to work as a vice president of the New York Road Runners Club (NYRRC), which organizes the New York City marathon. Seven years later, the Runners Club promoted the Western New York native to president and CEO. Over a decade as the race director for the NYC marathon, she grew the event to 50,000 runners while raising $35 million a year for charity. It is the largest marathon in the country for spectators and runners, and it is also an international spectacle with more than 300 million television viewers worldwide. Wittenberg also leveraged her position of power to raise money for several New York City charities.[107] In a *Running Times* magazine profile of Mary Wittenberg, the author stated, "Her fresh-faced good looks belie an iron will, fierce determination, and an uncompromising work ethic."[108] During her years as leader of the race, Mary Wittenberg was considered one of the world's most influential female sports administrators.[109]

About a decade after Mary Robertson left Canisius College, another student excelled on the track at the Jesuit school. Western New York native Mary Beth Riley Metcalf was a cross-country and track star, as well as an outstanding scholar. The 1991 *Summa Cum Laude* Canisius graduate set school records in the 800-meter indoor race and two relay races. In her sophomore year, she was diagnosed with Hodgkin's disease. Even while undergoing nine weeks of chemotherapy for lymphatic cancer, she continued her studies and training.[110]

In 1991, Riley was selected as a top ten finalist for the first-ever national NCAA Woman of the Year Award. The award honors the nation's top senior female athlete. On October 30 in Chicago, with the ten finalists eagerly awaiting the announcement of the winner, NCAA President Judith M. Sweet presented the award to Canisius's Mary Beth Riley. When Daniel Starr, history professor and former Canisius College Athletic Director, was asked about the highlight of his twenty-five years of leading the school's athletic department, he cited the selection of Mary Beth Riley as the NCAA's first Woman of the Year.[111]

South Buffalo and NHL Hockey

Buffalo Irish residents, especially from the city's south side, have impacted hockey on and off the ice. Former First Ward resident Edward John "E.J." McGuire played hockey for Canisius High School and Brockport State University. Later, McGuire was Mike Keenan's assistant coach for eleven seasons with the Philadelphia Flyers, Ottawa Senators, and Chicago Blackhawks. The Keenan/McGuire duo won five divisional titles and went to the Stanley Cup with the Flyers and Blackhawks. The First Ward native was also the head coach for American Hockey League (AHL) and Ontario Hockey League (OHL) teams. As a coach, McGuire was an innovator who used video to educate and motivate his players, incorporating statistics to analyze player matchups.[112]

But McGuire's most significant contribution was bringing credibility back to the NHL's scouting department. In 2005, he was hired to work in the Central Scouting unit and quickly became its director and the NHL's Hockey Operations vice president. Adding staff and analytics, the Central Scouting department provided more accurate profiles of draft-eligible prospects, enabling the twenty-nine scouts working for him to watch and rate the eligible players worldwide. At McGuire's death, NHL Commissioner Gary Bettman declared that the NHL "was privileged to benefit from E.J.'s expertise and enthusiasm" and added that how he ran the Scouting unit "made it vitally important to every one of our Clubs."[113]

McGuire created the annual NHL Combine—where teams analyze prospects before the draft—and advocated holding this yearly event in Buffalo, which has hosted it for eight consecutive years, bringing positive international attention to McGuire's hometown. McGuire also assisted in creating the NHL's first real-time replay system in Toronto. To honor the proud Buffalonian who died of cancer at 58, the NHL created the E.J. McGuire Award of Excellence, recognizing the draft prospect who best exhibits character, competitiveness, and athleticism. Now, McGuire's name will live on for years to come.

South Buffalo produced two NHL players at the beginning of the twenty-first century. Tim Kennedy, a South Buffalo native and the son of a police officer, attended Bishop Timon High School and played hockey at Michigan State University. In the 2005 NHL Draft, Kennedy was picked in the sixth round by the Washington Capitals and then traded to his hometown team, the Buffalo Sabres. As a journeyman professional hockey player, he later played left wing for several NHL and AHL teams and had stints playing in Swedish and Russian leagues. Two years after Kennedy was drafted, the Chicago Blackhawks drafted another Buffalo Irish American from the same tight-knit neighborhood. He would become one of the greatest professional athletes in Western New York history.

Patrick Kane—NHL Superstar

On June 9, 2010, the Chicago Blackhawks played the Philadelphia Flyers in Game Six of the Stanley Cup Finals in Philadelphia. Chicago led the best of seven series 3-2 and, with a victory, would become champions. With the score tied 3-3 at the end of regulation, the game went into overtime. About four minutes into the extra session, Chicago forward Patrick Kane sprinted down the left side of the rink, skated around a Philadelphia defender, and raced toward the net, ripping a wrist shot at the goal. For several seconds, no one in the arena except Patrick Kane knew that the puck was lodged in the upper right side of the net. With Kane's goal, the Blackhawks had won their first Stanley Cup Championship since 1961.[114]

Patrick Timothy Kane II was born in South Buffalo on November 19, 1988, to Patrick Jr. and Donna Kane. Patrick "Tiki" Kane recognized his son's talent for hockey when Patrick was a young boy. By age seven, Patrick dominated his peers on the ice, and within a short time, he played hockey year-round on travel teams with older children and continued to excel. The kid from South Buffalo regularly scored four or five goals a game at age eleven.[115] Three years later, Kane and his parents decided he could develop his skills further by joining the HoneyBaked Hockey Club, a development team based in Detroit, which required the fourteen-year-old to leave his family in Buffalo and relocate to Michigan. Besides playing with higher caliber teammates, Kane lived with former NHL star Patrick Verbeek—a Hall of Famer who mentored and guided the young Buffalo prodigy.

At age sixteen, Kane played for the United States Development Team Program, and in his second year (2005-2006 season), he broke the previous program record held by Phil Kessel by tallying 102 points in 58 games. The following year, he played for the London Knights in the Ontario Hockey League (OHL), winning the league's scoring title with 145 points and the OHL Rookie of the Year.

In 2006, the year before Kane was eligible to be drafted, NHL scouts had concerns about his skinny 5'8" frame and his toughness in the NHL. Some hockey experts thought the South Buffalo boy would be a third-round pick. However, the year before he was drafted, the self-confident Kane told one of his teammates that he would be the first pick in the draft.[116] Indeed, he was. The Chicago Blackhawks turned down trade offers for the first pick because they knew Patrick Kane was the best player in the draft. They were proven right.

In Chicago, Kane quickly became a fan favorite. Although the Blackhawks missed the playoffs his first year, the team was now competitive. In his inaugural Chicago season, Kane won the Calder Memorial Trophy as the NHL's rookie of the year. By Kane's third year, he led his team to the Stanley Cup Finals. As described above, Kane's overtime heroics in Game Six against the Philadelphia Flyers established him as a Chicago legend. The Blackhawks returned to the Stanley Cup in 2013, and more than two million Chicago fans congratulated Kane and his teammates at the victory parade. Chicago's dominance continued with their third Stanley Cup trophy in 2015. After three Stanley Cup wins, the Buffalo native brought relevance back to the Chicago Blackhawks franchise.

Patrick Kane has won almost every NHL award available to an offensive player. In 2013, he won the coveted Conn Smythe Trophy as the most valuable player in that year's NHL playoffs. Three years later, the South Buffalo native was the first American-born player to win the Art Ross Trophy as the NHL's scoring

leader. The same year, he was the first American-born player to win the Hart
Trophy, awarded to the player determined to be the most valuable to his team.
That year, Kane also received the Ted Lindsay Award for being the league's most
outstanding player.

As Kane's career advanced, he continued to break records. In 2015, he
established a new Chicago Blackhawk point streak at 26 straight games, and, in
the same year, he set the record for most consecutive games with a goal (seven) by
an American player. In January 2020, at age 31, Patrick Kane became the youngest
American-born player to tally 1,000 points. Three years later, he was third on the
all-time point list for American-born hockey players, and if he continues to score
at his current pace, he will almost certainly vault to first place. Even against the
best non-American-born players, Kane excels. During the decade of the 2010s, he
scored more points than any other NHL player, including future Hall of Famers
Alexander Ovechkin (Russian) and Sidney Crosby (Canadian).

Hockey columnist Mike Harrington once proclaimed that if there were a
pantheon of the four or five best Western New York athletes, Patrick Kane would
be on it.[117] This statement is high praise in a region that has produced the likes
of Warren Spahn, Bob Lanier, Cliff Robinson, Ron Jaworski, Christian Laettner,
Jimmy Slattery, Jennifer Suhr, and Rob Gronkowski. If Kane keeps up his current
pace, he could become the greatest United States-born player in NHL history.[118]

The majority of the greatest Buffalo Irish athletes have come from South Buffalo or
the First Ward: Jimmy Collins, Jimmy Slattery, Johnny McCarthy, Patrick Kane,
and George Breen. Bishop Timon High School (now Timon-St. Jude) and the
surrounding South Buffalo neighborhood have nurtured and produced exceptional
competitors. In addition to outstanding players, the school has produced several
stalwart coaches, such as Thomas "Tommy" Ryan and Paul Fitzpatrick, who have
left an indelible mark on hundreds of Western New Yorkers, Irish and non-Irish.
The future of Buffalo Irish women and men in sports is bright.

The Buffalo Irish produced champions not only on the sports fields but also on
the battlefield. Their stories are next.

CHAPTER ELEVEN

Military Figures

Major General Bennet Riley

In 1848 and '49, thousands of settlers rushed to the California territory with gold fever. At the time of the Gold Rush, Congress was stymied on the issue of California's statehood, debating whether to admit it as a slave or free state. While the legislators argued, some areas of this western territory suffered lawlessness because of the absence of a functioning government. There were reports of white miners shooting Native Americans in cold blood, and tempers flared between the Mexican miners and the newly arrived settlers from the East.[1] Both white and Mexican settlers were agitated because they had to pay taxes but lacked representation in Congress.[2] A group of San Francisco residents even tried to create their own government, and the federal government condemned their actions. Finally, the United States War Department dispatched one of its most experienced generals to remedy the chaotic situation. Major General Bennet Riley, a resident of Buffalo, New York, quickly brought order to a volatile situation.

On June 3, 1849, in Monterey, California, General Riley proclaimed that *he* was the authority over California's civil government, forbidding anyone from recognizing or paying taxes to any groups trying to establish their own government. Riley also deployed troops to protect Native Americans from lawless miners.[3] As the executive of the civil government, Riley appointed judges and set up elections for town councils and justices of the peace.[4] To soothe the angry residents, the Irish-American general initiated a constitutional convention in Monterey and ordered the election of representatives to this meeting, paving the way for a democratically elected governor and state delegates. His efforts restored peace and order and set up the groundwork for statehood. The following year, as part of Congress's legislative package called the Compromise of 1850, California was admitted to the Union as a free state. Riley had the distinction of being the final military governor of what became the Golden State.

Bennet Riley was born to Irish Catholic parents in St. Mary's County, Maryland, in 1787.[5] After working as a cobbler, he became a privateer and enlisted in the US Army during the War of 1812. Promoted to lieutenant, he served with distinction at the Second Battle of Sackets Harbor near Watertown, New York. At the war's end, Riley still found military life satisfying and remained in the army, serving as a captain. He was described as gallant, fearless in battle, and a natural leader.[6] Ulysses S. Grant described Riley as "the finest specimen of physical manhood I had ever looked upon...6'2" in his stocking feet, straight as the undrawn bowstring, broad-shouldered with every limb in proportion, with an eye like an eagle and a step as light as a forest tiger."[7]

After a few years of relative peace in the United States, Riley was deployed to battle Native Americans in conflicts across the country. In 1823, under the command of Colonel Henry Leavenworth, Riley fought against the Arikara Indians in present-day South Dakota. It was the first US Army battle against the Native Americans west of the Missouri River. Six years later, in 1829, Riley led the first military escort of traders along the Santa Fe Trail. He was also active during the Black Hawk War (1831-1832). In 1839, Riley, now a major, played a critical role in defeating the Seminole Indians at the Battle of Chokachotta (sometimes spelled Chakotta) in Florida. His superiors elevated Riley to brevet colonel for his bravery in the conflict.

In 1839, Riley was promoted to lieutenant colonel of the Second Infantry Regiment and was stationed in Buffalo, New York. Two years later, his superiors named him commander of the Buffalo Barracks, a sizable military base located north of the city's downtown.[8] Riley and his wife, Arabella, considered Buffalo their permanent home and raised six children in a brown frame home on Main Street. After the United States annexed the Republic of Texas, Riley was sent to the southern border to fight the Mexicans while his wife and children remained in Buffalo.

During the Mexican-American War (1846-1848), Riley was the commander of the 2nd US Infantry under General Winfield Scott. After the Siege of Veracruz, Riley was promoted to brigadier general and was now in charge of a brigade. General Scott credited Riley with winning the Battle of Churubusco and elevated him to brevet major general. But it was his actions off the battlefield that are still remembered in Mexico and Ireland today.

On August 26, 1847, in San Angel, a hamlet just outside of Mexico City, Riley presided over the second court martial trial of the St. Patrick's Battalion (also known as the San Patricios). During the war with Mexico, this Celtic fighting unit, comprised primarily of soldiers of Irish ancestry, had deserted the United States Army to fight on the Mexican side under General Antonio Lopez de Santa Anna. Some immigrant soldiers switched to the Mexican side because they suffered discrimination from the Protestant officer corps, while others pitied the innocent Mexican citizens. General Santa Anna pleaded with the Irish soldiers to switch sides by stressing the shared bond between Mexico's and Ireland's Catholicism.[9] On August 20, 1847, about two hundred former US soldiers fought on Mexico's side in the Battle of Churubusco, many defending a Catholic convent. Unfortunately for these deserters, the superior United States military defeated the Mexicans in the battle and captured many of the surviving Irish soldiers.

General Winfield Scott chose the Irish-American Riley to preside over one of the two court-martial proceedings. Despite their shared heritage, Riley showed no mercy to the captured Irish deserters and gave death sentences to all but two of them.[10] After much public condemnation, General Scott reduced some of the punishments. But on September 12, US soldiers executed fifty of the deserters in the largest mass execution in US Army history. But the deceased soldiers and their deeds have never been forgotten. Mexicans commemorate the Saint Patrick's Battalion every St. Patrick's Day and on September 12, their execution day. In San Angel, now a wealthy suburb of Mexico City, there are numerous plaques, monuments, and schools named after this famed Irish fighting unit. Even Hollywood thought their story was worth retelling when Orion Pictures released *One Man's Hero* (1999), a drama about the St. Patrick's Battalion, starring Tom Berenger.

In 1850, Riley's health began to decline after his exhausting duties in California, so he retired to his Buffalo home. On his arrival in April 1851, the city treated him as a national hero. The mayor, a large committee of citizens, and a military contingent greeted him at the Exchange Street rail depot, waving flags and banners throughout the streets.[11] Despite the joyous homecoming, Riley was battling cancer and would survive only three more years. When he died June 6, 1853, his funeral in Buffalo was a public event, with large crowds watching as soldiers from the 65th Regiment led a riderless horse with boots reversed in the stirrups.[12]

The Riley House, a landmark on Main Street near Barker Street, eventually became part of St. Joseph's Collegiate Institute, a Catholic boys' high school. For over one hundred years, the house looked the same as when the Rileys lived there, with a few modifications.[13] However, similar to the historically catastrophic leveling of Samuel Wilkinson's mansion—which became a gas station—the former Riley homestead was demolished and is currently the site of a massive car wash and gas station.

In June 1853, US Secretary of War Jefferson Davis honored Major General Bennet Riley by renaming a Kansas military camp Fort Riley. The mission of this military installation was to protect the movement of people and commerce on the major routes of the Oregon and Santa Fe trails. Riley County in Kansas was named after the Buffalo Irishman, as well. Six years after Riley's death, in 1859, Buffalo laid out a new street and named it after him.[14]

In 1945, a hundred years after Riley's death, the *Buffalo News* published an article declaring him "Buffalo's greatest soldier." One *News* reporter made a case for Riley's supremacy over others, like General Peter B. Porter (former US Secretary of War) and General William "Wild Bill" Donovan (First World War hero and Second World War spy chief). The reporter argued that Riley was involved in more chapters of US history than any other Buffalo military figure (the War of 1812, the Black Hawk War, the Seminole War, the Mexican-American War, and service as the governor of California).[15]

Riley's wife, Arabella, remained in Buffalo for more than four decades after his death (she was twenty years younger than him and lived until age 90). Prominent Riley descendants continued to reside in Buffalo a century after his death.[16] As the imperial history of the United States continues to be reevaluated, Riley's reputation, like many who were involved in the Mexican and Native American conflicts, may be reassessed. But as a man of his time, he was a force of nature. One historian referred to him as an "arch-typical frontier officer" whose outstanding thirty-seven-year career included twenty-five years on the frontier.[17] Major General Bennet Riley is buried under a modest white gravestone in Buffalo's Forest Lawn cemetery, not far from Samuel Wilkeson's final resting spot.

US Civil War

While Bennet Riley didn't live to fight in the Civil War, hundreds of Buffalo Irish laborers did. As the military campaigns of the Union Army continued to fail in 1861, it became clear that the federal government required more soldiers to defeat the Confederates. In the summer of 1862, the Irish in Buffalo desired a fighting regiment of their own—an idea supported by even Bishop John Timon. Some men enlisted for a sense of adventure, some out of patriotism for their new country, and others for the money.

On August 17, 1862, John E. McMahon, a practicing attorney from Pearl Street, was tasked with organizing a Buffalo Irish regiment as part of the Corcoran Irish Legion. McMahon was born in Wexford, Ireland, in 1834, and five years later, his family emigrated to Canada. His father eventually moved the family south of Buffalo, where he worked for the railroads. In 1851, John graduated from St. John's College (later called Fordham College) in New York City. The following year, New York Governor Horatio Seymour hired the intelligent and diligent Irish immigrant as his private secretary. A few years before the start of the Civil War, in 1857, John McMahon moved to Buffalo to set up a law practice.

McMahon's orders were to recruit four companies of men from Buffalo for a new regiment called the 155th. This unit recruited heavily from the working-class Irish along the waterfront and signed up five hundred men within a few weeks. In Buffalo newspaper ads, generous bounties were offered to entice the men: the federal and state governments provided $150 per soldier, and wealthy Buffalonians offered an additional $25-$50 per volunteer. After training, the 155th regiment left on October 10, 1862 and landed in Newport News, Virginia. The 155th was to join with other forces in New York State to fight in Corcoran's Irish Legion, also known as the Fighting 69th, led by Brigadier General Michael Corcoran. These Irish regiments across New York were also known as "Green Flag Regiments," and they were composed almost entirely of Irish immigrants or their immediate descendants.[18]

General Corcoran had to reorganize his brigade due to desertions and poor recruiting in some parts of New York State. So he split up the four companies of Buffalo's Irish regiment, with "I" and "K" staying with the 155th, and "C" and "D" moving to the 164th Regiment. However, the Buffalo Irish, who desired to fight as one unit, were incensed, and some deserted from the regiment, feeling the military leadership deceived them.[19] The two regiments (the 155th and 164th) did fight side by side in many battles throughout the last years of the war.

The 155th only had to wait a few months for their first engagement, which came on January 30, 1863 in Virginia at the Battle of Deserted House. The unit fought in several bloody engagements in the Virginia campaign, such as the Siege of Suffolk and the battles of Spotsylvania and North Anna; their most significant number of casualties occurred toward the end of the war at Cold Harbor.[20] They also fought in the Battle and Siege of Petersburg, and some survived to witness the surrender of the Confederate troops at the Appomattox Court House. By the war's end in 1865, the 155th suffered a nearly 60% casualty rate, with 189 deaths and 280 injured out of the 820 enlisted men.[21]

McMahon's 164th regiment, with two companies of Buffalo Irish men, fought in the critical Virginia campaign from 1863 to 1865, playing a significant role in the battles of Cold Harbor, Spotsylvania, Strawberry Plains, and Petersburg. The commanding officer and recruiter of the regiment, Colonel John E. McMahon, died of tuberculosis on March 11, 1863. His younger brother, James McMahon, a twenty-nine-year-old lawyer, replaced him as the regimental colonel twelve days later. At the savage Battle of Cold Harbor, James P. McMahon, with a green flag in his left hand and a sword in his right, tried to rally his men up the enemies' defenses; only a handful of men followed him. Colonel McMahon turned and exclaimed, "Now boys we got 'em." At that moment, he was struck with a hail of Confederate bullets; at least seven bullets pierced him. One historian poetically described the scene this way: "For an instant he [James McMahon] was there outlined, against the sky of the summer morning, the beau ideal of the Irish warrior. Then he was down and done and the Green Flag fallen across his body."[22]

All told, ten officers and over a hundred men from Buffalo were killed in conflicts throughout the Virginia campaign. Of the 766 men recruited into this regiment, 490 were lost to death, injury, or capture. In 1864, at Sangster's Station, Virginia, eight Buffalo Irish soldiers were captured and sent to the infamous Andersonville Prison in Georgia. Like many others in this prison, these prisoners died there.[23] Both John and James McMahon were buried in Holy Cross Cemetery in Lackawanna, but their bodies were moved in 1905 to a cemetery in Utica, New York to be closer to John's widow.[24] Years after their deaths, the *Buffalo Commercial* proclaimed "two noble offerings of a foreign nationality upon the altar of the great Republic."[25] John and James' younger brother, Martin T. McMahon, who was not involved with the Buffalo regiment, became a brevet major general by the war's end.

The valiant efforts of the Buffalo Irish during the Civil War helped change the perception of some of the Protestant establishment. In a history of the city of Buffalo, the authors commented that this band of Irish soldiers "sustained the reputation for impetuous valor borne by those of that nationality [Irish]."[26]

General Dennis Nolan—Director of Military Intelligence

Western New York produced two of the twentieth century's finest and most consequential US military intelligence officers. The first, Dennis E. Nolan, was a prominent member of General Pershing's staff during the First World War, serving as Chief of Intelligence Services for the American Expeditionary Forces (AEF). Dennis Nolan was born in Akron, New York, east of Buffalo, in 1872. His parents, Martin Nolan and Honora Cunningham Nolan, were Irish immigrants who landed in Western New York after the US Civil War. Nolan's Irish father, who could neither read nor write, worked in a cement mill near Akron. The Nolans also ran a small farm at their homestead to supplement the family income. Dennis, the oldest of six children, was a good student who wanted to become a teacher after graduating from Akron High School. While planning to attend Cornell University, he decided to try his luck with the admissions exam for military colleges—he earned the highest score and was accepted to West Point Military Academy.[27] At the military college, Nolan wasn't an exceptional student but showed leadership abilities. He was also one of the finest football players in the country, playing both the defensive and offensive end positions.[28]

Nolan graduated in 1896 and served in Cuba during the Spanish-American War, receiving two Silver Stars.[29] Next, his superiors sent him to the Philippines during the insurrection of Filipino nationalists, where he was elevated to major. While there, Nolan met, and left an impression on, Captain John J. Pershing, who promoted him a decade later. In 1901, Nolan returned to the United States and married Julia Dent Sharp, the niece of former First Lady Julia Dent Grant, in a Catholic ceremony.[30] After the wedding, the Nolans moved to West Point, where Dennis taught history and coached the school's football team—under his leadership, the team had its finest season since its founding. As an aside, Coach Nolan's pupil and team manager was Douglas MacArthur, a future five-star general.

In 1903, Secretary of War Elihu Root selected Captain Nolan to be on the General Staff (this was a group of the Army Chief of Staff's closest advisors) in Washington, DC. In this capacity, the Western New York Irishman earned a reputation as an excellent administrator. After several years in that role, Nolan was sent back to the Philippines in 1907 as the Acting Adjutant General to General John J. Pershing. After a brief move to Buffalo in 1911, where the Nolans welcomed their second child and spent time with Dennis's mother and siblings, the US Army transferred the family to California.

In 1914, as war broke out in Europe, Nolan served in various capacities in Washington, DC, including assessing the US military's readiness. His commanders charged him with drawing up plans for national conscription. One month after the United States joined the war, General Pershing sent Colonel Nolan to France to organize and lead the American Expeditionary Forces (AEF) intelligence service. Nolan toured the French and British army intelligence units to determine how to construct an American group. "Nolan built the Army's intelligence service from the ground up, creating a multidiscipline intelligence organization on a scale never seen before in the US Army," according to his biographer.[31] In a short time, Nolan's men gathered valuable information on enemy troop strength and positioning throughout the many European battlefields.

General Pershing appreciated the intelligence Nolan had gathered, but he also needed competent field commanders. So, the general assigned Nolan to lead an undersized brigade, ordering him to hold onto the area around the town of Apremont in northeastern France. Through his "indomitable courage and coolness" in this battle, Nolan inspired his men (about 400 soldiers) and repelled a German attack with two regiments (approximately 2,000 men) at Apremont. His brigade killed over 1,000 Germans and captured 250 others.[32] For his efforts, in 1919, after participating in the Peace Conference at Versailles, Nolan received the Distinguished Service Cross from President Woodrow Wilson for his extraordinary heroism in France. He was one of only eleven generals in the war to win this prestigious award. At the war's end, Nolan created the Military Intelligence Officers Reserve Corps, hoping to preserve some of the intelligence and tactics in the event of a future military conflict.

At the end of the First World War, Nolan became the Director of Military Intelligence (G-2) for the US Army. A few years later, in 1924, he became the Deputy Chief of Staff, the second highest-ranking commander in the Army; a year after, he was promoted to Major General.[33] There were rumors that Nolan would replace General MacArthur, his former pupil, as Chief of Staff, but President Franklin D. Roosevelt decided to renew MacArthur's appointment. Two years later, Nolan commanded the Fifth Corps Area in Columbus, Ohio, the largest of the nine corps areas in the entire army in terms of geography. Later, he commanded the Second Corps Area, which comprised forces from New York, New Jersey, and Delaware. In that role, the former Akron native also served as an unofficial ambassador for New York City, hosting foreign military personnel and other foreign dignitaries.[34] In 1936, Nolan retired as the Commanding General of the First Army—one of the highest-ranking generals in the military.

At the end of Nolan's career, President Roosevelt commended him: "For his long and brilliant service as an army officer in peace and war, General Nolan merits the gratitude of the people of the country. His splendid public service and his high character have won for him the love and esteem of all who know him."[35] It took another fifty years before his legacy was assured. On June 2, 1989, the Intelligence and Security Command's (INSCOM) headquarters at Fort Belvoir, Virginia, was named in honor of Major General Dennis Edward Nolan.[36] This Department of the Army has over 17,000 personnel who execute intelligence and security operations worldwide. In addition to the Distinguished Service Cross, Nolan also won the Croix de Guerre and the Distinguished Service Medal for organizing and administering the AEF intelligence service.[37]

General Dennis E. Nolan's contributions to US military intelligence were extensive. During the First World War, the Western New Yorker implemented several intelligence units that still exist today in the twenty-first century. Nolan established aerial reconnaissance, radio intelligence, interrogation teams, and counterintelligence agents.[38] And his tactics were effective in combat. During the Battle of Saint-Mihiel in the First World War, Nolan successfully utilized aerial photography to locate all of the German artillery batteries and formations. Nolan's Signal Corps intercepted German wireless communications that proved particularly useful. His unit also dropped millions of propaganda leaflets behind enemy lines, helping demoralize the German soldiers. By the war's end, thanks to Nolan's efforts, General Pershing believed the Americans had the best intelligence of any army in the conflict.[40] In retirement, Nolan continued to write about military intelligence, urging the country to be ready in the event of another war. Sadly, his warnings were not heeded.

General "Wild Bill" Donovan—Spy Master

During the Second World War, President Franklin D. Roosevelt needed a trusted hand to create a centralized US intelligence service, so he called on an Irish American from Buffalo. William J. Donovan was born in Buffalo's First Ward on January 1, 1883 to Timothy and Anna (Lennon) Donovan. As a result of William Donovan's eventual fame, the lives of his grandfather and father were well documented, and their biographies give us insight into the lives of other Irish men of their time. William's grandfather, Timothy Donovan—who will be referred to as Grandfather Donovan, so as not to confuse him with William's father, Timothy— was a schoolteacher from the fishing village of Goleen in County Cork. Despite his previous profession in Ireland, he worked as a grain scooper when he arrived in Buffalo, a city he chose because the wages were higher than in other surrounding towns and the Catholic Church was prominent.[41] Grandfather Donovan was one of the fortunate Irish immigrants to arrive in America with some money; this enabled him to eventually purchase one of the better-constructed homes in the First Ward. As a former teacher, he promoted learning among his children and filled his home with books—uncommon among working-class Irish families during that time.

Like many first- and second-generation Irish Americans, Grandfather Donovan was an ardent supporter of Irish independence and rumored to be affiliated with the Fenians. It is a fact that the elder Donovan housed and supported Irish independence leaders and intellectuals who traveled and stayed in Buffalo.[42] He also assisted his fellow Irishmen by turning his homestead into a safe house for Irish refugees who would sneak into Buffalo from Canada.[43] Numerous Irish natives arrived in Buffalo illegally from Canada and were then sheltered for a short while until they became established. Grandfather Donovan abstained from alcohol and was the leader of a local League of the Cross branch dedicated to encouraging temperance among working-class Catholic families. This was the environment in which Grandfather Donovan's son Timothy—the father of William—was raised, and he subsequently passed on to young William.

The younger Timothy Donovan initially worked as a greaser for the Erie and Lackawanna Railroad but was quickly promoted to rail yardmaster.[44] Like his father, Timothy promoted book learning to his children and abstained from alcohol. He was also a registered Republican—an almost unthinkable act among Irish Americans in those days. Despite these differences, the Donovans had struggles like others in the Ward. Of the nine children in Timothy Donovan's household, the first four died of meningitis, and only two survived to old age.[45]

This left William, the fifth in birth order, as the oldest. Like many young First Ward boys, Will Donovan attended St. Bridget's School but later transferred to Miss Nardin's Academy. Even as a young boy, Will had natural gifts that separated him from his peers. His classmates remembered him as a determined boy, and although not necessarily the brightest student, definitely one of the most tenacious.[46] In addition to possessing abundant natural gifts, Will was also lucky. His father was a close friend of Bishop James Quigley, who realized that Will was a child with unique talents, so he used diocesan funds to pay for Will's studies at St. Joseph's Collegiate Institute (a prominent local Catholic high school).[47] Donovan then went to Niagara University and later transferred to Columbia University, where he received his degree.

The handsome Bill Donovan had penetrating blue eyes, and although he was only 5'8", he seemed taller to those who met him in person. At Columbia, Donovan excelled as the quarterback of the school's football team and rowed on the college's varsity team. His athleticism, coupled with his charismatic personality, contributed to the perception that the Irish American was a natural leader. After completing his undergraduate studies, Bill earned his law degree from Columbia University in 1908, and shortly after that, he entered a private legal practice in Buffalo.

Before World War I, he and a group of blue-blood Buffalonians formed Troop I, a New York National Guard cavalry unit. Donovan served as captain of the squad, which was unusual since he was an Irish Catholic leading a group composed almost entirely of upper-class Protestants. Around this time, he met Ruth Rumsey, the daughter of one of Buffalo's wealthiest men, Dexter Rumsey. Even though Bill and Ruth came from two different worlds—the working-class First Ward and the monied Delaware Avenue elite—they married in 1914, and Bill Donovan officially entered Buffalo's WASP society. Shortly after the US entered World War I, Donovan was called to lead the 1st Battalion of the 165th Infantry, also known as the "Fighting 69th." This unit of mostly Irish Americans from New York City—the same unit in which dozens of First Ward men fought during the Civil War—was now, fifty years later, under Donovan's command.

There is a debate about how and when Donovan acquired his nickname: "Wild Bill." Some say it was from his ferociousness on the football field at Columbia University, while others attribute it to his fearlessness on the battlefield in France. Regardless, it stuck for the rest of his life. After proving himself in several battles, Major "Wild Bill" Donovan was promoted to Lieutenant Colonel, where he courageously led his unit in battle at Landres-et-St. Georges during the Argonne offensive. Leading one of the three regiments, Donovan captured a well-entrenched enemy post on a steep ravine surrounded by machine guns and artillery. Because of the danger of this mission, the other two supporting regiments refused to advance. But Donovan believed in following orders, so he rallied his company and led the advance under fierce conditions (the high command expected 60% casualties from this assault).

Despite being hit three times by enemy fire, Donovan refused to leave the battlefield until all his men were cared for.[48] This sort of courage fed the legend of "Wild Bill" Donovan. When the battle was over, Donovan's regiment was devastated: 600 of his 1,000 soldiers were killed, wounded, or missing in action. By the war's end, Donovan's unit had suffered 644 killed in action with 3,501 casualties. In a New York City parade at the war's end, over a million people turned out to cheer Donovan and the "Fighting 69th" regiment for their bravery. Donovan had captured the imagination of the nation and overnight became a true American hero. In 1940, Warner Bros. released the movie, *The Fighting 69th*, and George Brent played General "Wild Bill" Donovan.

As a result of his extraordinary bravery and his accomplishments in France defeating the Germans, the former First Ward boy became the most decorated soldier in American history. He earned the top three awards: the Medal of Honor, the Distinguished Service Cross, and the Distinguished Service Medal.[49] During the war, "Wild Bill" Donovan earned more medals than even the distinguished Brigadier General Douglas MacArthur. Donovan had made a name for himself on the national stage. However, his most important contributions to his country were still to come.

Between the wars, "Wild Bill" served in various political positions and was a partner in a successful Wall Street law firm where he reportedly became a millionaire. In 1922, as the US Attorney for Western New York, he was responsible for enforcing the Prohibition laws, which he did faithfully (in fact, some speculate that his overzealous enforcement efforts may have cost him a chance at higher political office). Herbert Hoover reportedly offered Donovan the position of Vice President on his ticket in 1928, but he turned it down, hoping for the Attorney General slot. However, at that time, there was too much animosity toward a Catholic enforcing US law, so Hoover couldn't offer Donovan his desired position. In 1932, Donovan unsuccessfully ran as the Republican candidate for governor of New York and was once considered a possible Republican presidential candidate. But political office eluded Donovan for the rest of his life for various reasons.

Donovan and President Franklin Delano Roosevelt, former classmates at Columbia University, were close personal friends despite their different political affiliations. When hostilities began in Europe preceding the entry of the United States into the Second World War, Roosevelt called on Donovan to assist him. The President dispatched Donovan on diplomatic missions to assess the evolving crisis, where he met with leaders such as Winston Churchill and King George

VI. At the start of the war between England and Germany, Ambassador Joseph P. Kennedy assessed that the English were finished and would capitulate to the more powerful Germans. Donovan's assessment was much more optimistic, and he urged Roosevelt to provide resources to assist England. Roosevelt trusted Donovan's opinion more than Kennedy's, so the United States started sending material aid to the British through the Lend-Lease program. Upon returning home, Donovan urged Roosevelt to prepare for war.[50]

After Donovan's information-gathering European mission, the disabled Roosevelt had even grander plans for the former First Warder, whom he once referred to as "my secret legs."[51] Before the US involvement in the war, the United States had an ineffective and fragmented foreign intelligence network, so Roosevelt tasked Donovan with centralizing these disparate organizations into one spy agency. On July 11, 1941, Bill Donovan was named the Coordinator of Information for the US Government. One year later, Roosevelt appointed Donovan as director of the newly created Office of Strategic Services (OSS)—a centralized intelligence agency, which aided the United States during the Second World War. Donovan propelled the US intelligence agency from outdated tactics into the twentieth century and hired the best and brightest from across the country; he reportedly claimed that his ideal candidate was someone who had a Ph.D. and could win a bar fight.[52] Donovan pushed for a diverse agency with a "cross section of racial origins, of abilities, temperaments and talents." He hired and promoted many women as well.[53]

Donovan's organization provided valuable information for the Allied Forces during the War, and in 1944 he was promoted to the rank of Major General in the US Army for his efforts. While Roosevelt admired Donovan greatly, his Vice President, Harry S. Truman, intensely disliked Donovan. After Roosevelt died in 1945, President Truman dismissed Donovan and dissolved the OSS at the war's end. One year later, Truman re-established the department under the name of the Central Intelligence Group, but did not appoint Donovan, the likely candidate, as director. Despite this egregious snub, Donovan is still considered the "Father of American Intelligence." His portrait hangs first in the gallery of CIA directors at CIA headquarters in Virginia. After his directorship of the OSS ended, Donovan was made associate counsel for the War Crimes Commission during the Nuremberg Trials, and he later served as an ambassador to Thailand.

William J. Donovan was one of the most remarkable twentieth-century Buffalonians. His accomplishments for his country rank up there with other recognized Buffalonians, including Presidents Millard Fillmore and Grover Cleveland. The United States recognized Donovan for his tireless efforts by honoring him with the nation's four highest decorations: the Congressional Medal of Honor, the Distinguished Service Cross, the Distinguished Service

Medal, and the National Security Medal.[54] Judge Salvatore Martoche, a Bill Donovan expert, claimed, "Buffalo never produced such a colorful figure on the national or international stage [as Bill Donovan]."[55] Sir William Stephenson, known as "Intrepid," was a British Intelligence director who worked closely with William Donovan during the Second World War. Stephenson boldly asserted that Donovan "was one of the significant men of our century." At the end of the War, Admiral Wilhelm Canaris, the German Intelligence chief, stated that of all the Allied leaders he wished to meet, he would choose William Donovan.[56] More importantly, Donovan biographer Richard Dunlop claimed that Adolf Hitler "feared and hated him [Donovan] more than he did any other American."[57] In 1959, after William Donovan passed away, President Dwight Eisenhower declared that the young man from the First Ward was "The Last Hero."[58]

Alice Lord O'Brian—Red Cross Hero

Not all Buffalonians involved in the First World War fought on the French battlefield. Numerous women worked as nurses and aid workers. One of the most well-known was Alice Lord O'Brian. Alice was the middle child of Elizabeth Lord, an Irish-born mother, and John O'Brian, a son of Irish immigrants. Alice's father, John, was a successful businessman and judge, which allowed the O'Brians to live on Cleveland Avenue in a well-off part of Buffalo. As discussed earlier, her brother John Lord O'Brian was an assistant attorney general. He worked under the US Attorney General in Washington, DC during the First World War. Before the world conflict, Alice worked in Black Rock as a social worker.

When the United States entered the war, thirty-seven-year-old Alice was the first Buffalonian to volunteer for the Red Cross in France, where she worked in a canteen (a facility that provided food and services to soldiers and local citizens). She became the founding director of the canteen in St. Germain des Fosses, caring for wounded French soldiers. The Buffalo Irishwoman then volunteered as a nurse in the United States Army field hospital during the bloody Saint-Mihiel offensive. As a passenger in an army truck that overturned in an accident, she sustained severe injuries but quickly returned to work as the head of the Red Cross canteen in Clermont-Ferrand.

After the war, in March 1919, the French government awarded O'Brian the French Recognition Medal (La Medaille de la Reconnaissance Française) for her efforts for the victims of the war.[59] She was the first American to receive the prestigious honor, which the French government rarely gave to women. At the time of her award, the *Buffalo Times* said O'Brian, "not only won fame for herself but has added distinction to American womanhood. America is proud of her, France is proud of her, Buffalo is proud of her! In the roster of brilliantly successful and unselfish service in the Great War shines the name of Alice Lord O'Brian."[60] The French government also bestowed The Military Health Service Medal (La Medaille d'honneur des Epidemies) to her for her dedication and generosity to the wounded and ill French people.[61]

When O'Brian returned from France, she settled in New York City and became an anti-war activist. In 1936, O'Brian published a book of letters that she had written to her brothers from France called *No Glory: Letters from France, 1917-1919*. In the book's foreword, she warned the readers not to glorify the Great War and not to repeat the same mistakes, as it seemed the world was about to do. When the world plunged into war during the 1940s, O'Brian became the director of the Officers' Club in New York City, where she cared for junior officers at home.[62] In 1965, O'Brian moved back to Buffalo, where she lived until the age of ninety-two.

Father Thomas Conway and Lt. James Crotty

Not all Buffalo Irishmen returned home alive from the Second World War. Father Thomas M. Conway, born on April 5, 1908 in Waterbury, Connecticut, was the oldest child of two Irish immigrants. After attending Niagara University, Conway entered the priesthood for the Buffalo Catholic Diocese and was ordained a priest on May 16, 1934. After various assignments throughout the diocese, he ended up at St. Brigid's in the Irish First Ward, where parish members fondly remembered him as a "priest in touch with and sympathetic to the blue-collar realities of his parishioners."[63] Conway also loved to sail his small boat on Lake Erie.[64] But his peaceful days sailing along the lake would soon end when the Japanese bombed Pearl Harbor in 1941.

In September 1942, Fr. Conway enlisted in the US Navy to serve as a chaplain. After serving at various naval bases on the East Coast, on August 24, 1944, he was assigned to the cruiser USS *Indianapolis*, which swiftly sailed to fight in the Pacific Campaign against the Japanese. The *Indianapolis* participated during the infamous Battle of Okinawa, and a kamikaze bomb claimed the lives of nine sailors on board; Father Conway, at his own expense, used his leave to fly to various parts of the country to comfort the families of these fallen men. He returned to the *Indianapolis* and resumed his duties, ministering to Catholics and non-Catholics alike, all unaware of the impending disaster awaiting this naval cruiser.

On July 30, 1945, shortly after midnight, just a month before the war's end, a Japanese submarine struck the *Indianapolis* with two torpedoes. The ship sank in just fourteen minutes. Of the 1,196 crew members, 300 went down with the vessel, while the other 900 were left floating in the debris-strewn, shark-infested waters of the Pacific. Numerous sailors later recalled the actions of Fr. Conway during those distressing times. For three days, this thirty-seven-year-old priest from Buffalo assisted the frightened sailors in many ways: he prayed with them to calm their fears, heard their confessions, performed last rites, and consoled those who had lost hope. Many remembered the constant encouragement he gave the scared, exhausted sailors and the confidence he inspired in them that their rescue was imminent. After three days floating in the ocean, and only one day before the remaining sailors were rescued, Father Conway died from exhaustion and drowned like 600 of his fellow sailors.

Shortly before Fr. Conway left for his US Navy duty, he recorded a tape for a close friend. On the recording, the assistant rector of St. Brigid's told his friend: "So, don't miss me. I'll be back. Remember me in your prayers, and I'll remember you." Despite Thomas Conway's optimism, he never returned to sail the boat that waited for him alongside the church rectory. Ten years after he perished, the Buffalo City Council named a park in the heart of the First Ward after the Buffalo priest. In 2006, leaders of The Buffalo and Erie County Naval and Military Park unveiled a Father Thomas Conway bust and memorial plaque.

At the same Buffalo military park, the Foundation for Coast Guard History erected a plaque in honor of Lieutenant Thomas James (Jimmy) Crotty in 2010. Jimmy was the son of Irish immigrants from County Clare: Patrick and Helen (McGarry) Crotty. Born in 1912, Jimmy Crotty was raised in South Buffalo and graduated from South Park High School, where he was a star athlete. Crotty attended the Coast Guard Academy, where he was the senior class president and captain of the football team. A natural leader, he was named a company commander.

In 1941, as the United States entered the Second World War, the South Buffalo Irishman, an expert in explosives, was assigned to a US Navy unit in the Philippines. As the second-in-command of a minesweeper in Manila Bay, Crotty was credited for his bravery as he worked in darkness to protect US ships and submarines.[65] He also led a mission to strip and disable a US submarine, the USS *Sealion*, to prevent the Japanese from capturing it. In May 1942, during the Battle of Corregidor, in the Philippines, Crotty was commander of an artillery battery, which was overrun by the enemy. Crotty and all of the Americans were captured and sent to an infamous Japanese prison camp where 3,000 POWs died. The South Park High School graduate was the first member of the Coast Guard captured since the War of 1812.[66] The thirty-year-old Crotty died in a diphtheria outbreak in the camp in July 1942. The Purple Heart winner's body was not returned home to Buffalo until 2019, seventy-seven years after his death. In August 2022, with the help of Congressman Brian Higgins, the Coast Guard renamed its Buffalo headquarters the LT. T. James Crotty Sector Command Building. During the dedication, the congressman stated that the naming of the building "will ensure Lt. Crotty's legacy is remembered, celebrated, and lives on indefinitely."[67]

While Father Thomas Conway and Lieutenant Jimmy Crotty died as heroes in the campaign to defeat the Japanese, another Buffalo Irishman played a pivotal role in destroying the Japanese Imperial Navy and turning the tide of the war.

C. Wade McClusky—Battle of Midway Hero

On Monday, June 19, 1944, a headline on the front page of the *Buffalo Evening News* declared, "South Buffalo Welcomes Hero."[68] The distinguished Naval airman returned to his hometown to aid the US war bond effort. He appeared at the Lafayette Square bond booth and toured his boyhood South Buffalo neighborhood in the Bondmobile (a vehicle with stenographers and equipment to produce bonds on the spot). The man was Captain Wade McClusky, Jr., and some historians credit his actions with turning the tide in favor of the Allied Forces in the Pacific Campaign during the Second World War.

Clarence Wade McClusky, Jr., born in Buffalo in 1902, was the second of five children of a father who shared his name and Mary Stearns McClusky. Clarence Wade Sr., an accountant for a local linseed oil company, was of Scots-Irish Presbyterian stock. Mary "May" McClusky was an Irish Catholic.[69] At the time of their wedding, mixed religious marriages were rare and often complicated; this was the case with the McCluskys. Wade Sr. refused to let May practice her Catholic faith and forbade her from raising their children in that faith. In 1928, after her husband died in an automobile accident, May returned to her Catholic faith and even converted one of her daughters. Meanwhile, Wade Jr. continued to practice the Episcopalian faith.[70]

Raised in South Buffalo, Wade Jr. was a talented athlete and exceptional student who graduated from South Park High School at age sixteen. After graduation, like many other neighborhood boys, he went to work for the railroads, where he cleaned oil and chemicals from the walls of tanker rail cars. It was a miserable job, and the experience convinced him he needed to return to school.[71] At age twenty, after scoring well on the entrance exam, the five foot nine-inch, blue-eyed boy from South Buffalo entered the United States Naval Academy in Annapolis. McClusky was a talented math student who played on Navy's football team. After graduating from the Academy, he became a Navy aviator with extensive experience flying multiple aircraft, including fighter and torpedo planes and dive-bombers. McClusky was remembered as a quiet, modest man who was a competent pilot and staff officer.[72]

Before the Japanese attack on Pearl Harbor on December 7, 1941, McClusky's superiors assigned him to the USS *Enterprise*, where he was the ship's fighter squadron commander. Prior to the epic Battle of Midway, he was promoted to Air Group Commander. In the late spring of 1942, US intelligence picked up signals that the Imperial Japanese Navy planned to destroy the US base on Midway Island, west of Hawaii, hoping to neutralize America's air and sea power in the western Pacific. With this intercepted information, the Americans crafted plans to ambush and destroy the larger enemy fleet.

On the morning of June 4, 1942, *Enterprise* Lt. Commander McClusky led his two dive-bomber squadrons on a mission to destroy as many Japanese aircraft carriers as possible. It was a risky mission because he and his fellow pilots faced the full might of Japanese air and naval firepower. McClusky's two teams arrived at the interception coordinates provided to them before the flight, but the enemy fleet wasn't there. Running low on fuel, McClusky would have been tempted to head south toward Midway to see if the Japanese arrived earlier than planned.[73] While deciding which way to go, McClusky spotted a lone Japanese cruiser heading north—in the opposite direction of Midway—and he surmised it was heading back toward the rest of the Japanese fleet. Fortunately for the Americans, the Buffalo native's instincts were exactly right.

Within ten minutes, McClusky and his dive-bombers spotted the massive Japanese armada. He and his men went to work fifteen minutes later and destroyed two of the enemy's four massive aircraft carriers. A third one was sunk shortly after by the USS *Yorktown* bomber squadrons. Later that evening, *Enterprise* pilots destroyed the fourth enemy carrier after another mission. By the end of the battle, the Americans had destroyed four massive Japanese aircraft carriers and more than three hundred Japanese planes, and had killed 3,000 Japanese sailors, including scores of the country's best pilots.

The Americans lost more than three hundred sailors and pilots and one aircraft carrier, but they accomplished their mission. McClusky was shot in the left shoulder during the engagement, and fifty-five enemy bullets hit his plane. Most of the aircraft under McClusky's command barely made it back to the *Enterprise* because of a lack of fuel, and ten planes, presumed to have run out of fuel, were never found. McClusky and his team, many pushed to the point of no return, made the difference for the United States that day.

The Battle of Midway was one of the most consequential engagements of the Pacific War, and the South Buffalo Irishman had saved the day. As McClusky biographer David Rigby stated, "As of 10:00 am on the morning of June 4, 1942… the United States was losing the war in the Pacific. One half hour later, at 10:30 am on June 4, 1942, the United States was winning."[74] Admiral Chester Nimitz claimed that McClusky's actions "decided the fate of our carrier task force and our forces at Midway."[75] The Japanese never recovered from their devastating defeat at Midway, which was the turning point in the Pacific War.

In Commanding Officer Captain George D. Murray's official report to Admiral Nimitz after the battle, the captain wrote the following:

> Both pilots and gunners displayed a spirit of utter fearlessness, resolution and determination throughout all air actions. This spirit, though shared by pilots and gunners alike, found its highest expression in the person of the Air Group Commander, Lt. Comdr. C.W. McClusky, Jr. U.S.N. On June 4, prior to intercepting the main enemy forces, it was his decision, and his decision alone, that made the attack possible which led to the destruction of a major part of the enemy forces. It is the considered opinion of the Commanding Officer that the success of our forces hinged upon this attack. Any other action on the part of Lt. Comdr. McClusky would inevitably have led to irreparable loss to our forces.[76]

For his efforts at Midway, McClusky was awarded the prestigious Navy Cross. After the famed battle, the Navy transferred McClusky to California to train the next generation of pilots. Toward the end of the war, he was promoted to Aide and Chief of Staff to Vice-Admiral Frederick Horne in Washington, DC, where he worked on logistical plans for the OVERLORD (D-Day) channel assault and operations in the Pacific campaign. In the fall of 1944, Captain McClusky was promoted to commander of the USS *Corregidor*, a small aircraft carrier active in the Pacific operation. In the 1950s, he moved to a suburb of Baltimore and worked as an engineer for the Martin Company, and later taught at a private girls' high school.[77] McClusky died of cirrhosis in 1976.

In 1983, the US Navy commissioned a frigate named the USS McClusky in his honor. In 2017, for the 75th anniversary of the Battle of Midway, the Buffalo Naval Park unveiled a bust of Wade McClusky crafted by artist Susan Geissler. In 2019, historian David Rigby wrote the first full-length biography of the Buffalo hero entitled Wade McClusky and the Battle of Midway. That same year, a major motion picture called *Midway*, in which British movie star Luke Evans played the role of Wade McClusky, was released in the United States by Lionsgate. Before this movie, several other television shows and films about Midway included actors who portrayed McClusky. The Buffalo Irishman will not be forgotten because the US Navy annually presents the "RADM C. Wade McClusky Award" to the most outstanding attack squadron in the US Navy.

The Buffalo Irish not only played a role on the battlefield in American and global conflicts, they also worked tirelessly to help Ireland achieve independence from Great Britain. Here is their story.

CHAPTER TWELVE

Irish Independence

At 12:45 p.m. on Monday, April 24, 1916, Irish rebel leader Patrick Pearse read his Proclamation of the Republic outside the General Post Office (GPO) in Dublin. It declared the Irish Republic a sovereign state, independent from British rule. The Easter Rising, as this event was later called, initially failed. Public sentiment changed, however, once the British executed more than a dozen Irish rebels and leaders. Within five years, Ireland was free. Early in his address, Pearse thanked Ireland's "exiled children in America" for their support. The impact of Irish Americans on Ireland's independence cannot be understated. As one historian declared, "No America, no New York, no Easter Rising—simple as that."[1]

Compared to Irish populations in similar-sized American cities, the Buffalo Irish punched above their weight in the undertaking of Ireland's liberation from Great Britain. As a border city with a sizable Irish population, Buffalo was a sanctuary for Irish nationalists. Not only did Buffalo host national conventions dedicated to Ireland's welfare, it was also a center for fundraising and a launching pad for the legendary 1866 Fenian Raid.

After centuries of British subjugation and colonization, many Irish Catholics hated their British rulers. From the seventeenth-century plantation system, where the British resettled thousands of Scots and English citizens on Irish soil, to the Penal Laws of the eighteenth and nineteenth centuries (restrictions on Catholics' religious practices, occupations, and political office-holding), the English repeatedly subdued the native Irish. The eighty percent of Irish who were Catholic resisted being controlled by a small Protestant minority. For centuries, there was an undercurrent of Irish discontent toward their rulers, with sporadic rebellions. While this resentment was centuries old, the Great Famine ultimately drove the Irish to overthrow British rule. The thousands of desperate Famine refugees who landed in Buffalo, mainly from the devastated south and west of Ireland, were united in their desire to remove the usurpers from their native land.

Fenians

One of Buffalo's most thrilling and vital contributions to Irish history occurred the year after the United States Civil War ended. Throughout the war, thousands of Irish soldiers in the Union Army secretly belonged to an Irish organization called the Fenians or the Irish Republican Brotherhood (IRB). Based in the United States and Ireland, the Fenian movement was created in Dublin on St. Patrick's Day in 1858. Its audacious mission was to use military force to secure Ireland's independence from Great Britain.

The Fenian organization had military leaders from the highest echelons of the US Army, including General Michael Corcoran, leader of a legion named in his honor and commander of Buffalo's two Irish regiments. When Corcoran died after falling off his horse, Fenian leaders chose US Army Brigadier General Thomas Sweeny as their Secretary of War. Prior to Sweeny's appointment in 1865, the Fenians had planned on sending Irish-American soldiers to Ireland to fight the British forces.[2]

But Sweeny had a different plan of attack. Instead of sending troops back to Ireland, he proposed that the Fenians remain on this side of the Atlantic and invade Canada.[3] While this idea seemed preposterous, Canada was geographically closer than Ireland and did not have a standing army or a strong central government to defend itself. The Irish rebels had also hoped to draw the US government into an armed conflict against England, as many political leaders in the North were still unhappy with Britain's neutrality during the Civil War. If the US government refused to assist the Fenians, the Irish military unit planned on capturing Canada and holding it ransom in exchange for Ireland's freedom.

Fenians held meetings across the United States to raise funds and rally soldiers. Irish women who could not fight busied themselves with preparations. The Buffalo chapter of the Fenian Sisterhood hosted a Fenian Ball in 1865 to solicit donations for the military mission. The following year, they continued raising funds for weapons and munitions. Later that year, Irish-born sisters Ann and Maria Cruice presented the Buffalo Fenian Brotherhood with a hand-sewn green silk battle flag, measuring nine feet long by six feet wide. The Fenians would later carry this silk banner onto the field at the Battle of Ridgeway.[4]

Buffalo was just one part of a multi-pronged attack that was to occur from several towns along the United States-Canadian border. Western New York support for the Fenians was so strong that they formed their own Irish Republican Army (IRA) unit, the Seventh Regiment (see Appendix F). Other units, like the Eighteenth Regiment, needed men from several states (Tennessee, North Carolina, South Carolina, Georgia, and Alabama) to staff a single corps. Interestingly, only one year after the Civil War, former fierce enemies from the North and South united to fight for freedom for their native Ireland.

During the last few days of May 1866, Fenian recruits disguised themselves as railroad laborers and steadily streamed into Buffalo from as far away as Kentucky, Tennessee, and Indiana. The enthusiastic young men jumped off trains a mile before the Exchange Street rail station, where they knew the police were waiting to arrest them.[5] Irish residents in the First Ward and other parts of South Buffalo welcomed the new arrivals. The Buffalo Fenians set up headquarters on lower Pearl Street at Patrick O'Day's Auction House, with a backup base at Hugh Mooney's saloon on Ohio Street.[6] They planned to capture Fort Erie, Ontario, and then seize control of the Welland Canal, hoping to disrupt British troop movements between Eastern and Western Canada.

Most Fenian soldiers were young men aged twenty to twenty-seven years old. Many wore green jackets and black hats—a few of which were stovepipe style. Some men wore "IRA" pins on their jackets, which may have been one of the first uses of the acronym. On the evening of May 31, Fenian soldiers marched to Black Rock, near the Pratt Rolling Mill at Ferry Street. Colonel John O'Neill, an Irish-born, thirty-five-year-old former Union officer, led the campaign.

In the dark of the night at 3:15 a.m. on June 1, the first wave of soldiers was ferried across the Niagara River on canal boats pulled by tugs. At least eight hundred heavily armed men had crossed the river to Canada. By 4:00 a.m., the Fenians proudly planted the Irish flag on Canadian soil, cheering so loudly that one could hear the revelry across the Niagara River in Buffalo. Irish soldiers then cut telegraph lines, destroyed a railroad bridge, and seized the Old Fort Erie ruins. Although the Fenians made progress, British Crown forces were streaming in from Toronto and Hamilton. It was becoming clear that a significant battle was imminent.

Having lost many men to desertion, O'Neill now had as few as five hundred active soldiers. Combined British and Canadian troops outnumbered the Fenians almost ten to one. O'Neill decided to strike the smaller Canadian force led by Lieutenant Colonel Booker before Booker could unite with a larger unit of volunteers in St. Catharines.[8] O'Neill's men engaged Booker's troops west of Fort Erie at Ridgeway or Lime Ridge on June 2, 1866. Despite fewer soldiers and a rugged terrain, the battle-tested and more experienced Fenians killed twelve Canadians and injured twice as many. Having won the battle, O'Neill ordered his men to retreat to Old Fort Erie to wait for reinforcements and supplies, promising to turn the old fort into a slaughter pen before he would surrender.[9] But Fenian reinforcements from Buffalo would never arrive. The USS *Michigan* gunboat, which had undergone repairs in the First Ward dry docks earlier that spring, was now patrolling the Niagara River and Buffalo harbor, preventing Fenian reinforcements and supplies from crossing the river.

However, the USS *Michigan* had been late in preventing the first wave of Fenians from crossing into Canada because of a sabotage mission. US District Attorney William Dart had alerted the commander of the *Michigan*, Commander Andrew Bryson, on the evening of May 31 that a Fenian launch on the Niagara River was imminent. Bryson readied the vessel with steam and loaded his guns. But the ship's pilot, Patrick Murphy, and second assistant engineer, James P. Kelley, were missing. Some suspected that Kelley was either a Fenian or a Fenian sympathizer. Indeed, Kelley embarked on a secret mission to put the *Michigan* out of commission, delaying Murphy from reporting for duty by distracting him with alcohol, cigars, and a "lady friend."[10] The typically punctual Murphy arrived with Kelley around 5:00 a.m., too late to stop O'Neill's forces. Commander Bryson arrested both men and forced Murphy to pilot the vessel to Black Rock. Bryson would later admit that Kelley's tactics in delaying the *Michigan* were ingenious.[11]

Lacking reinforcements, the Fenians were forced to retreat to Fort Erie and then across to Buffalo, admitting defeat only seventy-two hours after the invasion was initiated. Despite the cessation of military activities in Canada, however, Fenians continued to stream into Buffalo. By June 5, another 2,000 were waiting for orders. Ten days later, 5,166 Fenians were camped out in Buffalo.[12]

Many leaders in the US Federal government, including several members of Congress, sympathized with the Fenians, while President Andrew Johnson waited several days to intervene.[13] British diplomats, however, pressured Johnson to intercede or risk war with Great Britain, and the President ordered General Ulysses Grant to halt the movement of Fenian soldiers across the border into Canada. Grant sent Irish Catholic General George G. Meade (who had led the Army of the Potomac at the Battle of Gettysburg) to Buffalo on June 3 to take control of the situation. Meade immediately banned Fenian meetings and stationed troops along the shore. By June 15, he had successfully dispersed any further Fenian threat.[14]

After gunfire ceased at the Battle of Ridgeway and skirmishes near Fort Erie fizzled out, British and Canadian forces had suffered sixteen dead and 74 wounded. At the same time, the Fenians reported five dead, with seventeen wounded. During the Ridgeway Raid, Canadians took several Fenians prisoner, and a few of them were sentenced to death. Fenians in Buffalo readied a brigade to try to rescue the prisoners. Instead, President Johnson's administration members compromised with the Canadians for the prisoners' release.[15]

A Buffalo ship carpenter from the First Ward, Edward K. Lonergan, was among the deceased.[16] Fenian leaders erected a large monument for Lonergan in Holy Cross Cemetery in Lackawanna, New York, in 1867 with the epitaph:

"Edward Lonergan: Who fell gallantly fighting Ireland's enemies on the Famous Field of Ridgeway on June 2, 1866." One hundred and thirty years later, in 1997, the Police Emerald Society and the Ancient Order of Hibernians refurbished his monument.

Many newspaper reports of the Fenian invasion mocked their efforts, claiming they were as ill-planned as they were outrageous. Many still think this was just a group of drunken, hotheaded Irishmen dreaming up the impossible. The Fenians, however, were well-organized and well-funded, with strong leaders. Their organization was housed in an executive mansion in New York City, led by a chief executive, with an elected senate and a lower assembly of representatives. They also successfully raised funds by issuing bonds and received significant military assistance from officers such as Brigadier General Sweeny.

Although the military incursion failed, the Fenians did not disappear. In 1867, Buffalo had the nation's largest Fenian arms depot, with 4,000 Springfield rifles and 500,000 cartridges.

Fenian Leaders

So, what happened to the leaders of the Fenian Raid? Patrick O'Day, whose Pearl Street auction house was headquarters for the 1866 Raid, led the Fenian Circle in Buffalo. Born in Limerick in 1829, O'Day lived through the horrors of the Famine. With limited education, he arrived in New York City at twenty-six and moved to Buffalo the following year with his wife. After working as a locksmith, O'Day served as Buffalo's harbormaster and owned a successful auction business. But he never wavered in his desire for Irish independence.

O'Day financed three Irish nationalist newspapers (the *Buffalo Globe*, *Fenian Volunteer*, and the *Irish Republic*) to raise awareness and funds for the cause.[17] Before the 1866 Raid, O'Day concealed the Fenian's weapons and ammunition in his warehouse's basement. He also made arrangements for rations and clothing for the troops.[18] While O'Day worked tirelessly to execute the Buffalo operation of the 1866 Raid, the auctioneer made one critical mistake. He penned newspaper articles boasting of an impending military engagement, which encouraged the Canadian authorities to infiltrate his operation. O'Day hired Alexander McLeod as his company's bookkeeper, not realizing his new accountant was a Canadian spy who regularly updated the Crown Forces on details of the impending military operation, giving the Canadians time to prepare.

O'Day's leadership of the Fenians ended around 1871 when Irish nationalists formed a new organization, the *Clan na Gael*. Known for his "flashing wit and genial humor," O'Day opened a prosperous saloon in Buffalo.[19] Later, the successful Irish native purchased a large farm in West Seneca and occupied himself with a shipping business. He died in 1901 and was buried with a sizable funerary monument with the phrase "God Save Ireland" and an inscription that read: "He Loved His God, His Family and the Land of His Birth." One friend described him as "one of the best specimens of the Irish patriot that I have known…and nothing interested him to the last day of his life like his native country."[20]

After the invasion, the Buffalo Fenians continued to hold mass meetings and summer picnics. On August 21, 1866, General John O'Neill and twenty thousand people from as far as Boston and Cleveland attended a Fenian picnic outside of Buffalo.[21] Participants reenacted the Battle of Ridgeway, listened to speeches and Irish songs, and raised money for the national organization. In 1868, the Fenian Senate elected General O'Neill as the organization's president. One of his first stops that year was Buffalo, where he spoke to six thousand enthusiastic members at St. James Hall.

O'Neill returned to Buffalo on May 21, 1870, where he finalized his plans to invade Canada again, from Vermont and Malone, New York. While at Buffalo's Mansion House, he summoned his right-hand man, Henri Le Caron, to share his plans for a secret invasion (three days later, on May 24) and to promote Le Caron to brigadier general.[22] At the time, O'Neill did not know that his trusted aide, Le Caron, was a British spy named Thomas Beach.[23] As Beach funneled intelligence to the Canadians, O'Neill's second invasion never stood a chance.

After the failed 1870 military incursion, the Fenian membership declined. As their movement lost momentum, O'Neill advocated creating Irish colonies in Nebraska. In 1874, he founded one such town in the northern part of the state that settlers named after him. Four years later, at age forty-three, O'Neill died of a stroke. In 2022, the city of O'Neill, Nebraska, erected a life-size statue of the Fenian general and town's founder.

The Fenians failed to free Ireland from England's rule. However, fifty years later, in Dublin in 1916, the Irish Republican Brotherhood, which drew inspiration from the Fenians, engaged in a new armed struggle that ultimately led to Ireland's freedom. Fenian historian Christopher Klein wrote, "Although plagued by naivete, disunity, and indiscretion, the Fenian Brotherhood was a link in the chain of history that led Irish republicans to ultimately topple the British lion."[24] In 1919, when Irish revolutionary leader Eamon de Valera visited the gravesite of Ridgeway hero General O'Neill, he proclaimed, "The Fenian Brotherhood for which General O'Neill fought is the backbone of the Irish republic. We have vindicated O'Neill by establishing the republic."[25]

Few Fenians lived to see the 1916 Easter Uprising. But their efforts, which seemed fruitless at the time, contributed to the birth of the Irish nation.

The Land League

Leading up to Ireland's independence, there was a clash between those who advocated for militaristic methods and those who favored political reform. After the Fenian military failure, a new movement favoring political activism arose. Throughout the nineteenth century, one of the principal causes of Irish poverty was the lack of land ownership by the native citizens. Tenant farmers often worked the land of wealthy Protestant landlords, barely surviving on the money that was left after paying their rent. The Great Famine exacerbated this situation when property owners evicted thousands of tenants. Many Irish Americans who lived through those traumatic events or heard stories about them were inspired to prevent this injustice from recurring.

In October 1879, Irish political leaders Charles Stewart Parnell and Fenian Michael Davitt formed the Irish National Land League. Specifically, the organization fought to end "landlordism" by advocating for land transfer from absentee landholders to the farmers who worked the land. The League adopted the famous slogan, "The land for the people." The organization also pursued policies to end British political rule, tenant evictions, and arbitrary arrests.

Buffalo's Irish community—one of the largest in the country in the 1880s—was often a destination for fundraising and rallying support for the cause of freedom. One of the most notable visitors from the Emerald Isle was the co-founder of the Irish Land League, Charles Stewart Parnell. The "Uncrowned King of Ireland" visited the Queen City during his tour of America in 1880.[26] On January 25 of that year, a crowd of several thousand men and women greeted Parnell and John Dillon, a fellow Irish politician, at Buffalo's Exchange Street rail station.[27] Buffalo businessman James Mooney and politician John C. Sheehan organized the meeting. In Mooney's welcoming address, he proclaimed, "Irish hearts in Buffalo still burn with love for the old land, still beat with hope to see her rise from her sorrows and misfortunes."[28] At Parnell's sold-out address at the Academy of Music, he warned that another Irish famine was looming. Parnell cited the town of Ballina in Mayo, which lost 3,000 residents in the Great Famine, and where he feared the remaining 3,000 residents were at risk. He also reported that in six counties in the south and west of Ireland (Mayo, Galway, Cork, Kerry, Sligo, and Clare), up to 250,000 people would have no food through the winter.

Parnell railed against the current system that kept tenant farmers poor. In a crowd filled with wealthy Buffalo businessmen, clergy, judges, and politicians, he explained how greedy landlords evicted tenants with capriciousness, increasing their rent during abundant harvests, thereby preventing the renter from earning a profit. Parnell and his followers proposed a plan where the tenants could work the land and buy it from the landlords over time. The enthusiastic Buffalo crowd

donated liberally to his fund. Parnell described his visit to Buffalo—which
followed Philadelphia, New York, and Boston—as "by far the most respectable,
best organized, and I believe financially, the most successful of any reception we
have had yet."[29] A week after his Buffalo rally, Parnell addressed Ireland's dire
famine in the US House of Representatives. He was the fourth international
leader to address the House and the first Irishman.

Irish Land League branches sprang up across North America within a few
months, including Buffalo's first branch formed at Stephen's Hall. The Buffalo
chapter had a reputation as being one of the most vociferous and aggressive
in the nation.[30] Father Patrick Cronin, the Irish nationalist and editor of the
Catholic Union Times, served as president, encouraging local citizens to contribute
generously to a fund to assist Irish farmers. Moved by Parnell's speech, wealthy real
estate broker James Mooney also formed a local Land League branch. Mooney,
who had heard stories about the evictions from the last Famine as a young boy, felt
compelled to help overthrow the old system.

In 1880, Fanny Parnell, Charles Stewart Parnell's sister, called on Irish-
American women nationwide to support the Irish nationalist movement.
Tens of thousands of American women responded by forming Ladies' Land
League branches. About one hundred Buffalo Irish women founded a chapter
on December 17, 1880, electing physician Dr. Jane Carroll as president. While
women had already been active in parish fundraising, this was one of the first
mass movements where women of Irish heritage banded together to assist those
suffering in their native land.[31] Some in the Church hierarchy, including Buffalo's
Bishop Stephen V. Ryan, disapproved of their activities. Bishop Ryan denounced
the group's actions as not befitting of women.

Enthusiasm for the Land League intensified when Buffalo hosted the first
national convention on January 12, 1881, and one hundred and twenty delegates
from around the country descended on Buffalo.[32] Buffalo's Father Patrick Cronin,
a Famine survivor from Limerick, opened the convention with a passionate plea
to the delegates.

> You gather here to-day, amid the winter snows, to aid a long-suffering land,
> to fling from her bleeding bosom the crushing nightmare of oppressive
> centuries. The clank of Ireland's chains has come o'er the deep to you, her
> exiled children; and the memory of her wrongs and sorrows swells up in your
> hearts with fresh force, in this, the hour of her fearful crisis. You turn with
> anguish-stricken hearts to Ireland…which has become, through the black
> blight of landlordism, a dreary waste and a wilderness of starvation.[33]

Like Parnell's earlier visit, the Buffalo National Land League conference was a resounding success.

James Mooney—National Leader

The following year, in April 1882 in Washington, DC, Buffalo's James Mooney was unanimously elected (by over two hundred delegates across the country) as the Irish Land League's national president. Buffalo's John J. Hynes, son of Famine immigrants, was elected the national secretary.[34] After his election, Mooney declared, "I accept the trust and pledge my best efforts to further the good work inaugurated by Michael Davitt. It must not be relinquished till the soil of Ireland shall be as free as that of America."

James Mooney was born in 1834 in Queen's County, Ireland (now called County Laois). When he was five, the Mooneys emigrated to Canada, and seven years later, they settled in Buffalo. James attended Buffalo public schools but ended his formal education at fourteen to work for a local seed dealer. During Buffalo's property boom after the Civil War, Mooney became a partner in a real estate and insurance firm.

Mooney co-owned the original Arcade Building in Buffalo, which was destroyed in a fire in 1893. Two years later, Mooney and the brothers Albert and George Brisbane built the Mooney & Brisbane Building (known today as the Brisbane Building) in a prominent location on Lafayette Square. Mooney supervised the building's construction and co-owned it with the Brisbane brothers. Aside from being a successful real estate businessman, the civic-minded Mooney was one of Buffalo's twelve original park commissioners and one of the commissioners responsible for acquiring the land for the Frederick Law Olmsted-designed park system.[35] Politically and religiously active, he led the Erie County Democratic Party twice and served as president of the Young Men's Catholic Association.[36]

In his later years, Mooney's chief occupation was to fight for Ireland's freedom. Tales of cruel evictions in Ireland and the subsequent hardships shaped his belief in Ireland's need for self-government. In his thirties, he reportedly helped fund the Fenian Raid.[37] In the 1880s, Mooney was Buffalo's prime Clan na Gael figure and the center of "militant Irish nationalism."[38] As mentioned, he became a leader in the National Land League movement, defeating candidates from cities with larger Irish communities.

President Mooney and Secretary John Hynes collected money and communicated with over five hundred national Land League branches from Buffalo's Arcade building. They led a successful recruitment campaign to grow the membership and increase donations. During the winter of 1882 and 1883, the Buffalo Irishmen also hatched a plan to raise funds to relieve a famine in the west and north of Ireland.[39] Mooney urged every Irish-American citizen to send one dollar to the group, which they would transfer to a relief fund. While it is uncertain how many Americans contributed, the campaign was successful, and many of the 25,000 evicted Irish tenants received assistance from the League.

During this period, the other founder of the Irish Land League, Michael Davitt, visited Buffalo for a rally on June 29, 1882. Davitt spoke at St. James Hall to a standing-room-only crowd, recounting the accomplishments of the Land League and outlining its future endeavors. Davitt was warmly received and enjoyed a standing ovation from the crowd in Buffalo.[40]

By 1890, Parnell and Davitt had significantly improved Irish tenants' rights, and the number of absentee landlords plummeted. They were also building a powerful coalition of politicians who favored Irish self-government. Things had never looked brighter for the Irish people. But then, as had been the case for centuries regarding Ireland's independence, an unexpected crisis developed. Credible allegations surfaced that Parnell was having an affair with Katharine "Kitty" O'Shea, the wife of another member of Parliament. As a result of the affair, Irish Americans were split as to whether or not Parnell was morally fit to lead the movement. Without American financial support, Parnell was doomed. Ultimately, the majority sentiment turned against Charles Stewart Parnell, and the "Uncrowned King of Ireland" was removed from his leadership post. Within a year, Ireland's greatest statesman of his generation died a broken man at forty-five. Ireland's independence, which had seemed so close, would have to wait almost three more decades.

Unlike Parnell, Buffalo's James Mooney, who died of disease in June 1910, lived a long and prosperous life. He and the other Buffalo Land League members lived long enough to see reforms in the Irish landlord-tenant system favoring impoverished workers. Under Mooney's leadership, the organization also raised millions of dollars (at today's rate), alleviating Irish farmers' suffering during several desperate harvest years. At his death, the *Buffalo Times* wrote, "Mooney was one of the most patriotic Irish-American citizens in the state and displayed a loyalty for Ireland that attracted country-wide attention."[41]

Clan na Gael

Although most Buffalonians advocated for political movements (like the Land League and Home Rule) to improve conditions in Ireland, some radicals still supported the use of violence. After the failed Fenian Raid, some Irish nationalists formed a secretive revolutionary society in 1867, called Clan na Gael or "Family of the Gaels." This organization, America's sister organization to the Irish Republican Brotherhood in Ireland, was supportive of guerilla warfare against the British in Ireland. Initially, organizers opened five Clan "camps" in Buffalo, Boston, New York City, Jersey City, and Philadelphia, and the organization quickly spread across the country.[42] The Clan na Gael held a national convention in Buffalo in August 1888. Once again, Buffalo was one of the primary centers for an Irish independence organization. True to many Irish nationalistic groups, members disagreed on the methods to attain their goal. Some more radical Clan members advocated using explosives to terrorize the British Empire's citizens in what is now called the Dynamite Campaign (1881 to 1885). Buffalo's John "Exile" McBride was one of these radicals.

John "Exile" McBride—Dynamiter

John McBride was born in Dublin, Ireland, in 1842, and at a young age, he joined the Young Ireland movement as a passionate Irish nationalist.[43] During the early 1860s, he organized and trained other young men to prepare for a rebellion against the British, but it never materialized. The British authorities sentenced him to life in prison for his treasonous activities. After escaping prison, he fled to New York City and came to Buffalo to participate in the 1866 Fenian Raid. McBride later recalled his pride in carrying the American flag onto Canadian soil. He was captured but later released, due to Bishop John Timon's efforts. Like dozens of Fenians, McBride settled in Buffalo, where he devoted four decades to agitating for Ireland's freedom.

McBride was a member of the Buffalo branch of the Invincibles, a radical splinter organization of the Fenians that, in the 1880s, advocated violence to obtain Ireland's self-government. In 1882, the Invincibles in Ireland viciously assassinated Lord Frederick Cavendish, Britain's Chief Secretary of Ireland, and Thomas Burke, Britain's Under Secretary of Ireland, in Dublin's Phoenix Park. The brutal stabbing deaths sent a shock wave throughout England and beyond. The British authorities executed five of the accomplices, and later, they hanged Patrick O'Donnell, who had killed an informant. In response, Buffalo's John McBride published an article in a Buffalo newspaper vowing revenge against the British.

In a bizarre but true story, the British authorities sent Canadian agents to Buffalo to kidnap McBride. At about 11:00 p.m. on December 27, 1883, at the corner of Main and Niagara Streets, a stranger introduced himself to McBride as an old Fenian acquaintance from their time together in Dublin's Kilmainham jail. The man called himself Bill Carson and suggested they grab a drink together. After a few pints, Carson recommended they try another saloon, and McBride agreed. Some of McBride's friends then witnessed Carson forcing their friend into a carriage where a Canadian police detective named Finlay bound McBride's hands and feet.

The three men drove north of Buffalo toward the Niagara River. Suspecting something sinister, McBride's friends jumped into another carriage and followed their friend. After several miles, about a half mile south of Tonawanda, McBride's friends rescued him just before the kidnappers could cross into Canada by boat. It was discovered later that Canadians had wanted to question McBride concerning his public declaration to seek revenge for Patrick O'Donnell's execution.[44]

On the same day as the kidnapping, an even stranger story about "Exile" McBride appeared on the front page of the *Buffalo Daily Times*. There had been a massive explosion at Emil Gerot's, a French restaurant on Buffalo's Main Street; McBride was the prime suspect. The newspaper noted that McBride had been experimenting with dynamite and manipulating chemicals in East Buffalo several days prior. Just before his dinner on the night he was kidnapped, McBride had a drink at Gerot's bar but left an hour before the explosion. Authorities questioned the Irish nationalist about the rumors that he had carelessly dropped some dynamite powder on the floor of the bar. While McBride didn't deny the accusation, he claimed that if that was the cause of the blast, it was an accident. The explosion that ripped through the French restaurant caused more than $10,000 in damage ($250,000 in 2020 dollars). More importantly, six employees were left unconscious, some bleeding profusely.[45]

When McBride wasn't getting in trouble with authorities, he earned a living as a photographer, making political badges for politicians and ribbons for civic and fraternal organizations.[46] On Independence Day and other national holidays, McBride dressed in a suit adorned with the American flag and handed political pamphlets to people walking down Buffalo's Main Street. McBride earned a national reputation by organizing Fenian and Home Rule conferences. One noteworthy accomplishment was starting a petition of 30,000 signatures, including from US presidents and governors, demanding that Ireland be granted self-government. He later presented the document to British Prime Minister William E. Gladstone.

McBride died of bronchitis in 1911, five years before the Easter Rising. His *Boston Globe* obituary read, "McBride Dead: He Spent His Life Organizing Movements for Home Rule—Was in the Fenian Raid."[47] The *Buffalo Courier* referred to him as a "picturesque figure in Buffalo" who was known to most of the people who visited downtown.[48] John McBride was one of many Irish men and women who dedicated their lives to the cause of Ireland's freedom.

Other Irish Nationalists

John A. Murphy was a giant in the Irish nationalist movement. Born in County Cork, Ireland, in 1866, he graduated from the Royal University in Dublin and set sail for Buffalo in 1888.[49] Murphy entered the insurance business, eventually owning one of Buffalo's largest firms, and served as vice president of Buffalo's Chamber of Commerce and treasurer for the Board of Trade.[50] But Murphy's efforts on behalf of Irish independence make him noteworthy.

Murphy was an active member of Clan na Gael, and in 1908, he became one of the leaders of Buffalo's Sinn Fein organization. In 1913, he served on the executive committee of the Emmet Memorial Committee, which consisted of ardent advocates for Irish independence. The following year, he was secretary of Buffalo's Irish Volunteer Association, which sent aid to the Irish Volunteers (the Irish paramilitary organization that eventually became the Irish Republican Army.)[51] In 1916, six weeks before the Easter Rising, Murphy became one of the national leaders of the Friends of Irish Freedom (FOIF), eventually serving as chairman.[52]

The Friends organization was initially dedicated to Ireland's freedom and revival of Celtic culture. However, once Irish rebels launched their Rising, the American organization secured funds to rebuild parts of Dublin destroyed in the conflict and provided aid to the families of those killed during the Dublin insurrection. In the summer of 1916, the New York City-based group raised $100,000 ($2.5 million in 2021), and Buffalo's John A. Murphy and John Gill, a New York labor leader, traveled to Ireland to distribute the relief aid.[53] This trip would not be Murphy's last mission to Europe on behalf of the Irish people.

Three years later, in 1919, Irish American nationalists established an organization to advocate for Irish self-determination at the Paris Peace Conference (held in Versailles) following the end of the First World War. Murphy was sent from Buffalo as the American Commissioner of Irish Independence. As the Irish American envoy, he called attention to the atrocities committed by the British against innocent Irish citizens.[54] Murphy also pleaded with the French to advocate for an independent Ireland, reminding them that twenty million Americans claimed Irish ancestry. Murphy suggested that if the French intervened on behalf of the Irish, American public opinion of the League of Nations would become more favorable. Unfortunately, the Allies did not oppose the British, who blocked all discussions about Irish independence. American President Woodrow Wilson, a leading champion for self-determination for other small countries, had no sympathy for Irish nationalists, allegedly telling a legal advisor he wanted to tell the Irish delegation to "Go to hell."[55]

While Murphy's efforts in Versailles failed, he lived to witness the beginnings of an independent Ireland. In April 1922, Murphy died while visiting his sister in County Limerick. His body was shipped back to Buffalo, where Monsignor Nelson Baker presided over his funeral mass at St. Joseph's Cathedral. Irish nationalists from across the country attended the service.[56]

One of the most sensational and spectacular stories about Buffalo's connection with Irish independence involved a Buffalo lawyer named John T. Ryan. Born in Boston in 1874, Ryan, practicing law in Buffalo at the outbreak of the Spanish-American War, enlisted in the National Guard in July 1898 and fought as a second lieutenant in the Philippines. Discharged from the US Army in 1901 as a captain, he returned to Buffalo to practice law, where he was elected ward supervisor.[57] In 1912, after failing to replace the Erie County Republican Party leader, he became active in the Progressive Party (or "Bull Moose Party"). While his political career floundered, he immersed himself in matters related to Irish nationalism and took over the leadership of Clan na Gael in Buffalo.[58]

Irish nationalists on both sides of the Atlantic Ocean had cozied up to the Germans at the outset of the First World War, hoping to receive weapons and support in their campaign against the British. John Ryan was one of them. In 1916, US authorities accused Ryan and Clan Na Gael leader John Devoy of knowing about a German plot to destroy the Welland Canal in Ontario, hoping to obstruct British military transportation. German agents, including Major Horst von der Golz, had met with Ryan in Buffalo in 1914 to request funds for the operation.[59] Later, when US agents questioned Ryan about giving Golz the money, Ryan explained that he thought the money would finance a grain company, and he was not charged.

Ryan's alleged support for the Germans in 1914 was dismissed because Germany and the United States were not at war. By 1917, however, things changed, and in 1918, the Buffalo Irish lawyer was indicted on federal charges of treason and espionage, charged with conspiring to attack Canadian, British, and American interests during the First World War. Authorities also charged Ryan with harboring a German spy, Baroness Marie von Kretschmann, the daughter of a prominent Prussian general, and providing her with financial assistance and sharing information with her about US troop and ship movements during the war.[60] The Germans were, in fact, plotting to use explosives to destroy specific United States docks, piers, and ships. Ryan regularly traveled from Buffalo to Long Beach, New York, to meet with the German Baroness throughout 1917, and the authorities discovered secret messages between Ryan and the Germans. Clan na Gael was likely willing to share intelligence in exchange for German assistance in Ireland's quest for independence.

Ryan fled Buffalo on May 8, 1918, initiating a nationwide search. The story was front-page news for major newspapers, and officials assumed he had fled to Mexico or South America. There were numerous false sightings, and some unfortunate Irish Americans who looked like Ryan were arrested. But Ryan continued to evade the authorities while the morphine-addicted Baroness von Kretschmann was providing authorities with information implicating the Buffalo Irishman in various plots. John Lord O'Brian, the Buffalo lawyer who headed the US government agency that investigated foreign agents during the war, sought to bring Ryan to justice, claiming the Baroness "was the most dangerous agent in the country."[61]

Ryan's friends, who knew he loved Ireland and detested the British, were not surprised by his actions. One unnamed acquaintance claimed that Ryan's mysterious life was part of his nature. He used to send coded telegrams to friends. "Intrigue was food and drink to him—he loved it."[62]

In June 1921, three years after Ryan's disappearance, the British government claimed they had evidence that Ryan was a Sinn Fein envoy in Soviet Russia. This allegation was eventually proved false.[63] Ryan finally surfaced in November of 1922 in New York City and returned to Buffalo in January 1923 after US Attorney General Harry M. Daugherty dismissed treason charges.[64] The elusive Ryan reported hiding in cities such as Chicago and New York, staying in the finest neighborhoods, figuring that Secret Service agents wouldn't look for him there. In a 1923 interview, the unrepentant Irish American nationalist declared that the Irish Free State was a disaster and that he would continue to advocate for an Irish republic.[65] In February 1923, the national Clan na Gael leader, Joseph McGarrity, gave Ryan a large sum of money to purchase weapons from Germany for Ireland's anti-treaty (pro-republic) forces.[66] But the armaments were unnecessary because Sinn Fein president Eamon de Valera declared a ceasefire in May.

Ryan's collusion with German agents in return for assistance to arm Irish rebels was almost certainly treasonous, but he was never punished. In 1937, at the age of sixty-four, he died in New York City. At the news of his death, Irish Prime Minister Eamon de Valera proclaimed, "My colleagues and I greatly grieved to hear of the death of our good friend, John T. Ryan, whose work for Ireland has been so constant and devoted."[67]

William E. Shaddock—Sinn Fein

On August 8, 1908, Buffalo hosted the founding convention of the Sinn Fein League of America. At the conference, Irish nationalists from across the United States and Canada drafted a constitution. This organization—an offshoot of Arthur Griffith's organization in Ireland—advocated for an independent Irish state free of British control and for the perpetuation of the Irish language and culture.[68] Earlier in the year, the Sinn Fein Society organizers started a chapter in Buffalo and named William Shaddock president.[69] Shaddock was also elected to the Sinn Fein National Council at the Buffalo convention.

William E. Shaddock was born in 1879 in Buffalo's First Ward to parents who were Famine refugees from County Clare. After graduating from St. Bridget's School, William apprenticed for a local plumbing business. In 1910, Shaddock started a prosperous heating and cooling firm, receiving substantial contracts for projects with Buffalo's City Hall, the New York Central Railroad terminal, and state colleges in Buffalo and Albany.[70] Shaddock served as president of the Friendly Sons of St. Patrick and helped revive the St. Patrick's Day Parade. He was also active in fundraising for the local Sinn Fein Society chapter.

In March 1909, at a Sinn Fein gathering hosted by Shaddock in Buffalo's Lyric Theatre, Irish rebel leader John Devoy spoke at a commemoration ceremony for Irish martyr Robert Emmet. After Devoy's speech, organizers read a declaration of principles, which urged Irish Buffalonians to pledge themselves to Sinn Fein and the cause of Ireland's freedom. The group also thanked their fellow German Americans for preventing the proposed military alliance between the United States and England. Finally, they applauded the effort to establish a new National University of Ireland in Dublin to preserve the Irish language, literature, and history.[71]

When Shaddock died at age fifty-two in August 1932, the *Buffalo News* described him "as one of America's foremost agitators for the cause of the Irish Republic." It also claimed that he was a close friend of Irish President Eamon de Valera.[72]

Irish Visitors and Fundraising in Buffalo

Buffalo was a hotbed of Irish nationalist activities. As a border city between the United States and Canada, it was logistically convenient for the Irish diaspora from both countries to meet there. It also had a sizable population of Irish residents who emigrated from the hardest-hit areas during the Great Famine. They were passionate in their desire to overthrow British rule. As a result, Buffalo hosted many of the Irish independence movement leaders: Thomas Francis Meagher, Thomas D'Arcy McGee, Michael Davitt, Charles Stuart Parnell, John Devoy, John Dillon, Sir Roger Casement, and Eamon de Valera, as well as hosting many national meetings and conventions to benefit Irish America and Ireland throughout the nineteenth and twentieth centuries.

In February 1856, journalist and former Irish rebel Thomas D'Arcy McGee held Buffalo's first national Irish convention: The Emigrant Aid Convention. McGee advocated establishing colonies for Irish Americans in the Midwestern United States and Ottawa Valley in Canada. Over one hundred delegates from across North America came to wintry Buffalo to draft a plan to create Irish colonies. McGee's scheme ultimately failed because the Catholic hierarchy opposed it. A decade later, the Fenian Raid was launched from Buffalo, and in subsequent years, the Queen City hosted mass meetings, with thousands of Fenian nationalists coming to raise funds for the Irish cause.

Buffalo also hosted the United States' first Land League meeting (1881) and the inaugural national Sinn Fein convention (1908). In November 1899, John Redmond, leader of the Irish Parliamentary Party (IPP), and Dublin Lord Mayor Tallon came to Buffalo to organize a fund for a Charles Stewart Parnell memorial in Dublin's Glasnevin Cemetery. They also collected funds for the Parnell family to pay off their debts so they would not be evicted from their County Wicklow homestead.[73]

In September 1910, Buffalo hosted the United Irish League (UIL) national convention, an Irish nationalist political party that agitated for land reform and political change through constitutional measures. Less militaristic than some of the other nationalistic organizations, it was the successor to Parnell's Land League. John Redmond, the most powerful political leader in Ireland and head of the Irish Parliamentary Party, led a sizable Irish delegation at the Buffalo convention, which the mayors of Boston, New York City, and Philadelphia also attended. At Buffalo's Convention Hall, delegates from across North America pledged $151,000 ($4.3 million in 2020) for the cause of Ireland's freedom.[74] Buffalo's *Catholic Union and Times* declared this was the greatest UIL Convention ever held in America. Unlike previous conventions, the Buffalo gathering was noteworthy because a large delegation of women participated.[75]

Eamon de Valera's Visit

On December 22, 1919, Eamon de Valera, president of the Irish Republic, arrived at Buffalo's Main Street train station at 1:00 p.m., where he was met by two marching bands playing "The Wearing of the Green." That evening, de Valera spoke to over 8,000 enthusiastic people in the Broadway Auditorium. The *Buffalo Times* wrote, "Rarely has Buffalo seen such a demonstrative mass meeting as that which greeted the Irish leader last night."[76] At the beginning of the event, someone in the crowd shouted "Ireland Forever" and "de Valera," and those in the audience rose to their feet, cheering for eleven minutes, until de Valera pleaded with them to take their seats.[77] At the event, Buffalo's Irish-born Bishop William Turner proclaimed that as Americans, "we love justice and hate iniquity; we love freedom and hate oppression." The bishop reminded the crowd that the United

States had aided many nations and peoples in their quest for freedom. But none was held in bondage as long as Ireland.

De Valera started his address by speaking in Irish, saying that the British had unsuccessfully tried to destroy the Irish language for centuries and would be equally unsuccessful in destroying the Irish people's nationalistic aspirations. De Valera compared Ireland's struggle for freedom to the United States' struggle for independence from Britain, expressing optimism that the US government would soon recognize the Irish Republic.[78] The *Buffalo Courier* described the event as "a handclasp of friendship and sympathy which Buffalonians extended to struggling Ireland."[79] The following morning, de Valera spoke at Buffalo's Holy Angels Academy before heading to Rochester.

Irish Republic Efforts

While de Valera's trip to the United States was politically successful, the young Irish Republic was struggling financially. In March 1920, Buffalo Irish leaders William Shaddock and John Hynes led a bond drive to support the fledgling nation. The Buffalo Catholic Diocese endorsed the campaign and set a goal for each parish. Buffalo Catholics generously supported the drive, and even non-Irish congregations, such as St. Monica's and St. Lucy's, exceeded their goals. Our Lady of Perpetual Help, a parish in the First Ward, earned the distinction of being the parish with the greatest number of bolds sold. Michael Regan served as the leader of the parish's effort. Mary Lernihan, from St. Bridget's parish, was the individual who sold the most bonds. In addition to earning this distinction, she was proof that this was not an all-male effort. Buffalo's Bishop William D. Turner was also at the top of the list.[80] After meeting their goal in June, the organizers sent the money to President de Valera. Then, they held a banquet to celebrate the accomplishment, where Bishop Turner predicted that a free Ireland would turn westward and forever be friends with the United States.[81]

After Ireland won its freedom in 1923, Buffalo's Irish nationalist movements mostly disappeared. However, during the Troubles in Northern Ireland in the late 1960s, nationalistic sentiment reemerged. In 1969, the Irish Northern Aid Committee (NORAID) was formed in New York to reduce financial hardship for families of the hundreds of political prisoners in Northern Ireland. Some Buffalonians enthusiastically supported NORAID, which was accused of supplying weapons to the Irish Republican Army, though members of the group consistently denied these accusations.[82]

In 1976, during the Troubles, Irish-American Michael Collins, the CEO of Buffalo's public broadcasting service station (WNED-TV), agreed to interview two Irish Catholic leaders from the Northern Ireland women's peace movement: Betty Williams and Mairead Corrigan. The women came to the United States to urge Americans to stop funding Irish Republican Army weapons purchases. This interview was going to be conducted secretly in Buffalo and broadcast nationally on October 14. When word got out that the women were coming to Buffalo, they received death threats. Given the presence of Irish Republican Army sympathizers in Buffalo, the station was worried about the peace leaders' safety, so they secretly sent Williams and Corrigan to New Orleans to tape the interview. While New Orleans also had a large population of Irish Catholics, it did not have a significant fundraising connection to the IRA, like Buffalo and Toronto.[83]

Buffalo's Irish diaspora played a significant role in Ireland's struggle for independence. Buffalo's most ardent nineteenth-century Irish nationalists, some of whom dedicated their lives to the cause, never witnessed a free Ireland. But their descendants would know the critical role that Irish America played in securing a free Ireland.

CHAPTER THIRTEEN

Irish Heritage and Culture

The Irish in Buffalo have celebrated and honored their rich cultural heritage for nearly two centuries. Festivities honoring St. Patrick's Day are among the most recognizable celebrations. Mary O'Rourke hosted Buffalo's first public observance of St. Patrick's Day on March 17, 1839. Two years later, Martin Rowan presided over a St. Patrick's Day banquet at Huff's Hotel on Main Street. On St. Patrick's Day in 1846, the Friendly Sons of St. Patrick held a stately banquet, which became an annual tradition that lasted for decades.[1]

Buffalo's first St. Patrick's Day procession occurred on March 17, 1848, when the Friendly Sons of St. Patrick teamed up with the Sons of Erin to march through the principal downtown streets, finishing at St. Patrick's Church on Ellicott Street.[2] That evening, club members feasted on a banquet at the Mansion House on Main Street and offered enthusiastic toasts and speeches. The mayor and other local dignitaries joined the Irish residents in their evening merriment.

By 1876, the St. Patrick's Day parade comprised four divisions with nearly a dozen clubs and societies. The 3,000 marchers were described as "strong, well-dressed, sturdy fellows, good specimens of our working class."[3] At 1:00 p.m., the group marched from Niagara Square in "a wet, disagreeable snow storm" with two inches of mud on the pavement. After the marchers paraded through a few downtown streets, Mayor Philip Becker reviewed the cavalcade in front of City Hall before they marched through the streets of the First Ward. After a mile walk, the revelers headed back downtown, concluding their parade at Main Street and the Terrace.[4] Throughout the nineteenth century, the parades were some of the largest celebrations in Buffalo of any holiday.[5]

In 1887, the *Buffalo News* claimed that the 1876 parade, the largest in Buffalo's history, was the last one, as local Irish leaders and younger generations were of a "less revolutionary character."[6] Even though parades ceased after 1876, the Friendly Sons of St. Patrick's annual dinner and ball in honor of Ireland's most renowned saint remained a yearly tradition.

After a hiatus from public processions, organizers resumed the parade tradition in 1915.[7] That year, many prominent Celts from the city's south side assisted William J. Shaddock, the committee chairman, in organizing the event.

It was estimated that 3,000 to 5,000 marched in a lively procession led by Grand Marshal Edward J. Duggan—it was described as the greatest parade ever held in Buffalo in honor of the saint.[8] The march continued annually until at least 1918.[9]

The St. Patrick's Day Parade resurfaced in 1935, with Michael P. Quinn as grand marshal and George J. Evans as the parade chairman. Two boys flanked Grand Marshal Quinn: one was dressed up as Uncle Sam, carrying an Irish flag, and the other was dressed in green, carrying an American flag.[10] Large contingents from the Blackthorn Club, Knights of Equity, and Ancient Order of Hibernians were present, as were firefighters, police, and grain scoopers.

In 1941, the parade was moved from the First Ward to Main Street downtown to accommodate larger crowds. That year, members of the United Irish American Association of Erie County organized the event, and they continue to do so to this day. Over the years, prominent politicians such as Senator Daniel Patrick Moynihan have marched in Buffalo's parade. In 1981, because of the metro rail construction, the organizers moved the procession from Main Street to Delaware Avenue, where it is still held today. By the 1980s, nearly two hundred marching units participated in the event, and 175,000 people turned out on city streets to cheer on the marchers.[11]

The United Irish American Association (UIAA) leadership selects the Delaware Avenue parade marshals. While most parade leaders have been male, many women have been chosen in recent years. In 1978, the UIAA chose Belfast Summer Relief Program co-founder Martha Harkin as the first female grand marshal. Two years later, Mary Whalen, secretary for UIAA, was selected to lead the marchers. In 1981, Brigid Anne Courtney, the corresponding secretary of the UIAA since she was thirteen, became the third female head of the parade.

Buffalo is fortunate to have two major St. Patrick's Day processions. After reading a memoir detailing the original 1915 parade through the First Ward, Peg Overdorf, the Valley Community Center executive director, and a group of First Ward neighborhood leaders started the "Old Neighborhood" St. Patrick's Day Parade in 1994. Overdorf explained that the First Ward parade differs from the one on Delaware Avenue because "The people can identify and connect more. They can imagine what it was like at the turn of the century with their ancestors marching down the same streets, celebrating in the same way."[12]

Most grand marshals of the "Old Neighborhood" parade are prominent First Ward and Valley neighborhood advocates. When it began, this celebration originally had about twenty marching units; it now has more than one hundred entities.[13] The parade contains floats, Irish dancers, a variety of Irish organizations, and family marching units. With the Police Emerald Society leading the parade, followed by local firefighters and other union members, Irish public safety and labor heritage are prominently represented. Following the march, the Valley Community Association hosts a hooley (an Irish term for a party) to raise funds for the center.

Irish Festivals

While St. Patrick's Day parades occur toward the end of Buffalo's gray winters, the Irish also celebrate their culture during the sunny summers. In 1983, Shannon Pub owner Kevin Townsell and patrons Tom O'Carroll and Aby Marks decided over a drink that Buffalo's large Irish diaspora deserved an Irish festival like other American cities. The following year, they launched the inaugural event. Despite their careful planning, the event almost ended in disaster due to an unexpected visit from Mother Nature on the opening night. Around dusk, a strong gust of wind blew a hole open in the top of the main tent, almost ruining the celebration. Several enterprising attendees saved the evening by circling their cars around the tent and turning on their headlights so the show could go on.[14] Aby Marks thought the storm was "a blessing in disguise" because the television news reports "brought our project to the attention of people who had never heard of it before."[15]

Marks stated, "We knew we wanted to avoid a carnival atmosphere. We did not want rides and gambling games that one sees at many festivals. We wanted an event that fosters Irish culture." In 1994, Vincent O'Neill and Josephine Hogan of the Irish Classical Theatre Company joined the list of performers to bolster the cultural portion of the event. Popular participating bands have included Seamus Kennedy, the Dady Brothers, the Blarney Bunch, the Glengarry Bhoys, Kindred, The Leftovers, and Crikwater. By 1995, the three-day Buffalo Irish Festival, held at Weimer's Grove, later named Willow Grove, in Lancaster, consisted of Irish heritage booths, vendors, bands, Irish dancing, and food and drink. While the event's location has changed over forty years, the mission of the celebration has not. The festival continues to share Irish culture with Western New Yorkers, entertaining thousands of people with music and dance.

As with St. Patrick's Day parades, Buffalo is fortunate to have two annual Irish festivals. In 2001, South Buffalo Roots, a nonprofit organization promoting Irish culture, hosted the first South Buffalo Irish Festival. The day-long festival, held at the end of the summer in Cazenovia Park, features Celtic and Irish bands, Irish dance, cultural workshops, and food and drinks from local restaurants. The festival has attracted fan-favorite bands like Jackdaw, Crikwater, and Black 47. Some of the founders of this festival, including Ray McGurn, Thomas "T.E." Caufield, and Louis Petrucci, were honored with an Irish Echo Arts and Culture award in 2023.

283

Buffalo Irish Center

The Buffalo Irish Center in South Buffalo is the heart of Western New York's Irish culture. The Center, founded in 1970, owes its existence to several Irish immigrants, including Irish-born Michael "Ray" Byrne. In Ireland, Byrne and his wife Maureen owned a gas station and a bicycle repair shop, but they decided there were better opportunities for themselves and their four children in the United States.

In 1956, the Byrnes sold their house and businesses, flew to New York City, and arrived in Buffalo two days later. Ray Byrne secured a job in Bethlehem Steel's electrical department, and Maureen worked as a nurse's aide in the Mercy Hospital nursery. In the 1970s, Byrne opened MPB Travel Services, a travel agency on Abbott Road that offered charter flights to Ireland.

In 1966, Byrne, the president of the St. Patrick's Irish-American Club, crafted a plan to consolidate the Buffalo Irish clubs into one space, which would become "a home away from home" for the sizable Irish diaspora. In 1970, Buffalo attorney John Callahan approached Byrne with an opportunity to purchase the South Buffalo YMCA on Abbott Road for $50,000 (about $400,000 in 2023).[17] Byrne sold the idea to several local Gaelic clubs, and within a few months, construction on the Buffalo Irish Center began in earnest. Tom Johnson, a County Clare-born bricklayer, established the Gaelic American Athletic Association (GAAA) in order to purchase the building.[18]

To raise funds for the new building, Byrne worked tirelessly to secure Irish bands like the Carlton Showband from Toronto, which played to sold-out crowds at the Chuckwagon Hall in Lackawanna. He also brought the Irish Rovers, Dubliners, and Clancy Brothers to Kleinhans Music Hall to raise funds for the Abbott Road facility. Byrne's daughter, Dymphna Browne, explained that "people thought he was crazy" when he suggested purchasing the large athletic center. But Byrne, a natural leader, had "a way of pulling people along with him."[19]

In 1970, Byrne served as the first president of the newly formed Gaelic American Athletic Association (GAAA)—the organization that runs the Buffalo Irish Center. Over the years, countless others have volunteered and donated time and money to keep the center going.[20] But Michael Byrne was the visionary who conceived of the Buffalo Irish Center, benefiting thousands of people.[21]

Another critical provider of funds for the Irish Center was New York State Assemblyman Richard "Dick" Keane. The South Buffalo native, a descendant of County Cork and County Clare immigrants, was responsible for securing thousands of dollars for capital improvements. Keane also served as the president of the New York State American-Irish Legislators Society in Albany, New York and was one of the founding fathers of the Irish American Heritage Museum in Albany.

Assemblyman Keane and fellow South Buffalonian Tom Blake championed the Center's most successful fundraiser. During the financially bleak 1970s, chairman Tom Murray tasked Keane and Blake with spearheading a St. Patrick's Day luncheon celebration to raise funds for the fledgling operation. At the annual event on the Friday before the Buffalo St. Patrick's Day Parade, guests feasted on corned beef and cabbage while listening to Irish music and watching Irish dancers. Tom Blake's son, Rich Blake, described the luncheon event as "… a jam-packed beehive of political leaders and candidates, city and labor union officials, news media, parade organizers, clergy, various civic leaders and businessmen, from all parts of the city…together under one roof."[22] More importantly, the affair provided much of the annual operating funds for the facility. In later years, Megan (Corbett) Rizzuto organized the annual event with great success.

Mary Heneghan

Mary (Breen) Heneghan was the longest-serving president of the Buffalo Irish Center, and she provided strong leadership and solid dedication during her tenure. Born in South Buffalo in 1946, Heneghan was a second-generation Irish American whose father, John Breen, was from County Clare. John Breen emigrated to South Buffalo in 1922 for better job prospects and stayed after marrying Katherine Scanlon. Breen shared an appreciation for Irish culture with his daughter Mary and encouraged her to try Irish dance.[23] Heneghan, who traveled to Ireland several times with her dad, was inspired by the richness of Irish heritage.

Mary met her husband, Tom Heneghan, an immigrant from County Mayo, at an Irish picnic in Buffalo. Mary Heneghan worked as a school teacher, but after researching how to open an Irish import store, she decided to switch careers. She set up the Tara Gift Shoppe on Abbott Road across the street from the Irish Center around 1980. For over four decades, the gift shop has been the unofficial hub for information on all things Irish.

Mary Heneghan served as the Irish Center board chair for over two decades. Heneghan's vision for the Center was "to make sure it was an Irish heritage center" where people could learn about the Irish impact on Western New York.[24] She worked tirelessly to bring cultural programming (lectures, music acts, poetry, and theater) to the Center while renovating the pub, the library, and the Emerald Room. Under her leadership, the Irish Center became the heartbeat of Irish South Buffalo.

In a *Buffalo News* interview, Heneghan shared that she loved South Buffalo because of its "sense of community and the sense of family," where there is "a feeling of Irish heritage, no matter what time of the year."[25] Heneghan served as an unofficial mayor of South Buffalo's Abbott Road neighborhood, and local politicians picked up the phone whenever she called. At her funeral in August 2022, US Congressman Brian Higgins described her as "the charismatic leader (of the Center), its heart and soul, the mistress of discipline. She's the boss."[26] Mary's daughter, Mary Kay, added, "She was a force to be reckoned with."

One of Mary's last efforts at promoting Irish culture was assuming control of the 2022 Buffalo Irish Festival when the previous organizers retired from the project. Although dying of cancer, she lived to see the final day of the festival. Upon Heneghan's passing, the Irish Center board of directors issued a press release.

> Those who knew her, knew that she had a secret power; she could convince anyone to volunteer and join the mission to preserve traditional Irish culture. A tireless worker on behalf of the Irish-American community, she was the singer, the poet, the writer, the storyteller, the dreamer. Because she inspired others to do so.[27]

Social Clubs

Social clubs provided necessary community and support for nineteenth-century Irish immigrants. The first Buffalo Irish social club, the Friendly Sons of St. Patrick, operated as early as 1845. The Sons of Erin started a few years later. Both groups were involved with local St. Patrick's Day celebrations as far back as 1848.[28]

By 1891, Buffalo had two chapters of the Ancient Order of Hibernians (AOH), the country's oldest Irish Catholic men's fraternal organization, which was vocal in advocating for Irish self-government. The local AOH annually commemorated Irish patriot and martyr Robert Emmet on his birthday to advance the cause of Ireland's independence. Almost ninety years later, in 1980, Tom Carroll, Craig Spears, and John Ward decided to revitalize the AOH and founded a new chapter (Thomas W. Carroll, Division 1), which has been involved in many Irish heritage projects in Western New York.[29]

The Knights of Equity, another longtime Buffalo club, supported the Irish Center in 1970, when they left their Delaware Avenue headquarters and relocated to South Buffalo. This fraternal men's group formed a Buffalo branch in 1901 and, three years later, boasted 1,200 members.[30] Still active in the twenty-first century, the Knights founded the local Gaelic American Athletic Association and helped promote knowledge about Irish history and culture.

The Blackthorn Club was incorporated in 1917 when five men gathered at Hagan's Tavern on Elk Street (now South Park Avenue), which served as the club's headquarters for decades. While not the oldest Irish-American club in Buffalo, it might be the most colorful. According to their charter, the social club's purpose was to provide "social intercourse among the members" and "to cultivate a friendly and fraternal spirit among such members, and to generally promote their pleasure and well-being."

The Blackthorns secured regular speakers for their monthly meetings, including local or national sports figures and politicians. The Blackthorn Club's membership comprises men from all walks of life, including physicians, business people, law enforcement officials, lawyers, and government employees. Some prominent former members include US Senator James Mead, Congressmen William H. Ryan and Daniel J. Driscoll, and James Molloy, the former doorkeeper of the US House of Representatives. Another loyal member, Tim "Big Russ" Russert, was known to many nationwide because of his son's fame from NBC's *Meet the Press*. The younger Russert once spoke at a Blackthorn meeting, and the famous political satirist Mark Russell was a regular speaker.

The Blackthorn Club will always be associated with the St. Patrick's Day Parade, where they are one of the first companies to march in the parade, not far behind the grand marshal. They have consistently been awarded the "Best Dressed" unit, with their outfits consisting of black top coats, tall black hats, and blackthorn walking sticks.

While the Blackthorn group catered to men in the South Buffalo area, other social clubs formed as the Irish migrated to the suburbs. One of them, the Amherst Gaelic League, was in full force starting in the early 1970s, with their annual headlining event, the St. Patrick's Day party, starting in about 1972. The late *Buffalo News* columnist Bob Curran once wrote, "I do not hesitate to say that I consider the Amherst Gaelic League to [have] the best St. Patrick's Day party in Western New York."[31]

The Gaelic League's event in the 1990s regularly drew 1,300 guests. Since 1982, the club has selected an "Irish Person of the Year," including local politicians, entertainers, and community activists. For many years, the funds raised from the event went to the Belfast Summer Relief program. But in recent years, the club has supported the Irish Famine Monument, the Buffalo Fenians Gaelic Athletic Association, and the James Joyce Collection at the University at Buffalo. Some of the notable founders of the group include Mike Flynn, Dr. Leo Kane, Rev. Jim Browne, Jack Kelleher, Tom Kenny, John Lane, Mike McGuire, and Patrick G. Lucey. The Town O' Tonawanda Irish American Club was another suburban fraternal group that catered to Irish enthusiasts north of Buffalo.

Some well-known Irish women's social clubs include the Daughters of Erin and the Ladies Ancient Order of Hibernians. The Daughters held their national convention in Buffalo in 1960, and Buffalo native Madeline M. Sheehan served as the group's national president in the 1970s. The group marched annually in the parade in kelly green cloaks modeled after their patron, St. Brigid.[33]

Another organization connected to Buffalo's Irish Center is the Buffalo Irish Genealogical Society (BIGS), started in 1997 by Kevin O'Brien and Jim and Donna Shine to assist people in finding information about their Irish ancestors. After the Famine, many records were lost, and names were changed when the immigrants landed in the United States, making ancestral details difficult to come by. The BIGS volunteers have created databases of genealogy information and opened a research library at the Heritage Discovery Center on Lee Street, now assisting people from all over North America.

Belfast Summer Relief Program

Buffalonian Tom Harkin, a native of County Leitrim, returned to Ireland in 1975 during "The Troubles." While there, Harkin was shocked to find no children playing in the streets because of the ongoing violence. When he and his wife Martha Harkin returned to Buffalo, they started the Belfast Summer Relief Program (BSRP) to bring Northern Irish children to Buffalo, providing them a safe respite. Every other summer, the Harkins and other volunteers brought fifty to sixty children to Buffalo, with an even split between Catholics and Protestants, and boys and girls, for a six-week stay. Helping with logistics, volunteers hosted fundraisers to pay for airfare and insurance, while host families provided free room and board for the children. The Amherst Gaelic League was the most generous financial supporter of the organization for at least thirty-five years. In recognition of the Harkins' charitable efforts and her service to the United Irish American Association (UIAA), Martha was named Buffalo's first female St. Patrick's Day Parade grand marshal in 1978.

Jack and Maureen (Leary) Fecio, lifelong South Buffalo residents active with the Irish Center, became involved with the Belfast program in 1981. Jack, a one-time chairman of the GAAA, served as the BSRP's fundraising chairman while Maureen was associate director. In the mid-1990s, when Martha Harkin's health was failing, she asked the Fecios to lead the organization. After peace returned to Northern Ireland, the organizers dismantled the Belfast Relief program in 2015. During the program's four decades, the organization brought over 1,600 boys and girls, ages ten to twelve, to Western New York. For their service to the United Irish American Association and all of their efforts in the Irish community, Jack was named the grand marshal of the St. Patrick's Day Parade in 1996, and Maureen had that honor three years later.[34]

Irish Dance

In 1901, Buffalo's *Catholic Union Times* published an article about a Gaelic revival, where Irish Americans were learning how to perform Irish dances and play the Irish pipes, activities that had fallen out of favor with the children of the diaspora.[35] In July 1912, a Buffalo branch of the Gaelic League sponsored a revival of Irish dance, where men and women were taught traditional Irish dancing.[36] There were competitions in jigs, hornpipes, reels, and a contest for the best dancer, with the Hibernian Drum and Fife Corps providing music. For St. Patrick's Day in 1922, newspapers reported local Irish dancers performed Irish dance (jigs and reels) at the Elmwood Music Hall. However, Irish dance participation was not widespread in Buffalo for a few more decades.

One report claimed that formal traditional Irish dance in Buffalo began in Nora (Darcy) Quealy's basement in the early 1950s. Quealy, an Irish immigrant from County Leitrim, started teaching a friend's daughter, eventually offering weekly classes out of her home, and word spread.[37] Quealy formed a group of dancers called the Shamrockettes, who performed in local parades, sharing traditional Irish dance with the public.[38]

In the mid-1960s, Mae Butler opened Butler Academy, the first formal local school for Irish dance. Others, such as Desmond Penrose, Dublin-born Paul Tynan, and Paula Woodgate, opened their schools during that decade or shortly after. Western New York had several thriving Irish dance schools by the twenty-first century, including Rince na Tiarna, O'Sullivan Irish Dance Academy, Rochez-Lahey Academy, McCarthy School, Clann na Cara, and the Harris Grieco Academy of Irish Dance.

In the 1960s, Irish dancers traveled from Buffalo to Cleveland and Syracuse to compete in Irish dance competitions (called a Feis), but Buffalonians wanted to host their own locally. So, in 1965, they organized Buffalo's first Feis at Lackawanna Stadium. Out of this event, organizers founded the Irish Cultural and Folk Art Society of Western New York to secure funding for future competitions. For the next three decades, the Buffalo Feis changed locations, until settling on the Hamburg Fairgrounds, which could accommodate a thousand performers and their families.[39] The Buffalo Feis is considered one of the elite competitions in North America.

Irish Music

As with Irish dance, there was an effort at the beginning of the twentieth century to revive Irish music among the Buffalo diaspora. Irish marching bands were active in the nineteenth-century St. Patrick's Day parades, but not much is known

Karen Brady was a trailblazing newspaper columnist for the *Buffalo News*.

Margaret Sullivan was the first female top editor of the *Buffalo News*. Later, she had prominent roles at the *New York Times* and the *Washington Post*.

Kevin O'Connell was a long-time weather anchor for WGRZ-TV and one of the most popular people on local television. He also raised millions of dollars for local charities.

Tim Russert, a South Buffalo native, was one of the leading political journalists of his time.

44

First Ward-born John C. Sheehan became a New York City police commissioner and later the leader of Tammany Hall.

45

William "Blue-Eyed Billy" Sheehan served as Lieutenant Governor of New York and used his connections to become a multimillionaire in New York City.

46

John Lord O'Brian worked in senior positions in five presidential administrations. The University at Buffalo Law School building is named for him.

47

Joseph J. Kelly, a Democrat, was Buffalo's first Irish Catholic mayor (1942-1945). He was followed by another Irish Catholic, Bernard Dowd, a Republican.

James Mead was the first and only Buffalo native to serve as a United States Senator. Mead was a popular politician and active in the labor movement.

James T. Molloy, the Doorkeeper of the House of Representatives, visited the Edward M. Cotter fireboat in 1979.

Democratic Chairman Peter J. Crotty (center) at a rally for President John F. Kennedy (far right) on the steps of Buffalo's City Hall, October 14, 1962.

Erie County Democratic Chairman Joe Crangle (far right) shares a laugh with Senator Robert F. Kennedy (second from left) in January 1968. Crangle was one of Buffalo's most powerful political party chairmen.

52

53

Walter J. Mahoney was a longtime Republican majority leader in the New York State Senate and one of the most powerful state Republicans. A prominent building downtown is named in his honor.

Paul Fitzpatrick was the New York State Democratic Chairman and a close associate of President Harry S. Truman.

54

Congressman Richard "Max" McCarthy and his wife Gail (Coughlin) McCarthy campaigning in 1970. They both helped raise public awareness of a secret US government biological weapons program.

56

55

Buffalo native Jimmy Collins was a Hall of Fame third baseman who led his Boston Americans to win the first World Series in 1903.

Player and manager Jimmy Collins of the Boston Americans raises the first World Series flag on Opening Day in 1904 as members of the Boston Americans and Washington Nationals look on.

57

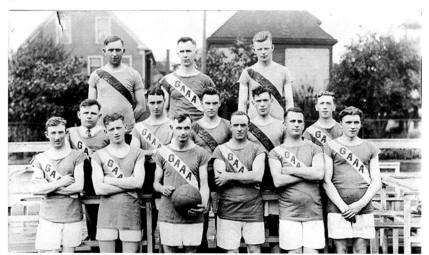

Buffalo's Gaelic football team in 1923. Top row: Ed O'Dea, Pat King, John Browne. Middle row: Manager Pat King, John Ahern, Pat Maroney, Bill McNerty, Joe Conners. Bottom row: John Breen, Martin Browne, Joe Breen, Mike Cummings, Pat Flanigan, John Connors.

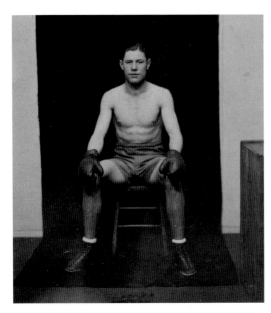

58

First Ward's Jimmy Slattery
won the 1927 World
Light Heavyweight boxing
championship and was one of
Buffalo's first celebrity athletes.

59

Former Buffalo Bills quarterback Jim Kelly
was a hero on and off the football field. In this
photo, Kelly received an award in 2013 for one
of the many charities he was associated with.

60

Emily Regan (left) with her mom, Barb
Regan (right), a few hours after Emily won
an Olympic rowing gold medal in Rio de
Janeiro, Brazil.

61

Alice Lord O'Brian was a prominent First
World War Red Cross leader in France and
an author.

62

South Buffalo native Clarence Wade
McClusky was a hero during the Battle of
Midway in the Second World War.

63

President Harry Truman pinning a medal on General William "Wild Bill" Donovan. Donovan was
a hero in the First World War and the founder of the OSS, the precursor to the CIA, during the
Second World War.

64

The University at Buffalo (UB) holds the world's largest collection of James Joyce's manuscripts, working papers, memorabilia, and portraits. In this photo, James Joyce is seated with his publisher Sylvia Beach, who donated two sets of materials to UB's Joyce Collection. A museum dedicated to this renowned Irish author is planned on UB's South Campus.

In the twenty-first century, Crikwater is one of the premier Irish-American traditional folk bands in Western New York. From left to right, Charlie Coughlin, Matthew Sperber, Liam Caulfield, and Peter Zalocha.

USS *The Sullivans* is one of the main attractions of the Buffalo Naval & Military Park and one of the many Irish monuments and memorials along the waterfront. Martha Harkin (center with Grand Marshal sash) was the first female grand marshal of Buffalo's St. Patrick's Day Parade and former director of the Belfast Summer Relief Program.

Grand Marshal Brigid Anne Courtney leading Buffalo's St. Patrick's Day Parade in 1981.

For over 100 years, the Blackthorn Club has marched in the St. Patrick's Day parade, and they are almost always selected as the "Best Dressed Unit" in the parade.

Mary Heneghan was the longest-serving leader of Buffalo's Irish Center and did much to enhance Irish heritage in Western New York.

The Irish Center in South Buffalo has been the headquarters for Buffalo's Irish culture for more than fifty years.

Irish immigrant John Brinkworth's saloon on Chicago Street. The Brinkworth family has been in the tavern business in Buffalo from 1868 until the present.

Patrons enjoy a drink at Gene McCarthy's tavern in the First Ward. Saloons and taverns have been important to the social fabric of the Buffalo Irish.

Michael Shea's Wonder Theatre in the heart of Buffalo's Theatre District. Shea was Buffalo's most prolific impresario for decades and helped shape Vaudeville.

Irish American Louis Sullivan designed the Prudential Building (later called the Guaranty Building), one of Buffalo's most architecturally significant buildings. Other Irish builders, architects, and business people left a significant mark on Buffalo's downtown.

US Senator Daniel Patrick Moynihan (left) did much to preserve Buffalo's architectural and natural treasures. Frank McGuire (center) was a successful businessman and philanthropist who played a role in many local development projects.

Governor Kathy Hochul, the granddaughter of Irish immigrants and the first female governor of New York State, proudly marched in Buffalo's St. Patrick's Day parade. Hochul has been a strong advocate for Western New York, championing its growth and development. Behind her, Congressman Tim Kennedy, wearing a hat and waving to the crowd, has also been instrumental in supporting Buffalo, including strengthening ties between Western New York and Ireland.

Mayor Jimmy Griffin (right) and Larry Quinn (middle) discuss a development project with Governor Mario Cuomo (left). Griffin and Quinn helped transform Buffalo's downtown and waterfront during the 1980s.

Congressman Brian Higgins has done more for Buffalo's waterfront development than anyone in the modern era. Higgins was a significant catalyst in Buffalo's twenty-first-century renaissance.

about individuals or musical groups that performed. On August 25, 1906, George P. Robinson, a native of County Wicklow and the Erie County president of the Ancient Order of Hibernians, with eight AOH members, organized an Irish band called the Hibernian Fife and Drum Corps. It grew to over thirty regular performers, playing at AOH conventions, Buffalo Labor Day parades, and union conventions. They were frequent guests at the annual German-American Day picnic at Teutonia Park.[41] In 1913, the Hibernian Drum Corps hosted an Irish cultural program with Irish athletes from New York City, Toronto, and Rochester. Held at Buffalo's Columbia Park, the event included hurling, Gaelic football, running, jumping, shot put, hurdles, baseball, and Irish jig and reel contests.[42] As Buffalo's premier Irish band, in 1915, the Hibernian Drum Corps marched at the head of the St. Patrick's Day Parade, singing songs such as "Wearing of the Green," "The Minstrel Boy," and "It's a Long Way to Tipperary."[43] Robinson and his band members were heavily involved in Buffalo's Gaelic revival before Dublin's 1916 Easter Rising.

During the latter half of the twentieth century, many popular Buffalo Irish bands hailed from South Buffalo. One of the best-known was the Blarney Bunch, an Irish folk band formed in 1972, consisting of Cathy Beecher, Frank Finn, Eileen O'Sullivan, Dan Bonner, and Frank Hilliard. The band was a favorite at the Buffalo Irish Center and Buffalo Irish Festival.[44] They also performed on television and for the vice president of the United States and other prominent politicians.

Jackdaw is another South Buffalo band, and all its members have some Irish ancestry. In 2002, the *Buffalo News* music critic wrote, "To experience Jackdaw in concert is to see a band whose dedication to craft is readily apparent."[45] The band was described as a working-class band playing melodies that were part country, part bluegrass, and all Irish. Their guitar-heavy style resembled rock groups like The Pogues or The Clash. Other popular local Irish bands include The Leftovers, Penny Whiskey, Kindred, and the Dady Brothers. (Although the Dady Brothers were based in Rochester, they frequently performed in Buffalo.)

South Buffalo's Crikwater, founded in 2010, has become the area's premier Irish traditional folk band. Band members Liam Caufield, Charlie Coughlin, Matthew Sperber, and Peter Zalocha perform frequently across Western New York, keeping the Irish folk music tradition alive. Buffalo is also home to Limerick-born musician and singer Owen Ó Súilleabháin, who performed locally and worldwide, bringing Ireland's rich tradition of storytelling, poetry, and song to thousands. In 2023, Ó Súilleabháin performed a popular concert in Buffalo honoring Buffalo's Chauncey Olcott.

Gaelic Sports

On August 28, 1901, the Gaelic Athletic Association hosted a hurling match and Gaelic football competition in front of a large crowd at Buffalo's Pan-American Exposition. After that, the Buffalo club hosted regular hurling, handball, and Gaelic football games against teams from as far away as Detroit and Cleveland. In 1925, the club built a new sports field on Abbott Road near Elk Street, where local games were played.[46] The Gaelic football club thrived from the early twentieth century until it folded in 1979. However, it was revived by Tim Flanagan when he started the Na Fianna Gaelic Football Club in 1996.[47] A few years later, some members of Na Fianna broke off and formed the Cuchulain club until they merged in 2005 to form the Buffalo Fenians under the leadership of Paul Mulcaire and Jack Hanley.[48]

Paul Mulcaire came to Buffalo in 1986 from County Clare. In addition to organizing the Fenians, he helped organize the Buffalo Fenians' youth program, with over one hundred boys and girls participating in the club. Mulcaire and Mayo-born Padraic Walsh spearheaded the efforts to bring the Gaelic Athletic Association's Continental Youth Championships to Western New York. During the four-day hurling and Gaelic football competition in July 2017, 250 teams with 2,000 young players came to Buffalo from across the globe. They were cheered on by eighteen thousand enthusiastic spectators.[49]

Irish Studies and Scholars

In the area of academics, Irish studies programs became popular on college campuses in the 1960s. Earlier, at the University of Buffalo, English professor Dr. Thomas E. Connolly was a James Joyce scholar and author of *The Personal Library of James Joyce* (1955) and *Joyce's Portrait: Criticisms and Critiques* (1962). Across town, Canisius College's Dr. Charles Brady had taught courses on James Joyce and W.B. Yeats, and Father William T. Noon wrote a well-received book titled *Joyce and Aquinas* (1957).

While there were some Irish literature scholars, there were no formal Irish studies programs in Buffalo. That changed in 1973, when English professor Dr. Richard J. Thompson created an Irish Studies minor at Canisius College. Thompson, whose paternal grandparents were from County Louth, became interested in Irish culture on a sabbatical to Ireland, where he fell in love with all things Irish.[50] Thompson "developed a broad range of courses in Irish literature" and turned the college into "a vital center for the study of Irish culture."[51] The same year Thompson started the Irish program, he led student summer tours to

Ireland, eventually opening up his popular excursions across the Atlantic Ocean to faculty, staff, and alums.

In the 1980s, Thompson brought in prominent Irish poets, including John Montague, Thomas Kinsella, Richard Murphy, and Seamus Heaney. Due to budget constraints, several of these internationally renowned scholars lodged at the Thompson house.[52] The popular, esteemed Irish-American professor also created the Irish Club at Canisius College and was one of the committee members for the St. Patrick's Scholarship Fund (an endowment established to send Buffalo students to Ireland). Thompson served on the board of directors in the early years of the Irish Classical Theatre Company, regularly published articles in Irish studies periodicals, and authored a book on Irish short story writers, titled *Everlasting Voices: Aspects of the Modern Irish Short Story* (1989).

While Dr. Thompson shared his love of Irish literature at Buffalo's Jesuit college, Dr. Fraser B. Drew worked with students a few miles away at Buffalo State College. After he earned a Ph.D. in English literature at the University of Buffalo, Buffalo State College recruited Drew in 1945, and he remained there for thirty-eight years. Drew, who was half-Irish, traveled extensively throughout Ireland and enjoyed a one-on-one meeting with his boyhood hero, President Eamon de Valera, with whom he corresponded after their meeting.[53] Drew's graduate courses in Irish literature exposed hundreds of students to Celtic culture and literature.

In 1973, when the State University of New York system initiated the inaugural SUNY Distinguished Professor award, Drew was among only nine professors to win across the state. He also chaired the St. Patrick's Scholarship Fund for many years and was a member of the United Irish Societies of Buffalo and Erie County. The Friendly Sons of St. Patrick named him "Irishman of the Year" for his extensive work promoting Irish culture. The popular Irish professor passed away only a few hours after turning one hundred years old.

Several years after Dr. Drew Fraser retired, Buffalo State College hired another Irish literature expert. Laurence Shine, a County Kilkenny native, came to Buffalo to study James Joyce at the University at Buffalo and never left. Shine was a popular lecturer at Buffalo State College, where he taught Irish and English literature and led student trips to the Emerald Isle for over a decade.

In June 1998, Shine initiated Buffalo's first annual Bloomsday celebration on June 16, the day James Joyce's *Ulysses* takes place. Until recently, Shine hosted and served as the master of ceremonies almost every year, getting help from his good friends Vincent O'Neill and Alphonse "Al" Kolodziejczak. In 2007, in conjunction with the University at Buffalo Humanities Institute, Shine co-hosted "Joyce with Gusto," an international conference on James Joyce, inviting various Irish scholars for public lectures. In 2008, Shine founded and led the *Ulysses* Reading Circle on the Buffalo State College campus, helping dozens of residents understand and appreciate *Ulysses*, Joyce's masterwork. For over two decades, he separately led a reading group for *Finnegans Wake*, Joyce's notoriously difficult text. Buffalo State College created the Laurence Shine Undergraduate Research Fellowship to acknowledge his accomplishments and contributions.

In 2012, philosophy professor Dr. Timothy J. Madigan was named the first director of St. John Fisher University's Irish Studies program in Rochester. Madigan, a Buffalo native, was the great-grandson of "Snake Oil" Johnny McMahon and a cousin of Hollywood actor Joe Conley (*The Waltons* TV show), both of whom were previously mentioned in an earlier chapter. St. John Fisher's Irish Studies program attracted students from across Upstate New York, establishing it as a nexus of all things Irish in Rochester. Madigan organized annual conferences on topics such as the Great Famine, Frederick Douglass and Ireland, the Fenians, the Irish and the Building of the Erie Canal, and the Irish in the American Civil War, attracting scholars and community enthusiasts from throughout the Northeast. Some graduates of his Irish Studies program have secured jobs in Irish cultural organizations across the country and abroad.

Rochester and Syracuse, with significantly smaller Irish populations than Buffalo, have supported Irish studies programs (St. John Fisher University and Le Moyne College, respectively). With experts and scholars of Irish literature and history at the University at Buffalo (UB), Buffalo State University, and Canisius University, coupled with UB's James Joyce Collection, the Queen City could become a regional center for Celtic studies.

Buffalonian Patrick Martin also played a significant role in enhancing Buffalo's Irish culture. Born in Spartanburg, South Carolina, Martin graduated from Duke University and pursued graduate studies in English at the University of Buffalo. While in Buffalo, he married Mary Kennedy and clerked for Judge John T. Curtin, working on the school desegregation cases.[54] A lover of literature, Martin co-directed and co-wrote a James Joyce documentary for the National Library of Ireland in 2004. The film, titled *Following James Joyce, Dublin to Buffalo*, traced the famous writer's life in Dublin, Trieste, and Paris. Martin's documentary, which also told the remarkable story of how the Joyce manuscripts ended up in Buffalo, was viewed by Joyce fans across the globe, further solidifying Buffalo's reputation as a critical destination for the renowned Irish writer's work.

The same year Martin produced his film, he also created Cinegael—an Irish film festival. His annual event at the Albright-Knox Art Gallery screened critically acclaimed Irish films that had not yet premiered in the United States. The Buffalo lawyer also started riverrun, Inc. (named after the first words in James Joyce's *Finnegans Wake*), which promoted local cultural programs and provided fellowships for students at the University at Buffalo.[55] One of Martin's most noteworthy accomplishments was helping the Buffalo & Erie County Public Library reacquire Mark Twain's handwritten copy of the first half of the *Adventures of Huckleberry Finn*. Twain had gifted it to Buffalo, but it had been missing for one hundred years.[56]

Buffalo's James Joyce Treasure

Various Buffalo institutions possess important literary treasures, but none more remarkable than the James Joyce Collection. In the fall of 1949, University of Buffalo English Professor Oscar Silverman was on sabbatical in Paris when he visited an exhibit of James Joyce memorabilia at the Librairie La Hune, including drafts of Joyce's *Ulysses*, *Finnegans Wake* notebooks, and numerous personal effects like the author's family portraits. The bookstore proprietor informed the Buffalo professor that the items would be for sale after the exhibition. Professor Silverman recognized "the intellectual significance of the materials on display," which, in his words, would "give rise to scholarship for generations."[57] He quickly contacted Charles Abbott, the first director of the University Libraries at UB, to alert him to the availability of this literary treasure trove.

With the financial assistance of Margaretta F. Wickser, UB officials acquired this first lot of priceless Joyce materials. Two more installments came in 1951 and 1959 when the University obtained materials donated by Joyce's first American publisher. Another portion of the collection came in the winter of 1959 when Constance and Walter Stafford purchased one-of-a-kind memorabilia from Sylvia Beach, the owner of the Shakespeare and Company bookstore in Paris and the first publisher of Joyce's *Ulysses*. More of Beach's Joyce artifacts arrived in Buffalo a few years later. In 1968, the library obtained the final installment, including galley proofs from *Finnegans Wake*.[58] Sylvia Beach told Professor Silverman she was "glad to think that the University of Buffalo is to be the centre for the study of Joyce's work."[59]

Buffalo's James Joyce collection is the largest and most prestigious one in the world and the envy of universities across the globe.[60] This unique archive contains 10,000 pages of working papers, manuscripts, correspondence, and notebooks from Joyce's works, such as *A Portrait of an Artist*, *Finnegans Wake*, and his masterpiece, *Ulysses*. It also includes the author's private memorabilia, including his eyeglasses, passports, walking sticks, original oil paintings of his family members, including his parents and grandparents, and an extensive personal photograph collection. The Poetry Collection also has Joyce's private library from his days in Paris. The University owns a complete set of first editions of Joyce's works, including most issues and states, translations of his works, magazine appearances, and most criticism of his writings.[61]

While this archive certainly enhances the University's international reputation, it also elevates the profile of Buffalo's Irish community. As long as the Joyce collection resides in Buffalo, Irish politicians, dignitaries, and artists will continue to travel to Buffalo to view the collection. In recent years, visitors have included the Irish Ambassador to the United States, several consuls general, the mayors of Dublin and Belfast, and prominent Irish artists, writers, and actors. On an April 2018 visit to Buffalo's Irish Center, the former Lord Mayor of Belfast and *Irish Echo* publisher, Máirtín Ó Muilleoir, boldly proclaimed that Buffalo is the capital of Irish America because the city owns the most extensive James Joyce Collection in the world.

UB's collection has attracted Joyce scholars, some settling in Buffalo after receiving their degrees. The corpus also allowed Buffalo to host the North American James Joyce Conference (*Eire on the Erie*) in June 2009. That year's gathering, organized by professors from the University at Buffalo and Buffalo State College, brought together over 185 scholars worldwide. National Book Award-winner Colum McCann spoke during the conference, and Buffalo hosted an international Bloomsday celebration.[62]

For many years, the University at Buffalo had proposed building a dedicated James Joyce Museum to house the collection. On June 16, 2023, the University announced that Governor Kathy Hochul and Senator Tim Kennedy secured $10 million to build a 5,000-square-foot museum dedicated to the Irish writer in Buffalo. The museum will be located in Abbott Hall on UB's South Campus and will have an endowed curator, digital displays, and permanent and changing exhibitions. A public museum with a permanent exhibition space and a more accessible location will allow the University to showcase this crown jewel to more visitors and create a significant tourist and scholarly destination for Buffalo.

James Maynard, Curator of UB's Poetry Collection, declared, "We have an opportunity to do something spectacular, not just for the University at Buffalo but for all of Western New York, and our goal is nothing less than to invite the entire world to experience the life and literary accomplishments of Ireland's James Joyce." UB also promises that the new center will "promote Irish heritage in Western New York by celebrating one of Ireland's most significant cultural exports and providing Buffalo and its large Irish community with a notable, new landmark."[63] Senator Kennedy said it will not only attract visitors from around the world but also "further strengthen the relationship between the United States and Ireland."[64]

Buffalo's tradition of celebrating and honoring its rich Irish culture shows no signs of slowing. Now, we turn to some other Irish imprints on Buffalo's landscape.

CHAPTER FOURTEEN

Pubs, Monuments, and Buildings

Irish Pubs

Pubs have been integral to Irish culture for a thousand years. When the Irish came to Buffalo, they brought this tradition with them. Pubs, short for public houses, were popular with working-class Irish Buffalonians, who could not afford to drink in private clubs. In the United States, drinking establishments were often called saloons or taverns, so we will use these terms interchangeably.[1]

Saloons in nineteenth-century Buffalo were the epicenter of leisure activities for many Irish men. But saloons served these men more than a drink after a hard day's work. "Workers often utilized the saloon as a cafeteria, a hiring location where networks were forged and the news was spread, a place to sleep, and a location for general conviviality." They were also popular places to pass the time in the winter when work along the waterfront crawled to a halt. In the early part of the twentieth century, women were not allowed in drinking establishments; thus, married men would escape to a saloon for refuge from the demands of their wives and children.[2] Even as late as 1910, Buffalo Police Chief Michael Regan issued orders to clamp down on taverns that allowed women into their establishments.[3]

Since saloons were so popular, saloonkeepers were generally wealthier and more powerful than their patrons. "Ownership of a saloon was viewed as a key avenue of upward mobility within the community...."[4] Congressman Richard McCarthy recalled his father saying that saloon owners were often godfathers of their patrons' children because they could "usually be counted on to give the new baby a $5 bill."[5] During the saloon-boss era, the saloon keepers controlled who worked, and they often held sway over the votes of their customers.[6]

The First Ward was filled with saloons and taverns in the nineteenth century. In the 1880s, one hundred and nineteen saloons were scattered throughout this waterfront neighborhood.[7] In 1869, County Clare-born Patrick Kane opened a tavern and boarding house at the corner of Ohio and Chicago Streets. A few years later, Kane, a Civil War veteran and Fenian captain, added a grocery store to the back of his building to cater to the needs of his boarders.[8] During Buffalo's bustling waterfront days, sailors and dock workers frequented Kane's pub. In 1870, twenty-one Irish laborers and two Irish domestic servants boarded at his establishment.[9] Kane's saloon changed hands over the next century but continued serving neighborhood patrons. In 1975, Irish American Edward Malloy and his wife Julie purchased the then-called Harbor Inn, and ran it for two decades. In 2003, the new owner of the building tore down the storied 134-year-old establishment.[10]

The Hagan brothers, born in County Sligo, owned several taverns in the First Ward. Peter, Henry, and John Hagan started their careers on the docks and later established separate saloon and liquor businesses. In the 1880s, Henry Hagan opened his saloon at the corner of Elk and Hamburg Streets, a popular place for political rallies and an annual Election Day gathering, with large bonfires and celebrations.[11] Other saloon owners used their establishments for business purposes. William J. Conners' saloon at 444 Ohio Street was home to one of the most powerful dock labor companies on the Great Lakes. During the Great Strike of 1899, laborers formed a union at McMahon's Tavern on Elk Street, which ended Conners' control over the grain trade.

In the twentieth century, other notable saloons included Quinn's Tavern on Chicago Street, which Mike Quinn opened in 1913 in a former German hotel built in the 1850s. Quinn's eventually became Kitty O'Malley's and then McBride's Irish Pub. In 2008, the building was torn down after a storm with 60-mph winds ripped the roof off.[12] Gene McCarthy's in the First Ward, opened by Gene and his wife Mary in 1963, was a mainstay in the neighborhood for decades. Years later, tavern owners Bill Metzger and Matt Conron added a brewery and upscaled the food menu, and locals and others still frequent the establishment. For several decades, Gene McCarthy's brother Sam also operated a popular corner tavern on O'Connell Avenue in the First Ward.

The Prohibition Era from 1919 to 1933 adversely affected Irish neighborhoods and their tradition of public houses. Some bars closed up entirely while others, like Jimmy Kane's saloon, adapted by selling home brews and cider.[13] Many others, like Chick McCarthy's, were boarded up in front but secretly operated in the back of the saloon.[14]

The Brinkworths

One Irish family that started in Buffalo's First Ward has left an indelible mark on the local pub scene. The Brinkworth family opened their first saloon in 1868, and family members continue serving customers one hundred and fifty-five years later. They are perhaps the longest, continuous pub operators in Buffalo's history.

The patriarch John Brinkworth, born in Tipperary, settled in America in 1834 at the age of twenty-two.[15] Brinkworth, a pre-Famine immigrant, could read and write, giving him an advantage over most of the illiterate Irish immigrants who came after him. Within a few years of landing in Buffalo, John owned a nail-making shop. By 1868, three years after the end of the Civil War, John had saved enough money to open a saloon to service the masses of thirsty Irish laborers in the Ward. The Brinkworth Tavern on Perry Street near Chicago Street benefited from its location in a thriving manufacturing district teaming with laborers and residents. Brinkworth's son, Jeremiah (Jerry), inherited the family saloon and restaurant and ran it for fifty years. Another son, John, opened his own pub and eventually managed several local hotels, including the Humboldt Parkway Hotel, which is no longer in operation.

In 1945, Dennis Brinkworth and his wife Eleanor (Coughlin) opened the Diplomat at Main and Seneca Streets. Later, they opened three popular restaurants: the Downtowner, the Saratoga, and the Pony Post. But it was their children who grew the family business. By the early 1970s, the Brinkworth family owned over sixteen bars and restaurants in Western New York, including House O'Quinn, Gavin's, Brunner's, Brinks, the Park Meadow, and the Locker Room.[16] *Buffalo News* reporter Tom Buckham wrote, "In this quintessential pub town, the Brinkworths were kings to their shot-and-a-beer subjects—hard-working, blue-collar Buffalo Irishmen...."[17] Over the years, the Brinkworths employed hundreds of Western New Yorkers and built a loyal customer base of prominent lawyers, politicians, judges, and business people. In the early years of the twenty-first century, John Brinkworth's descendants had ownership interests in popular saloons such as Brinks, Colter Bay, the Blue Monk, and W.J. Morrissey.

Downtown and South Buffalo Pubs

Irish pubs were also scattered outside the First Ward in Buffalo's downtown district. Ray Flynn's Golden Dollar on Main Street near Virginia was described as "a classic World War II era drinkery."[18] It was particularly popular with the *Courier Express* news staff until the paper closed in 1982. In later years, *Buffalo News* employees and actors from the Theatre District were regular patrons. The owner's son Tom Flynn was a famous bartender who never forgot a face. Not far away, the Shebeen on Delaware Avenue was described by Dale Anderson "as having the air of an Irish roadhouse" and was "downtown Buffalo's most thoroughly Irish establishment."[19] Ulrich's Tavern on Ellicott Street was opened in 1868 by a German family. But in 1954, James Daley, a First Ward native with a dry Irish wit, and his German-born wife, Erika, purchased it. The tavern had both Irish and German sensibilities.[20] Their son James (Jamie) took it over and operated the bar until 2013. Pat McGinty's Pub, across the street from the Buffalo Bisons' Sahlen Field, advertised itself as "a neighborhood pub in the heart of the city." The owner, Patrick C. McGinty, grew up in Buffalo's Riverside neighborhood and opened his first tavern, the Sonata Lounge, in 1968 on Seneca Street. He was one of the first pub owners in Buffalo to offer live Irish music acts.[21] In 1985, he opened McGinty's in an old livery stable on Swan Street, and it became a favorite destination for Sabres and Bisons fans. It was later renamed the Irish Times.

Founding Fathers on Edward Street off Delaware Avenue, while not Irish-themed, is owned by Irish American Mike Driscoll. In 1990, Eddie Brady opened a bar on Genesee Street and named it after himself. Brady, of Irish descent, was a legendary bar owner and was featured in an off-Broadway play, *Bartenders*.[22] The bar business was in Brady's blood. His father tended bar at Crotty's Peace Pipe on Niagara Street, another downtown Irish mainstay. Bartholomew Crotty and his wife Helen owned Crotty's, a popular spot for politicians and social clubs. Close by, Garcia's Irish Pub on Pearl Street opened in 1984 and benefited from its proximity to both Memorial Auditorium (the former home of the Sabres) and the Buffalo Bisons ballpark. There was nothing Irish about Garcia's—apparently, the owners tried different names and liked the sound of "Irish Pub."

In 2001, entrepreneur Mark Croce opened D'Arcy McGee's Irish Pub on Franklin Street. He named it after Irish-born Thomas D'Arcy McGee, a former Buffalo resident and assassinated Canadian politician. An Irish firm designed the 6,000-square-foot bar, and almost all the materials (stone fireplace, teak bar, and furniture) were imported from Ireland.[23] At the time, it was one of only 130 pubs in the United States that met the Irish Pub Concept standards. One of Croce's close business associates, Belfast native Conor Hawkins, managed D'Arcy McGee's and several of his other establishments. After Croce died, Hawkins and Dublin natives Kevin Dargan and Neil Coogan, along with Buffalonian James Corda, opened The Banshee Irish Pub in the former McGee's space in 2021. The Banshee has become a popular spot in the Chippewa district, where patrons enjoy authentic Irish pub food while watching a football (soccer) match or listening to live Irish music.

Many more Irish watering holes were located south of downtown in the Irish stronghold of South Buffalo along Abbott Road, South Buffalo's main thoroughfare. The Buffalo Irish Center has a bustling bar that serves a good pint of Guinness and a variety of food choices while patrons enjoy live music. Down the road, Doc Sullivan's is known for its delicious Smitty-style chicken wings.

Still further down Abbott is the popular Molly Maguires. O'Daniels Gin Mill (previously called O'Malley's) is another popular tavern on Abbott.

On Seneca Street, patrons can find a perfectly poured pint of Guinness at the Blackthorn Restaurant and Pub, formerly called Early Times Tavern. The pub hosts monthly gatherings for the storied Blackthorn Club. Other Irish South Buffalo bars include Talty's on South Park Avenue. Forgotten Buffalo Tours described Talty's as "one of the liveliest pubs in South Buffalo" and owner Dennis Talty as "one of the friendliest barkeeps in the entire city."[24] The Talty family has operated taverns on South Park for over a century. South Park was also home to Crehan's Club Como, opened in 1952 by Vincent Crehan, and it was the site of many political and family functions. In 1977, Irish Americans Bill Murphy and Richard Keane purchased the thriving club, offering big band routines, live theater, and comedy acts. Other notable South Buffalo taverns include Potters Field, Hopper's Rush Inn on Seneca Street, Daly's Bar on Seneca Street, and the Blarney Castle on South Park Avenue.

As some Irish moved out of South Buffalo, pubs emerged in their new communities. McPartlan's was established on South Park Avenue in 1955 and moved to Amherst in 1971, where it was known for its delicious fish fry. In about 1990, J.P. Fitzgerald's, named after the owner's grandfather, opened in Hamburg as a sports bar and restaurant with an Irish flair. The owners organize an annual trip to Ireland for their patrons.

In 1982, Buffalo-born Kevin Townsell, whose family roots are in County Clare, opened an Irish-themed music pub at the Airways Hotel, an establishment his father co-owned near the Buffalo airport. He named the Shannon Pub after the Irish airport, not the river.[25] Four nights a week, the pub featured some of the finest Irish folk music in the area. In addition to hosting popular entertainment such as the Dady Brothers, Eugene Byrne, Cahir O'Doherty, Fiona Molloy, and Bill Craig, Townsell also brought in a couple of young Irish actors, the O'Neill brothers. Vincent and Chris O'Neill performed at this bar before settling in Buffalo and establishing their critically acclaimed Irish Classical Theatre Company. *Buffalo News* columnist Bob Curran referred to Townsell's pub as the "Irish Center East" because, like South Buffalo's Irish Center, it served authentic Irish beers and recruited top-notch Irish musicians.[26]

In about 1994, Townsell moved his celebrated Shannon Pub to Main Street in Amherst and later to Niagara Falls Boulevard in Tonawanda. The Shannon Pub became a regional hot spot for Irish music and bands such as Tommy Makem & the Clancy Brothers and the Saw Doctors. In 1986, the Irish-American restaurateur also opened the Buffalo Brewpub, Buffalo's first new regional brewery.[27] In 1991, Townsell hosted the first Buffalo Beer Festival, which ran for several years, offering beers from microbreweries across the country.[28]

Townsell also supported Irish heritage and culture. He served on the committee for the Irish Famine Memorial and donated the funds and services to host a website that promotes all things Irish in Buffalo. The tireless entrepreneur also hosted tours to Ireland for more than thirty years. For Townsell's work on behalf of the Irish community, the Amherst Gaelic League awarded him their "Irish Person of the Year" award in 1999. But Townsell's most significant contribution was probably his work co-founding the annual Irish Festival, which takes place every summer.

In Buffalo's northern suburbs, the Shatzel family opened Brennan's Bowery Bar on Transit Road in Clarence in 1970. The Irish-themed bar and restaurant closed in 2022 after over five decades in operation. In Williamsville, The Irishman Pub and Eatery opened in 2008 and has been so successful that owner Gene O'Donovan opened a second pub in East Aurora. The Irish pub tradition, which started in the Old First Ward and spread throughout Buffalo and Western New York, remains strong.

Irish Landmarks, Monuments and Buildings

Beyond the community's fine pubs throughout Western New York, Buffalo's waterfront is filled with Irish monuments. One of the most poignant is the Irish Famine Monument located at the Erie Basin, near the former Erie Canal, which brought many Famine and post-Famine Irish immigrants to Buffalo. After a long journey from New York City via the Hudson River and the Erie Canal, immigrants would disembark from the boats and head off to Irish strongholds along the water's edge (typically south to the First Ward or north to the West Side). Planning for the monument began in 1995 when twenty-six Western New York cultural organizations formed a committee to design and raise funds for a memorial dedicated to famine immigrants. They received funds from the City of Buffalo, Erie County, and Cork, Ireland.

Rob Ferguson designed the site with a 12-foot granite stone in the center surrounded by a well. The single stone reminds visitors of the ancient standing stones throughout the Irish countryside. The central stone came from County Galway, one of the hardest-hit areas of Ireland during the Famine. The outer edges of the monument's site are surrounded by a ring of thirty-two large limestone blocks representing the thirty-two counties of Ireland.

Each stone in the Buffalo monument was taken from Penrose Quay in County Cork, where ships departed for the United States from Ireland. The emigrants would have walked on these stones as they boarded ships to North America. For many, it was the last time they would stand on Irish soil. In the middle of the site are eight hundred granite stones inscribed to honor Irish and Irish-American

Buffalo families and individuals. Some stepping stones are left blank to honor the thousands of nameless victims who perished in the Famine. An inscription from the Gospel of Luke is at the base of the main stone: "If they were to keep silent, I tell you the very stones would cry out."

At the dedication ceremony on August 23, 1997, Irish American Chuck Treanor, the fundraising committee president, explained that the memorial commemorated the 150th Anniversary of Black '47—the worst year of the Great Hunger. The monument serves as a memorial to the thousands of immigrants from the Emerald Isle who settled in and shaped Buffalo. Mike Flynn served as the master of ceremonies, Buffalo's bishop blessed the monument, and Erie County Sheriff Thomas Higgins offered words about world hunger. A delegation from Cork City, including Lord Mayor David McCarthy, was also in attendance.

Each summer, an annual Famine mass at the site commemorates those lost to the Famine and reminds the public of the ongoing struggle to defeat hunger worldwide. Some of the prominent organizers of the monument include Ed Patton, Laurence Shine, John Carney, Kevin Townsell, and Charles Treanor.

Military and Irish Independence Monuments

As previously outlined, Buffalo provided the Union Army with five infantry units during the US Civil War. One of them, the 155th New York State Volunteers, was primarily composed of Irish and Irish-American laborers. In the early twenty-first century, a group of Buffalo reenactors decided the men of the 155th deserved a memorial to honor their sacrifice during the war. This famous regiment suffered massive casualties in the War's Virginia Campaign. In 1997, members of the reenactment regiment, led by President Gary N. Costello, raised money for a monument in their honor. Fellow reenactor and sculptor Henry J. Schmidt was hired to make a clay model for the memorial, which was cast in bronze and mounted onto a granite slab.[29] In September 2002, hundreds of reenactors marched from the Soldiers and Sailors Monument to the Buffalo Naval Military Park, near the Vietnam Memorial, to unveil the monument that will ensure that these Irish soldiers will not be forgotten.

Some men who fought with the 155th during the Civil War also participated in the 1866 Fenian Raid launched from Buffalo into Canada. This military incursion was instigated to force Great Britain to grant Irish independence. The year following the failed invasion, the Fenian leadership erected a tall monument in Holy Cross Cemetery to honor Buffalo's Edward Lonergan, who died in the battle.

New York State Senator Timothy M. Kennedy and other prominent Irish Americans spearheaded plans for another memorial to commemorate this daring attack on British forces. At the memorial's opening on March 16, 2012, Senator Kennedy explained, "The Fenian Invasion was a global event, and this monument celebrates one of the many contributions Buffalo and Western New York has made to the global community."[30] The polished granite slab stands in Tow Path Park along the Niagara River, close to the launch site of the incursion. To commemorate the event, members of the Black Rock Historical Society, led by William "Chip" Butler III, and leaders of the Thomas W. Carroll Ancient Order of Hibernians Division 1, hosted an annual march from the site of the monument through Black Rock. When Irish dignitaries and politicians come from Ireland to Buffalo, they often visit this newest memorial.

USS *The Sullivans* and the Cotter Fireboat

The USS *The Sullivans* is one of the main attractions at the Buffalo and Erie County Naval and Military Park. The US naval ship is named after five Sullivan brothers from an Irish Catholic family from Waterloo, Iowa. The brothers joined the Navy after Pearl Harbor on the condition that they could serve together. All five were killed on the USS *Juneau* in the horrific 1942 Battle of Guadalcanal during the Second World War. On April 4, 1943, the US Navy named a Fletcher-class destroyer in honor of the deceased brothers. After the warship was decommissioned, the Navy moved it to Buffalo in 1977. On July 17 of that year, 2,000 people glimpsed the vessel at the dedication of the new Naval Park, and John Sullivan, a son of one of the deceased Sullivan brothers, was the event's honored guest.[31] The Navy destroyer, which has a giant green shamrock with the motto "We Stick Together," attracts thousands of visitors annually. Designated a National Historic Landmark in 1986, it is one of the top attractions at the Naval Park. In April 2022, the 79-year-old ship suffered a hole in its hull, causing it to take on water, and it was in danger of sinking. To rally support to repair the vessel, the New York State Ancient Order of Hibernians issued a statement:

> While The *Sullivans* should hold a position of respect for all Americans, it has a special place in the hearts of Irish Americans. The Sullivan family sustained the most extensive loss in combat by any one American family during the war. The Sullivan brothers are symbolic of the best traditions of service to family and nation that have been the hallmark of Irish Americans.[32]

Subsequently, over $1 million was raised from private and government sources to repair the ship and preserve it for generations.

On the Buffalo River, south of the USS *The Sullivans*, the *Edward M. Cotter* fireboat resides in a slip near the Michigan Avenue bridge. The boat was named after the

Irish American Edward Cotter, who founded the Buffalo Firefighters Association Local 282 in 1930. Cotter, born in 1891, was the son of Irish immigrants who landed in Buffalo's First Ward. After schooling, he worked as a steamfitter and then joined the fire department, where he later founded a firefighters' union and served as its president. Cotter was the "recognized public spokesman for Buffalo's firefighters during his 36-year career in the department."[33]

The *Cotter* fireboat, built in 1900, was initially named the *W.S. Grattan*. In 1954, at Cotter's death, the fire department renamed the fireboat in his honor. The *Cotter*, which could pump 15,000 gallons per minute, was critical in extinguishing numerous waterfront industrial fires. In the winter, the City of Buffalo used the *Cotter* to break up ice buildup in the Buffalo River. Declared a National Historic Landmark in 1996, it is considered the oldest working fireboat in the world.

A Walk Through Buffalo's Irish Downtown

The imprint of Buffalo's Irish is found throughout Buffalo's downtown. Starting at the Inner Harbor, one can view the outline of Samuel Wilkeson's harbor, which enabled Buffalo to become the Erie Canal's western terminus. While there, a visitor may explore the sites at Canalside, thanks primarily to the efforts of Congressman Brian Higgins, who secured the funding to rebuild this district. Looking west toward the Erie Basin Marina, one can observe the thriving waterfront neighborhood of townhouses and high rises, which Irish American Mayor James Griffin and Larry Quinn spearheaded in the early 1980s. Moving north on Main Street, you come to a Marriott Courtyard and the law offices of Phillips Lytle. This structure was formerly the Donovan Building, a state office site named after General William "Wild Bill" Donovan, one of Buffalo's most celebrated citizens.

Past Seneca Street on the east side of Main Street, one would find the restored five-story Glenny Building, which now houses luxury apartments. This structure was the headquarters for Irish-born William Glenny's national dry goods enterprise. Across the street, The Sweeney Building, the site of Irishman John F. Sweeney's department store, has been fully refurbished. One block east of these buildings stands Buffalo's Sahlen's Field baseball stadium, conceived and spearheaded by Mayor James Griffin. The plaza outside the stadium is named for Griffin, and it includes a life-size statue in his likeness.

Another Irish-influenced Buffalo landmark stands across the street from Griffin's ballpark. The Erie Community College city campus (formerly the Main Post Office for Buffalo) was designed by Jeremiah O'Rourke, an Irish-born architect, who was the United States Supervising Architect responsible for federal buildings nationwide. From 1894 to 1897, O'Rourke designed the Gothic

Romanesque-styled Main Post Office building, which architect James Knox Taylor finished in 1901. The six-story building, with over 200,000 square feet of space, was built with pink Maine granite, marble columns, and a 244-foot tower.[34] Adorned with statues of eagles and gargoyles, it is one of the most prominent structures in the city. After the Main Post Office moved to a modern building on William Street in 1962, O'Rourke's landmark building sat empty until it was converted into the city campus for Erie Community College (ECC).

Bishop John Timon's St. Joseph's Cathedral, dedicated in 1855, is a couple blocks west of ECC. Irish-born architect Patrick C. Keely designed this Gothic Revival church. Irish laborers provided much of the labor during the construction of the bishop's church. The structure continues to serve as the mother church of the Buffalo diocese. Several blocks north of the cathedral, Patrick Keely also designed St. Michael's Church on Washington Street, the former home of the Jesuit community for more than one hundred and fifty years. A few blocks west of the cathedral, another Irish-American architect, Michael C. Sheehan, designed St. Anthony of Padua Church, a Romanesque house of worship for Buffalo's Italian community. The cornerstone was laid in 1891 by Bishop Stephen Ryan, and it was a center for Italian Catholic life for decades.

One block from St. Joseph's Cathedral is the most significant Buffalo building associated with an Irish American: The Guaranty Building. Boston native Louis Sullivan, the son of an Irish-born father, designed the Buffalo high-rise. Sullivan became one of the most influential architects of the nineteenth century and is referred to as "The Father of the Skyscraper." Sullivan's Guaranty building was made of steel and adorned with terra-cotta tiles that form a tree of life pattern. Completed in March 1896 at a staggering cost of $1 million, it was considered "one of the finest buildings in the country," and the thirteen-story building was the tallest building in Buffalo at the time."[35] Today, the masterpiece is rated one of Buffalo's top five architectural sites, in a city filled with spectacular structures.[36]

Going north again on Main Street, at Lafayette Square, there are two significant Irish structures. The Brisbane Building, formerly the Mooney-Brisbane Building, was co-owned by James Mooney, an ardent Irish nationalist and real estate agent who helped oversee its construction. Across the street stands the Soldiers and Sailors Monument, designed by Cork-born George Keller. The cornerstone for the 85-foot war memorial was laid in 1882, and the monument was dedicated two years later. Within five years, however, the structure started sinking and was declared a public hazard. The aforementioned upstart Irish-American granite firm McDonnell & Sons won the contract to rebuild the monument so that it could last for generations. It still stands straight over one hundred and thirty years later.

Two blocks west of Lafayette Square, on Court Street, sits another of Buffalo's former prominent state office buildings. In October 1982, fifty-one years after this structure opened, Governor Hugh Carey came to Buffalo to rename the state building for Buffalo Irishman Walter J. Mahoney, a powerful state legislator and a State Supreme Court justice. Across the street on Court Street is the former Michael J. Dillon US Courthouse, named for a local IRS revenue officer who was killed collecting a debt in 1983. This block-long building along Niagara Square housed all of Buffalo's federal courts.[37]

Further north, on the 400 block of Main Street, the Hens & Kelly building is a fixture in that district. Irish immigrant Patrick J. Kelly and German immigrant Mathias Hens completed the six-story, state-of-the-art department store in 1925. It currently houses a government agency and residential apartments. Further up Main Street in the Theatre District, on the east side of the street, is the home of the Irish Classical Theatre Company. Dublin immigrants Vincent O'Neill and Josephine Hogan created the company, and Irish American Peter Andrews and his wife Joan donated a sizable contribution to the buildout of the theater building. Across the street, Shea's Buffalo Theatre, Irish American Michael Shea's cathedral to entertainment, hosts a lineup of premier Broadway productions each year.

Still on Main Street and crossing Goodell Street sits the Catholic Diocese of Buffalo's headquarters. This building was the former *Courier-Express* newspaper headquarters owned by Irish American William "Fingy" Conners. About two blocks over on Ellicott Street is the Thomas R. Beecher Innovation Center, named in honor of the Irish-American leader of the Buffalo Niagara Medical Campus. From there, up a block to Virginia Street, heading west to St. Louis Place, is a plaque to commemorate Buffalo's first hospital built by Bishop John Timon and the Irish Sisters of Charity. Back down Virginia to Main Street is the Granite Works block. This restored district is anchored by the former McDonnell & Sons granite-façade headquarters building erected in 1886.

This tour of Buffalo's downtown is only a partial list of places that the Irish built or shaped.

At the turn of the twenty-first century, Buffalo experienced a renaissance, and several Irish-American men and women made significant contributions to it. We turn to that topic now.

CHAPTER FIFTEEN

Modern City Shapers

Mayor Jimmy Griffin and Larry Quinn

Buffalo's economy in the 1970s was dreadful. The region was still struggling after the significant loss of jobs from the 1959 opening of the St. Lawrence Seaway, which destroyed the city's bustling waterfront economy. Companies moved jobs overseas or to lower-cost southern states. The financial outlook for Buffalo was bleak as people moved to the suburbs or left the area completely. The city desperately needed a strong leader and found one in an Irish-American politician from Buffalo's south side.

James D. "Jimmy" Griffin was born in the First Ward in 1929, four months before the start of the Great Depression. His father, Tom, the son of Irish immigrants, worked as a hardware clerk for Beals, McCarthy and Rogers. The Griffin family home was on South Park Avenue, and as a boy, when not playing baseball, Jimmy hauled bags of potatoes at the Elk Street Market. Griffin dropped out of high school to work on the waterfront, returned to complete his diploma, and then fought in the Korean War as a paratrooper. The First Ward native worked for Maritime Milling as a laborer and scooped grain from railcars.

In 1961, Griffin won a seat on the Buffalo Common Council, representing the Ellicott District, and five years later, he was elected to serve in the New York State Senate. He had great political instincts, a knack for connecting with people, and a gift for remembering names and faces. In 1977, after meeting with his top advisors, Griffin was convinced he had to run for mayor of Buffalo. However, the Democratic leadership in Buffalo had decided on Arthur Eve, an African-American candidate. It appeared that Griffin would have to wait a little longer. But the former infantry platoon leader thought *he* should lead Buffalo, so he ran on the Conservative Party line instead. In a heated three-way race, Griffin beat the favored Democratic candidate Arthur Eve, and then won four consecutive mayoral terms. His sixteen years as Buffalo's mayor stood as a local record until 2021, when Mayor Byron Brown won five straight elections.

Griffin shared his common-sense management philosophy as mayor:

I campaigned on very simple ideas. Everybody said, 'You've got a simple solution to everything.' Well, that's the way life is. You can't make it complex. If the people in a neighborhood say that they want a stop sign, that stop sign goes up. I don't wait for surveys. If I think there should be more policemen on the streets, I don't wait for FBI statistics. I believe in the simple way of doing things. More than experts, we need people with common sense in government.[2]

Griffin had many admirers, as well as detractors. The Irish from South Buffalo and the First Ward mostly loved him. After Griffin's first term, 65% of Buffalo's citizens felt he was doing a good or excellent job handling the city.[3] Griffin stacked his administration with his trusted advisors from the Irish First Ward and South Buffalo, such as his long-time friend John "Scanoots" Scanlon, Dave Comerford, James Comerford, Rick Donovan, Donald "Bughead" Smith, Stan "Boots" Buczkowski, George "Ortsie" Gould, John B. Myers, and Danny Bohen.

Despite his best efforts, Griffin couldn't slow the closing of local plants and mills. Pillsbury closed the Great Northern Elevator in 1981. Two years later, the shuttering of the Bethlehem Steel plant—which employed 22,000 workers at its peak—dealt a devastating blow to the region. Republic Steel in South Buffalo closed a year later, and thousands more Western New Yorkers lost their jobs.

Still, Griffin accomplished a great deal despite the loss of Buffalo's manufacturing base, declining population, and lower tax revenue. Significant projects included the gentrification of the Theatre District on Main Street and the restoration of the historic Market Arcade building. He oversaw the construction of a metro rail line from downtown to the University at Buffalo on Main Street and over 1,000 affordable homes. Perhaps Griffin's most significant accomplishment was on the waterfront, where he led the development of housing and commercial buildings on the Erie Basin Marina.

Griffin, a former semi-pro baseball player, led the effort to bring Triple-A baseball back to the city, hoping to secure a major league team. By 1970, professional baseball had disappeared in Buffalo. Almost ten years later, Mayor Griffin gathered a group of investors to purchase the Double-A Jersey City franchise.[4] While most cities built stadiums in the suburbs, Griffin wanted to construct a world-class baseball facility downtown as part of a revitalization project. On April 14, 1988, two years after a groundbreaking ceremony, Buffalo opened the $42-million-dollar ballpark, home of the Buffalo Bisons. Critics across the country responded with rave reviews, and it became a model for other minor league baseball stadiums.[5] It wasn't just the critics who loved it. The fans did, too. In the ballpark's first year, attendance was over one million, setting a minor league record.

Hundreds of thousands of Western New Yorkers have enjoyed professional baseball in Buffalo because of the efforts of Griffin and the Rich family. The Buffalo Bisons' organization honored Griffin by renaming the area outside the stadium as James D. Griffin Plaza and installing an 800-pound bronze statue of Griffin at the entrance to "The House that Jimmy Built."[6]

In his 1978 inaugural address, Griffin promised, "I won't let you down." And he didn't. Griffin's accomplishments with the waterfront, downtown revitalization, the baseball stadium, the Theatre District, mass transit, and thousands of affordable houses continue to benefit Buffalonians. At Griffin's farewell party, Buffalo developer Frank Ciminelli said, "Here's a guy who broke his neck for this city, and people just don't realize it. There were deals I never would have touched if it wasn't for him."[7] Upon his death, the *Buffalo News* wrote, "[Jimmy Griffin] might rank as the most dominant political figure of modern Buffalo."[8]

Every successful mayor has at least one person like this in their administration: you pick up the phone, and the person on the other end will make the seemingly impossible come true. For Mayor Griffin, that person was Larry Quinn.

In 1957, five-year-old Larry Quinn and his family moved from Trenton, New Jersey, to Buffalo. His father, Harry Quinn, was hired as the chief engineer to build the Kensington Expressway.[9] Larry's mother, Loanne (Casey) Quinn, was an Irish Chicagoan. After attending Christ the King Elementary School, Larry Quinn graduated from Canisius High School and Notre Dame University.

In 1977, Mayor James Griffin chose twenty-four-year-old Larry Quinn as his economic development director. When Quinn accepted, Griffin gleefully replied, "Just wait until this certain woman who complains about all of the Irish Catholics in my administration hears your name!"[10] The young Irish Catholic quickly demonstrated that he was adept at making deals. Just four years later, the mayor promoted twenty-eight-year-old Quinn to commissioner of community development, and Quinn became the city's youngest commissioner. Mayor Jimmy Griffin once declared, "They always talk about who you want in a foxhole with you when the shooting starts. I want Larry Quinn."[11]

"Building things" was in Larry's blood. When Larry was a young boy, his father took him to see building projects in downtown Buffalo, urging his children to have "a deep respect for the community in which you live."[12] Under Griffin, Quinn's building projects enhanced Buffalo, including the Hilton Hotel (1979), the Genesee Building restoration (1984), which became the Hyatt Regency, and Fountain Plaza. Quinn also worked on the original waterfront housing development at the Erie Basin Marina.

Quinn played a significant role in developing Buffalo's Theatre District. One of Mayor Griffin's first initiatives after his election in 1977 was to redevelop upper Main Street. Quinn worked with University of Buffalo Professor Harold Cohen to develop a plan to transform the area. Quinn started with the derelict 600 block of Main Street, securing federal monies to rebuild the Otto Building, the structure just south of Shea's Theatre, and the E.B. Green-designed Root Building next door, which he called Theater Place. The project comprised retail and commercial space on the lower floors, with artists' lofts above. It was a gamble because the city spent $3.5 million before securing any tenants. However, investors quickly signed on with an idea for a nightclub and music venue—the Tralfamadore Café (later known as The Tralf) became the mecca for music in downtown Buffalo.[13] This section of Main Street anchored other revitalization efforts in what was then called Buffalo's Entertainment District, which grew rapidly in the next decade. Later, Quinn also found a new home for the critically acclaimed Irish Classical Theatre Company (ICTC), helping solidify the Theatre District.

William "Bill" Donohue, a former commissioner in the Griffin administration, credited Quinn with helping small businesses during the economically depressed 1980s by securing block grants from the Erie County Industrial Development Agency (ECIDA). Quinn viewed it as a tremendously successful program contributing to "probably the greatest building boom Buffalo's ever had."[14] Donohue said, "Quinn always did what was good for economic development in Buffalo."

In December 1992, Buffalo Sabres Chairman Seymour H. Knox III hired the forty-year-old Quinn to spearhead building a new home for the Buffalo Sabres, which was desperately needed to keep the franchise in Buffalo. As the vice president of the Crossroads Arena Corporation, Quinn secured $52 million in public financing for the project, which was later called Marine Midland Arena.

Quinn then oversaw the construction of the $127 million project, which he completed on time and under budget. The 700,000-square-foot arena with 19,500 seats opened in September 1996.[15] According to columnist Mike Harrington, it was Quinn's idea to use the arena for other purposes, such as hosting NCAA basketball tournament games. Many people doubted Quinn, but by 2000, Buffalo was hosting NCAA tournament games, which the city has hosted seven times since then.[17]

In 1996, the Knox family named Quinn president of the Sabres and Marine Midland Arena. Under Quinn, the team held the sixth-best record in the NHL, won the Northeast Division championship, and advanced to the conference finals in the Stanley Cup playoffs. The Sabres' season ticket base grew from 6,000 to

14,000 ticket holders. Quinn's other notable accomplishments included arranging the return of legendary Buffalo Sabre Gilbert Perreault to the organization, signing Dominik Hasek, and bringing Lindy Ruff in as the coach.

When Adelphia Communications founder John Rigas purchased the Sabres in 1998, he fired Quinn. Four years later, authorities arrested Rigas on fraud charges, forcing the NHL to take control of the team while searching for a new owner. There was a serious concern that the team would leave Buffalo. But Larry Quinn urged Rochester billionaire Thomas Golisano to purchase the Sabres. Despite Golisano's misgivings, Quinn's salesmanship skills worked; Golisano bought the team in 2003 and kept the Sabres in Buffalo. Without Quinn, the Buffalo Sabres may have moved out of town.

Quinn also played a role in the success of the NHL Winter Classic game. In 2008, the Buffalo Irishman brought the first outdoor game to open-air Ralph Wilson Stadium on New Year's Day. No other teams were willing to take the risk, but Quinn didn't hesitate at the opportunity. Tickets for the game in Buffalo's 70,000-seat Ralph Wilson Stadium sold out in eighteen minutes, and it became a marquee NHL event.[18] Later, Quinn declared that Buffalo was the only city that could have pulled off the inaugural event. He continued to work for the Sabres until 2011, when Golisano sold the team. The Sabres won two conference finals and Northeast Division titles during Quinn's time with the team.

Additionally, Quinn served as the vice chairman of the Erie Canal Harbor Development Corporation (ECHDC), where he helped shape the development of the Erie Canal terminus site and the beginnings of Canalside. Quinn also managed the building of Hauptman Woodward Institute's (HWI) state-of-the-art research facility on the Buffalo medical campus. In 2020, Great Point Media, a London production studio, turned to Quinn to help build a $60 million film and television studio on the West Side of Buffalo.[19] The project, which includes a 20,000-square-foot stage and 70,000 square feet of office space, will attract national and international media companies to Buffalo.

Larry Quinn has been described as intelligent, a maverick, and a go-getter with an unconventional style.[20] Friend and business partner Frank McGuire said that Quinn "is one of the smartest people I've known, [and] one of the most creative people I've known."[21] The Buffalo Irishman has been one of the most influential leaders in Buffalo's two significant renewal periods of the 1980s and the 2000s. Fortunately for Buffalo, Larry Quinn has shown no signs of slowing down. He's still ready to pick up the phone.

Thomas R. Beecher—Medical Campus Leader

A local Irish American was a primary force in creating one of Buffalo's most significant twenty-first-century economic drivers. In 2001, Thomas R. Beecher and a small group of local leaders envisioned a world-class medical campus in Buffalo, similar to what Cleveland and Boston had built. Beecher had witnessed how his friend Dr. Lawrence Jacobs had discovered a revolutionary multiple sclerosis treatment in Buffalo. But the city could not bring it to market, so a Boston-based biotech company purchased it, creating thousands of well-paying jobs in Massachusetts, not in Buffalo.

Beecher knew that Buffalo needed an integrated medical campus that would create high-paying jobs and improve public health. Building a medical campus, which city leaders had discussed for years, required someone with diplomacy, resiliency, and vision. Someone who could unite disparate private and public sector groups, while keeping an eye on the big picture. As we will see, Thomas Beecher was the man to complete this project.

Thomas Beecher, Jr. was born in Buffalo in 1935 to Thomas and Dolores (Shea) Beecher. A graduate of College of the Holy Cross and the University of Buffalo Law School, Beecher became a partner at the Phillips Lytle law firm.[22] In 1969, he joined the newly formed Rand Capital board, a Buffalo venture capital firm. Beecher eventually served on over thirty community boards and a dozen company boards, building connections across the region.[23] He left the law firm to become president of Barrantys, LLC, an estate planning and wealth management firm.

The Beecher family history is an inspiring immigrant story. Tom Beecher's paternal grandfather, Michael Beecher, was born in 1863 on a farm in County Cork, where he lived with his parents and his ten siblings in a modest thatched-roof farmhouse. With six brothers, scarce family land, and limited formal education, Beecher left Ireland in 1881 and eventually moved to Buffalo to become superintendent of the Buffalo Weaving and Belting Company, where he worked for fifteen years.[24] But the Irish immigrant wanted to run his own business.

In 1916, Michael Beecher founded Globe Woven Belt Company, a manufacturer of conveyor belts for various food and industrial applications. The enterprise grew from a single building on Clinton Street into a campus of twenty interconnected buildings in the Clinton-Bailey neighborhood. It was one of the largest conveyor belt manufacturers in the United States. Throughout the years, Globe employed over two hundred men and women in Buffalo, many of them first-generation immigrants. Michael's grandson, Tom Beecher, eventually became chairman of the Buffalo company.

In the early 1990s, Tom Beecher also served as the chairman of Buffalo General Hospital, where he helped lay the foundation for merging several local hospitals to create Kaleida Health. In 1999, he became chairman of the board of directors for this newly formed entity, giving him a front-row seat to the region's healthcare needs. Around this time, momentum for a medical campus was growing. Not surprisingly, in 2002, Beecher was named the founding chairman of a new entity: the Buffalo Niagara Medical Campus (BNMC).

The BNMC is a consortium of the region's health and life sciences companies, medical education institutions, and local neighborhoods.[25] This non-profit organization helps with entrepreneurship, business innovation, and enhancing its 120-acre campus. Some of the notable projects since the inception of the BNMC include the John R. Oishei Children's Hospital ($270 million), the Gates Vascular Institute ($291 million), the Conventus Building ($90 million), the University at Buffalo School of Medicine ($375 million), the Hauptman-Woodward Institute ($24 million), and the Roswell Park Cancer Institute's Clinical Science Center ($50 million). All told, New York State and private organizations have invested over $1 billion in hospitals, university buildings, and commercial institutions, with plans to move other University at Buffalo healthcare programs to the campus.[26] The medical campus now employs 17,000 workers, with a goal of 20,000. Plans are in place to have ten million square feet of space for academic, research, and commercial purposes.[27]

Beecher's BNMC is one of the critical drivers in Buffalo's renaissance. As board chairman, Tom Beecher brought together politicians, healthcare executives, community activists, and university leaders to forge a world-class medical campus. He has been praised for his ability to "see things in a bigger scheme than people who tend to see only the things that are right in front of them."[28] The BNMC named their campus's innovation center in Beecher's honor.[29] The University at Buffalo recognized Thomas Beecher with two of its highest awards: the Edwin F. Jaeckle Award (2005) and the Chancellor's Award (2010).

Preserving and Beautifying Buffalo

Turning away from building and industry, Irish Americans have done much to preserve and beautify Buffalo. One such person, not himself a Queen City resident, was US Senator Daniel Patrick Moynihan. The Irish-American politician, raised in New York City, became one of Buffalo's most passionate advocates for preserving its architectural and heritage treasures. Timothy Russert, a central figure in the senator's inner circle, spurred and aided Moynihan's interest in Buffalo.

One of the critical moments in Buffalo's preservation history occurred in June 1979 when Erie County Legislator Joan Bozer invited Senator Moynihan to be the keynote speaker at an event focused on preserving Buffalo's Olmsted parks. The senator urged Buffalonians to create an Olmsted Conservancy as New York

City did.[30] This organization, independent of politicians' control, would preserve and maintain the six Buffalo Olmsted Parks and the parkway system. Concerned residents formed a group called the Friends of the Olmsted Parks, which became the nucleus for the Buffalo Olmsted Parks Conservancy. In 2004, the Conservancy, which had advocated for the parks and raised money for capital projects, finally wrested control of the parks from the City of Buffalo. Since the takeover, many city residents think the parks have never looked better. Moynihan was right.

Senator Moynihan's Buffalo visit in 1979 was about more than just parks. It also had a "lasting impact on the city's nascent preservation movement."[31] According to Mark Goldman, "His [Moynihan's] strong support for both the conversion of the Post Office [the former main post office building], as well as the insistence that the city save the Prudential Building, turned the tide politically and financially for both projects."[32] Moynihan urged Buffalonians to create "a broad, comprehensive and assertive approach to historic preservation that would preserve the whole of Buffalo's built environment."[33] Within a few years, concerned citizens formed the Preservation Coalition of Erie County.

A little more than a decade later, on March 18, 1991, the day after Buffalo's St. Patrick's Day parade, Senator Moynihan arrived unannounced at the Darwin Martin House, a Frank Lloyd Wright-designed masterpiece in Buffalo's Parkside neighborhood. After seeing the house in disrepair, the senator declared the estate was "a ruin and a disgrace."[34] He wrote a scathing letter to the *Buffalo News* urging local citizens to step up and save this historic home from ruin; in addition, he started a private fundraising campaign. Moynihan's efforts have been credited as the turning point in protecting one of Buffalo's architectural treasures. The following year, the University at Buffalo, the owner of the estate, transferred ownership of the home to the Martin House Restoration Corporation, which restored this Buffalo gem for $52 million. The Martin House is now Buffalo's most popular tourist attraction.[35]

Journalist Tim Russert once related a story about Senator Moynihan's vision for one of Buffalo's architectural treasures—the Guaranty Building (also called the Prudential Building). In the 1970s, the building was in foreclosure after a five-alarm fire. There were concerns that investors would purchase it and demolish one of Louis Sullivan's most important architectural creations. Moynihan vowed this would never happen and launched an uphill battle to save the landmark. Russert remembered Moynihan saying, "People [in Buffalo] may not appreciate this politically, but some things are worth doing."[36]

Moynihan secured several grants and loans, pleading with Mayor Griffin to do everything he could to preserve the Guaranty Building. "I will tear down the pyramids before they tear down the Guaranty Building."[37] After Sullivan's Guaranty Building was restored in 1983, Moynihan told Mayor Jimmy Griffin,

"Mark my words: There will be a day when people get on Lufthansa Airways in Munich and fly to Buffalo to admire that building." As Russert recalled, even the mayor, one of Buffalo's biggest boosters, was skeptical and reportedly replied, "Bullshit, Paddy."[38] To Moynihan's credit, this building ranks as one of Buffalo's most popular tourist sites. Senator Daniel Patrick Moynihan was in the vanguard in recognizing that architectural tourism would become one of Buffalo's top draws for out-of-town visitors.

Not all Buffalo preservation leaders were out-of-town politicians. Susan "Sue" McCartney, one of the local preservation movement leaders, grew up in Buffalo with a Northern Irish father and an Italian Catholic mother. Although she studied business, receiving her MBA and Ph.D. from the University at Buffalo, McCartney was passionate about Buffalo's rich architectural treasures. Unfortunately, as she was growing up in the 1960s and '70s, many of them were being demolished.

In 1979, McCartney was spurred into action when Sportsystems, Inc. (now Delaware North) proposed destroying the McKim, Mead & White-designed Metcalfe House on North Street to create parking for the firm. Despite an outcry from some politicians and citizens, Sportsystems destroyed the stately Metcalfe House.[39] In reaction to this loss, McCartney and five other passionate citizens founded the Preservation Coalition of Erie County in 1981 to fight the destruction of Buffalo's other architectural gems.[40] "It was the fact that the Metcalfe could go down so easily, we had to prevent it from happening again."[41] For two decades, McCartney, the president and chair of the organization, challenged politicians, developers, and even the local leaders of the Catholic Church to protect Western New York's historic structures.

During McCartney's tenure, the Preservation Coalition created new historic districts, including the Joseph Ellicott and Hamlin Park areas. It also designated the St. Vincent's Orphan Asylum and the Buffalo Savings Bank building as landmarks, and secured the title for the Buffalo Central Terminal, ensuring its protection. Additionally, the organization sued New York State to preserve the H.H. Richardson Complex and Buffalo's Erie Canal terminus.[42] McCartney played a leading role in saving the Connecticut Street Armory, the New York Telephone Building, the Genesee Building, and St. Mary of Sorrows Church. She and her associates also aided in the preservation of the Allendale Theater, Plymouth Methodist Church, and the Great Northern grain elevator (her group saved the historic structure from demolition in the early 1990s but lost the fight in 2023).[43]

According to Mark Goldman, McCartney and Tim Tielman have been "the city's most powerful and prescient preservationist[s]."[44] Goldman also credited McCartney's Preservation Coalition with helping him designate his Calumet building as a protected structure.[45] The Calumet project was the catalyst for revitalizing the neglected Chippewa Street neighborhood.

In 2011, the Campaign for Greater Buffalo History, Architecture & Culture recognized Susan McCartney for saving Buffalo's architectural heritage by bestowing her with the "Preservationist of the Century" award.[46] Buffalo's business journal, *Business First*, included her on their Power 200 Women list (the most powerful women in Western New York).

Olmsted Parks

While McCartney was saving buildings from destruction, another Irish-American woman was preserving historical landscapes. Patricia O'Donnell, a Buffalo native, is an internationally renowned landscape architect and urban planner. O'Donnell's father, Francis, was a thoracic surgeon, and her mother, Eileen, was a nurse. Her father, a grandson of Irish immigrants, performed Buffalo's first open-heart surgery in 1962.[47] Her sister, Elizabeth O'Donnell, founded the Skating Association for the Blind and Handicapped (SABAH), teaching thousands of blind, deaf, and disabled people how to skate.[48]

A graduate of Buffalo State College, Patricia earned a master's in landscape architecture at the University of Illinois Urbana-Champaign. In 1975, Patricia O'Donnell led a restoration project of Delaware Park's Rose Garden. She surveyed Buffalo's 1,700-acre Olmsted Park system, and her report was integral to submitting Buffalo's Olmsted Parks system for inclusion in the National Register.[49] She was a founding member of the National Association of Olmsted Parks.

In 1987, the trailblazing O'Donnell founded Heritage Landscapes, the nation's only firm dedicated solely to preserving and revitalizing historic landscapes.[50] In addition to her work with Delaware Park's Rose Garden, she was also consulted on projects at Buffalo's Martin Luther King Park and South Park. O'Donnell prepared the cultural landscape report for one of Buffalo's architectural jewels: the recently restored Richardson Olmsted Complex. She also composed the report for Graycliff, the summer home Frank Lloyd Wright designed outside of Buffalo for Darwin and Isabelle Martin. O'Donnell spearheaded a master plan to reforest Buffalo's 269-acre Forest Lawn Cemetery, estimating that the cemetery lost 75% of its canopy from elm disease in the 1960s and the 2006 October ice storm. Her master proposal, which would usher in a "new era for Forest Lawn," called for replanting 1,700 new trees (maples, oaks, and elms) to restore the forest.[51]

Outside of Buffalo, O'Donnell's firm has completed over six hundred cultural landscape projects, including forty National Historic Landmarks and eight World Heritage Sites.[52] O'Donnell and her associates helped revitalize park systems in Pittsburgh and Louisville, and her company teamed up with other firms for major commissions in Washington, DC, including the US Capitol Grounds and the National Mall. The Buffalo trailblazer helped to pass the UNESCO Recommendation on the Historic Urban Landscape (HUL), earning her recognition as one of the "mothers of HUL."[53]

In 2021, the National Trust for Historic Preservation awarded O'Donnell its highest lifetime achievement award. She was the first landscape architect in the award's sixty-year history to receive this prestigious award. O'Donnell currently focuses on landscape challenges of climate change, sustainability, accessibility, and inclusion.[54] Anyone who has enjoyed strolling through the restored Olmsted Parks, the grounds of the Richardson Olmsted Campus, or Forest Lawn Cemetery on a fall day can thank a trailblazing Irish American woman from Buffalo.

Garden Walk

Buffalo's Garden Walk, one of Buffalo's most anticipated summer outings, was co-founded by Gail McCarthy. Born Gail Coughlin, McCarthy grew up in South Buffalo and studied the cello at Seton Hill College, a small liberal arts school outside Pittsburgh. Her father, Edmund Coughlin, son of two Irish immigrants, was a Buffalo fire department captain. While in college, Gail, an accomplished musician, met Richard "Max" McCarthy, a Buffalo newspaper reporter eight years older. They eventually married and had five children.

As mentioned earlier, Gail McCarthy was a powerful force in Max McCarthy's political career. While in Washington, DC as a congressman's wife, Gail was active in Mrs. Claudia "Lady Bird" Johnson's Beautification Project, which improved neighborhood pride and stabilized transitional neighborhoods by planting gardens.[55] It was a lesson she never forgot and one that she brought back to Buffalo.

Later in her life, Gail was married to Marvin Lunenfeld. After attending Chicago's inaugural garden walk event in 1993, Gail and Marvin were inspired to start something similar in Buffalo. Two years later, they founded Garden Walk Buffalo, with their house at the corner of Norwood Avenue and West Utica Street serving as the event's headquarters. They insisted that the Walk be open to everyone, with no admission charge. Within two to three years, the annual event led to a beautification movement in their community, later spreading to other parts of the city.

Buffalo's Garden Walk, with self-guided tours of over four hundred gardens, has surpassed Chicago's; it is now the largest garden walk of its kind in the country.[56] Over 65,000 people from the United States and Canada descend on Buffalo the last week of July to tour more than 400 residential gardens. The Garden Walk organizers have given out $100,000 in grants to more than one hundred projects for community gardens, hanging baskets, corner gardens, and other street enhancement projects. Other towns throughout Western New York have modeled their events after McCarthy's. Gail McCarthy has left a lasting legacy that continues to blossom every year.

Neighborhood Gentrification

Other Irish-American women have dedicated themselves to strengthening Buffalo neighborhoods. We have already learned about Sister Denise Roche's efforts to solidify the D'Youville University neighborhood on the West Side. Similarly, Mary Heneghan led efforts to beautify South Buffalo's Abbott Road neighborhood for over thirty years.

In the First Ward and Valley, Margaret "Peg" Overdorf, who is three-quarters Irish, was a passionate advocate for the neighborhoods adjacent to the Buffalo River. As the executive director of the Valley Community Association, Overdorf championed projects, including the Valley Child Care Center, an academic center, and the Geraldine Butler Senior Center to provide care for neighborhood residents.

One of Overdorf's long-term goals was to improve access to the Buffalo River, an underutilized natural resource that meanders through her community. She worked closely with local politicians to build two public parks. For the first one, Mutual Riverfront Park, Overdorf negotiated with the New York Power Authority to create a one-acre recreation space at the foot of Hamburg Street in exchange for storing their ice boom.[57] This park has public kayak and canoe access areas and a boathouse, and it is home to the Waterfront Memories and More Museum. Thousands of water enthusiasts access the Buffalo River from this park each year.

In 2010, Overdorf hosted a ribbon cutting for a second park—Buffalo River Fest Park—further up Ohio Street. This three-acre park, located on the banks of the Buffalo River, hosts the annual River Fest festivities and is open to the public year-round. The park includes a beautiful green space, a band shell, a boardwalk, a boat slip, a pavilion, and a banquet hall called the Tewksbury Lodge. Adjacent to the park is a heritage trail that connects the First Ward to the Inner Harbor. This bike path and walking trail offer convenient access to the Buffalo River and points of interest in the Ward.

Overdorf also created the First Ward's first museum, Waterfront Memories and More. The museum opened in June 2012 and is home to a treasure trove of First Ward and Valley artifacts, photos, and books. Peggy May-Szczygiel, Bert Guise-Hyde, and Joan Graham-Scahill manage the museum and welcome people from all over Western New York and beyond who visit to learn more about the neighborhood where they or their ancestors grew up.

In 2022, after more than four decades of serving the neighborhoods south of downtown, Peg Overdorf retired as director of the Valley Community Association. Congressman Brian Higgins proclaimed, "Her [Overdorf's] compassion for the people she serves and persistence for the community she loves is like none other. Peggy is the force behind the rebirth of the Buffalo River and the neighborhood around it."[58]

Roswell Park Alliance and The Ride For Roswell

Buildings, landscapes, and neighborhoods weren't the only way the Irish shaped Buffalo. They also founded and led numerous civic and cultural institutions. One Irish-American woman channeled her grief from losing a child into co-founding one of the most successful foundations in Western New York, positively impacting thousands of people. Anne Driscoll grew up on Coolidge Road in the Irish stronghold of South Buffalo. Her father, William Driscoll, was a lawyer and the son of Irish immigrants. Her mother, Anne (Reedy) Driscoll, also of Irish ancestry, raised the couple's four daughters. The younger Anne Driscoll graduated from Canisius College and worked as a teacher.

In July 1989, the now-married Anne (Driscoll) Gioia and her husband, Richard Gioia, suffered the tragic death of their five-year-old daughter, Katherine, to a rare cancer. From this tragedy, Anne, with the help of her sister-in-law Donna Gioia, conceived and founded the Roswell Park Alliance Foundation the following year.

The Roswell Park Alliance allocates funds for research, treatment, and prevention programs at Western New York's largest cancer center. The Alliance also focuses on improving cancer patients' quality of life and meeting their psychological needs.[59] The founding of Gioia's organization was timely because, in 1991, New York State threatened to reduce funding for the hospital. With the help of others such as Pam (Ryan) Jacobs, Anne and Donna Gioia made countless trips to Albany to advocate for Roswell Park. The group even purchased full-page ads in the *Buffalo News* to alert the public to the dire situation.[60] After that crisis, the organization focused on its core mission of fundraising.

As of 2022, the Foundation has raised over $455 million to support this critical cancer hospital. Other subsidiary groups within the Roswell Park Alliance Foundation include The Ride for Roswell, the All-Star Night, and Carly's Club. In addition to Anne Gioia's more than thirty years of involvement with Roswell Park, she has served seven terms on the Roswell Park Cancer Center board of directors. The tireless South Buffalo native also co-chaired the $21 million campaign to raise money for the Roswell Park Center for Genetics and Pharmacology, a state-of-the-art research and drug development center.

In addition to galvanizing community support for Roswell Park, Anne Gioia has served on the Buffalo Niagara Medical Campus board and has worked in various service roles at Women and Children's Hospital, Buffalo General Hospital, and Canisius College. In 2017, Roswell Park named their new pediatric hematology center after Anne, her late daughter Katherine, and her sister-in-law Donna Gioia. In 2020, Anne Gioia received a New York State Women of Distinction Award for her decades of service to improve cancer patients' lives.

Within Gioia's Roswell Park Foundation, another local Irish American founded one of the most successful fundraising events: The Ride for Roswell. Mitch Flynn, whose Irish roots are from County Clare, graduated from Canisius High School and Georgetown University. Flynn, a Roswell Park Alliance Foundation board member, was asked to create a fundraiser to support the cancer hospital. His suggestion—a community bike ride—flourished in its first year, with 1,000 riders and $100,000 raised. Flynn suggested that the event succeeded because it became a rallying point for patients, family, and friends.[61]

Flynn's firm, Flynn & Friends, provided free marketing and advertising resources for the event's first fifteen years to get it started. Since the start, he has personally raised $570,000 for the event and set a goal to raise $1 million by 2025.[62] Since the Ride began in 1996, organizers have raised over $60 million for cancer research. As of 2022, Flynn's Ride for Roswell is Western New York's largest and highest-grossing fundraising effort, with increasing community participation each year. Mitch Flynn continues to be an enthusiastic spokesperson for the event.

Philanthropists

Many Irish Americans have made philanthropic contributions to Buffalo, but a few families stand out. One of them is the Walsh family. Their family firm, the Walsh Duffield Company, has had roots in Buffalo for the last one-hundred and sixty years.[63] One of the firm's founders, James Mooney, the builder of the Brisbane building and an ardent Irish nationalist, was discussed in another chapter. His descendants have been generous Buffalo philanthropists for over a century, with family members in leadership positions in dozens of non-profit organizations. In recent years, John "Jack" Walsh III, former chairman of the family's insurance firm, has served as board chairman for the Buffalo Philharmonic Orchestra, American Red Cross, and Children's Hospital. Jack Walsh's most significant contribution may have been his service as president of the Martin House Restoration Corporation. He led the organization for six years during a critical period in restoring this Frank Lloyd Wright masterpiece, now Buffalo's most popular tourist destination.

Jack's nephew, Edward "Ted" Walsh Jr., has also served as president and CEO of the Walsh Duffield Company and has also contributed to civic causes, especially in healthcare. In 2022, he was named board president of Buffalo Niagara Medical Campus, where he led the continued momentum of this vital organization. Ted previously served as board treasurer of the John R. Oishei Foundation and board chairman for Kaleida Health, United Way of Buffalo and Erie County, and Hospice Buffalo.

The Cullens are another philanthropic Irish family. Their family foundation has become the fifth largest in Western New York.[64] In 1961, John "Jack" Cullen founded Multisorb Technologies, North America's largest manufacturer of drying agents. Cullen was born in Pittsburgh, raised in the Buffalo suburb of Amherst, and graduated from Notre Dame University, where he studied chemistry. As a summer intern at Union Carbide, Cullen discovered that a desiccant (a substance that induces dryness) could prevent the problem of moisture from car air conditioners shorting out the car radios. From that discovery, he launched Cullen Industries, which later became Multisorb Technologies. His company, which made packets that protected food and electronics from damage due to exposure to moisture, employed more than five hundred people at manufacturing plants in Western New York, Alabama, and England.[65]

Cullen was active with several Western New York cultural and charitable organizations. He was a trustee or significant donor for many local enterprises such as Artpark, the Irish Classical Theatre Company, Shea's Center for the Performing Arts, Studio Arena, the YMCA, and the United Way. Cullen was passionate about theater and was one of the leaders who helped save Shea's Theater from the wrecking ball. His daughter Kathleen described him as having "an engineer's mind and poet's soul."[66] In 2006, Jack donated $2 million to his alma mater, St. Joseph's Collegiate Institute; it was the largest gift ever given to a Buffalo high school.[67] The Cullen Foundation has $153 million in assets and donates nearly $5 million annually to area charities related to education and the arts.

Congressman Brian Higgins

We end this story of Buffalo's Irish the same way we began: with an Irish American who transformed the city by way of Buffalo's waterfront. Samuel Wilkeson, a son of Northern Irish immigrants, built Buffalo's harbor in the 1820s and secured the Erie Canal's western terminus for his hometown. Almost two hundred years later, Congressman Brian Higgins, the grandson of immigrants from the Republic of Ireland, led Buffalo's transformation at the start of the twenty-first century. Brian Higgins is one of Buffalo's most influential Irish figures.

Congressman Higgins grew up on Milford Street in the Irish Catholic stronghold of South Buffalo. His paternal grandfather, Patrick Higgins, an orphan from County Mayo, emigrated from Ireland and settled in Detroit. Brian's paternal grandmother, Theresa Driscoll, came from County Kerry, while his maternal Irish family came over several generations earlier and initially settled in Canada.[68] Higgins' father, Daniel J. Higgins, Sr., was a bricklayer and a Buffalo Common Council member (1969-1977). The senior Higgins was a lifelong member of the Bricklayers & Masons union, Local 45. Brian Higgins' mother, Mary Breen, was a school teacher in the First Ward, and she worked for the Erie County Auto Bureau.

Higgins' Irish heritage has been an essential part of his personal and political life.[69] He has traveled extensively to Ireland as a US congressman and forged friendships with former Sinn Fein leaders Gerry Adams and the late Martin McGuiness. In March 2008, Higgins invited Adams, one of the architects of the Northern Ireland peace process, to Buffalo to speak to an Irish Center crowd and march with Higgins in the First Ward's St. Patrick's Day parade.

Brian Higgins graduated from South Park High School and Buffalo State College. Like his father, he was elected to the Buffalo Common Council, representing the South District in 1988. A decade later, he was elected to fill Richard Keane's vacated New York State Assembly seat. Higgins won the election by defeating former mayor Jimmy Griffin in the Democratic primary. In the Assembly, Higgins focused on improving Buffalo's waterfront, starting with an area called Gallagher Beach, south of downtown. He began with a small project to show those in his hometown and Albany that Buffalo could finally develop its waterfront, as Baltimore and Cleveland had done.[70] For the buildout of Gallagher Beach, Higgins secured enough funds to build a boardwalk, picnic area, watercraft launches, fishing pier, and a parking lot. It was this project that initiated Buffalo's waterfront renaissance.[71]

In 2004, Assemblyman Brian Higgins was elected to Congress, representing South Buffalo. He was committed to making progress on Buffalo's greatest asset— its expansive, underdeveloped waterfront. Over the years, other Buffalo politicians set up agencies to develop this area and accomplished almost nothing. Higgins knew Buffalo needed more than committees; the city needed a well-developed vision and the financing to implement it. Higgins would provide that vision and get the New York Power Authority (NYPA) to provide the funds. In 2005, the South Buffalo politician insisted that the NYPA offer Buffalo a fairer deal with their Niagara Power Project revenue-sharing agreement. The Power Authority was renegotiating their 50-year leasing deal with the city, and Higgins wanted more than just cheap hydropower for local companies—he wanted funds to redevelop the waterfront.

At the beginning of Higgins' quest for a new deal with the state agency, he was "a voice in the wilderness, a one-man army."[72] Undeterred, Higgins publicly called out other regional politicians and leaders for their silence in seizing this once-in-a-lifetime opportunity. Eventually, other politicians joined the cause, forcing the NYPA to make a more generous offer. The Power Authority agreed to a licensing settlement that would provide $279 million for waterfront development and $14 million annually for Greenway Projects. This deal provided the financial resources to complete large-scale Inner and Outer Harbor projects. Higgins had won one of the most important political battles in a generation.

Encouraged by the relicensing agreement, Higgins proposed a locally owned corporation to manage the waterfront projects. The state created the Erie Canal Harbor Development Corporation (ECHDC) to oversee waterfront project planning and implementation. That same year, the congressman secured $70 million in a federal highway bill to redesign Fuhrmann Boulevard, the access road along the waterfront. This project commenced in 2008, creating more green space and improving access for residents and visitors along miles of the Lake Erie shoreline.

In May 2008, Western New Yorkers celebrated the opening of the restored commercial slip and a new central wharf boardwalk. The $53 million project was the start of Canalside. From that point forward, ECHDC made significant annual progress in improving the site. In 2009, demolition crews leveled the mothballed Memorial Auditorium to make room for more development. That same year, Higgins procured funds to reconstruct four cobblestone streets at Canalside to recreate the authentic streetscape from the Erie Canal era and renegotiated the NYPA settlement to front-load $55 million in funds for more development projects.

In addition to Higgins, a few other Irish Americans helped spearhead projects connected to Canalside. Tom Dee, a former senior executive at Cannon Design, served as president of the Erie Canal Harbor Development Corporation (ECHDC) board for almost a decade. Dee oversaw critical projects at Buffalo's Canalside and the Outer Harbor, including the replica Erie Canal waterways. By the end of Tom Dee's tenure, more than 1.5 million tourists visited the area annually. Maureen (O'Connell) Hurley was another influential ECHDC leader who worked tirelessly to bring family attractions to Canalside. The Irish-American businesswoman's most significant achievement included encouraging the Explore & More Museum to move from East Aurora to the waterfront.[73] As the museum's board president declared, "There really is no Explore and More at Canalside without Maureen Hurley."[74] This family-friendly museum, which has a plaque dedicated to Hurley, brings more than 200,000 visitors to Canalside annually.

Congressman Higgins also secured resources to reconfigure the US Coast Guard site, allowing public access to the historic 1833 lighthouse. He also procured funds to improve Times Beach and Gallagher Beach, forcing the Niagara Frontier Transportation Authority (NFTA) to relinquish its grip on acres of prime waterfront real estate. River Fest Park opened along the Buffalo River the same year, thanks partly to Higgins. He also provided federal funding to reconstruct a 1.6-mile dilapidated stretch of Ohio Street, which was converted into a beautiful riverfront parkway with walking and bike paths and historical markers. Within a few years, apartment buildings, businesses, and retail establishments were built along the $11 million parkway, rejuvenating this historically significant neighborhood.

As part of the 2013 NYPA licensing agreement, a park on Buffalo's Outer Harbor was built and named in Samuel Wilkeson's honor. That same year, Higgins secured federal funds for a US Environmental Protection Agency (EPA) project to dredge the Buffalo River of contaminants from its industrial past. Higgins had been demanding a cleanup of the Buffalo River since the 1980s when he served as a Buffalo councilman; his request was finally realized. This $44 million Buffalo River cleanup project extracted 40,000 truckloads of riverbed sediment to remove the pollution and improve the fish habitat. An additional $20 million in projects were implemented to stabilize the river bank and habitat along the shoreline. Higgins said, "This is miraculous. The Buffalo River is emerging as a recreational waterfront of exciting new possibilities after decades as a contaminated, poisoned industrial waterway."[75]

In 2014, the NFTA finally relinquished control over 354 acres of waterfront land and transferred it to the ECHDC. In the same year, state and local agencies built pocket parks along the Outer Harbor, as well as an Industrial Heritage Trail and the popular Tifft Street Pier.[76] That year, construction crews converted a portion of the former Memorial Auditorium site into an outdoor ice-skating rink.

For years, Higgins had proposed turning eighty acres of land on Buffalo's Outer Harbor into a state park. With the help of Governor Andrew Cuomo, the congressman's dream was realized with the construction of Buffalo Harbor State Park in 2015. With some of the most spectacular views of the lake, this park includes a 1,100-slip marina, boat launches, restrooms, walking paths, and a playground. Funds from the NYPA agreement also funded a bike ferry to transport pedestrians and bicyclists from the Inner Harbor to the Outer Harbor.

While Higgins directed much of his energy to the waterfront, he also spearheaded other initiatives contributing to Buffalo's renaissance. Brian Higgins believed that the New York State Thruway tolls going into and out of Buffalo were unjust and made Buffalo an unwelcoming place for people to visit. In 2006, the Authority stopped collecting money from drivers and dismantled the unsightly toll booths the following year. While the issue might seem inconsequential, it was a turning point. It showed that with strong leaders, Buffalo could force Albany authorities and politicians to respond to their needs.

In 2009, Higgins was a catalyst behind the effort to reconstruct Buffalo's Main Street so that it permitted both cars and Metro trains to share the road. This ongoing project has helped rejuvenate the city's central commercial district. The South Buffalo congressman also spearheaded a Congressional resolution to fund the $127 million Robert H. Jackson Courthouse. In recent years, Congressman Higgins has devoted much energy to supporting Roswell Park Cancer Institute, including securing federal funds to help build the Clinical Science Building. He has also become a vocal proponent for increasing funds and awareness for cancer screening.

North of Buffalo, Higgins led the effort to remove the northern section of the Robert Moses Parkway in Niagara Falls, New York. This stretch of highway made it unnecessarily difficult for Falls residents to visit the waterfront, and it also stifled economic activity in the city. In 2016, at the congressman's urging, the New York Power Authority paid $40 million to remove the paved four-lane highway and replaced it with green space and a biking and walking trail.

Without Higgins' leadership and wrestling of funds from the New York Power Authority, Buffalo's Canalside and waterfront development would never have happened. What Higgins brought back to Western New York politics was a fighting Irish spirit, which the community had not seen since the days of Mayor Jimmy Griffin. Higgins had a clear vision for Western New York, coupled with the courage of his convictions. He was sometimes the lone voice, speaking out against obstructionists in Albany and New York State and regional agencies. Without Brian Higgins, there may have been a Buffalo Renaissance early in the twenty-first century, but it would have looked vastly different without his efforts and accomplishments. The *Buffalo News* editorial board wrote, "Buffalo has the kind of congressman other districts can only dream about. He [Higgins] is honest, intelligent and relentlessly focused on making Western New York a better place."[77]

Brian Higgins is the most recent Irish American to shape our city. He will surely not be the last.

Conclusion

Despite many hardships and challenges, the Irish started to shape and transform Buffalo within a few years of their arrival. Various factors contributed to their success.

With their gift of gab and Celtic charisma, the Irish immigrants were natural politicians. Moreover, they came to this country already speaking English, which gave them an advantage over many of their fellow European immigrants. Also, since the Irish arrived before the Poles and Italians, they were able to seize leadership roles in the Democratic Party, which the Irish were then reluctant to share. Savvy politicians wielded their political clout to dole out many civil servant jobs to those who hailed from the Emerald Isle, improving the welfare of their constituents. These new Buffalonians were also natural storytellers. Irish American editors and journalists told their stories and published editorials about the injustices suffered by those who were disadvantaged.

Having suffered gravely at the hands of the British during the Great Famine (1845-1850), the Irish came to this country with a hunger for justice. As they settled in Buffalo, some gravitated toward the field of law, serving as lawyers and judges. Labor strikes along the canal and on the waterfront made Irish workers realize that by banding together, they could advocate for better working conditions and a just wage. Buffalo's descendants of the Great Hunger, many of whom came from the hardest-hit areas of Ireland (see Appendix A), also contributed substantially to Ireland's cause for independence.

Throughout most of the twentieth century, the Queen City was a workingman's paradise. There were plentiful jobs, and the Catholic Church, led chiefly by Irish bishops and religious sisters, was a force for good. Memories of the pain and suffering brought on by the Famine inspired countless Irish Catholics to establish and support many of Western New York's charitable organizations, which improved the lives of their fellow Celts and other desperate immigrants.

Some of the Irish who settled in Buffalo eventually moved further west. But many more stayed. Families that arrived after the Famine still owned homesteads a century later in communities like the First Ward. The Irish stronghold in South Buffalo provided a protective and nurturing environment that enabled many Irish to realize the American Dream. Finally, notwithstanding Buffalo's notorious snowfall, our northeastern climate resembled the one they knew back in Ireland.

It was these factors that enabled these most "poor and wretched" immigrants to found a New Ireland in Buffalo, living more prosperously than they could have ever imagined living back home.

Buffalo's demographics are rapidly changing. In a recent census report, fewer than 17% of the population in the Buffalo metropolitan area identified as having Irish ancestry. With Irish immigration to Buffalo down to barely a trickle, the Irish influence in the Queen City will likely wane. In the first two decades of the twenty-first century, Buffalo was one of the top ten American cities for refugee resettlement. Unlike earlier European immigrant waves, the new refugees settling in Buffalo hail from Asia, Africa, and the Middle East. Immigrants from Latin America and Bangladesh are also shaping and transforming the city's neighborhoods. Following their Hibernian counterparts' footsteps, they will leave their distinctive imprint on this city of good neighbors.

As the Irish imprint begins to fade, this book is one man's humble attempt to preserve Buffalo's rich Irish legacy. There is indeed an emerald thread running through the fabric of our city. To imagine Buffalo without the Irish is to imagine a very different city.

Appendix A

Below is a list of the Irish county of origin for some of the Buffalo Irish men and women discussed in this book. To keep it consistent, I chose the paternal line, unless only the maternal ancestry was known. Nearly sixty percent (60%) of those mentioned in the book are from five counties in Ireland's south and west (Cork, Clare, Kerry, Mayo, and Limerick). These counties were some of the areas hit hardest by the Great Famine, an event that profoundly impacted those who immigrated to Buffalo.

County Antrim
Hugh Mooney (town of Rasharkin)

County Cavan
Charles Brady
Bishop John Timon

County Clare
Richard Blake
Boland family (town of Kilrush)
John Carney
Peter Crotty (town of Kilrush)
Lieutenant Thomas (Jimmy) Crotty
Kevin Cusick
Dottie Gallagher-Cohen
Joseph Hassett (Clare and Cork)
Mary (Breen) Heneghan (town of Kilmihil)
Capt. Patrick M. Kane
Maureen Kennedy (town of Kildysart)
Joseph P. Molony
Paul Mulcaire (town of Kilrush)
Sister Mary Mechtilde O'Connor (Anna Margaret O'Connor)
Monsignor John Nash
Daniel O'Day
Peggy O'Neil
William Shaddock (town of Kilkee)
Stephen Talty
Kevin Townsell

County Cork
Thomas Beecher
Timothy Bohen
Michael J. Broderick
William Carland (City of Cork)
William J. Conners
Jack Connors (Cork and Kerry)
Dr. John Cronyn
Sean Cullen—maternal side
Michael Danahy (town of Millstreet)
Michael Desmond
William Donohue
General William J. Donovan
Congressman Daniel A. Driscoll (Dunmanus, Cork)
Maureen Leary Fecio
Seamus Gallivan
Daniel Guiney
Edward Hartnett (Macroom, Cork)
Sheriff Thomas Higgins
John Hurley
Daniel Kenefick
Ray Lawley
Ronald "Whitey" Martin—maternal side
Congressman Richard "Max" McCarthy
Robert McCarthy
John A. Murphy
Jack O'Brian —maternal side, Kelleher
Barbara O'Brien
Chauncey Olcott—maternal side, Doyle
John Phelan
Emily Regan
Captain Mike Regan
Jeremiah F. Sheehan (town of Bantry)
John Sheehan
William F. Sheehan
John "Jack" White

County Derry
Fiona Dargan
Kevin Dargan
Kevinah Dargan

County Donegal
James Nicoll Johnston
Margaret McGrath

County Down
Joe Crangle
Jim Kelly—maternal side, McGinn
Eugene C. Murphy

County Dublin
Sister Mary Anne Burke
Edward H. Butler, Sr.—maternal side
Augustine Keogh
Kevin B. O'Callahan
Vincent O'Neill
Chris O'Neill
Dr. James Warde

County Fermanagh
F. Scott Fitzgerald—maternal side, McQuillan
Frank McGuire (town of Enniskillen)

County Galway
Tim Flanagan
John J. Hynes

County Kerry
State Supreme Court Judge John J. Callahan
Brigid Courtney Knott
Dr. Fraser Drew
Kathy (Courtney) Hochul (village of Maharees)
Len Lenihan
Congressman Rowland B. Mahany
Thomas Ventry "T.V." O'Connor

Loraine O'Donnell- (town of Killarney)
Jerry Sullivan

County Kilkenny
Richard J. Burke (town of Freshford)
Fr. Patrick Cronin
John Hughes (town of Dunmore)
Laurence Shine

County Laois
James Mooney

County Leitrim
Tom Harkin
Nora Quealy
James McCarroll

County Limerick
Fr. Patrick Cronin
Paul Neville
John Neville
Patrick O'Day
Owen Ó Súilleabháin
Thomas W. Ryan
Bishop William Turner

County Longford
Emily (Dinegan) McDonnell

County Louth
John "Exile" McBride
Thomas D'Arcy McGee
Dr. Richard Thompson

County Mayo
Bishop Joseph Burke (town of Islandeady)
Congressman Brian Higgins
Mickey Kearns
John Murphy (town of Balla)
Peg Overdorf

Congressman Jack Quinn
Padraic Walsh

County Monaghan
Patrick McGroder, Jr.

Northern Ireland
William Glenny
Michael Harrington
Jim Heaney
Mary Jemison
Susan McCartney
Samuel Wilkeson

County Offaly
Michael Byrne

County Roscommon
John P. Fecio, Jr.—maternal side, Hanley
Mitch Flynn
Maureen Hurley
John McDonnell
Mary Lynch O'Rourke

County Sligo
Henry Hagan
John Hagan
Peter Hagan

County Tipperary
New York State Senator Tim Kennedy
Archbishop James E. Quigley
New York State Senator Sean Ryan

County Tyrone
Bishop Charles Colton

County Waterford
Patrick Antony Powers

County Westmeath
Brigid Hughes (town of Athlone)
Bill Polian (town of Coole)

County Wicklow
Sean Cullen
George P. Robinson

Appendix B

Irish and Irish-American bishops led Buffalo's Roman Catholic Church for its first one hundred and fifty years.

1. John Timon (1847-1867)
2. Stephen Ryan (1868-1896)
3. James Edward Quigley (1896-1903)
4. Charles H. Colton (1903-1915)
5. Dennis Joseph Dougherty (1915-1918)
6. William Turner (1919-1936)
7. John Aloysius Duffy (1937-1944)
8. John Francis O'Hara (1945-1951)
9. Joseph Aloysius Burke (1952-1962)
10. James Aloysius McNulty (1963-1972)
11. Edward Dennis Head (1973-1995)

Appendix C

Here is a list of Irish authors and poets who have visited Buffalo as part of the Hassett Family Reading Series at Canisius University.

William Kennedy	2003
Eavan Boland	2005
Paul Muldoon	2006
Eamon Grennan	2007
Sebastian Barry	2008
Alice McDermott	2009
Roy Foster	2010
Colm Tóibín	2011

Bernard O'Donoghue   2012
Seamus Heaney   2012
Paula Meehan   2014
Theo Dorgan   2015
Anne Enright   2016
Emma Donoghue   2016
Belinda McKeon   2017
Michael Longley   2019
Marina Carr   2022
Vincent O'Neill   2023

Appendix D

Below is a partial list of books written by Buffalo Irish authors. The bibliography for this book contains additional authors.

Brady, Charles. *Stage of Fools* (Dutton, 1953).
Brady, Charles. *Sword of Clontarf* (Doubleday & Co., 1960).
Brady, Charles. *Viking Summer* (Bruce Pub. Co, 1956).
Dooley, Roger. *Days Beyond Recall* (Bruce Publishing, 1949).
Dooley, Roger. *From Scarface to Scarlett: American Films in the 1930s* (Harcourt, 1984).
Dooley, Roger. *The House of Shanahan* (Doubleday, 1952).
Farrell, Michael. *Running with Buffalo: A Novel* (No Frills, 2007).
Farrell, Michael. *When the Lights Go Out* (No Frills, 2015).
Fitzgerald, F. Scott. *Tender is the Night* (Fitzgerald's most autobiographical and most references to Buffalo).
Gaughan, Kevin. *At First Light: Strengthening Buffalo Niagara in the New Century* (Canisius College Press, 2003).
Hannon, Mark. *Every Man for Himself* (Apprentice House, 2016).
Hassett, Joseph M. *Yeats and the Poetics of Hate* (Gill and Macmillan, 1986).
Hassett, Joseph M. *W.B. Yeats and the Muses* (Oxford Press, 2010).
Higgins, Rosanne. *Orphans and Inmates* (2014).
Higgins, Rosanne. *A Whisper of Bones* (2014).
Horgan, Paul. *Great River: The Rio Grande in North American History* (Rinehart, 1954).
Horgan, Paul. *Lamy of Santa Fe* (Wesleyan University Press, 1975).
Horrigan, Jack. *The Other League: The Fabulous Story of the American Football League* (Rutledge Book, 1970).

Horrigan, Joe. *NFL Century: The One-Hundred-Year Rise of America's Greatest Sports League* (Crown, 2019).

Kinder, Colleen. *Delaying the Real World* (Running Press, 2005).

Kinder, Colleen, ed. *Letter to a Stranger: Essays to the Ones Who Haunt Us* (Algonquin Books, 2022).

Marren, Joe. *Buffalo's Brush With the Arts: From Huck Finn to Murphy Brown* (Western New York Wares, 1988).

Johnston, James Nicoll. *Donegal Memories and Other Poems* (1908).

McCarthy, Richard D. *The Ultimate Folly: War by Pestilence, Asphyxiation and Defoliation* (Vintage Books, 1969).

Polian, Bill, *The Game Plan: The Art of Building A Winning Football Team* (Triumph Books, 2014).

Russert, Tim. *Big Russ & Me: Father and Son: Lessons of Life* (Miramax, 2005)

Russert, Tim. *Wisdom of Our Fathers* (Random House, 2006).

Shannon, Timothy. Da's Shillelagh: *A Tale of the Irish on the Niagara Frontier* (2012).

Sullivan, Margaret. *Ghosting the News: Local Journalism and the Crisis of American Democracy* (Columbia Global, 2020).

Sullivan, Margaret. *Newsroom Confidential: Lessons and Worries* (St. Martin's Press, 2022)

Sullivan, Richard. *The First Ward* (2011).

Sullivan, Richard. *The First Ward II: Fingy Conners and the New Century* (2012).

Talty, Stephan. *Agent Garbo: The Brilliant, Eccentric Secret Agent* (Mariner Books, 2012).

Talty, Stephan. *The Black Hand: The Epic War Between A Brilliant Detective and the Deadliest Secret Society in American History* (Mariner Books, 2017).

Talty, Stephan. *Black Irish: A Novel* (Random House, 2013).

Talty, Stephan. *Saving Bravo: The Greatest Rescue Mission in Navy SEAL History* (Mariner Books, 2013).

Appendix E

Other Buffalo Irish journalists whom I did not profile in the book but who should be remembered include:

James Brennan (*Buffalo News*, TV topics)
Jean Callahan (*Courier-Express*, society editor)
Paul Carroll (*News*, reporter)

Ronald J. Colleran (*News*, photographer)
Ed Collins (*News*, copy editor)
Jimmy Collins (*News* financial reporter/editor)
Maurice Condon (treasurer of the *Buffalo Times*)
Greg Conners (*News*, editorial writer)
Jack Connolly (*News*, city editor)
Thomas J. Dolan (*News*, investigative reporter)
Kevin Doherty (*News*, assistant news editor)
Fletcher Doyle (*News*, sportswriter)
John Dwyer (*News*, music critic)
Michael Farrell (*News*, columnist)
Bob Feeney (*News*, sportswriter)
Katherine Fitzgerald (*News*, sports)
Matt Glynn (*News*, financial)
Cornelius Kennedy (*News*, photographer)
Margaret Kenny Giancola (deputy managing editor of *News*)
Elizabeth Licata (former editor of *Buffalo Spree*)
John Manion (*News*, art department)
Mark Mulville (*News*, photographer)
Kevin Noonan (*News,* copy desk)
Ryan O'Halloran (*News*, sports columnist)
Don O'Hara (*News*, financial)
Patricia Swift MacClennan (*News*, columnist)

*I apologize to the female reporters/editors of Irish descent whose heritage I couldn't identify because I was not sure of their maiden names. I hope the record can be corrected in the future.

Appendix F

Below is a list of Buffalo Irish men connected to the Fenians in the Buffalo 7th Regiment or in Fenian leadership positions.

Lt. Colonel Michael T. Bailey
Major Bigelow
William Booker
John Byrne
John Cadogan
John Cannady

John C. Canty

George Chambers

Patrick K. Cleary

William Clingen

John Convey

John Cooney

Thomas Cooney

Jeremiah Crowley

Daniel Cruise

Thomas Cruise

Michael Danahy

James Danbridge

James Dillon

John Donohue

Patrick Donohue

Daniel Drummond

William Dugan

Mike Duggins

Thomas Ellis

James Etchingham

John Farley

Michael Farley

John M. Fogarty

John Francis

Frank B. Gallagher

John Gleason

John Gorman

Thomas Grant

Michael Hagar

Thomas Hanlon

Daniel Hern

Patrick Hickey

Thomas Higgins

Colonel John Hoy

Patrick Kane

Charles Kelley

Daniel Leahy

Edward Lonergan (died)

Michael T. Lynch

Thomas Madden (wounded)

John J. McBride

James McConvey

James McGliney

Patrick McGurely

Samuel Merriam

Hugh Mooney

Patrick Norton

Joseph O'Brien

Pat O'Connor

Patrick O'Day

Barney O'Donohoe

William Osborn

Michael Porter

James Quinlan

John Quinn

John Reid

James Reilly

John Rogan

James Roll

Michael Ryan

James Scanlan

Thomas School

Michael Shannon

William B. Smith

Henry Rutgers Stagg

Patrick Stanton

Jeremiah Sullivan

William Tiernan

Morris Vaughn

David Whelan

James Whelan

Thomas Wilkes

Chronology

1804   Thomas Moore, the famous Irish poet and lyricist, visits Crow's Tavern in the village of Buffalo during a tour of North America

1815   Arrival of Patrick and Mary O'Rourke, the first Irish Catholic family to settle in Buffalo

1821   Samuel Wilkeson creates Buffalo's harbor

1824   Samuel Wilkeson secures Buffalo as the western terminus of the Erie Canal

1839   (March 17) Buffalo's first public observance of St. Patrick's Day at Mary O'Rourke's home

1841   St. Patrick's Church dedicated (the first predominantly Irish church in Buffalo)

1847   Bishop John Timon is installed as Buffalo's first Roman Catholic bishop

1848   (March) The first St. Patrick's Day parade is held in Buffalo

1848   (August) Sisters of Charity open Buffalo's first hospital

1851   Father Theobald Mathew, an Irish temperance reformer, comes to Buffalo to administer the alcohol abstinence pledge to 6,000 men

1852   Brigadier General Thomas Meagher comes to Buffalo to raise funds for Ireland

1855   (July) The Know-Nothing Party (anti-Irish-Catholic party) holds its convention in Buffalo

1856   (February) Irish Colonization Convention in Buffalo hosted by Thomas D'Arcy McGee

1858   The Sisters of Mercy arrive in Buffalo

1866   (May 31) The Fenians launch their invasion of Canada from Buffalo

1867   (March) William Roberts, American Fenian Leader, speaks a year after the Fenian invasion

1867   (July 17) Fenian General John O'Neill addresses 10,000 people at a Fenian picnic near present-day Forest Avenue

1868   (December) Mrs. Jeremiah O'Donovan Rossa, wife of the famed Irish nationalist, speaks at the Opera House

1880   (January) Michael Davitt, founder of the Irish Land League, rallies the Irish at the Academy of Music

1880   (January 26) Charles Stewart Parnell and John Dillon speak in Buffalo for a fundraiser

1881   (January 12) The Land League holds its first national convention in Buffalo, with 120 delegates from across the country

1882   (June 29) Michael Davitt, founder of the Irish Land League, speaks andraises funds

1882   (February 8) Oscar Wilde gives a lecture on the English Renaissance at the Academy of Music

1882   (June 4) The Ladies' Land League hosts a mass meeting in Buffalo

1883   (March 22) Patrick Egan, the Irish Land League treasurer, speaks to a crowd at St. Stephen's Hall

1883   (April 26) Three Buffalo men are elected to the Irish Land League's national board: James Mooney (president), John Hynes (secretary), and William F. Sheehan (assistant secretary)

1884   The Irish-American Savings and Loan Association is founded

1884   (July 22) John Devoy, Clan Na Gael leader, speaks at the Irish National League meeting in Buffalo

1888   (June) The National Clan Na Gael Convention is held in Buffalo

1899   (May) The Great Strike of 1899, led by Irish laborers, shuts down shipping on the Great Lakes

1899   (November) Irish political leader John E. Redmond and Richmond Tallon, Lord Mayor of Dublin, come to Buffalo to raise funds for a Parnell Memorial in Ireland

1890   (November 19) Irish nationalists John Dillon and William O'Brien, along with T.D. Sullivan, Lord Mayor of Dublin, speak in Buffalo

1892   Buffalo's William "Blue-Eyed Billy" Sheehan is elected Lt. Governor of New York

1895   John Sheehan becomes Tammany Hall boss in New York City

1900   William "Fingy" Conners forms the *Courier-Express* newspaper

1901   (April 10) Maud Gonne and Major John McBride speak at St. Stephen's Hall

1906   (May 13) Douglas Hyde, future president of Ireland and founder of the Gaelic League, lectures about his work with the League

1908   (August 8) Sinn Fein League of America holds its national convention in Buffalo; William Shaddock is Buffalo's representative, and John Devoy is a keynote speaker

1909   (January 24) Labor leader James Connolly speaks in Buffalo at Columbian Knights' Hall, Main and Mohawk; he also addressed crowds in Buffalo in 1902 and 1910

1910   (September 28) John Redmond speaks at the national convention of the United Irish League at a three-day conference at Convention Hall

1914   (February 16) William Butler Yeats lectures on "Contemporary Lyric Poets" at the Twentieth Century Club

1914   (August 9) Sir Roger Casement, Irish nationalist, fundraising speech for the Irish Volunteers at Shea's Buffalo; the British executed Casement two years later

1917   (March 4) Hannah Sheehy-Skeffington speaks in Buffalo at the Star Theatre; her husband, Francis, was executed by the British the prior year

1919   (May 18) New York State Supreme Court Justice Daniel Cohalan speaks to a crowd at Elmwood Music Hall, where he implores President Woodrow Wilson to allow Ireland to become an independent nation

1919   (December 22) Irish leader Eamon de Valera speaks to 8,000 people at Broadway Auditorium

1920   (April 13) John McCormack, the great Irish tenor, performs at the Elmwood Music Hall

1926   (January) Michael Shea opens Shea's Buffalo on Main Street

1938   Buffalo's James Mead becomes US Senator from New York

1941   John Kelly is elected as Buffalo's first Irish Catholic mayor

1950   The first installment of the University at Buffalo's James Joyce collection
        of manuscripts and artifacts arrives

1960   (September 28) John F. Kennedy holds a campaign rally at
        Memorial Auditorium

1962   (October 15) John F. Kennedy participates in the Pulaski Parade
        in Buffalo

1964   (September 8) US Senate candidate Robert F. Kennedy attends a rally
        where more than 100,000 line the streets of Buffalo to see him; he later
        speaks at Kleinhans Music Hall

1965   US Senator Robert Kennedy takes a tour of the polluted Buffalo River

1970   Buffalo Irish Center opens in South Buffalo

1977   The USS *The Sullivans* arrives in Buffalo as part of the new Naval Park

1977   (November) James D. Griffin is elected to his first of four terms as
        Buffalo's mayor

1978   Martha Harkin is the first female grand marshal of Buffalo's St.
        Patrick's Day parade

1981   Seamus Heaney, future Nobel laureate, speaks at Canisius College

1981   (April) World premiere of Samuel Beckett's *Rockaby* in Buffalo

1985   Chris O'Neill, Dublin actor, performs in Buffalo for the first time

1990   The Irish Classical Theatre Company is founded by Chris O'Neill,
        Vincent O'Neill, Josephine Hogan, and Dr. James Warde

1997   (August 23) The Irish Famine Monument is dedicated at the Erie
        Basin Marina; David McCarthy, Lord Mayor of Cork City, speaks
        at the event

1999   (January) The Andrews Theatre, home of the Irish Classical Theatre
        Company, opens

2003   (September 18) William Kennedy, Irish-American author, speaks at the inaugural Hassett Reading series at Canisius College

2008   (March 15) Gerry Adams, Sinn Fein leader, addresses a crowd at the Irish Center and marches in the First Ward's St. Patrick's Day parade.

2009   (April 7) Alice McDermott, Irish-American writer, speaks at Canisius College

2009   (June) International James Joyce Symposium, "Eire on the Erie," occurs in Buffalo

2009   (June 12) Colum McCann, author, speaks in Buffalo as part of the Cinegael conference

2011   (March 3) Colm Toibin, Irish author, speaks at Canisius College

2012   (March 16) Unveiling of the Fenian Monument commemorating the 1866 invasion of Canada

2012   (March 29) Irish President Mary Robinson speaks at the University at Buffalo

2012   (October 23) Seamus Heaney speaks at Canisius College as part of the Hassett lecture series

2014   (January 9) Liam O'Neill, the GAA president from Dublin, visits Buffalo

2016   (May 25) Criona Ni Dhalaigh, Lord Mayor of Dublin, tours Buffalo

2016   (October 4) Emma Donoghue, Irish author, lectures at Canisius College

2017   (March 24) Edna O'Brien, Irish writer, speaks at the Babel Series

2018   (April 12) Former Lord Mayor of Belfast Máirtín Ó Muilleoir speaks at the Irish Center

2019   (July 11) Daniel Mulhall, Irish Ambassador to the United States, speaks at a University at Buffalo event.

2021   (August 24) Kathy (Courtney) Hochul becomes New York's first female governor

2023   (June 16) NY State Senator Tim Kennedy and the University at Buffalo announce $10 million in funding to build a James Joyce Museum on UB's South Campus

Bibliography

Anbinder, Tyler. *Nativism & Slavery: The Northern Know Nothings & Politics of the 1850s* (1992).

Anderson, Dale. *A Beerdrinker's Guide to Buffalo Bars* (1985).

Armitage, Charles. *Grover Cleveland as Buffalo Knew Him* (2010).

Bevis, Charlie. *Jimmy Collins: A Baseball Biography* (2012).

Blake, Richard. *Slats: The Legend & Life of Jimmy Slattery* (2015).

Bohen, Timothy. *Against the Grain: The History of Buffalo's First Ward* (2010).

Brown, Anthony Cave. *Wild Bill Donovan: The Last Hero* (1982).

Bruccoli, Matthew. *Some Sort of Epic Grandeur: The Life and Times of F. Scott Fitzgerald* (1981).

Carroll, Francis. *American and the Making of an Independent Ireland* (2021).

Chernow, Ron. *Titan: The Life of John D. Rockefeller, Sr.* (1998).

Cochrane, Mary, ed. *Hearers and Heartners" The First 16 Years of the Hassett Family Reading* (2019).

Condon, George. *Stars in the Water: The Story of the Erie Canal* (1974).

Conley, Joe. *Ike Godsey of Walton's Mountain* (2009).

Deuther, Charles. *The Life and Times of the Right Rev. John Timon* (1870).

Donohue, Thomas. *History of the Catholic Church in Western New York* (1904).

Donohue, William J. *Himself: A Civil War Veteran's Struggles with Rebels, Brits, and Devils* (2014).

Dunlop, Richard. *Donovan: America's Master Spy* (2014).

Finkelman, Paul. *Millard Fillmore* (2011).

Gerber, David. *The Making of an American Pluralism: Buffalo, New York 1825-60* (1989).

Ghiglione, Loren. *CBS's Don Hollenbeck: An Honest Reporter in the Age of McCarthyism* (2008).

Gilbert, James. *World War I and the Origins of Military Intelligence* (2012).

Goldman, Mark. *City of My Heart: Buffalo, 1967-2020* (2021).

Goldman, Mark. *High Hopes: The Rise and Decline of Buffalo, New York* (1983).

Hauser, Thomas. *Reflections* (2014).

Jenkins, William. *Between Raid and Rebellion: The Irish in Buffalo and Toronto* (2013).

Kelly, Jim. *Armed & Dangerous: Football's Toughest Quarterback Gives His Candid View* (1992).

Klein, Christopher. *When the Irish Invaded Canada: The Incredible True Story* (2019).

Koeppel, Gerard. *Bond of Union: Building the Erie Canal and the American Empire* (2009).

Lovering, Joseph P. *The Well-made Historical Novels of American Regionalist Charles A. Brady, 1912-1995.*

MacManus, John. *Mary Lynch O'Rourke: The Simple Story of an 18th Century Gentlewoman* (1903).

Maynard, James, ed. *Discovering James Joyce: The University at Buffalo Collection* (2009).

McGreevy, Patrick. *Stairway to Empire: Lockport, the Erie Canal, and the Shaping of America* (2009).

Nelson, Sioban. *Say Little, Do Much: Nurses, Nuns and Hospitals* (2001).

Olcott, Rita, *Song In His Heart: The Story of Chauncey Olcott's Life* (1939).

Overfield, James, ed. *The Seasons of Buffalo Baseball: 1857-2020* (2020).

Richardson, Jean. *A History of the Sisters of Charity Hospital, Buffalo, New York, 1848-1900* (2005).

Rigby, David. *Wade McClusky and the Battle of Midway* (2020).

Russert, Tim. *Big Russ & Me: Father and Son: Lessons of Life* (2005).

Shannon, Mariam. *The South Buffalo Boy Who Became Bishop* (2014).

Shannon, Mariam. *The South Buffalo Girl Who Built a Hospital: Sister Mary Mechtilde* (2015).

Shelton, Brenda. *Reformers in Search of Yesterday: Buffalo in the 1890s* (1976).

Smith, H. Perry. *History of the City of Buffalo and Erie County, two volumes* (1884).

Vogel, Michael N. *America's Crossroads: Buffalo's Canal Street* (1993).

Williams, William. *'Twas Only an Irishman's Dream* (1996).

Wilson, David. *Thomas D'Arcy McGee: Passion, Reason, and Politics, 1825-1857, v1* (2012).

Weekly, Nancy, ed. *Kevin B. O'Callahan and the Buffalo Print Club* (1988).

Image Credits

1. Colin Waters/Alamy Stock Photo.
2. Collection of the Buffalo History Museum. Pan American photograph collection, Picture. P36, Box 12, PA VI A22.
3. Author's collection.
4. From Rev. Thomas Donohue's *The History of the Catholic Church in Western New York*, (1904).
5. Collection of The Buffalo History Museum. General picture collection, Buffalo Harbor - 1820-1829.
6. From the Collections of the New York State Library, Manuscripts and Special Collections, Albany, New York.
7. Collection of The Buffalo History Museum. General photograph collection, Buildings - Transportation & Storage - Elevators - Grain.
8. Courtesy, Daughters of Charity Province of St. Louise, St. Louis, MO.
9. Collection of The Buffalo History Museum. General photograph collection, Buildings - Residences - Hospital - Sisters.
10. Collection of The Buffalo History Museum. General photograph collection, Persons - G.
11. From Rev. Thomas Donohue's *The History of the Catholic Church in Western New York*, (1904).
12. Author's collection.
13. Collection of The Buffalo History Museum. General photograph collection, Persons - Mooney.
14. Author's collection.
15. From Rev. Thomas Donohue's *The History of the Catholic Church in Western New York*, (1904).
16. Preferred Citation: Collection of The Buffalo History Museum. General photograph collection, Persons - B.
17. The *Courier-Express* Photograph Collection, Archives & Special Collections Department, E.H. Butler Library, SUNY Buffalo State.
18. The *Courier-Express* Photograph Collection, Archives & Special Collections Department, E.H. Butler Library, SUNY Buffalo State.
19. The *Courier-Express* Photograph Collection, Archives & Special Collections Department, E.H. Butler Library, SUNY Buffalo State.
20. Library of Congress, Prints & Photographs Division, LC-DIG-ggbain-33672.
21. The *Courier-Express* Photograph Collection, Archives & Special Collections Department, E.H. Butler Library, SUNY Buffalo State.
22. Billy Rose Theatre Division, The New York Public Library. (1877).
23. Author's collection.

24. Library of Congress. Bain News Service, Publisher. Peggy O'Neil., ca. 1915.

25. ZUMA Press, Inc./Alamy Stock Photo.

26. The *Courier-Express* Photograph Collection, Archives & Special Collections Department, E.H. Butler Library, SUNY Buffalo State.

27. Photo by Jordan Matter, with permission from Sean Cullen.

28. Permission from Irene Haupt.

29. Permission from Katie Addo.

30. Collection of The Buffalo History Museum. Howard D. Beach photograph collection, 28758-02.

31. Permission from Kevin Brady, photo by Fred Kosslow.

32. Photo by Kristin Etu from Canisius College.

33. Courtesy of Brigid Hughes.

34. Courtesy of Stephan Talty, photo by Nathacha Vilceus.

35. With permission from Bruce Blair to use his father's etching.

36. Permission from Rory Allen.

37. The *Courier-Express* Photograph Collection, Archives & Special Collections Department, E.H. Butler Library, SUNY Buffalo State.

38. The *Courier-Express* Photograph Collection, Archives & Special Collections Department, E.H. Butler Library, SUNY Buffalo State.

39. The *Courier-Express* Photograph Collection, Archives & Special Collections Department, E.H. Butler Library, SUNY Buffalo State.

40. The *Buffalo Evening News*.

41. Permission from Margaret Sullivan.

42. The *Courier-Express* Photograph Collection, Archives & Special Collections Department, E.H. Butler Library, SUNY Buffalo State.

43. Zuma Press, Inc./Alamy Stock Photo.

44. From *Notable New Yorkers* (1899).

45. Library of Congress. Bain News Service, Publisher. Wm. F. Sheehan.

46. Library of Congress, Prints & Photographs Division, Farm Security Administration/Office of War Information Black-and-White Negatives.

47. The *Courier-Express* Photograph Collection, Archives & Special Collections Department, E.H. Butler Library, SUNY Buffalo State.

48. Harris & Ewing, photographer. Sen. James M. Mead. 1939. [or 1940] Photograph. https://www.loc.gov/item/2016876992/.

49. The *Courier-Express* Photograph Collection, Archives & Special Collections Department, E.H. Butler Library, SUNY Buffalo State.

50. Collection of The Buffalo History Museum. General photograph collection, Persons - Kennedy, John F.

51. Collection of The Buffalo History Museum. General photograph collection, Persons - K.

52. The *Courier-Express* Photograph Collection, Archives & Special Collections Department, E.H. Butler Library, SUNY Buffalo State.

53. Collection of the Buffalo History Museum, General photograph collection, Persons.

54. The *Courier-Express* Photograph Collection, Archives & Special Collections Department, E.H. Butler Library, SUNY Buffalo State.

55. Library of Congress. Chickering, Elmer, photographer. *James Collins, Boston baseball club*. ca. 1897.

56. Boston Public Library, Michael T. "Nuf Ced" McGreevy Collection.

57. Permission from Mary Heneghan.

58. The *Courier-Express* Photograph Collection, Archives & Special Collections Department, E.H. Butler Library, SUNY Buffalo State.

59. ZUMA Press, Inc./Alamy Stock Photo.

60. Photo by Larry Regan, with permission from Larry Regan.

61. Collection of The Buffalo History Museum. Howard D. Beach photograph collection, 46820.

62. NH 93189, courtesy of the Naval History and Heritage Command.

63. Collection of The Buffalo History Museum. General photograph collection, Persons - D.

64. The Poetry Collection of the University Libraries, University at Buffalo, The State University of New York.

65. Photo by Sara Heidinger, courtesy of Crikwater.

66. Courtesy of the Buffalo and Erie County Naval & Military Park.

67. The *Courier-Express* Photograph Collection, Archives & Special Collections Department, E.H. Butler Library, SUNY Buffalo State.

68. Permission From Tom Burns Photography.

69. Permission from Thomas Heneghan.

70. Permission from Paul Pasquarello.

71. Permission James Hartnett and Susie Rydza.

72. Permission from Paul Pasquarello.

73. Permission From Tom Burns Photography.

74. Library of Congress. Detroit Publishing Co., Publisher. *Prudential Building, Buffalo, N.Y.* ca. 1900. Photograph.

75. The *Courier-Express* Photograph Collection, Archives & Special Collections Department, E.H. Butler Library, SUNY Buffalo State.

76. Wirestock, Inc./Alamy Stock Photo.

77. The *Courier-Express* Photograph Collection, Archives & Special Collections Department, E.H. Butler Library, SUNY Buffalo State.

78. Permission from Megan Corbett Rizzuto and Congressman Brian Higgins.

Endnotes

In order to include more content and photos in the book, the endnotes for *Emerald Thread* can be found on my website: **www.timothybohen.com**

Please feel free to contact me at tim@oldfirstward.com.

Index

Acknowledgements

This project wouldn't have happened without the support and encouragement of my wife, Kimberly Blessing. I am forever grateful for many hours of brainstorming and advice. Readers will be grateful that she shortened the book by about a hundred pages. I am deeply indebted to my Irish-American family: my mother, Betsy (McLaughlin) Tomasulo, modeled intellectual curiosity and a love of research; my late father, Timothy, passed down his love of storytelling and history in general; my brother, Brian, shared his love of Irish history in particular; and my sister, Kate, provided helpful feedback at all stages of the project and encouraged me to find more Irish women for the book.

I want to thank Chuck LaChiusa from Explore Buffalo, who encouraged me to keep working on the Buffalo Irish; David Gerber, William Jenkins, and Mark Goldman, who have previously captured the history of the Irish in Buffalo; Edward Patton, Mike Vogel, and Paul Redding, authors of *America's Crossroads* (1993), who introduced me to Irish characters from the Canal District; and Karen Brady Borland, who helped with the Irish in journalism.

I am grateful to Dan DiLandro at Buffalo State University's E.H. Butler Library, who provided me with numerous photos from the Courier-Express collection, and Cynthia Van Ness, director of library and archives at the Buffalo History Museum, who honored countless requests for information and photographs.

There are many people to thank for providing historical information, stories, and photographs for this book: Timothy R. Allan, Chris Andrle, Raymond Ball, Thomas Beecher, Marian Betrus, Bruce Blair, Rich Blake, Colleen Bohen, Molly Beecher Bohen, Patrick Bohen, Karen Brady Borland, Kevin Brady, Dymphna Browne, Philip Burke, John Carney, Mary Cochrane, Kevin Corbett, Joe Crangle,

Jr., Peter Crotty, Colleen Cullen, Matt Cullen, Sean Cullen, Fiona Dargan, Kevinah Dargan, Tracy Marks Dargan, Kathleen Delaney, Deborah Desilets, Mike Desmond, Stewart Desmond, Terry Dunford, John Feeney, Tim Flanagan, Mark Goldman, Mike Harrington, Erin Hartnett, James Hartnett, Joe Hassett, Mary Heneghan, Tom Heneghan, John "Jake" Herlihy, Sheriff Tom Higgins, Josephine Hogan, Brigid Hughes, Bert Hyde, William Jenkins, Theresa Kennedy, Al Kolodziejczak, Frank Kowsky, Len Lenihan, Kathleen Lesniak, Ann Marie Linnabery, Jim Madden, Timothy Madigan, Mary Kennedy Martin, Whitey Martin, James Maynard, Amy Miller, Robert McCarthy, Jenn Fecio McDougall, Herman Mogavero, John Montague, Prish Moran, Paul Mulcaire, Matt Murphy, Anne Neville, John Neville, Kevin O'Brien, Jack O'Donnell, Loraine O'Donnell, Vincent O'Neill, Liz Oldfield, Emilie Bournaud Pack, Sasha Pack, Paul Pasquarello, Louis Petrucci, Bill Polian, Derrick Pratt, Larry Quinn, Larry Regan, Pat Regan, Emily Reid, Megan Corbett Rizzuto, Aidan Ryan, Susan Rydza, Ralph Salerno, Chris Schoepflin, Dan Shanahan, Dan Starr, Jerry Sullivan, Margaret Sullivan, Mariam Shannon, Tim Shannon, Shane Stephenson, Peggy Szczygiel, Stephan Talty, Richard Thompson, Kevin Townsell, Padraic Walsh, Paul Wangler, Noelle Wiedemer, and my loyal friends at Waterfront Memories and More Museum.

To my niece, Anabella, and my nephews, Jack, Harry, Peter, Dan, and Santiago, may you always appreciate your Irish heritage.

About the Author

Tim Bohen is the author of *Against the Grain: The History of Buffalo's First Ward*. He has appeared on C-SPAN and in two PBS productions: one on Buffalo's First Ward and another on the Erie Canal. Many of his Irish ancestors settled in Buffalo, some as early as 1849. Tim and his wife live in Buffalo.

He can be emailed at tim@oldfirstward.com

www.timothybohen.com